REEFER MADNESS

The History of Marijuana in America

D0373651

WITHDRAWN

Larry "Ratso" Sloman

Introduction by William S. Burroughs

Afterword: The Madness Continues
by Michael Simmons

St. Martin's Griffin New York

SAN BRUNO PUBLIC LIBRARY

We are grateful for permission to reproduce lyrics and excerpts of musical scores from the following compositions:
"If You're a Viper," words and music by Rozetta Howard, Horace Malcolm, and Herbert Moren, © copyright 1938 by MCA Music Inc., New York, New York. Used by permission. All rights reserved.
"Knocking Myself Out," by Marshall Jones and Carl Smith, © copyright 1938 by Bess Music Inc. Used by permission. All rights reserved.
"Sweet Marihuana Brown," by Leonard Feather, © copyright 1945 by Global Music, Inc. Used by permission. All rights reserved.
"The Man From Harlem," by Will Hudson, © copyright 1933 by American Academy of Music, Inc. Copyright renewed. Used by permission. All rights reserved.
"The Stuff Is Here (Let's Get Gay)." Words and music by Alex Hill and J. M. Williams, © copyright 1934 by Northern Music Co., New York, New York. Used by permission. All rights reserved.
"When I Get Low, I Get High," by Marion Sunshine, © copyright 1936, 1937, by Sanson-Antobal Music Co., Used by permission. All rights reserved.

We gratefully acknowledge permission to reproduce sections from the following books:
Louis: The Louis Armstrong Story, by Max Jones and John Chilton, published in the United States by Little, Brown and Co., © copyright 1971. Reprinted by permission of the publisher.
Really the Blues, by Milton (Mezz) Mezzrow and Bernard Wolfe, © copyright 1946 by Random House, Inc. Copyright renewed 1974 by Bernard Wolfe and Milton Mezzrow. Reprinted by permission of Harold Matson Co., Inc.

REEFER MADNESS. Copyright © 1979 by Larry Sloman.
Introduction copyright © 1983 by William S. Burroughs.
Afterword copyright © 1998 by Michael Simmons.
All rights reserved. Printed in the United States of America. No part of this book may be used or reproduced in any matter whatsoever without written permission except in the case of brief quotations embodied in critical articles or reviews. For information address St. Martin's Press, 175 Fifth Avenue, New York, N.Y. 10010.

Library of Congress Cataloging-in-Publication Data

Sloman, Larry.
Reefer madness : the history of marijuana in America / Larry "Ratso" Sloman.
p. cm.
Includes index.
ISBN 0-312-19523-0
1. Marijuana. 2. Drug abuse—United States—History. 3. Drug abuse—United States. I. Title.
HV5822.M3S54 1998
362.29'5'0973—dc21 98-36366
CIP

First published in the United States by The Bobbs-Merrill Company, Inc.

10 9 8 7 6 5 4 3

For

Tom Forcade (1945–1978)

and

Emmett Grogan (1942–1978)

Final score: ALL FREE

ACKNOWLEDGMENTS

Thanks first to Tuli Kupferberg and Danny Moses for suggesting this project and offering sound advice every step along the way. Erich Goode made some documents available to me. Mike Brown, George Barkin, and Jim Cusimano read and made valuable comments on the manuscript. On the archival front, Jane Zack, Edith Crutchfield, Michelle Jones, and Helen Lightfoot made my stay at the Drug Enforcement Agency library an experience I'll never forget. Ron Phillapelli and Margaret Derrickson did likewise at the Anslinger Archives at Pennsylvania State University. Michael Aldrich opened up the Fitz Hugh Ludlow Memorial Library doors to me. Allen Ginsberg and Peter Orlovsky supplied files and a great meal. Leslie Morrison and the folks at *High Times* magazine provided support.

On the secretarial front, Robin Lerner, Beverly Cusimano and Susan Smoot did a great job transcribing the garbled tapes. Gary Frankel worked endlessly on a countless number of research tasks and contributed tirelessly of his time and effort.

On the road, Bill Cluck, Jim and Carolyn Hougan, Mark Green and Denny Frand and Mike made the journeying reporter feel at home. Gina provided a song. Keith Stroup and Frank Fioramonti opened the NORML files. Dangerous Dan supplied the Panama hat. Brother Artemus talked in vain. Roger Friedman came along, then introduced me to Edith the Egg Lady. Jim Drougas and Mo Cohen of New Morning Bookstore gave me a library card. And Jim and Bev Cusimano and, of course, Lynn made it all possible and worthwhile. I suppose I should also mention my parents, who never turned me in. The Rangers didn't help much; they got eliminated early.

CONTENTS

INTRODUCTION

Harry J. Anslinger becomes comprehensible only as part of a conspiracy. Many will remember his reign of terror, the pointless fear that ugly troll occasioned when no one was safe smoking a joint in his own home—at any second twenty narcs could bust in, guns drawn; when a single joint could mean ten years in jail. . . . "Marijuana! Marijuana!" says the illiterate judge, "Why, that's deadlier than cocaine! All right, let's see your arms." And what was the point of all this? We can see the point of Stalin's or Hitler's terror: it was done in self-defense. A man like that has to keep them scared and weed out any potential threat, otherwise they would gang right up on him.

Dare one hope that Anslinger and Watergate were the prelude to a Fascist takeover that aborted? Seen in this light, Anslinger's terror seems very logical indeed: criminalize the real or potential opposition . . . disrupt with fear. . . . Hoover was trying the same thing against the Hippies and Yippies, whom he considered the greatest threat to America, along with eggheads. Hoover's people had to keep under cover, and any clear thinking linked to expression was a deadly menace to their attempt.

It would seem that somewhere the tide turned against them. It was a long war of attrition, fought in many areas: censorship, liberalization of drugs, and sexual freedoms. The Vietnam War was certainly one of the turning points. The stupidity of the military mind is such they may have thought this was a war that could be won, and that they could step from a glorious victory in Vietnam to a good old-fashioned America. And Hoover—what did he really hope to gain by recording the copulations of Dr. Martin Luther King? And Anslinger, with his reefer madness and all his other bullshit, laughable except for his power at the time. And the press, who faithfully reported and verified his outrageous flood of disinformation and sensational rubbish. . . . I would say that the Fascist revolution was aborted by downright stupidity.

Anslinger's reefer madness did not contain even the seeds of efficient, intelligent, ruthless action. But the propaganda utterances of Stalin and Hitler did. The same goes for Hoover, sniveling Nixon, the whole miserable, wretchedly evil lot of them . . . not a man among them who could have pulled off a successful coup in a banana republic. They bungled and failed, right down the line, going too far here and not far enough there, until they were washed away screaming in Watergate. The dam had indeed broken, but it had been eroded and weakened for years before Watergate. The enforcers just didn't have what it takes to run a police state. They cried for it, like children used to cry for Castoria, the vilest medicine ever forced on a child. But they would have fumbled the ball if it was handed them on a platter. They plain struck out.

Of course there were freedom fighters aplenty. Not on the life-and-death scale; the conflict was never so clearly defined. Once again they faltered and fumbled, ready to jump in three directions . . . lying so obviously it stinks out on TV and anyone can see the shameless lie. So we're not doing so well in Vietnam? Well, that's easy, just juggle the casualty figures. Rather like the famous scene in Rabelais . . . surrounded by his advisors and concubines, the monarch reclines in his tent:

"Tell me of our glorious victories, General."

"Yes your majesty. Our right flank has broken through, the enemy is fleeing in panic."

"And what of our left flank?"

"They have not been idle: they are even now at the gates of the City of Moscow. A special commando team has been sent in to capture the enemy leaders alive."

"Excellent, excellent. We have treats in store for these enemies of mankind. . . ." At this point his fleeing army rushes through the tent, snatching food on their way, the enemy close on its heels.

Hoover bellows piteously: "Oh heaven help a poor old Queen. . . ."

They fade and die away like inglorious old hams, selling their disgraceful memoirs . . . no takers on their souls: "Tell you straight, Harry, it ain't worth shit. Nothing and nobody there. I buy souls, not tape recorders."

At best, this sorry team of political adventurers displays a certain jaunty imbecility, like a private detective's: nothing too low or too dirty for old George, down on his luck . . . a jarringly false we're-all-good-thieves-and-villains-together camaraderie that just doesn't get off the ground. Hunt says about Leary: "So we both went on to greater things. . . ." Tired old actors, tired old lines. The Fascist takeover ended not with a bang, but a whimper. I can see Mitchell as a security guard, Hunt and the other old Company boys back to some marginal off-the-record CIA operations. The Company takes care of its own. . . .

This was never a serious takeover attempt, except: around about 1965 the big brass had a war scheduled with China, see? "It starts by an atom bomb on New York and that takes care of a lot of spics and niggers and smartass Jew intellectualized liberals. We pin it on China, draft the whole fucking country, and take over. Got some mighty fine land in Alaska, all ready for some settlers. . . ."

Yes, there is always a moment when something *could* happen . . . they did not know that it was already behind them, somewhere back there in that vast obscurity beyond Washington, The City, where the dark field of the Republic rolled on under the night, and somewhere in that vast obscurity they were defeated. There was no magic in these men, to recognize the moment and act.

November 1982 WILLIAM S. BURROUGHS

Overture

May 2, 1977. Eleven o'clock Monday morning. Sloman had forgotten to turn his answering machine on. He groped for the receiver, the weight of ten free Tom Collinses, courtesy of his friend Michael the Bartender, pinning him to that mattress, where he had dropped his inert body some seven hours ago. "Larry, baby, wake up." Tuli Kupferberg's gravelly voice cut through the last shreds of sleep. "I got a project for you. Bobbs-Merrill wants a book on pot. How it's changed in the seventies—like that. I had mixed feelings, but maybe you want to do it."

Kupferberg, of course, was the logical choice. He was an early head, frequenting the bohemian circles of Manhattan in the late forties and early fifties, later to emerge as one of those legendary pot, porn and pussy balladeers we knew in the sixties as the Fugs. Besides, Tuli had always been interested in the sociology of drug use; in 1960 his small press magazine *Birth* had devoted a whole issue to stimulants and addiction, with extensive sections on alcohol, opium, tobacco, marijuana and peyote. But Tuli passed in 1977 and offered the plum to Sloman.

"Another book on marijuana? Isn't that a dead issue?" Cusimano scoffed as Sloman related the phone call later that day. Sloman also felt a curious sense of *déjà vu* about the project, but there was something tugging at the back of his mind, something dark and mysterious. Maybe it was just the Tom Collinses. The call from Tuli had intrigued the writer, had set him to thinking about grass, something he hadn't really done for years. And with good reason. Sloman was never your typical pothead. Oh, he started smoking in 1967, when he was a sophomore at Queens College. He would never forget that first time, at the pad of A. J. Weberman, the self-proclaimed Dylanologist. Sloman was fascinated by Weberman's obsession with Dylan and was visiting A.J. to see his fabled Dylan concordance, a computer printout of every line the singer ever wrote, all cross-indexed. And it was there, in Spanish Harlem, that Sloman first partook of the weed. And he still remembers, as though it happened yesterday, that ancient lightheadedness, stumbling down the rickety stairs, pouring out onto 105th Street, feeling at one with the heaped mounds of garbage, the charcoaled air, the cacophony of the city sounds. He remembered, however, to keep his right hand on his wallet all the way to the subway.

So, pot became an occasional experience for the middle-class student. And in 1971, in Madison, Wisconsin, while in graduate school, Sloman incurred a severe case of the heebie-jeebies after one intense pot debauch; after that, he became an even more occasional user, which was the case until this very day. So his visit to Cusimano was not purely ceremonial. Sloman had met Cusimano in Madison while in graduate school, and a strong affinity had grown between the two men, a bond largely forged through their mutual admiration for the Velvet Underground, one of the early decadent rock bands. Cusimano was known around Madison in the early seventies as a connoisseur, albeit a self-proclaimed one. He wrote a very popular food column for the school newspaper—the *State Street Gourmet*. He could tell you who the greatest guitarist in the world was without blinking an eye.

And when it came to dope, Cusimano was the litmus test. Functioning as a sort of underground drug analysis unit, most of his friends would bring the English graduate student a taste of their proposed stash. Cusimano would light up, suck the smoke deep into the caverns of his chest, scratch his scraggly beard, and finally exhale. If the dope was strong enough to permeate every layer of his corpulent frame, then it would be bought, and the revelers would retire to Gargano's to celebrate by having a pizza with everything on it.

So with the spirit of Madison riding in the back seat, the two set off for Washington, D.C., a month later. It was Sloman's idea to cover the Fourth of July smoke-in, an annual event where masses of marijuana-mottled mobs, under the guise of demonstrating and agitating for their right to smoke, come together and party for days. The event has traditionally been organized by the Yippies, the remnants of that genetic strain that once populated America in the sixties—politicized hippies. Sloman always felt a kinship with the Yippies—his politics ran with Jarry and the Dadaists, and the Yippies always seemed to have a sense of humor about what they were doing.

But what made this year's smoke-in more interesting was that this was the first time the event was to be co-sponsored by NORML. NORML, of course, is the National Organization to Reform the Marijuana Laws, a mouthful, an organization largely made up of mouthpieces. That is to say, NORML is a traditional lobby group attempting to effect social change through the time-honored American tradition of "grab and pump and I'll scratch your back and you scratch mine and then we'll get the laws changed." Except these intense young esquires aren't trying to get milk subsidies, or Model Cities money, or CAP grants. They're trying to get elected representatives to vote for bills that, bottom line, sanction the use of the drug marijuana. Which puts them, at least in the eyes of most of our Byzantine congressmen, right in the same camp with the Yippies; and it was there, in Jefferson Park, a stoned throw from the White House across the street, that Sloman and Cusimano had traveled to join the issue.

The reporters arrived at the park as part of a massive march of Yippies who were encamped at the Reflecting Pool near the Jefferson Monument. The scraggly troupe had snaked its way through the strangely deserted streets of a holiday Washington, D.C., under the watchful eyes of city and park police. It was a pleasant trek, punctuated by chants of "Smoke dope" every block or so; but the real surprise came when the regiment marched into the park, only to find that a few thousand heads had preceded them and were lolling around, passing joints and catching rays. All told, there were at least 4,000 or so partisans there, which impressed Sloman and Cusimano.

As the band set up at the makeshift stage where the proceedings would attempt to be focused, a lone Yippie was discoursing on one of the inhabitants of the big White House across the street. "Did sleazy men slink up to him in bars and try to guilt-trip him into selling them pot? Hey! Did they bust Carter's kid for marijuana? No! They kicked him out of the navy."

This speech was making Keith Stroup nervous. Stroup is the chief honcho of NORML—a lean, blondish, wire-rimmed lawyer who reminds one a bit of John Denver on speed. Even though he's the head of an outlaw lobby, he has achieved a modicum of Washington status, most young bureaucrats being closet heads anyway; and with this wild-eyed, unauthorized speaker raving about the Carters, for godsakes, Stroup looked as if his fragile respectability was about to go up in—well, smoke. So he instinctively grabbed a pert young reporter from one of the Washington dailies, snapped on that winning Kennedy smile, and shuffled, "Oh, that's just some crazy guy. He's not part of our program."

"They threw him out of the navy," the Yipster repeated with syrupy sarcasm. "Now, that's not a punishment, that's a reward!" Stroup smiled wanly and grabbed Dana Beal.

Dana Beal is the Lenin of pot. And probably the Stalin and Trotsky too. That is to say, he has devoted the last ten years of his still-under-thirty life to an active practice and reflection on the dilemma of being a radical in America. Beal was always acknowledged as the leading theoretician of the original Yippies, Hoffman, Rubin and their ilk bowing to his rhetorical prowess. But a series of LSD arrests kept him in jail or underground for much of that decade, and when he resurfaced to pick up the pieces of YIP, he was left a small diehard coterie. Although YIP politics embraces a total world view, it is the pot issue that has become the cornerstone of the YIP's frontal attack on the Moloch culture, the culture that denies them their sacramental herb.

Except that day. What a strange sight it was: thousands of ragged kids in various stages of repose, clustered around a thin cigarette or a fat bong, openly violating the laws of the great District of Columbia. Yet there was an artificiality about this license, a tension that was inhaled with each draw of grass. Sloman recognized that feeling and traced it to high school, in the bathroom, passing around a Kool and expecting Mr. Cooper to barge in any minute . . .

"You're confusing the issue, Dana!" Stroup was shouting. "Let's get started!" But while Beal checked to see if the band was ready to go, another speaker began by articulating the day's demands: "Okay, we got four demands: One, free all drug prisoners in this country." A large cheer issued from the crowd. "Two, decriminalize immediately as a first step until we can get legalization in. Three, bring home all dope prisoners from abroad —Mexico and all over. And four, abolish and investigate the

DEA—Drug Enforcement Agency." The crowd broke into another cheer just as Cusimano joined Sloman in the roped-off section in front of the speaker's platform.

And a parade of partisans began: a black woman from Washington, a white liberal from the ACLU. The heat and the rhetoric and the grass began to get to Cusimano; rivulets of sweat began pouring off his nearly bald dome, soaking his torn blue Banlon shirt. "Fuck, it's hot," he cursed under his breath. "I gotta get something to drink."

But just then a curious squealing noise began issuing from some of the young girls gathered around the reporters. After a few seconds Sloman made it out. They were squealing "Keith! Keith!" And sure enough, Stroup was striding confidently toward the mike. "All right, Keith!" one kid cheered, and Stroup flashed the candidate smile and raised his arms in benediction.

"All right—well, it is indeed nice to see so many of you . . . of our friends here . . . from a lot of parts of the country—Ohio . . ." A great Carson tactic, as the large Ohio sector of the audience burst into whoops. "I suppose, in a very brief way, I'd like to say that I think what we're trying to say to the White House today, and to the Congress perhaps as much as the White House, is that the marijuana laws are absurd today. They don't make any sense." He lifted his arms to deflect the cheers, revealing a yellow NORML T shirt under his collegiate blue blazer and tucked into his prefaded denims. "Look at this! We have a thousand people openly smoking grass in this park, and the police wouldn't even think about making an arrest; they wouldn't dare come in and arrest somebody." Cheers. "Free Keith Richards," someone yelled. "Across the street the Carter boys smoke grass, and they don't get arrested, either," Keith continued in his midwestern drawl. "Now the only question I have left is, why the hell is marijuana still illegal? Everybody's smoking it; nobody's getting arrested; what is this? Now, we've heard mentioned briefly that we won a major victory this week in New York, and I want to underscore that. I don't know if you people realize that in New York State last year there were 30,000 minor marijuana arrests—in that state alone.

"Well, next year there should be no minor marijuana arrests in that state. It was a long fight, and a lot of people in New York worked for years to get these laws changed. I'm sure you remember the Rockefeller approach to drug use. Well, we've just shown them that when people get together, even in a state like New York, we can determine our drug policy; we don't have to sit and let other people make our drug policy for us. Now, I think we should also talk about . . ."

Suddenly a kid darted up and handed Stroup a thin joint. He accepted it even as he kept on talking in his machine-gun style. "I think you should also realize that despite the fact that we're standing here in this park in the nation's capital across the street from the White House openly smoking dope, and no one's doing a thing about it . . ." He paused for cheers and then slowly took a long hit on the reefer and flashed another shit-smoking grin, to wild applause. "Now, I want to make the point . . ." But wait—the YIP film crew, who were documenting this historic event on their Portapack video equipment, missed the goddamn toke. They screamed up at Stroup, trying to get his attention and get another puff for posterity. "Despite the fact we're doing this today, 2,500 were arrested in D.C. last year for marijuana, and that's got to stop!" Stroup paused, and finally caught on and brought the joint up to his lips as the camera zoomed in for a close-up. "Toke two!" Sloman screamed, himself a little stoned at this point.

"What the hell was that?" Stroup asked, smiling coyly. "Well, let me mention a couple of things about the bills that are pending in Congress . . ."

"No!" some kids intent on partying shouted out.

". . . then we'll get back to partying," Keith promised. "We've got some more speakers. Let me underscore what Jay Miller of the ACLU said. We do have three separate marijuana decriminalization proposals pending in Congress. But the important thing is to make sure your congressman knows that ten grams of marijuana is not enough. Ten grams won't do it; we'll all still be criminals. So contact Jimmy Carter, your local and federal elected representatives, and let them know that at a minimum, we don't want any penalties for the private possession and use and cultivation of marijuana. Thank you, folks."

A loud cheer arose from the crowd as Stroup ceded the mike to the M.C., who was from *High Times* magazine. "Okay, the next person is someone who many of us would probably envy. He's the only person in this country who is legally allowed to possess grass for his own use. His name is Bob Randall, and he has a disease called glaucoma that grass relieves, and he's been given a prescription and a supply from the government to save his sight."

Randall stepped up, a pleasant, almost wispy young man. He turned down an offer of a joint. "No, thanks, I get my own from the government," he said, and clutched the mike. "There are about 15 million people in this country who smoke it recreationally. There are about another 15 million who need it medicinally, and they're beginning to find out. I've met a lot of people in their sixties, seventies, eighties—there's even a guy who's ninety in Georgia who just got arrested. He sold two joints to a pig. He's been using it for forty years for asthma. So it's gonna get a lot more interesting, and I'm gonna go away . . ." And with that, Randall oozed away from the mike, to a chorus of protests from the engrossed crowd.

Tod Mikiyura was next—an M.D., dressed in colonial garb to underscore the tradition of protest being articulated that day. And, after a long, loquacious speech tracing the prohibition of cannabis, highlighted by the display of an authentic tincture of cannabis medicine bottle from the 1800s, Mikiyura read a petition on which NORML had amassed over 50,000 signatures, a petition that he and a few volunteers would personally deliver to the White House that afternoon.

Following Tod, the speeches dragged on and on, as the mid-afternoon sun baked the protesters. Cusimano, who by now had consumed eight cans of Pepsi, three ice creams, and about forty-nine tokes of sweet marijuana, looked like he was about to pass out. But then Dana, a little ball of red-haired Yippie energy, grabbed the mike to announce his faction's action: the mass turn-in.

The plan was to incite, cajole, nudge, somehow move these couple of thousand dormant bodies and enlist them for a march to the nearest police station, whereupon each marijuana user, supplied with one fresh joint as evidence, would turn himself in, in a mass display of contrition. Thereby dumping hundreds and hundreds of young nubile stoned bodies onto the jurisdiction of the District of Columbia Police Department to be processed, jailed, allowed calls, fed and maintained in whatever other ways young hippies require. A thankless task for the chief of police, a publicity coup for the Yippies in pointing out the absurdity of the grass law. That is, if they could find just one cop who would agree to enforce the law of the district that day.

That dilemma had to be in the back of Dana's mind as he stood before the stoned masses. "Boy, it's hot!" Dana said, wiping his brow. "I'm gonna go on the turn-in, and then I'm gonna go lay down." Beal was cruising slowly into his recruitment speech, when suddenly a section of the crowd to his right leaped up, began charging toward him en masse, and strangely, ran right past the stage to a statue at the rear. Cusimano craned his neck and saw the object of the dash: a tall, skinny kid in Arab mufti was standing inside the fence around the statue and was throwing handful after handful of joints into the crowd, as if he were feeding seals at a zoo. Cusimano gasped. "Jesus, that's beautiful!" By now Beal had realized what was happening and was trying to use the interruption to his own advantage. "Hey! This way! Over here!" Dana pointed toward the bulk of his audience. "Hey! Bring that free pot over here." A huge roar from the kids out front washed over the reporters in front of the stage. "All right, calm down!" Beal shouted. "I'd like to bring up the case of a kid in Texas who was shot in the head by his father as he was sleeping." The audience groaned as one. "Eighteen years old, this kid was shot through the head because he smoked marijuana, and his father couldn't live with it." The jeers and catcalls cascaded. "Wait"—Dana threw up his hands—"let me give you the end of the case. Please be silent. The end of the case was that a jury of the father's peers sat together and found the father not guilty!" Beal paused for the boos. "It was a decision that said that the potheads are second-class citizens. What that means is, sure, they can give you a hundred-dollar fine, they love to give you a hundred-dollar fine, like a traffic ticket when they haul away your car. But what will they do to keep other kids from getting their heads blown off by their fathers and then have no equal protection? I thought it said in the Fourteenth Amendment that we're supposed to have equal protection. Are the potheads gonna be the victims forever of any redneck that comes along, like in *Easy Rider*, and decides to blow their heads off?"

"No!" Cusimano and Sloman added their voices to the crowd.

"What we need is some action that'll make them respect us." Dana had worked himself into such a state that he didn't even realize that the large speakers had kicked out in the middle of his last sentence.

"We can't hear you!" a girl screamed.

"I'm sorry if I'm not loud enough!" Dana screamed, still unaware of the technical problem. "That's why we're gonna do this turn-in. The time has come to fan the flame. We're gonna be gathering here double file. But first I've got two more points." About one-tenth of the crowd can understand him by now. "A lot of people don't understand why we say 'Free the heads and jail the feds.' They say 'Why not leave the feds alone? They didn't do anything bad.' " A scowl crossed the patrician features of the speaker. "C'mon, man, how many people here have had their doors busted down at five A.M. The real threat to America is not marijuana, but the secret police . . ."

Just then a kid in his twenties vaulted the rope separating the speaker's area from the audience and advanced onto the platform. Sloman edged closer to the kid, sensing trouble. "Wait a minute; hold it right there"—the interloper was trying to get Beal's eye—"hold it right here and now, people. You'll have to get better sound equipment than this crap we have here. I got better stuff in my bedroom." The distraction worked. Beal stopped in midsentence; the Yippie Palace Guard, led by Pie-Kill expert Aaron Kay (who lists Mayor Abe Beame, Senator Moniyan, and Howard Hunt on his résumé under "Successful Pie Attacks") was inching closer, and the momentum was shattered.

"NORML sells undershirts for $5.50 and . . ." the stranger went on, but suddenly found himself surrounded by the Yippie enforcers. "Don't touch me, brother"—he raised an arm—"don't touch me."

"NORML did not put this on!" Beal shouted at the kid. "This equipment was donated by the Yippies, man!"

"C'mon"—Aaron seized the time—"let's get this motherfucker out. He's a police agent."

"He's a police agent. Get him out." Another Yip picked up the cry and grabbed the kid, who resisted. Aaron, who had been sucking on a can of Pepsi, charged to the center of the scuffle, caromed the Pepsi can off the kid's head, and swiftly retreated, in his best pieing fashion. Meanwhile Sloman and Cusimano charged into the fray, trying to restore order.

"Hey, the guy's got a point to make; don't hit him with your fist." Sloman peeled one Yip off the action. Cusimano bear-hugged the stranger, and a few others served as a buffer zone.

"What the fuck is this?" a young girl screamed at the top of her lungs. "This guy's with NORML and they're beating the shit out of him!"

"Get that fucking cop." One of the Yips was still beside himself with rage.

"He's no cop," Sloman scoffed.

"The guy tried to interrupt Dana." Aaron was back with a fresh can. "He's a fucking *provocateur*. Stomp his ass!" the angry Yip continued.

"Did you hear what he was saying?" Sloman asked Aaron.

"Yeah, he was trashing NORML and YIP, so I hit him over the head with a can."

"No, he wasn't trashing YIP. He was trashing NORML. He was saying they sell T shirts for $5.50, and they won't even give you a fucking sound system," Sloman noted.

"It was right at the point where Dana was gonna announce the turn-in." The enraged Yip was joined by his girlfriend. "He was sabotaging the fucking action. He's a cop." The Yip leaped for the kid, but Cusimano got him in a half nelson.

"He's a cop! He's a cop!" The Yippie struggled to get at the enemy.

"He's a cooooooppppppp!" His girlfriend emitted a blood-curdling howl that succeeded in dispersing everyone from stage right. The band was still working on the sound system, so Dana decided to round up the troops sans mike. He was stumbling forlornly around the perimeter of the crowd when Sloman and Cusimano caught up with him.

"I know, I know, it's a bummer. How come the sound always goes off when I'm speaking? I practically got sunstroke." Dana moaned. "I didn't get a chance to work the people up to the level I wanted."

" 'Cause of the interruption?" Cusimano asked, leaning toward the theory that the intruder was a *provocateur* of some sort.

"We pretty much blew the turn-in because those people started throwing joints around just as I began to do my thing." Beal shook his head as Aaron ran up. "So, Aaron, you gonna get this turn-in together?" Beal barked.

"What do I do?" Aaron asked.

"The bullhorn. Where's the bullhorn, Aaron?" Dana looked annoyed.

"All right, who's taking part in the turn-in?" Aaron started shouting, in lieu of a horn.

"C'mon, line up two by two." Dana was revitalized. "Let's go get busted."

Aaron started to wander, still shouting.

"Aaron, stay put instead of wandering around," Beal snapped, grabbing Aaron and his small girlfriend. "You two make the first couple, and everyone else line up behind them." The only problem was, except for Sloman and Cusimano and about six curious onlookers, nobody else knew what was going on, leaving Aaron and his girlfriend proudly and crisply standing at attention, heads erect, shoulders back, magnificently alone.

Dana had come back now, trailed by about thirty or so people, and about ten more milled around the park soliciting recruits. After a while, about 200 scraggly soldiers had been found, and the turn-in was about to commence. Except for one small detail—the pot.

"Do you guys have any joints?" Dana asked Sloman and Cusimano, who were clean. "There's supposed to be people here with the joints for the turn-in." Dana was beside himself at this lack of organization. "Where are the joints?"

Finally the reefer man was located, and everyone queued up for one stick. Immediately some of the kids lit up.

"No!" Dana screamed. "Don't smoke them!"

"Then the evidence will go up in smoke," one kid sagely pointed out.

"How about if we break them in half?" another suggested.

"Then it's only half a joint," came the answer.

At last a bullhorn was found, and Dana made the last preparations. "All right, do you hear me? OKAY, DO NOT SMOKE YOUR JOINTS. DO NOT BRING ANY OTHER DRUGS YOU CAN GET BUSTED FOR. DO NOT COME IF YOU ARE A FUGITIVE OR A RUNAWAY. This is a serious act of civil disobedience. Is everyone that wants to turn in here? Are you sure you didn't leave a friend around by a tree or something?"

The mob was about to march when Cusimano poked Sloman, pointing toward the front of the pack. And what a poignant sight! Aaron and his girlfriend were tenderly, awkwardly embracing, sharing a sweet good-bye before the boys in blue would swallow Aaron and his skinny joint up.

Then Dana barked out the orders and the crowd followed him and his bullhorn out. First they started circling the park, picking up stragglers, strangers, whoever might on impulse join their ranks.

After one turn around the park, the mass advanced to within

200 feet of the Avenue, providing them with their first real glimpse of enforcement strength that day. In defense of the White House, there were five helmeted cops guarding the gutter next to the park, eight motorcycle cops complete with cycles forming a barricade down the center of Pennsylvania Avenue, and finally, ten or so mounted policemen milling outside the gates of the White House. This sight immediately inspired the crowd to chant loudly, "Free Amy Carter"—a chant that attracted a few hundred more people over the curb, where the first confrontation was about to take place.

The crowd surged to the edge of the sidewalk as the cops braced themselves, clutching their nightsticks calmly.

"Are we getting busted for having a joint, or for trespassing?" one kid had the foresight to ask Dana.

"Are we getting busted for having a joint, or for trespassing?" Dana screamed through the bullhorn at the cops—two feet away.

"I don't want them dragging us down there, thinking we're getting arrested for pot, and it's for trespassing." The kid was still wary.

"But they have to inventory the pot!" Dana screamed. "That's why you shouldn't smoke it. That way, they have to inventory it, and they have to bust you for pot."

"That's the point; they won't bust us for pot."

"Walk up to them and see," Dana said, smiling.

"That would be trespassing," the kid maintained.

"No, that isn't trespassing to walk on the street," Dana scoffed just as a huge paddy wagon drove into view.

"It's jaywalking," another kid chuckled.

"It's jaywalking." Dana brightened. "Walking with a J. We got pot; come on, bust us!" He was screaming into the bullhorn now. "We got it; you got to enforce the law! I wanna make a citizen's complaint!"

The cops remained stonefaced as four hippies inched off the curb and advanced on them, armed with joints.

"We got four brave brothers who are coming forward!" Dana was screaming into the bullhorn. "Are there any people from the media here to see this? We have people holding up a joint right in front of the White House! Let's get these people busted here!"

And the chant was picked up: "Bust us! Bust us! Bust us!"—until it seemed that half of the revelers from the park were lining the curb now, screaming with glee and abandon. And suddenly the party shifted, and the mob settled into the curb area, lighting their joints, flaring their bongs, playing their guitars, drinking their Pepsis. And when the horses were trotted out to contain the swelling mob, a huge cheer arose.

Sloman and Cusimano found themselves at the front of the crowd, near the statue that had been occupied by hippies. The kids had overrun the southeastern corner of the park and were spilling over the sidewalk, engulfing ice cream vendors, holiday strollers, and even one lone priest with a "Ban the Neutron Bomb Now" sign. Which prompted one older ACLU-type to try and mediate rationally.

"Look, I'm the father of five kids!" he shouted, waving his arms while standing in the middle of the intersection. "You want to get marijuana legalized, don't you? Well, c'mon over in the park and let's talk about it." He tried to corral the kids near him and head back onto the sidewalk.

"Hey!" a stoned Yip screamed hoarsely. "The decision will be made by where the people stand! If the people want to vote for the street, let them come into the street! Those that don't, let them go over there!"

"Well, let's go into the park and vote on that . . ." The liberal smiled a smile of reconciliation.

"Fuck it; vote right here!" The Yip raised an octave.

". . . and if everybody wants the park. Look, do you guys want legalized marijuana, or do you want to stand out here in the street and raise hell?" The furrow in his brow deepened.

"Let's stand in the street and raise hell!" the Yippie exploded, hopping around as if he were on a pogo stick. "Whoop, whoop, whoop, whoop! Fuck this guy; fuck this asshole! We're smoking fucking dope right now! It's legal right now! Fuck the pigs!" He punched wildly into the air with his clenched fist. "We don't have to say 'May we please smoke dope?' We smoke dope!"

At that moment the mounted police were called into action. They rode their horses up the adjoining street, scattering the demonstrators in their path, laughing like they were at a rodeo. In fact, one cop kept terrorizing the kids, coming within inches of their prone bodies, until he pushed his horse a bit too far and the steed shot up on its hind legs and bolted, narrowly missing a young girl's head. "Jesus, what a hot dog!" Cusimano shouted over the screams of the terrified kids. "Look, they're disciplining him; they're taking him away!" And it was true—two commanding officers had ridden over and grabbed the hot dog's reins and led him back to Pennsylvania Avenue.

The Yippies retaliated by throwing firecrackers at the police, and succeeded in terrifying the horses. After a few minutes a long trail of horseshit littered Pennsylvania Avenue, and the Yippies, bored with the confrontation, regrouped in a square just past the Treasury Building. Beal set up shop at the top of the stairs leading to the building, and his bullhorned voice bounced impressively off the buildings and out over the park across the street.

"And what about the little guys who've been dealing nickel bags? The little people who suffered and went to jail? The little people! Do we want to give marijuana to Liggett and Myers? Do we want to give it to Reynolds Tobacco? We have a plan! It's the only plan to keep the Indians from getting wiped out. And the plan is"—Dana paused dramatically—"One, agricultural supports."

The delegates from that good state of Mary Warner broke into cheers. If he had had a gavel, Dana would have used it. "They have agricultural supports for peanuts, don't they?" he sneered. "Did you ever wonder why they have free peanuts on the airlines, even after they've taken away the free meal? Did you ever think it might have something to do with who's over there?" He pointed a bony finger in the direction of 1600 Pennsylvania Avenue. "So we want support programs so that the people who slaved to grow sinsemillia to get really good pot will be able to eat. We don't want the big tobacco companies coming in and usurping the neighborhood dope dealer . . ."—a cheer interrupted him—". . . with their monopolistic practices. We saw what Standard Oil did during the oil shortage. We don't want no marijuana shortage ten years down the road."

Someone threw an ash can at the fringe of the crowd, and the deafening explosion was met with sighs of approval. "And the neighborhood pot dealers should be given control, not just over pot, but over all herbs. We say take the ginseng away from the Moonies." Sloman roared himself hoarse with approval. "So we're gonna have to go out onto the streets for this one." Dana was wrapping it up, building for another assault on the jails to try and get busted. "The way we see it is that decriminalization is their solution. It's so they can keep the myth alive that there's something wrong with marijuana, when in fact its tragic people get busted because the laws against marijuana have no more sense to them than the laws against Jews in Germany."

"Personally, ah thought those was pretty good laws," a redneck head in front of Sloman leaned over and shouted at his friend, as he took a long hit on a passing joint, "the laws against the Jews in Germany." They exchanged the joint and slapped palms.

Suddenly Sloman's attention was caught by an odd-looking couple strolling slowly past the aggregation. The male was black, with long, curly, matted dreadlocks, the insignia of the Rastafari, a religious cult centered in Jamaica—a cult that uses ganja, or marijuana, as a vital part of its social and spiritual life. The Rastafarian's dreadlocks were barely contained by a huge wool cap. He wore army green fatigues and carried a large wooden walking stick. His mate was dressed in a long African-looking garment and wore a turban. But oddly enough they looked untouched by the ninety-five-degree heat.

Sloman scurried over and intercepted the pair. "Are you from Jamaica?" he blurted out.

The Rastafarian stopped and looked at the reporter with soft red eyes. "Who, I? *Sí.*"

"Are you Rastafari?" Sloman pressed.

"*Sí.*" A trace of a smile curled around his mouth.

"What do you think of this thing? This smoke-in?" Sloman moved his small tape recorder closer to the pair.

"Just love, mon, just love." The stoned soldier punctuated his response with firm taps from his walking stick on Sloman's tape recorder. "Love monifesting itself, in various aspects."

"But you don't ahsk for legalization," the woman offered.

"You don't ahsk for legalization," the Rastaman reiterated, making Sloman extremely nervous by tapping harder. "I, mon, gonna show you say what. How can you ahsk someone to give you freedom?"

"I-ree." The woman approved.

"I-ree." The man nodded. "You no ahsk someone to give you your freedom. You must take it." And with that the Rastaman lowered his stick and signaled the end of the conversation.

"But remember," the woman turned back and shouted a few seconds later, "you must maintain a respect for the herb!"

Sloman's meditation on that last response was broken by the surging crowd, who were heading back down toward Pennsylvania Avenue. "We're going to turn ourselves in." Dana was shouting into the horn. "We tried to turn ourselves in before by the White House, but they wouldn't take us; so now we'll turn ourselves into a jail!"

The crowd snaked its way down Pennsylvania Avenue, hundreds strong, but orderly for the most part. They waited for the green, stayed on the sidewalks, and politely avoided trampling little old ladies walking their dogs.

"Take it to the streets!" A few kids bolted the crowd and swarmed into the street. A few others joined them and soon a hundred people poured into the intersection of 15th Street and New York Avenue.

After that it was all downhill. Oh, the Yippies marched and chanted and shouted and milled and marched some more. A lot more. By this time it was late afternoon, and Cusimano and Sloman had succumbed to their age and were following the progress of the march through downtown Washington in an air-conditioned car driven by some *High Times* staffers. After a while Cusimano got thirsty, and the two jumped out and picked up some Pepsis during a lull in the proceedings.

Sloman was intrigued by the role of a few black men in short-sleeved white shirts with walkie-talkies. It turned out that they were observers from the mayor's office, making sure the rights of the demonstrators were not trampled upon by the hot, over-timed police. "This is the damnedest thing I've ever seen," one of the observers said, laughing. "These kids are trying to get themselves arrested."

"Pretty big turnout, huh?" Sloman joined in.

"Certainly bigger than we thought it'd be," the observer barked with an official air. "The folks were all geared up for something last year, and nothing happened. We had a million people here for the bicentennial and only a few arrests." He leaned closer toward the two reporters. "But I don't think these folks here are seriously interested in getting busted."

"Why's that?" Cusimano rushed for the bait.

The official laughed and shook his head. "Well, they've walked right past three jails already."

That broke Sloman's and Cusimano's will. It was clear that by now the cops had the upper hand. The Yippies were being herded back toward the Reflecting Pool, their outdoor motel for this holiday weekend. They hadn't even succeeded in getting themselves busted, after trying for four hours in nearly one-hundred-degree weather. Sloman wanted to march back to the Memorial, but Cusimano prevailed, and they slipped out of the shrinking procession around 9th and D streets and went into a Chinese restaurant for a drink and to assess the day's events.

Cusimano slowly sank into a booth and quickly grabbed for the only menu. "What shit!" He spat. "Am I exhausted! Pretty futile afternoon, huh. Those goddamn Yippies couldn't even get themselves arrested. They spent the whole afternoon marching around in this damn heat, until the media all split, most of the protesters dropped out, and the cops rounded them up like little kids and paraded them back to their playpen." The fat PR man mopped the sweat from his brow.

"Yeah, but what vitality; what an initial turnout." Sloman was on his second wind.

"But it was futile." Cusimano grabbed Sloman's napkin and continued to dry off. "I don't know, I think grass might be a dead issue today. Everybody smokes, and nobody gives a shit about the laws."

"What dead issue?" Sloman got animated. "Did you see the vitality of those kids? And the diversity of the speakers and the crowd? It was fascinating. Marijuana's not passé. It's routine, maybe. And that's a whole story in itself. I think there's a book here." The reporter took a long, satisfied hit of his Tom Collins.

"Yeah," Cusimano agreed weakly, preoccupied with the menu, "There just might be a book here. Listen, wanna split some mu shu pork? I got the munchies."

Part 1
Grass Roots

MEXICAN FAMILY GO INSANE
Five Said to Have Been Stricken by Eating Marihuana

Mexico City, July 5—A widow and her four children have been driven insane by eating the Marihuana plant, according to doctors, who say that there is no hope of saving the children's lives and that the mother will be insane for the rest of her life.

The tragedy occurred while the body of the father, who had been killed, was still in a hospital.

The mother was without money to buy other food for the children, whose ages range from 3 to 15, so they gathered some herbs and vegetables growing in the yard for their dinner. Two hours after the mother and children had eaten the plants, they were stricken. Neighbors, hearing outbursts of crazed laughter, rushed to the house to find the entire family insane.

Examination revealed that the narcotic marihuana was growing among the garden vegetables.

—*New York Times*, July 6, 1927

The Aztec Indians called the weed "malihua," and from this word eventually grew the word "marihuana," as the Spaniards then called the weed and as the weed is still known. The word "mallihua" or "mallihuan" comes from the combination of the words "mallin" (which means prisoner), "hua" (which means property or substance), and the termination "ana" (which means to seize or take possession of). Therefore, it would seem that when the Indians spoke of the "mallihua" or "mallihuan," they wished to impart the idea that the substance of the weed seized and took possession and made a prisoner of the person using the weed.

—From the papers of Harry J. Anslinger

CHAPTER 1:
Early Heads

The act of smoking marijuana with the intention of effecting a change in the user's consciousness first became defined as a social problem in the late 1910s and early 1920s, when early reports of a "drug" being carried across the border by Mexican immigrants surfaced in states in the Southwest. However, long before that time Americans had been quite familiar with other usages of the multifaceted cannabis plant.

Hemp was one of the first crops cultivated by the early colonial settlers. Used in making paper and sturdy garments, many of the early colonial legislative bodies encouraged its growth as a cash crop. In fact, in 1762 Virginia imposed penalties on those who did not produce it.

One of the early colonists who grew hemp was George Washington. In his diary entry of August 7, 1765, Washington noted: "began to separate the Male from the Female hemp at Do—rather too late." And two days later: "Abt. 6 o'clock put some Hemp in the Rivr. to Rot—." And in September of that year, our gentleman farmer chronicled: "Began to pull the Seed Hemp—but was not sufficiently ripe."

Washington's concern for separating the male plants from the female plants has led some to believe that our first chief executive was using the hemp for psychoactive purposes. But since George was putting his hemp into the river to rot rather than drying the plant, one is led to believe that the father of our country was merely soaking and not smoking his pot. Separating the male from the female is flimsy evidence that Washington desired a resin-soaked female plant for personal recreational or medicinal use. In all likelihood, he was stashing the strong fibrous male plants and discarding the psychoactive females.

From 1629, when it was introduced in New England, until the invention of the cotton gin and similar machinery, hemp was a major crop in the United States. And as its utility for clothing and the like diminished, the resilient marijuana plant appeared in a new form—as a medicine for a wide variety of ailments. It was first recognized in 1850 by the *United States Pharmacopaeia*, the highly selective drug reference manual. In 1851 the *United States Dispensatory*, a less rigorous listing, recommended cannabis for a wide variety of disorders:

> Extract of hemp is a powerful narcotic (used here to indicate sleep-producing substance) causing exhilaration, intoxication, delirious hallucinations, and, in its subsequent action, drowsiness and stupor, with little effect upon the circulation. It is asserted also to act as a decided aphrodisiac, to increase the appetite, and occasionally to induce the cataleptic state. In morbid states of the system, it has been found to cause sleep, to allay spasm, to compose nervous disquietude, and to relieve pain. In these respects it resembles opium; but it differs from that narcotic in not diminishing the appetite, checking the secretions, or constipating the bowels. It is much less certain in its effects, but may sometimes be preferably employed, when opium is contraindicated by its nauseating or constipating effects, or its disposition to produce headache, and to check the bronchial section. The complaints in which it has been specially recommended are neuralgia, gout, rheumatism, tetanus, hydrophobia, epidemic cholera, convulsions, chorea, hysteria, mental depression, delirium tremens, insanity and uterine hemorrhage.

Quite an impressive array. In fact, tincture of cannabis was produced by the leading pharmaceutical companies in the late 1800s, including Parke-Davis, Lilly and Squibb. A German firm even marketed cannabis cigarettes for use in combating asthma. The cigarettes also contained belladonna, and the more aware patients in the population rushed to their general practitioners, studied in the art of the wheeze.

In fact, for the early immigrants to the United States from eastern Europe, cannabis had traditionally played a major role in their folklore for centuries. In the fifth century B.C., the Greek historian Herodotus observed that the Scythians would hurl hemp seeds onto heated stones and then inhale the vapor to become intoxicated. This ritual would occur after a Scythian had died, and seems to presage the Irish wake. "The Scythians howl with joy for the vapour bath" was the way our ancient scribe put it.

Cannabis remained connected with the cult of the dead, even up to the present day in eastern Europe. The anthropologist, Sula Benet, reported that today in Poland and Lithuania, on Christmas Eve when the dead come back to visit, a soup made of cannabis seeds called semieniatka is served to the dearly departed. On Shrove Tuesday in Poland married women dance the "hemp dance," and young brides are sprinkled with cannabis seeds in lieu of rice. The creative Poles also use marijuana for divination, especially with respect to affairs of the heart. The eve of Saint Andrew's (November 30) is the best time to determine marital plans, and certain rituals, utilizing cannabis seeds, are believed to hasten the marital union. Benet, in an article in the anthology *Cannabis and Culture*, notes:

> Girls in the Ukraine carry hemp seeds in their belts, they jump on a heap and call out: "Andrei, Andrei, I plant the hemp seed on you. Will god let me know with whom I will sleep?" The girls then remove their shirts and fill their mouths with water to sprinkle on the seed to keep the birds from eating them. Then they run around the house naked three times.

Benet also reported the wide use of hemp in folk medicine in Russia and eastern Europe. In Poland, Russia and Lithuania, hemp was used to treat toothache by inhaling the vapor from seeds thrown onto hot stones. Years later, in New York City during the 1920s, it was not uncommon for Russian and Polish immigrants to trek over to Nassau Street, buy bulk cannabis, return to their Lower East Side tenements, throw the cannabis on the radiator, and, using a towel to form a smoke chamber, inhale the fumes for respiratory ailments.

Although tincture of cannabis was widely used in America from the mid-1800s until 1937, very few reports of its psychoactive properties were made. Perhaps this was due to the psychological set of the patients; they were taking a medicine, not indulging in a vice. At any rate there were a few early psychic explorers, and the most famous of these was a young man who lived in upstate New York: Fitz Hugh Ludlow.

Ludlow was born September 11, 1836, in New York City and grew up in Poughkeepsie, New York. In 1855 he was attending college in Schenectady, New York and chanced upon an article by the writer and traveler Bayard Taylor. Taylor described his experiences with the fabled drug hashish, which, as we know today, is a concentrated form of marijuana. It was the first personal account of hashish use by an American (which in France had reached semi-institutionalized status through the Club des Haschischins, whose prominent members included Baudelaire, Gautier, Dumas, Balzac and Nerval).

Being a curious lad, and fueled by the fantastic reminiscences of Taylor, Ludlow began to frequent the apothecary shop of his friend Anderson. The potions and utensils held a fascination for the twenty-year-old, and soon he was experimenting with consciousness alteration by inhaling chloroform. From chloroform, Ludlow advanced to ether, then opiates, "until I had run through the whole gamut of queer agents within my reach."

But then in 1855 a chance occurrence:

> One morning, in the spring of 185—, I dropped in upon the doctor for my accustomed lounge. "Have you seen," said he, "my new acquisitions?" I looked toward the shelves in the direction of which he pointed, and saw, added since my last visit, a row of comely pasteboard cylinders inclosing vials of the various extracts prepared by Tilden and Co. . . .
>
> A rapid glance showed most of them to be old acquaintances. "Conium, taraxacum, rhubarb—ha! what is this? Cannabis Indica?" "That," answered the doctor, looking with a parental fondness upon his new treasure, "is a preparation of the East Indian hemp, a powerful agent in cases of lock-jaw." On the strength of this introduction, I took down the little archer, and, removing his outer verdant coat, began the further prosecution of his acquaintance. To pull out a broad and shallow cork was the work of an instant, and it revealed to me an olive-brown extract, of the consistency of pitch, and a decided aromatic odor. Drawing out a small portion upon the point of my penknife, I was just going to put it to my tongue, when "Hold on!" cried the doctor; "do you want to kill yourself? That stuff is deadly poison." "Indeed!" I replied; "no, I can not say that I have any settled determination of that kind"; and with that I replaced the cork, and restored the extract, with all its appurtenances, to the shelf.

Ludlow immediately consulted his *Dispensatory* and recognized the cannabis extract to be none other than the famed hashish that Taylor had described. So, sneaking a ten-grain pill, Ludlow began his experimentation. At first he observed no effects, and he gradually increased the dosage to thirty grains. And suddenly America's first recreational cannabis user found himself stoned:

> Ha! what means this sudden thrill? A shock, as of some unimagined vital force, shoots without warning through my entire frame, leap-

ing to my fingers' ends, piercing my brain, startling me till I almost spring from my chair.

I could not doubt it. I was in the power of the hasheesh influence. My first emotion was one of uncontrollable terror—a sense of getting something which I had not bargained for. That moment I would have given all I had or hoped to have to be as I was three hours before.

No pain anywhere—not a twinge in any fibre—yet a cloud of unutterable strangeness was settling upon me, and wrapping me impenetrably in from all that was natural or familiar. Endeared faces, well known to me of old, surrounded me, yet they were not with me in my loneliness. I had entered upon a tremendous life which they could not share.

What loneliness! This bookish son of a prominent abolitionist preacher continued his hashish adventures, using the innocent extract for phantasmagorical flights of imagination, voyages that took him from his drab, small-town environment to fabulous Middle Eastern, African and Asian lands, immersed in alien cultures. Ludlow gobbled up all the Tilden's Extract at Anderson's and, a few weeks later, scored a weaker preparation at another chemist's. So naturally, to compensate, he upped the dosage to fifty grains, and proceeded to freak out:

I do not know how long a time had passed since midnight, when I awoke suddenly to find myself in a realm of the most perfect clarity of view, yet terrible with an infinitude of demoniac shadows. . . . Beside my bed in the centre of the room stood a bier, from whose corners drooped the folds of a heavy pall; outstretched upon it lay in state a most fearful corpse, whose livid face was distorted with the pangs of assassination. . . .

But—oh, horror immeasurable! I beheld the walls of the room slowly gliding together, the ceiling coming down, the floor ascending, as of old the lonely captive saw them, whose cell was doomed to be his coffin. Nearer and nearer am I borne toward the corpse. I shrunk back from the edge of the bed; I cowered in most abject fear. I tried to cry out, but speech was paralyzed. The walls came closer and closer together. Presently my hand lay on the dead man's forehead. I made my arm as straight and rigid as a bar of iron; but of what avail was human strength against the contraction of that cruel masonry? Slowly my elbow bent with the ponderous pressure; nearer grew the ceiling—I fell into the fearful embrace of death. I was pent, I was stifled in the breathless niche, which was all of space still left to me. The stony eyes stared up into my own, and again the maddening peal of fiendish laughter rang close beside my ear. Now I was touched on all sides by the walls of the terrible press; there came a heavy crush, and I felt all sense blotted out in darkness.

> I awaked at last; the corpse was gone, but I had taken his place upon the bier.

And so the first American bad trip was recorded. Ludlow continued his experiments with the extract, publishing the results in a widely read article in the September 1856 issue of *Putnam's Monthly Magazine*, and in his book, *The Hasheesh Eater*, first published in 1857 by Harper and Brothers.

Apparently Ludlow's experience was not an isolated one for long. In 1860 Mordecai Cooke, an English writer, noted in *The Seven Sisters of Sleep:*

> Young America is beginning to use the "bang," so popular among the Hindoos, though in rather a different manner, for young Jonathan must in some sort be an original. It is not a "drink," but a mixture of bruised hemp tops and the powder of the betel, rolled up like a quid of tobacco. It turns the lips and gums a deep red, and if indulged in largely, produces violent intoxication. Lager beer and schnapps will give way for "bang," and red lips, instead of red noses, become the "style."

As a medicinal agent, marijuana generally fell into disfavor before the turn of the century. For one, it was insoluble, and therefore couldn't be injected. So there were delays of up to three hours when administered orally. Secondly, there was tremendous difficulty in standardizing the dosage, as different batches showed great variations in potency. Also, there were variations among individuals in their response to the drug. So, when the new synthetic drugs were introduced—drugs which, like morphine, were capable of administration by the newly discovered hypodermic syringe—cannabis use decreased.

However, as a recreational drug, cannabis was just beginning to be discovered by adventurous Americans. In 1876 the Turkish display at the Philadelphia Exposition featured hash-smoking, and by 1885 clandestine hashish clubs catering to a well-heeled clientele composed of writers, artists, doctors and society matrons had been established in every major American city from New York to San Francisco.

In 1883 H. H. Kane, writing anonymously in the November issue of *Harper's Monthly*, gave a lurid description of a Hashish House in New York. The naïve author was taken by a friend in the know to a house on Forty-second Street, near the Hudson River. The house was run by a Greek and frequented by Americans and foreigners of "the better classes"—some masked, all garbed in Oriental costumes, all indulging their "morbid appetites." Kane recalled his entry into this strange world:

> A volume of heavily scented air, close upon the heels of which came a deadly sickening odor, wholly unlike anything I had ever smelled, greeted my nostrils. A hall lamp of grotesque shape flooded the hall with a subdued violet light that filtered through crenated disks of some violet fabric hung below it. The walls and ceilings, if ever modern, were no longer so, for they were shut in and hung by festoons and plaits of heavy cloth fresh from Eastern looms. Tassels of blue, green, yellow, red and tinsel here and there peeped forth, matching the curious edging of variously colored beadwork that bordered each fold of drapery like a huge procession of luminous ants, and seemed to flow into little phosphorescent pools wherever the cloth was caught up. Queer figures and strange lettering, in the same work, were here and there disclosed upon the ceiling cloth.

And that was just a description of the hall, while Kane was still straight! Once at the end of the hall, they were greeted by a "colored" servant, where they exchanged their clothing for long silk gowns, tasseled smoking caps, and noiseless slippers. After paying two dollars each, they received a small pipe filled with gunjeh (potent marijuana) and then repaired to one of the many smoking rooms, outfitted with numerous pillows and divans. Finally our adventurers were ready to smoke. With his companion acting as a guide, Kane began the smoking ritual:

> . . . As I smoked I noticed that about two-thirds of the divans were occupied by persons of both sexes, some of them masked, who were dressed in the same manner as ourselves. Some were smoking, some reclining listlessly upon the pillows, following the tangled thread of a hashish reverie or dream. A middle-aged woman sat bolt upright, gesticulating and laughing quietly to herself; another with lacklustre eyes and dropped jaw was swaying her head monotonously from side to side. A young man of about eighteen was on his knees, praying inaudibly; and another man, masked, paced rapidly and noiselessly up and down the room, until led away somewhere by the turbaned servant.

Like Ludlow before him, Kane did not know his limitations, and soon was hallucinating strange visions. At the end of his trip he saw a "thousand anguished faces" toiling at the bottom of a flame-encrusted abyss. Incarnate spirits of individuals who sought "happiness in the various narcotics." Their task in this netherworld? "To be obliged to yield day by day their lifeblood to form the juice of poppy and resin of hemp in order that their dreams, joys, hopes, pleasures, pains, and anguish of past and present may again be tasted by mortals." After awakening from this reverie in a cold sweat, Kane left his companion and high-tailed it for home.

> The dirty streets, the tinkling car-horse bell, the deafening "Here you are! twenty sweet oranges for a quarter!" and the drizzling rain were more grateful by far than the odors, sounds, and sights, sweet though they were, that I had just left. Truly it was the cradle of dreams rocking placidly in the very heart of a great city, translated from Baghdad to Gotham.

And again, like Ludlow before him, Kane ended his adventures on a moralistic note. Consumption of cannabis for the purpose of idle recreation was clearly a costly endeavor to Kane, one approached and evaluated with mixed feelings.

CHAPTER 2:
The Killer Weed Heads North: Enter Mr. Anslinger

By 1898 mariguana (Mexican for "intoxicant") was widely used in Mexico, usually in the form of cigarettes. It was thought that Pancho Villa's army fortified their struggle by the use of the weed, and the popular Mexican folk song "La Cucaracha" seems to refer to Villa's troops.

> The cockroach, the cockroach
> Now cannot walk
> Because he does not have, because he does not have
> Marihuana to smoke.

Among the first Americans to smoke the flowering tops of the cannabis plant were the Black Cavalry units stationed along the Mexican border at the turn of the century. The use of marijuana was also promulgated by sailors who brought back the drug from South and Central American ports. Of course the Mexican "wetbacks" who came to America to labor in the beet fields of the Southwest naturally continued their custom of smoking the plant.

Among the first Americans to adopt the practice were the blacks in the South, and some reports claim that as early as colonial times slaves smoked the hemp plant, having been familiar with it in Africa. At any rate, it is clear that the first users of marijuana—that is, the first people to smoke cannabis for mostly recreational purposes—were members of minority groups.

The first cities to perceive the use of marijuana as a problem were the Texas border towns, like El Paso, and New Orleans. A 1917 Department of Agriculture investigation noted that El Paso passed a city ordinance banning the sale and possession of marijuana in 1914. The town at that time was characterized as a "hot bed of marihuana fiends," and consumption of the drug was attributed not only to Mexicans, but also to "Negroes, prostitutes, pimps and a criminal class of whites."

Similarly, marijuana first appeared to be used in New Orleans around 1910 by blacks, and early fears were that the vice would spread to the white schoolchildren.

Along with blacks, another social type that figured in the early use of marijuana was musicians. In a letter dated August 21, 1920, to Governor John Parker, Oscar Dowling, the President of the Louisiana State Board of Health and an early marijuana alarmist, wrote:

> There is in Parish Prison a young man, Lewis Ernest Stephens, white, age 21, musician . . . charged with forging name of Dr. Lindner to prescription for Mariguana. Mariguana is the Spanish name for Cannabis Indica and according to Stephens is used to "make you feel good."

Dowling also sent a copy of the letter to Dr. Hugh Cummings, the Surgeon General of the United States, and added: "It seems to me it is imperative that the Federal Government take some action to enforce strict supervision of all drugs coming into this country."

But by and large, from 1915 until 1933, marijuana use was perceived to be a local problem, Dowling's views notwithstanding, and state after state enacted some form of prohibition against the nonmedical abuse of the drug. California in 1915, Texas in 1919, Louisiana in 1924, New York by 1927—one by one most states acted, usually when faced with significant numbers of Mexicans or Negroes utilizing the drug.

Usually the legislation was prompted by lurid newspaper stories depicting marijuana as a causative agent in crime or insanity. The Hearst chain were leaders in this regard, but even the newspaper of record, the *New York Times*, reported these horror stories.

However, the issue was also one that provided the state legislators with a chance for a bit of levity in the midst of their serious duties. On January 27, 1929, the *Montana Standard* reported the progress of a bill that amended the state's general narcotics law to include marijuana:

> There was fun in the House Health Committee during the week when the Marihuana bill came up for consideration. Marihuana is

> Mexican opium, a plant used by Mexicans and cultivated for sale by Indians. "When some beet field peon takes a few rares of this stuff," explained Dr. Fred Fulsher of Mineral County, "he thinks he has just been elected president of Mexico so he starts out to execute all his political enemies. I understand that over in Butte where the Mexicans often go for the winter they stage imaginary bullfights in the 'Bower of Roses' or put on tournaments for the favor of 'Spanish Rose' after a couple of whiffs of Marihuana. The Silver Bow and Yellowstone delegations both deplore these international complications." Everybody laughed and the bill was recommended for passage.

While the Montana legislature was "debating" their marijuana bill, a career bureaucrat, whose name would later go down in history linked hand-in-stem with the Marijuana Menace, was having a difficult time enforcing the prohibition of America's favorite recreational drug: alcohol. Harry Jacob Anslinger had just been appointed Assistant Commissioner of Prohibition, after working three years on the problem in Washington as Chief of the Division of Foreign Control with the Treasury Department.

If there was ever a better prohibitionist, Uncle Sam had never received his civil service application. Anslinger was born on May 20, 1892, in Altoona, Pennsylvania, a Taurus on the cusp of Gemini. Of sturdy Pennsylvania Dutch parentage, the young lad suffered a traumatic experience at the age of twelve that was to change the course of his life. In *The Murderers—The Shocking Story of the Narcotic Gangs*, Anslinger painfully recalled that incident:

> As a youngster of twelve, visiting in the house of a neighboring farmer, I heard the screaming of a woman on the second floor. I had never heard such cries of pain before. The woman, I learned later, was addicted, like many other women of that period, to morphine, a drug whose dangers most medical authorities did not yet recognize. All I remember was that I heard a woman in pain, whose cries seemed to fill my whole twelve-year-old being. Then her husband came running down the stairs, telling me I had to get into the cart and drive to town. I was to pick up a package at the drug store and bring it back for the woman.
>
> I recall driving those horses, lashing at them, convinced that the woman would die if I did not get back in time. When I returned with the package—it was morphine—the man hurried upstairs to give the woman the dosage. In a little while her screams stopped and a hush came over the house.
>
> I never forgot those screams. Nor did I forget that the morphine she had required was sold to a twelve-year-old boy, no questions asked.

But not only did young Harry harbor a crusader's zeal against the narcotic menace; he was possessed of a hankering for sleuthing and a remarkable aptitude for that work that produced results. At twenty he was an investigator for the Pennsylvania Railroad, while working his way through State College. A woman had been killed by the Broadway Limited at a grade crossing, and her aggrieved husband was suing for $50,000 damages, claiming that her shoe had become caught in the track while crossing and that the oncoming train was not visible due to a sharp curve in the track. Just as the railroad company lawyers were about to settle the claim, Anslinger came forth with evidence that the accident was, in fact, suicide. Suspicious that anyone would cross at such an isolated spot, the young sleuth searched the area and found the victim's market basket in some bushes. On questioning the couple's neighbors, he learned that the pair had quarreled violently the morning of the accident. Finally the husband admitted that his wife had threatened to kill herself, and the spurious suit was dropped.

Anslinger's work impressed his superior, who, on promotion to head the state police, enlisted Anslinger to take charge of arson investigations. Harry left college and investigated fires until World War I. At twenty-five he became an inspector for the War Department; after a year he applied for foreign service and in 1918 was assigned to the American Legation at The Hague. Situated behind enemy lines, young Anslinger carried out many espionage missions. As a result, he somehow obtained the field utility kit and other minor personal possessions of His Imperial Highness Kaiser Wilhelm II, which were donated to the Smithsonian Institution in 1957. "How I obtained them must remain a state secret," the modest official wrote later.

From The Hague, he became Vice-Consul at Hamburg, Germany, which was at that time a worldwide center for illicit drugs. After two years Anslinger was promoted to a consulship at La Guaira, Venezuela, where he encountered pearl-smuggling. These were good times for the Altoona native, and he and his wife, the former Martha Denniston, enjoyed the life of the foreign corps.

But duty reared its ugly head and interrupted Anslinger's idyllic stay in Venezuela, when he was transferred to the Bahamas as consul in 1926. In Nassau Anslinger came face to face with rumrunning, and his prohibitionist instincts were honed.

And on the creative front, being in the Bahamas gave him insight into another social problem: the shark scares. In his spare time, Harry wrote an article exposing the myth that sharks attack humans, and revealed that it was, in fact, barracudas who are the culprits of the deep. Published in the June 12, 1926, issue of the *Saturday Evening Post*, Anslinger debunked the shark's bad image with: "It may be safely stated that unless a shark is ravenously hungry he will not attack a human being, unless he is positive that the man has been drowned or is absolutely helpless. He has never been known to attack anything that is perfectly healthy."

It didn't take long for a torrent of letters to swamp the magazine's desks. People from all over the world sent in protesting letters, documenting horrible experiences where sharks had attacked humans. The editors at the *Post* forwarded the letters to Anslinger and asked for a follow-up article.

The result was "Shark Fins," and it bears scrutiny:

> Australians regard with astonishment persons who claim that the vicious barracuda is responsible for attacks by sharks. They have many arguments to back up their claim that the shark is a man-eater.
>
> Early in 1927, a fifteen-year-old boy died as a result of being attacked by a shark at Port Hacking, Australia. . . . It was found that the flesh of the right leg had been torn completely off from thigh to ankle, leaving the bones exposed and causing death shortly thereafter. . . .
>
> A sailor shipwrecked on Surprise Island reef in New Caledonia in 1916 saw a native Kanaka disappear in a flurry of blood and foam. The Kanakas remarked, "Too much blurry shark.". . .
>
> In the summer of 1926, a shark captured at Koolau, Hawaii, was found to contain human bones and a pair of swimming trunks. The bones consisted of more than half of the upper part of a skull, a hand, a knee, two whole arms, one leg bone and the first and second cervical vertebrae. (Photograph) A quantity of short black hair was attached to the skull. . . .

At last this document reveals the full maturation of the inimitable Anslinger style, the style that would titillate thousands of readers of *The Murderers*, *The Protectors*, and *The Traffic in Narcotics*. It was two-fisted journalism, pulling no punches, leaving no bone unturned. Here we have our first inkling of his tremendous feel for anatomical detail. Here we see the first usage of the litany of case histories. Finally, we note the obvious concern for the individual as opposed to the statistic. Nine years later Anslinger would be published again in a mass-media magazine. This time it would be the *American Magazine* of July 1937, but the style echoes the Bahamas, 1928. It began:

> The sprawled body of a young girl lay crushed on the sidewalk the other day after a plunge from the fifth story of a Chicago apartment house. Everyone called it suicide, but actually it was murder. The killer was a narcotic known to America as marijuana, and to history as hashish. It is a narcotic used in the form of cigarettes, comparatively new to the United States and as dangerous as a coiled rattlesnake. . . .

It was the flowering of a long, distinguished career. In one paragraph one can hear the echoes of the bloody railroad tracks that the Broadway Central hugged, the moans of the innocent swimmers cut down during a moment of relaxation by a dark vicious denizen of the deep. And of course the shriek of that desperate woman in that lonely farmhouse. Harry Anslinger was forty-five when his article appeared, and he was the head of the Bureau of Narcotics. And he had finally found his sharks in America, masquerading as a harmless little weed the Mexicans called marijuana, or "good feeling."

CHAPTER 3:
The Bureau Responds

Before we closely examine that "Marijuana: Assassin of Youth" article, we must return to 1929 and see how marijuana came to be defined as an object of national scorn and fear. In 1929 Anslinger was still fighting a losing battle against alcohol. Whereas in 1928 the young bureaucrat was convinced that alcohol prohibition could work (he even entered a contest sponsored by the "Prize Committee on the Eighteenth Amendment" where he suggested severe penalties of a fine not less than $1,000 and imprisonment of not less than six months in jail for the manufacture, sale, transport or *purchase* of liquor), by the next year he seemed to have soured on enforcing a law that lacked popular support. He later submitted a plan called "Common Sense Tolerance" that argued:

> The law must fit the facts. Prohibition will never succeed through the promulgation of a mere law observance program if the American people regard it as obnoxious. Temperance by choice is far better than the present condition of temperance by force. . . .

Anslinger's solution was the solution of the bureaucratic mind. He devised a three-pronged attack, with quasi-public control over liquor production (a remarkable proposal coming from a Neanderthal right-winger and an avowed enemy of the Bolsheviks in Russia and, later, the Communists in China), supplying individual consumption, and educating the public. Recognizing the fact that prohibiting liquor for *personal* use was next to impossible, the pragmatic Anslinger proposed:

> A person who desires to purchase liquor for domestic use must make a written application to the system company in his district, stating his age, occupation, salary, reason for wishing to purchase liquor, etc. This application should then be considered by the system company, and if it be approved, the applicant receives a purchase

> book entitling him to buy regularly a certain limited quantity of liquor.

According to Anslinger, another unanticipated drawback of Prohibition was public health violations. Smugglers were filthy and brought with them disease as well as contraband:

> Vessels sailing from filthy Central American and West Indian ports, having the lowest scum of the earth as members of the crew, sail into ports without passing quarantine, members of the crew contaminating the people of the slums with whom they mingle with contagious and loathsome diseases. . . .

So, if anything, we see a complex individual poised to become the first Commissioner of the Bureau of Narcotics in 1930. Anslinger was part ideologue, to be sure; his conservative upbringing, his hatred for the Bolsheviks while serving in The Hague and in Germany, and his soon-to-be-nurtured loathing for narcotics and the weak individuals who purvey and use them certainly add a resonance to an examination of his actions with respect to marijuana. However, as his consular career and his brief bout with Prohibition show, by 1930, with some twelve years of government service under his belt, Anslinger was also a consummate bureaucrat, responsible to superiors, and ever mindful of the impact of policy on the maintenance of office.

As Anslinger assumed control of the newly formed Bureau of Narcotics, which was subsumed into the Treasury Department of the federal government, the concern over marijuana was just beginning to have a national impact. In the states where marijuana usage was visible, namely, the Southwest and Louisiana, pressure began to mount to enact legislation against its use. Although most Americans couldn't care less about this strange exotic drug, a handful of newspaper editors, legislators and concerned citizens began to put pressure on Washington to move on the issue. However, there were complications with respect to enacting federal legislation against the drug.

Narcotic drugs were regulated at the federal level by the Harrison Act of 1914. For a time cannabis was included in the early drafts of that legislation; however, due to the vocal opposition of the pharmaceutical and medical professions, it was later dropped. The Harrison Act, as passed in 1914, seemed merely to be a law which raised revenue by the orderly marketing of narcotics on the part of doctors, pharmacists, manufacturers and importers. However, as interpreted by the courts, the Act became a tool which prevented physicians from maintaining opiate addicts as part of their treatment.

However, these decisions revealed a sharply divided court (on two occasions, 5 to 4, and later, 6 to 3), and when marijuana regulation became an issue, the natural impulse to place it under Harrison Act controls was resisted by Washington bureaucrats. The first evidence of that reluctance to jeopardize the slim majority view with respect to the Harrison Act was a letter dated June 10, 1929, from Cummings, the Surgeon General, to the *Journal of the American Pharmaceutical Association.*

An editor to the journal had requested information with respect to marijuana, and, after noting that its use was a problem "in the southwestern and far western States," Cummings replied:

> There has been some discussion respecting the desirability of including Indian hemp or marihuana in the present Federal narcotic law. I am inclined to think that such a plan would be difficult of administration and would probably be a factor in nullifying the constitutionality of the existing law.

Again, in January 1930, District Judge John Killit of Ohio wrote to James Doran, the Commissioner of the Department of Prohibition Enforcement and Anslinger's immediate superior, apprising him of a case in his court where the defendant possessed, in addition to "white mule," two quarts of a decoction of "Mexican loco weed" or "maruana, a very nasty narcotic."

Doran, in his reply, noted that his office has resisted subsuming marijuana under the Harrison Act "on the ground that the constitutionality of the Harrison Law may thereby be imperiled since the drug is producible from a plant grown domestically and is not included within the terms of the International Opium Convention of 1912. . . ." Instead, Doran suggested that the states "reduce or even restrict absolutely the growth of marijuana and a Federal Law might be drawn regulating the interstate commerce in the drug."

Anslinger took over as acting Commissioner of an autonomous Federal Bureau of Narcotics in June 1930, fully cognizant of the increasing demand for federal regulation of marijuana and at least in some sense familiar with the drug itself. For in April of that year, Anslinger, in his position as Secretary of the Federal Narcotics Control Board (under the Prohibition Unit), had instituted a survey of sorts into the cannabis problem. The survey was prompted by proposed legislation that sought to bring cannabis under the purview of the Narcotic Drugs Import and Export Act.

One of the people to whom Anslinger addressed a series of fundamental questions about cannabis was William Woodward, the Director of the Bureau of Legal Medicine and Legislation of the American Medical Association. The AMA, who by 1930 was a potent political force in medical matters, had had uneasy relations with the Treasury Department, especially since the Harrison Act had set the stage for a large number of cases where doctors were arrested and prosecuted for treating drug addicts by maintaining their habit.

So Woodward's reply to Anslinger on April 28, 1930, reeks with sarcasm and ill-disguised contempt:

> Undertaking to answer as far as practicable your specific questions, the following information is offered in response to the particular questions propounded by you:
>
> I—*What is the quality of Indian Hemp produced in the United States?* Ans.—The American Medical Association has no knowledge with respect to this matter.
>
> II—*What is the geographical distribution of the areas where Indian Hemp is grown within the United States?* Ans.—The American Medical Association has no information with respect to this matter except such as may be found in books and journals, with which information, it is presumed, you are already familiar.
>
> III—*What are the medical needs and uses of the drug or drugs produced from Indian Hemp?* Ans.—The answer to this question can be found in standard books on pharmacology and therapeutics, which are available in large numbers in the Surgeon General's library in Washington.
>
> IV—*What is the comparative medical value of Indian Hemp as domestically produced and as produced in foreign countries?* Ans.—The answer to this question can be found in standard books on pharmacology and therapeutics, which are available in large numbers in the Surgeon General's library in Washington.
>
> V—*What further information can you furnish concerning cannabis indica or Indian Hemp that does not fall within the questions propounded above, but which may be of assistance to the Federal Narcotics Control Board in making its report on S.2075, to include cannabis indica and cannabis sativa within the purview of the Narcotic Drugs Import and Export Act?* Ans.—The expediency of including cannabis indica and cannabis sativa within the scope of the proposed uniform state narcotic law has been made the subject of

> extensive correspondence with manufacturing pharmacists during the past year. I had assumed, as apparently you have done, that there was no question concerning the habit-forming properties of the drugs named. My recent correspondence, however, seems to throw some doubt with respect to the matter. . . .

To this chilly letter Woodward appended a thirteen-page document consisting of extracts from letters he had received from pharmaceutical manufacturers relative to the pharmaceutical use and habit-forming properties of cannabis. Twenty-nine out of the thirty respondents objected strongly to including cannabis under the Narcotic Drugs Act. One pharmacist railed: "Absolute rot. It is not necessary. I have never known of its misuse." A few maintained that the government should let sleeping dogs lie:

> With reference to Cannabis Indica, also Cannabis Americana, as far as our experience goes, the drug is practically abandoned in regular medicine. In veterinary medicine it is used to some extent. We make and offer the tincture and fluid extract and sell almost none. As far as we know there are only three products we offer in which it is one of the unimportant ingredients. Our opinion is that an action of this kind would only call attention to something which is already dormant and of no consequence, at least in the Eastern section of the United States.

The one respondent who cautioned Woodward about cannabis was saved for last. This correspondent reported meeting a physician from Indiana who contracted the cannabis habit during World War I. "He said that for three years he was as much a slave to the addiction of the drug as was ever a user of opium in any of its forms. . . . He had to take treatment, which he described as being similar to the treatment for morphine addiction. He said it was at least four months after he left the sanatorium before he fully regained his strength and nerve equilibrium. This may be an exceptional case."

That it was. Of thirty responses, only one reported negatively about cannabis. And, predictably enough, that was the one answer that Anslinger marked off in the margin of the letter with a broad bracket, destined to be filed for future use in the rapidly expanding file marked "Marihuana" of the infant Bureau of Narcotics.

Anslinger had also asked some of his field agents in the Prohibition Unit to investigate the cannabis situation. In June 1930 one narcotics agent made purchases of marijuana cigarettes and interrogated the vendors. He found that most of the marijuana sold in New York was sold by Spaniards and East Indians to trade consisting mostly of members of those races. The drug was obtained by these street peddlers from crews of boats belonging to the United Fruit Lines. Up in Harlem the marijuana was selling for twenty-five cents a cigarette, \$1.00 to \$1.50 for fifteen or twenty grams and \$75.00 to \$100.00 a pound. However, the agent noted that the price was considerably cheaper along the border and in cities of the Southwest and West, where single cigarettes went for five cents and pounds could be purchased for \$5.00 or \$6.00.

The agent concluded:

> Marihuana is used for smoking by Indians, Mexicans, Philipinos [*sic*], Spaniards, and East Indians. In the larger cities of the United States it is used, distributed and sold in the Spanish, Philipino, Greek, East Indian and Mexican quarters, and it is used by some white habitués of the Tenderloin districts. In Texas, Oklahoma, and Southern California it is used to a great extent in cities surrounding the oil fields where there is a large population of Mexicans and Indians, and by habitués of the Tenderloin. The smokers use it for its enlivening effect which is described as making things appear brighter, and relieving the user of care and worry. Overindulgence in smoking it causes temporary insanity, makes the user irresponsible and vicious, and deeds of violence have been committed under its influence.

By December 18, 1930, Anslinger had finally attained Senate confirmation as the Commissioner of the new Narcotics Bureau, a confirmation that came on the heels of a record \$5 million dope bust in New York the day before. It was a perfectly timed publicity play, something Anslinger would become very adept at, and it so moved one senator that he entered a newspaper report of the arrest into the *Congressional Record* with a preface: "This commendable act gives evidence that Mr. Anslinger is going to make an effective and useful commissioner."

Anslinger's rise to Commissioner of the Bureau of Narcotics seemed meteoric, since he had spent only three years in the Prohibition Unit. However, some commentators have pointed out the fact that his wife Martha came from the well-connected Denniston family who made a fortune in steel, and was also a niece of Andrew Mellon, who, as Secretary of Treasury, was Anslinger's immediate superior. At any rate Anslinger was a good solid Republican, taking office during the Hoover administration, and it would be two years before the New Deal would threaten his control over the Bureau.

When Anslinger took over, the Narcotics Bureau had an annual budget of $1,411,260 up from the previous year's total of $1,350,440—not bad for a depressed economy. But, operating with a staff of only some three-hundred-odd agents, it was clear that priorities would have to be set with respect to law enforcement. While morphine and opium addiction were known evils, Anslinger, during 1931, received many queries from all over the country regarding this new "menace" marijuana. Typical of these was a letter sent to the Narcotics Division on March 14, 1931, from Carl Murphy, the president of the *Afro-American*, which billed itself as the "World's Biggest All-Negro Weekly." Murphy wrote:

> I find theatrical folk smoking a cigarette which they term Reefer of Magijuana [the spelling is phonetic and probably incorrect], a Mexican importation.
>
> I understand that it is a drug and injurious to the health.
>
> Please advise what the real name of this plant is and what its effects are on the human body.
>
> Its use has spread so that it seems necessary to call attention to it if it is injurious.

Anslinger replied with a standard letter describing *Cannabis indica*, detailing its deleterious effects, and noting the "grave question" as to its constitutionality if it were to be placed under the Harrison Act. Instead, he borrowed Cummings's ideas and raised the possibility of placing interstate commerce controls on its distribution and/or preventing its growth within the country.

But if Anslinger essentially passed the political hempball, newspapers all over the country began agitating for federal regulations with respect to the new drug. In New Orleans, where marijuana consciousness had been high since the 1920s, a number of magazine articles helped to increase the pressure on the newly formed Bureau to act on this grave social issue.

One of these agitators was Dr. A. E. Fossier, an M.D. from New Orleans, who, on April 14, 1931, read a paper before the Louisiana State Medical Society called "The Mariahuana [*sic*] Menace." Fossier's paper began with a recounting of the legendary Assassin myth, a myth that links hashish to the commission of brutal murders in Persia around 1090. Although the myth was later discredited, it served as demonstrable proof that marijuana use was intimately tied up with brutal crime. Fossier argued that one in every four people arrested in New Orleans was "addicted to mariahuana." Seventeen of the thirty-seven murderers smoked "muggles," the marijuana cigarette.

But Fossier revealed the implicit racism that the early anti-marijuana crusaders shared when he speculated on the causes for the alarming rise of "mariahuana addiction":

> As far as it can be ascertained this addiction has assumed formidable proportions since the advent of that "noble experiment," that fiasco, prohibition. In fact, it is the offspring which bids fair to surpass its dissembling parent in destroying moral inhibition. The lesser of the two evils is alcohol. . . . The debasing and baneful influence of hashish and opium is not restricted to individuals, but has manifested itself in nations and races as well. The dominant race and most enlightened countries are alcoholic, whilst the races and nations addicted to hemp and opium, some of which once attained to heights of culture and civilization, have deteriorated both mentally and physically.

The paper was very well received, and much praise was heaped on the hemp theories of Dr. Fossier during the discussion period. Dr. Frank Gomila, the Commissioner of Public Safety of New Orleans, assured the good doctors present that the police department had been ordered to crack down on the "muggles" trade, since it was a drug "in the same class as heroin." In closing, Fossier had one last warning:

> If overnight, after the advent of prohibition, this nation became so adept in the brewing of beer, the making of wine and the distilling of alcohol, so much so that even children are adept in their manufacture, what will happen in the near future, with such a dangerous plant that may grow in our very backyards?

Another influential article which appeared that year was "Marihuana As a Developer of Criminals," by Eugene Stanley, the District Attorney of New Orleans. Originally published in the *American Journal of Police Science*, it recommended that marijuana be placed among the narcotic drugs covered under the Harrison Act. Again the old Assassin myth was trotted out, along with the notion that the drug is favored by the underworld for its value in "subjugating the will of human derelicts to that of a master mind." As if that weren't enough, Stanley further cautioned that it is commonly used as an aphrodisiac, although its continued use leads to impotency.

Stanley's article was widely circulated among law enforcement officials, and one copy was sent to Anslinger by the New Orleans Narcotic Agent in Charge. In an accompanying letter, the perceptive agent wrote:

> This is forwarded for information of the Bureau, and of any interest the Bureau may have in the proposition now and in the future, as Mr. Stanley had given newspaper interviews along the same line urging public opinion to compel the Federal Government to have a law passed with regard to "Marihuana" similar to the anti-narcotic statutes.
>
> Of course, it is a self-evident fact that the Federal Government would be seriously handicapped in the enactment and enforcement of law upon "Marihuana." Here in New Orleans, and in the Southland, this plant grows promiscuously. The Police Department here in New Orleans advises this office that this vegetable is grown generally on vacant city lots and out in the open country. The difficulty of enforcing a restrictive law with regard to production of "Marihuana" is obvious. It would appear that the suppression of the growth, use and dealing in Cannabis Indica is very clearly a police matter, hardly to be reached effectively by an Internal Revenue Statute of the Federal Government.

In his reply, Anslinger agreed with the agent's views and further stated that before federal legislation could be proposed, "it would be necessary to give the subject very careful consideration, particularly with reference to the extent to which cannabis sativa is grown in the United States, the extent of its use for bona fide medical purposes, and whether such use could be supplied by the substitution of a less harmful drug." He then requested that these views be communicated by the agent to Mr. Stanley.

So, early in his first year in office it was clear that Anslinger did not desire to burden his small staff with the additional responsibility of regulating traffic in a weed that was so widely available. The pressure on the Bureau to do so was coming from the southwestern, western and Gulf states and, by and large, the users of this new drug were minorities.

In an interview with Yale Professor David Musto in 1970, Anslinger recalled that early enforcement was directed at Mexicans whom the "sheriffs and local police departments claimed got loaded on the stuff and caused a lot of trouble, stabbing, assaults, and so on." But the New Orleans authorities were the first to warn the nation of the real danger marijuana offered. It was one thing that Mexicans were cutting each other up in the barrios during these lean Depression years. It was quite a different cause for concern when the "muggles" were actually being sold to impressionable white schoolchildren. Gomila, in one of his mid-1930 articles on the dangers of marijuana, reported: "One gentleman of the byways explained: 'The worst thing about that loco weed is the way these kids go for them. Most of them, boys and girls, are just punks and when they get high on the stuff you can write your own ticket.' "

But by 1931 the hysteria was largely confined to New Orleans, and Anslinger sought to temper it in the Bureau's annual report: "The Traffic in Opium and Other Dangerous Drugs." He wrote:

> This abuse of the drug (Marihuana) is noted particularly among the Latin-American or Spanish-speaking population. . . .
>
> A great deal of public interest has been aroused by newspaper articles appearing from time to time on the evils of the abuse of marihuana, or Indian hemp, and more attention has been focused upon specific cases reported of the abuse of the drug than would otherwise have been the case. This publicity tends to magnify the extent of the evil and lends color to an inference that there is an alarming spread of the improper use of the drug, whereas the actual increase in such use may not have been inordinately large. . . .

Anslinger urged state laws to regulate marijuana use, and this remained the position of the Bureau over the next few years; all inquiries to the Bureau with respect to marijuana got the standard reply that it was a matter for the states and their localities to deal with. It was clear that marijuana was not a priority of the Bureau.

During 1933 and 1934 the pressure on the Bureau mounted. Newspapers carried lurid accounts of the spread of the marijuana habit. For example, the *Los Angeles Examiner*, on November 5, 1933, screamed: MURDER WEED FOUND UP AND DOWN COAST—DEADLY MARIHUANA DOPE PLANT READY FOR HARVEST THAT MEANS ENSLAVEMENT OF CALIFORNIA CHILDREN. Two days later the *San Francisco Examiner* headlined: DOPE OFFICIALS HELPLESS TO CURB MARIHUANA USE.

However, in 1934 the marijuana phenomenon received attention from professional quarters as well as the sensationalistic press. At Bellevue Hospital in New York, Walter Bromberg, an assistant psychiatrist at the time, reported a clinical study of *Cannabis sativa* in the September issue of the *American Journal of Psychiatry*. Bromberg, who was presenting the first scientific data on marijuana since the scare began in the early 1930s, found that marijuana itself was not primarily responsible for crime. Rather, he argued that the drug simply uncovers the underlying antisocial aggressive and sadistic elements of persons who may use it. Using as an informant "an intelligent negro who has had an extensive criminal career and a wide acquaintance in the underworld," Bromberg delved into the sociological aspects of marijuana use. "Most folks in show business smoke it," Bromberg quoted his source as saying. "For the last five years it has increased to my knowing. . . . You can leave it at the start but not after a while. You want the exhilaration it gives you. . . . After a while, you just go on the bum. You can't do anything. You are dull. . . . Dancers especially like it because it makes you feel light. Only a few of those who smoke marihuana go in for morphine or heroin. Most of those who have the habit are satisfied with it and stay in it, increasing the dose."

Returning to the crime thesis, Bromberg reported that not a single case of confirmed marijuana addiction was found in a group of 2,216 criminals convicted of felonies in the Court of General Sessions in New York City in 1933. "None of the assault crimes could be said to have been committed under the drug's influence. No crimes were committed in this group at a time during or after the intoxication," he concluded.

One year later, in 1935, in an article for *Medical Record* called "The Menace of Marihuana," Bromberg continued to debunk the "breeder of crime" theory regarding marijuana:

> In considering marihuana as a "breeder of crime" one must bear in mind the psychopathic types that use the drug. It is more than probable that alcohol is at least as responsible for crime as is marihuana. It is inaccurate to assign such a role to the drug when the basic antisocial nature of the persons who use it is understood. From the material quoted and the experience with users, it is clear that marihuana cannot be considered a primary cause of crime. We cannot fasten on it responsibility for each new crime wave that appears. . . .

From all indications, Bromberg's empirical work had little effect on Anslinger. The Commissioner did appropriate the quotes from Bromberg's Negro source for the Bureau files; as for the doctor's thesis, Anslinger seemed to have little interest. That is, until February 1937, when he wrote to the Assistant Surgeon General inquiring whether Bromberg was in good standing in the medical profession.

However, we must note that Anslinger had other preoccupations at the time. After narrowly surviving when FDR and his Democratic New Deal swept into office, Anslinger came under serious attack near the end of 1934. A slew of letters descended on the White House, criticizing the running of the Bureau of Narcotics. One such letter, addressed to Roosevelt intimate James Farley, went:

> Anslinger, shaking and trembling, knowing you are going to can him, is making a big noise recently (seeking publicity) pinching a lot of poor *sick addicts*. And here's the *sad part*—a *genuine tragedy*—he conveys to society the impression that drug addicts are *desperate criminals*.
>
> Mr. Farley, drug addicts are the most *harmless* class of people in the country. A smart dick will tell you the same. *Not a narcotic agent.*

But the protests came from higher places too. In a letter to Stephen B. Gibbons, the Assistant Secretary of the Treasury and one of Anslinger's superiors, newly elected Senator Joseph Guffey of Pennsylvania called for Anslinger's dismissal:

> Enclosed herewith please find copy of a circular letter issued by Mr. H. J. Anslinger, Commissioner, Bureau of Narcotics, Treasury Department to District Supervisors and others concerned regarding Mr. ———.
>
> This circular letter has become public and the colored population of the State of Pennsylvania have been advised thereof. I am being deluged with complaints from our colored population because Mr. Anslinger has been so indiscreet as to refer to one of their race as a "ginger-colored nigger."
>
> It would seem to me that a man in such a responsible position as that held by Mr. Anslinger should have more discretion than to refer to one of such a large part of the population of this Country in the manner quoted above, and I doubt very much that one so indiscreet should be allowed to remain in such a responsible position. Personally, I think he should be replaced, and I submit the matter to you for your consideration.

But Anslinger had developed a strong following which included many highly placed pharmaceutical executives, many right-wing newspaper editors, and some influential congressmen; and, in the pre–Earl Butz atmosphere of the 1930s, he weathered the storm of his indiscreet remarks.

On the marijuana front, he maintained his position that the drug's control was a state and local matter, and he threw the weight of the Bureau behind the newly proposed Uniform State Acts that were being drafted in the early 1930s. The drug proposals went through five drafts and, in the final proposal, the cannabis section was withdrawn. However, any state could optionally add cannabis to their definition of "Narcotic Drugs." These drug controls apparently did not evince a strong interest from the National Conference of Commissioners, who had drafted this legislation. In the five-year period it took to hammer out the Uniform State Narcotics Laws, there was a total of one hour of debate by the full body. And, in the final draft, the bill passed the commissioners on October 8, 1932, by a vote of 26 to 3, meaning nineteen state commissioners did not even bother to show up for the roll call. Clearly the drug issue was not paramount in the midst of the Depression.

From 1932 to 1936 Anslinger strongly supported the Uniform State Laws, urging that the cannabis section be included by each state. The Bureau lobbied before each legislature in which the act was pending, oftentimes with agents doing the actual political pressuring. Anslinger himself made numerous speeches and radio broadcasts, drumming up public support for the legislation. However, by April 1933, only two states had enacted the Uniform Act in full, and by March 1935, only eight more had acted.

So by late 1934 Anslinger devised a new strategy to secure passage and arouse public opinion. Rather than merely noting the need for the Uniform Narcotic Act by states to combat drug problems, he focused specifically on the marijuana menace. By the 1935 issue of "Traffic in Opium," a substantial portion of that report dealt with marijuana. Whereas in the past marijuana might have received a page or two, thirteen pages of that year's report dealt with this new problem, including four full pages of photographs showing marijuana plants, leaves, cigarettes and seized bulk shipments.

By the end of 1935 it seemed that Anslinger's new strategy was working. Perhaps too well. By focusing on marijuana to secure the passage of the Uniform State Act, a Frankenstein was set loose on the land, driving our Mexican citizens loco, setting Negro against Negro, and tempting the innocent youth of our nation through an army of peddlers who would lurk by the schoolyards and entreat the innocents with "Wanna have fun? Hey, kid! Wanna have fun?"

The newspapers renewed their assault with a vengeance. In early 1936, under the headline "Murders Due to 'Killer Drug' Marihuana Sweeping United States," Universal News Service writer Kenneth Clark wrote this lead for a widely syndicated story:

> Shocking crimes of violence are increasing. Murders, slaughterings, cruel mutilations, maimings, done in cold blood, as if some hideous monster was amok in the land.
>
> Alarmed Federal and State authorities attribute much of this violence to the "killer drug."
>
> That's what experts call marihuana. It is another name for hashish. It's a derivative of Indian hemp, a roadside weed in almost every State in the Union. . . .
>
> Those addicted to marihuana, after an early feeling of exhilaration, soon lose all restraints, all inhibitions. They become bestial demoniacs, filled with the mad lust to kill. . . .

And the solution, of course, was not only the Uniform State Act, but a broader and stronger federal law that would bring marijuana under control:

> Do you know the Federal Government has no authority to arrest and imprison traffickers in death-dealing marihuana?
>
> Unfortunately, it's true. Uncle Sam can deal with opium, heroin, morphine, cocaine, but the production and use of marihuana within the United States are NOT PROHIBITED BY FEDERAL LAW. Strange, isn't it?

But, newspaper reports notwithstanding, the marijuana "problem" appeared to be overstated even by 1936. The majority of the public felt no concern for this issue, which was still, for all intents and purposes, limited to a small geographical and demographic segment of the country. And it is fair to say that the drive to federally outlaw marijuana had strong racial overtones. Not only were marijuana-crazed Mexicans and blacks objects of fear, but the possible association of blacks and young whites for the purpose of illicit thrills was enough to send any Rotarian, W.C.T.U. card-carrying member, Women's Clubber, or any church-going WASP running for the cover of oppressive laws.

Indicative of the thinly veiled racism surrounding the issue was a letter to Anslinger from Floyd Baskette, a friend of the Commissioner's, who was City Editor of the Alamosa, Colorado, *Daily Courier*. On September 4, 1936, Baskette wrote the Bureau:

> Two weeks ago a sex-mad degenerate, named Lee Fernandez, brutally attacked a young Alamosa girl. He was convicted of assault with intent to rape and sentenced to ten to fourteen in the state penitentiary. Police officers here know definitely that Fernandez was under the influence of marihuana.
>
> But this case is one in hundreds of murders, rapes, petty crimes, insanity that has occurred in Southern Colorado in recent years. . . .
>
> The people and officials here want to know why something can't be done about marihuana. . . .
>
> Is there any assistance your bureau can give us in handling this drug? Can you suggest campaigns? Can you enlarge your department to deal with marihuana? Can you do anything to help us?
>
> I wish I could show you what a small marihuana cigaret can do to one of our degenerate Spanish-speaking residents. That's why our problem is so great; the greatest percentage of our population is composed of Spanish-speaking persons, most of whom are low mentally, because of social and racial conditions.

While the pressure on the Bureau mounted, Anslinger cast about for solutions. In March 1936 he proposed a way around the constitutional objections of including marijuana in the Harrison Act. Anslinger proposed to his superiors in the Treasury Department that a treaty be enacted among the United States, Canada and Mexico. Basing this suggestion on the doctrine of *Missouri* v. *Holland*, the famous migratory bird case, the Commissioner felt that a cannabis treaty between these countries would enable Congress to enact legislation to enforce the treaty's terms, even if in so doing it would touch on matters ordinarily regarded as within the legislative province of the states. The *Missouri* v. *Holland* case of 1920 stated that treaties have precedence over local police powers.

On March 13 Herman Oliphant, a counsel for the Treasury Department, wrote a memo to Stephen Gibbons, Assistant Secretary of the Treasury, stating that "both the time and the subject appear to be appropriate from the Government's point of view to test the treaty power." Anslinger then entered into negotiations with Mexico and Canada, but in a few months the negotiations had broken down.

By October 1936, things seemed to be reaching a breaking point. Gibbons happened to meet the Dean of the Medical School of the University of Texas en route to Europe, who was very perturbed that the Bureau of Narcotics was dragging its feet on federal legislation of marijuana. Gibbons himself, as early as April 13, 1935, had overruled Anslinger and threw the Treasury Department's support behind early draft versions of bills by Senator Hatch and Congressman Dempsey of New Mexico to prohibit the shipment and transportation of cannabis in interstate or foreign commerce.

On returning to Washington, Gibbons fired off a memo to Oliphant on October 5, 1936. In it he recounted his meeting with the Medical School Dean and reinstated Anslinger's view on the constitutional difficulties:

> I, of course, appreciate what is in the back of Commissioner Anslinger's mind. While he hasn't stated definitely, I am of the opinion that he and nearly everyone having anything to do with the Harrison Narcotics Act are continually fighting shy of making any move which might bring any feature of this Act before the United States Supreme Court. As you will recall, the law was upheld by a five to four decision. However, be that as it may, steps should be taken legally or otherwise that will definitely control this product, for if we are to believe a small fraction of what is written it is frightfully devastating.

Much of those "frightfully devastating" reports, of course, were emanating from Mr. Anslinger's office and being received by a grateful yellow-tinged press. The Bureau was beginning to amass scores and scores of case histories of crime and insanity due to marijuana. Even the most tenuous connections were accepted with open files. Anslinger at times would go overboard in his zeal to generate negative publicity about the green plant. On December 23, 1936, responding to an inquiry about crime and marijuana from P. F. Collier and Son, magazine publishers, Anslinger was forced to admit that the Bureau's data was suspect:

> So far as I know, no student of crime has as yet made any direct study of the relative percentage of violent crime which is attributable to the use of Marihuana. [He obviously was not yet aware of Bromberg or had conveniently forgotten.] Recently we have received quite a number of reports showing crimes of violence committed by persons while under the influence of Marihuana; usually by dramatic methods. . . .

> Apparently many of the users of Marihuana are quickly reduced to insanity and to criminal acts; and it is my opinion that the incidents shown in the enclosed summary bear rather eloquent testimony as to the relation of crime with Marihuana.
>
> However, in many of the cases, we are unacquainted with the previous mental and moral characteristics and habits of the persons committing crimes while under the influence of Marihuana, so it can readily be seen that a final and conclusive statement in this regard is not yet in order. In most of the cases under observation, we do not have their criminal records; we do not know whether they were psychopaths, neurotics, moral delinquents, or normal individuals.
>
> The Marihuana problem is of comparatively recent origin in this country, and further investigations, both scientific and statistical, must be made and carefully studied. In the meantime, conclusions must be drawn from the facts at hand, which in themselves are enlightening, as witness the enclosed.

The letter went out intact except for the last sentence, which was deleted at the request of one of Anslinger's superiors, Assistant Secretary Gaston. It would mark the last time Anslinger would be so candid with respect to the highly questionable nature of the "facts" the Bureau was propagating about marijuana. In seven short months, in *American Magazine*, there would be no inkling that psychopaths might be committing these murders; or that severely disturbed persons might be crushing their bodies to a pulp in long suicide leaps. No, by July the sociological questions raised in the letter would be irrelevant to the Commissioner. By July the nation would be poised on the brink of its second great Prohibition; and Anslinger, good soldier that he was, would be merely doing his best to isolate the enemy, strip it of sympathy, infuse it with supernatural powers which, in the hands of the weak-willed, spelled certain doom. Even if it was, after all, just a sturdy old weed.

CHAPTER 4:
The Gore File

By 1937 the Treasury Department was poised to strike. Gibbons and Gaston, working with Oliphant, were convinced that federal legislation was inevitable and necessary even if the steps taken were "legal or otherwise." So proposed legislation was drawn up. And with an eye toward preparing a satisfactory legal definition of marijuana, a conference on *Cannabis sativa* was called at the Treasury Department in Washington on January 14, 1937. Represented were the foremost pharmacological authorities and consultants on the weed in government, along with representatives from Oliphant's office, the Alcohol Tax Unit laboratory, the National Institute of Health, the Department of Agriculture, and, of course, Anslinger and his right-hand man Tennyson from the Bureau of Narcotics—in all, fourteen conferees.

The conference began by attempting to isolate the constituent parts of cannabis that produce the deleterious physiological effects upon the body. They agreed that it was cannabinol, but no one was certain how much of it was present in different parts of the plant. Wollner, the Treasury Department chemist, complicated things further by raising the possibility that copious quantities of the active ingredient might be generated from the stalk of the plant, which had been thought harmless. "We might be in a bad position if we eliminated the stalks and later found it [cannabinol] to be present in them," Anslinger moaned, in one of his rare contributions to the discussion.

Dr. Munch, a Professor of Pharmacology from Princeton, made things worse by implicating the seed in the nefarious drug syndrome. Munch was Anslinger's discovery. They met shortly after Munch had developed a new method of determining whether racehorses had been doped. It was a splendid test involving an injection of a sample of the horse's urine into laboratory mice and observing the mice to see if they exhibited the symptoms of narcosis. Using Munch as a consultant, Anslinger went on to make headlines for the Bureau by exposing a horse-doping scandal. Subsequently, Anslinger asked Munch to bring his innovative skills to bear on the marijuana issue, and one of Munch's first contributions was the discovery that both the male and female plants contained enough cannabinol to wreak havoc with one's psyche.

"The active material from the fruits does not produce the same type of pharmacological response as the active material from the leaves," Munch noted. "We have instances recorded in literature of narcotic effects on children from the fruit."

"When you speak of fruits, do you include seed?" Tennyson, one of Anslinger's aides, seemed puzzled.

"Technically, this is a fruit, and not seed," Munch replied.

"The words are more or less synonymous in the way they are used," clarified Dr. Fuller, a chemist.

"There is a case on record"—Anslinger delved deep into his case-file memory bank—"I believe, of a prisoner who had a canary bird in the cell, and the warden found that he was taking the seed they brought in for the bird."

All this talk seemed to upset Tennyson. Alfred Tennyson was Anslinger's first lieutenant, generally conceded to be the most intelligent and cultured man in the Bureau. As such, he was invaluable to Anslinger, whose deficiencies in those areas had a certain charm of their own.

"It occurs to me, Dr. Wollner, that if we get a law, we have to support it and everything in it when we go before the Committee." Tennyson was catching on. "We have here some other uses—I don't know whether I am anticipating one of these questions or not. There is a use for fiber, for birdseed, and for oil in the varnish industry. Those people will probably come in and complain about what they consider a foolish attempt to control if we try to make this all-inclusive. If we are going to cast suspicion on every part of the plant we certainly will have to be fortified."

Of course Tennyson was right. In 1937 cannabis still had a multitude of legitimate industrial uses, the above-mentioned including a good bulk of them. And, as we shall see later,

Tennyson was also right about the protests on behalf of those industries during the deliberations on the bill.

The problem was complicated by the fact that there was no technology available to determine how much of the active part of the plant was in each constituent part. After throwing around a few more suggestions, Valaer of the Alcohol Tax Unit suggested that the bill should tax the green resin, rather than any constituent parts of the plant. "I would rather see us go further and, say, identify a green resin which is apparently in both male and female plants. . . . If it is not a definite structure we could say it is a green resin. We have been very successful in court. I don't know of any case where anybody has fallen down. If we go too far I'm afraid we are going to get into trouble. . . . If you want to get this into effect within the next year or so, if we get as far as a green resin characteristic of the plant, we will accomplish something."

This suggestion seemed to disturb Anslinger. "I'm afraid of making it too complicated," the Commissioner broke in. "The agents out in the sticks would be confused."

Wollner then suggested that the bill's definition of marijuana include the resin, the leaves, and the flowering tops of the plant. The seeds would be excluded from the bill. Anslinger demurred again. "The reason I'm after the seed is the preventive measure. Getting the seed out will make our trouble disappear." It was a pipe dream. Sievers, a Department of Agriculture pharmacologist, noted the parallel situation with respect to poppies from which heroin was made. "Isn't that the same situation you have with regard to poppy? You can grow them in this country for seed legally, can't you?"

"That's probably true," Tennyson admitted, "but we like to discourage that as far as possible."

"There is no law at present that would prohibit me from growing poppy as seed poppy," Sievers continued.

"In every case I know of where it was done, we got the defendant," Anslinger boasted ominously.

Tipton, who was from the General Counsel's office of the Treasury Department, the drafters of the bill, attempted to sum up. "Your suggested definition is the flowering tops, the leaves, and this greenish resin?" he asked Wollner.

"But that doesn't satisfy Commissioner Anslinger because potentially every seed is harmful?" Wollner repeated respectfully.

"Our experience has been that in almost every large seizure made we got a large quantity of the seed from the defendant for growing purposes," Anslinger cautioned.

Wollner's face lit up. "What would happen if we proscribed the use of seed for birdseed?"

"Dr. Munch told me it would stop the birds from singing," Anslinger noted ruefully.

After more discussion centering on the advisability of using the term marijuana or cannabis in the language of the bill, Wollner began interrogating Tipton with respect to the motivation of the Counsel's staff in regard to the bill.

"Would you be authorized to issue specific regulations interpreting this?" he asked.

"You have to be pretty specific in your act," Tipton replied.

"Would you be undertaking too much if you exempted the oil?" Wollner wondered.

"In our transfer tax we could make exemptions for the paint companies." Pierce, also from the General Counsel's office, was mindful of the paint industry that utilized large volumes of cannabis seed oil.

"If you're going to take care of those things in your transfer tax, why not take care of the stalk there too?" Wollner suggested.

"We could," Pierce agreed. "We are attempting to thrust the marihuana traffic into legal channels where it will be taxed some."

Wollner pressed on. "What is that predicated on?"

"Physical transfer," Tennyson piped in.

Wollner then had a brainstorm. "Suppose I grew the stuff myself?"

"You are taxed as a producer," Tipton, the eternal bureaucrat, replied.

"Would the tax on that be prohibitive?" Wollner was acting as the devil weed's advocate.

"No; by paying twenty-five dollars, I think you can grow and smoke all the marihuana you like," Tipton theorized.

"Is it incumbent upon you to see that no one else smokes it?" Wollner's questions were beginning to have a practical ring about them.

"There is a transfer tax which is prohibitive and, of course, criminal penalties," Pierce explained patiently.

"And the responsibility rests on the enforcement officer to

show that there was a transfer?" Wollner's thumb was getting greener by the minute.

"Yes," Pierce answered succinctly, and the conference moved on.

But what an exchange! Here was the principal architect behind the federal bill that would be the major marijuana prohibitionist legislation for the next thirty-two years candidly admitting that the intent of the bill was not to outlaw personal use. And here was Anslinger, prohibitionist extraordinaire, remaining silent as Tipton allowed Wollner his theoretical grass for personal consumption. So it seemed that the alcohol prohibition model was really in operation here, the sanctions being directed against the exchange and transfer of marijuana, not the individual personal consumption per se. But could this revisionist interpretation of the 1937 Marijuana Tax Act be valid? Wasn't someone going to mention the state laws that, in some cases, outlawed possession of the dread substance? Surely Anslinger was about to say something—he who was so concerned with every last birdseed being accounted for. Wollner, after this incredible exchange with Tipton and Pierce, gave Anslinger his chance.

"Commissioner Anslinger, have you any suggestions?" The talk had shifted to the proposed definition.

"No, I think that's going to be a great improvement over the definition we started with," Anslinger crowed. "I wanted to show the extent of the traffic and give some of the gentlemen an idea of this problem to show we are not on a fishing expedition." How defensive! Were these the words of a moral entrepreneur or a good soldier? "Last year there were 296 seizures we know about. The illicit traffic has shown up in almost every State. There was a question about forms of Cannabis derivatives employed medicinally. This will take care of that trade, won't it? Is the tax to be prohibitive as to the trade? We prepared for the legal division a statement as to what was used. We had a list of about three hundred compounds."

"We have allowed exemptions in another part of the law for medical or veterinary uses." Pierce was succinct.

"Even that's going to be awfully expensive, Mr. Pierce," Tennyson worried.

"I was surprised to hear some medical experts at Geneva recently say that it has absolutely no medical use," Anslinger broke in. "I think the Indian delegate wanted to know what he was going to do for his corn plaster, and one of the medicos said it wasn't the cannabis, but something else, that had this analgesic effect."

"We have shown that cannabis has no local analgesic effect," Munch, the horse expert, concluded glibly.

Apparently the conference was getting to Anslinger. All this talk about resin and corn plasters and bio-assays seemed to have given the Commissioner what would be known in the late sixties among acidheads as the "Swiss Cheese Effect." Anslinger's contributions were getting more and more inappropriate. But then again, perhaps it was only the dread manifestations of Case Envy rearing its ugly head. After all, it had been a few hours, experts from all sides of this issue had wielded their knowledge so adroitly with respect to this issue, and there sat the Commissioner of the Bureau of Narcotics, the agency that for godsakes was entrusted to enforce this damn proposed Act—there he sat like a bump on a log, reduced to counting birdseed. It was ignoble, and Anslinger would put a stop to it. After all, he was the master of the case history. Ever since the first rumblings from the provinces suggesting that some political hay be made from this psychic hay, Anslinger was there, snip-snipping newspaper articles, magazine pieces, letters, building up a file on this new deadly drug. All those hours of research, documenting the depravity in the wake of the weed, and not one of these goddamn chemists or medicos or legal-beagles was going to ask him about spattered cerebrums or stone-wild libidos or addlebrained adolescents. Anslinger could take it no longer. If these out-to-lunch academics wouldn't ask the right questions, he'd ask himself. This he did.

"What are the proofs that the use of marijuana, in any of its forms, is habit-forming or addictive, and what are the indications and positive proofs that such addiction develops socially undesirable characteristics in the user?" Anslinger was reading question number fourteen from the marijuana questionnaire that his own Bureau had circulated in anticipation of this conference. And of course he answered himself.

"We have a lot of cases showing that it certainly develops undesirable characteristics. We have a case of a boy about fifteen." At last he was reading from one of his files. He was giving expert testimony! Unfortunately for the sake of history the poor stenographer who was taking down this meeting apparently blanched at the grisly details of this horror story, for the transcript discreetly reads "reads from report of case" at this point. However, given the track record of the Bureau, we may rest assured that our wildest, most lurid, debased and grotesque fantasies probably do not hold a candle to what happened on that playground to those innocent youngsters in Finley, Ohio. Perhaps it is better that we remain ignorant. "This took place in a community playground in Finley, Ohio. The playground supervisors were the men who were selling the stuff. It all developed from the case of this youngster who was evidently going crazy. That's only one of the many cases we have."

A silence fell on the room. This was strong stuff for these gentle chemists, so used to administering their measured doses of cannabis extract to their lab dogs or cats or cute furry little mice. Anslinger had dragged those angry urban streets into their sterile environments, and they were uneasy. But the story struck a cord in the cagey Mr. Tipton. He saw just the thing he needed to ramrod this objectionable bill down the throats of a lackluster Congress. Something that could shut up those noisy birdseed manufacturers or those paint distributors or paper makers or whoever would suddenly get very pissed to find out that their legitimate industry was about to be wiped off the face of the earth because a few loco spics and some sex-crazed niggers were smoking a goddamn wild weed and going bananas behind it. No, Anslinger had really whetted Tipton's appetite, and a sly smile crossed the counselor's face.

"Have you a lot of cases on this?" Tipton politely inquired. "Horror stories—that's what we want."

That's what they got, too. Anslinger had always had a bent for the tawdry, as the shark episode demonstrated. And with a green light from his superiors, the Commissioner gave full rein to the seamiest, darkest side of his personality. Anslinger the ghoul reigned supreme. A gore file was started and the ghastliest, most heinous cases, some with very flimsy substantiation, became grist for the "horror story" mill. And, not surprisingly, many of these stories involved interracial contact. The following were some of Anslinger's "Top Ten":

West Va.—Negro raped a *girl eight years of age.*

Two Negros took a girl fourteen years old and kept her for two days in a hut under the influence of marihuana. Upon recovery she was found to be *suffering from* syphilis.

Negro, charged with burglary, so impressed jury with his story of people jumping out of their graves and grabbing him that he got a hung jury. He admitted that he was a marihuana smoker.

Colored students at the Univ. of Minn. partying with female students (white) smoking and getting their sympathy with stories of racial persecution. Result pregnancy.

Undercover agent invited to marihuana party. Suggestion that everyone take off their pants, both male and female. Agent dropped blackjack while disrobing and had to arrest immediately.

In New Jersey in 1936, a particularly brutal murder occurred, in which case one young man killed another, literally smashing his face and head to a pulp. One of the defenses was that the defendant's intellect was so prostrated from his smoking Marihuana cigarettes that he did not know what he was doing. The defendant was found guilty and sentenced to a long term of years. The prosecutor was convinced that Marihuana had been indulged in, that the smoking had occurred, and the brutality of the murder was accounted for by the narcotic, though the defendant's intellect had not been totally prostrate, so the verdict was legally correct. The fury of the murderer was apparent. Not content with killing his friend, he tore out his tongue, his eyes, and so mutilated him that even the hardened coroner had to turn his eyes away from the gruesome sight.

Corpus Christi—Gov. of Texas told me of a case he knew about personally, and one which in some measure influenced him to destroy 600 acres of hemp. An oil worker, good character, smoked a cigarette, raped his six-year-old daughter. When his wife returned home in the evening, she found him lying across the bed in a stupor and the little child torn and bleeding. He couldn't remember. Was sentenced to death.

A gang of seven young men, all under 20 years of age, who for more than two months terrorized central Ohio with a series of about thirty-eight stick-ups, were arrested in March 1937 in Columbus, Ohio, on robbery charges. They confessed that they operated while "high" on Marihuana. One of the youths admitted that he had smoked "reefers" on and off for at least two years, and said that when he went with the others on stick-ups he was "ready to tear anybody apart" who opposed him. He claimed the practice of smoking marihuana first started among his friends about four or five years ago, while most of them were still in high school. He also stated that dozens of his youthful acquaintances are addicts. *In describing his crimes he said: "If I had killed somebody on a job, I'd never known it."* This was verified by the officer obtaining the

> confessions, who explained that the hardest problem was to get these youths to remember who committed the stick-ups, or when or where they happened. When police told them how a filling station attendant reported a robber threatened to beat his brains out with a revolver butt, one admitted he was the robber, but had forgotten his own words. It was almost impossible for them to break off the habit when they could still get "tea" so easily, they claimed. "When you try to break off, you get jumpy, your hands shake and you hear the least little noise. A dopey feeling comes when you're going down, and you get mopey. You get so you smoke a 'stick' a day, and you can't stop."
>
> Nov. 1935—As for the girl—three months of smoking the weed have not spoiled entirely her beauty. She is still attractive, but her glazed eyes, her deathly pale face and her restless fingers are visible aspects of her degradation. A few quickly sucked pulls at a marihuana weed, and her eyes sparkle, her tongue is unloosed and for a little while she is the vivacious girl her years entitle her to be.
>
> While under the influence of the drug, the subject thrust his hand through his hair, and found that his fingers passed through his crackling skull and into his warm, cheesy brain. Another time, his head rolled off his shoulders, broke and burst like a huge egg upon the carpet. Another time, his innards fell out with a hideous splash. Nightmares were of horror, disgust, rebellion and fiendish vengefulness and exultation.

And this from a man who had never smoked one joint in his entire life! What vivid, pulsating detail for such a linear thinker. And what an improvement over the "shark" period. Washington seemed to bring out the most creative side of the Commissioner.

But there was one case that became Anslinger's favorite; his pet marijuana story, a story that was circulated to all the media with the regularity of a big-titted, two-bit whore at a fraternity party. It was the *Victor Licata* case, and it was one of the foundations on which the marijuana-crime-insanity edifice rested.

Anslinger first became aware of this case on February 1, 1937, when he received a letter from the Chief Inspector of the Florida State Board of Health. The letter came a scant two weeks after Tipton's admonition to get "horror stories" and, as such, it was indeed a godsend. In fact, Anslinger was so grateful for this information that he fired off a letter that same day to the Inspector, thanking him for the information and the photograph and asking him to forward similar cases in the future.

But a case like Licata's was one-in-a-lifetime, and the Florida Inspector could never hope to top it. In his files Anslinger would later sum up the case succinctly:

> A twenty-one-year-old boy in FLORIDA killed his parents, two brothers and a sister while under the influence of a Marihuana "dream" which he later described to law enforcement officials. He told rambling stories of being attacked in his bedroom by his "uncle, a strange old woman and two men and two women," whom he said hacked off his arms and otherwise mutilated him; later in the dream he saw "real blood" dripping from an axe.

The *Licata* case became a cause célèbre in Anslinger's newly renewed war against marijuana. It was picked up in the popular press of the time, and it was repeated many times over the years in Anslinger's own writings. Dr. Munch mentions it prominently in a widely circulated article called "Marihuana and Crime" that originally appeared in the United Nations *Bulletin of Narcotics* in 1966.

But a closer examination of the case reveals the unreliability of the data that Anslinger was so quick to herald. In his book *Marijuana—The New Prohibition*, Stanford Law Professor John Kaplan dug a little deeper into this case. The slaying occurred on October 17, 1933, and Kaplan reported that the next day's *Tampa Times* carried the following story:

> CRAZED YOUTH KILLS FIVE OF FAMILY WITH AX IN TAMPA
>
> . . . dazed and staring wild-eyed [he] was arrested at the scene as officers broke into the home. . . . Licata was crouched in a chair in the bathroom and offered no resistance as officers searched him for weapons. He mumbled incoherently when asked about the crime.

The first mention of marijuana came a few paragraphs into the story:

> W. D. Bush, city detective chief, said he had made an investigation prior to the crime and learned the slayer had been addicted to smoking marihuana cigarettes for more than six months. This he said had unbalanced his mind at least temporarily. A similar statement was made by Frank S. Caston, state drug and narcotic inspector, who said he had aided Bush in the investigation and was prepared to make charges against the youth when he heard of the ax slaying. He had also heard of several places where Licata bought the doped cigarettes.

The incident brought a quick reaction from Tampa's police chief, who vowed in the same paper: "Maybe the weed only had a small indirect part in the alleged insanity of the youth, but I am declaring now for all time that the increasing use of this narcotic must stop and will be stopped." Two days later the paper expressed these same sentiments in their lead editorial:

STOP THIS MURDEROUS SMOKE

> . . . it may or may not be wholly true that the pernicious marijuana cigarette is responsible for the murderous mania of a Tampa young man in exterminating all the members of his family within his reach—but whether or not the poisonous mind-wrecking weed is mainly accountable for the tragedy its sale should not be and should never have been permitted here or elsewhere. . . . It required five murders to impress the Tampa public and Tampa officials with the serious effects of the habit.

Of course Anslinger was not at all hesitant to impute the casualty directed to the "influence of marihuana." If he had followed the case, he would have learned that eleven days later, a psychiatric examination of Licata revealed that he was criminally insane, his condition being "acute and chronic." Licata was said to be "subject to hallucinations accompanied by homicidal impulses and occasional periods of excitement." The psychiatrist also asserted that his insanity was probably inherited, since the parents were first cousins, his paternal granduncle and two paternal cousins had been committed to insane asylums, and his brother, who was one of the victims, had been diagnosed as suffering from dementia praecox. As if that weren't enough, it was revealed that a year before, the Tampa police had filed a lunacy petition in an attempt to have Licata committed, but withdrew it when his parents pledged that they could take better care of him at home.

On November 3 Licata was committed to the state mental hospital, where he was diagnosed as suffering with "Dementia Praecox with homicidal tendencies." His behavior was adjudged "overtly psychotic," and nowhere in his file was his marijuana use mentioned. Licata resided at the Florida State Mental Hospital from 1933 until December 4, 1950, when he hanged himself.

But of course the Commissioner was too busy tracking down new gore reports to examine any one case thoroughly. So, in his famous *American Magazine* article of July 1937, four years after these killings, Anslinger would write of Licata:

> An entire family was murdered by a youthful addict in Florida. When officers arrived at the home, they found the youth staggering about in a human slaughterhouse. With an ax he had killed his father, mother, two brothers, and a sister. He seemed to be in a daze. . . . He had no recollection of having committed the multiple crime. *The officers knew him ordinarily as a sane, rather quiet young man; now he was pitifully crazed.* They sought the reason. The boy said he had been in the habit of smoking something which youthful friends called "muggles," a childish name for marihuana.

And even years after Licata's tragic suicide, Anslinger, in numerous articles, would invoke the ghost of this once "sane, rather quiet young man."

But what are we to make of this early link between marijuana and crimes of violence? Were all of Anslinger's examples as flimsy as the *Licata* case? Or was there a strong correlation between the weed and mayhem?

It seems obvious that in the 1930s there was a self-selection process operating here with regards to the drug. That is, individuals who were more prone to be violent for environmental or cultural reasons (*i.e.*, lower-class people) were, in fact, the majority of the users of the substance. And since marijuana was a relatively new consciousness-altering substance in American culture, the experience of getting stoned was not so thoroughly defined. Whereas in 1883 in the hashish houses, users had strict normative guidelines which helped shape their reactions to the use of hashish. It was to be an exotic, dreamlike experience, and the long gowns, the tasseled hats, the strange ambiance—all this contributed to assuage any untoward reactions to the drug. What's more, the novice smoker was usually accompanied by a "guide" who would act to allay any fears.

In the cities during the thirties, it appears that the informal peer system may not have been that structured with respect to the marijuana experience. As the use of the drug spread from Mexican immigrants and early black slaves who, by all accounts, had had direct cultural contact with the plant, the early pioneers who smoked "muggles," or reefers, seem to have been embarking on relatively uncharted psychic terrain. It wouldn't be until the jazz musicians adopted the drug in the mid-thirties that a strong peer culture would emerge to regulate its use. So in the absence of that, and with a growing stream of propaganda shrilling about the crime-causing properties of the weed, a situation became ripe where to engage in criminal activities while under the weed might be to assert a self-fulfilling prophecy. Certainly, one of the unanticipated consequences of Anslinger's crusade was that every smalltime hood from Altoona to Santa Fe began pleading insanity due to the ravages of those "mootas" that they had smoked just hours before the crimes. But, in the final analysis, what irked Anslinger and his crusaders so much seems not to have been the cheesy brains or the gouged eyes or the decapitated bodies. Harry was probably pissed that the Mexicans and the blacks were using this drug as a pretext to get close to sweet young white things. It was clear something had to be done.

CHAPTER 5:
The Marihuana Tax Act Hearings of 1937

For the next few months after that January conference, Anslinger began gearing up his campaign. With a collaborator he worked on the *American Magazine* story. He gave speeches, went on the radio, sent out his agents; he sicced the Anslinger army of women's clubbers, temperance freaks, and P.T.A. moyens on an unsuspecting public. And all in preparation for the hearings on H.R. 6385, Representative Doughton's House version of the Treasury Department's Marihuana Tax Act. And on Tuesday morning, April 27, 1937, the hearings began.

The show began with Clinton Hester, Oliphant's assistant, giving a broad background into the bill, explaining the constitutional difficulties that would ensue if marijuana were simply tacked onto the Harrison Act. But it was clear after a few minutes, that—the protestations of the legitimate hemp industry notwithstanding—Oliphant's boys were out to deal the evil weed a deathblow, even while allowing ludicrous loopholes in the act with respect to personal consumption.

Near the end of his summation, Hester provided a brief glimpse into the department's strategy:

> In the final analysis, after the committee has given full consideration to the subject of marihuana, it is not beyond the realm of possibility that the committee may conclude that the legitimate uses of marihuana are so negligible as compared to the injurious effect it has upon the public health and morals of the people of this country, that the committee will conclude to impose a prohibitive tax upon the production, manufacture, and sale of marihuana, and thus discourage its use in any form in this country.

The proposed bill was unique in that the meat of its provisions called for a prohibitive tax upon unauthorized transfers of marijuana. For transfers among people who register and pay a yearly tax under the bill, that is, legitimate transfers, the tax was one dollar an ounce; for illegitimate transfers, the tax was a mere $100 an ounce. At that time, cannabis was going for thirty-eight cents a pound on the licit market. The idea of this prohibitive tax was borrowed from the recently enacted National Firearms Act and its use here, according to Hester, was "to stop high school children from getting marijuana."

The first witness was Mr. Anslinger. And from his opening statement on, it seems clear that Harry had scoured all his files, scanned all his old notes, copped whatever he could from articles, letters, pulp magazines—and had strung them together for the benefit of the unenlightened congressmen.

> Mr. Chairman and distinguished members of the Ways and Means Committee, this traffic in marihuana is increasing to such an extent that it has come to be the cause for the greatest national concern. This drug is as old as civilization itself. Homer wrote about it, as a drug which made men forget their homes, and that turned them into swine. In Persia, a thousand years before Christ, there was a religious and military order founded which was called the Assassins, and they derived their name from the drug called hashish, which in now known in this country as marihuana. They were noted for their acts of cruelty, and the word "assassin" very aptly describes the drug. . . . Marihuana is the Mexican term for cannabis Indica. We seem to have adopted the Mexican terminology, and we call it marihuana, which means good feeling. In the underworld it is referred to by such colorful, colloquial names as reefer, muggles, Indian hay, hot hay and weed. . . . Here we have a drug that is not like opium. Opium has all the good of Dr. Jekyll and all the evil of Mr. Hyde. This drug is entirely the monster Hyde, the harmful effect of which cannot be measured. . . .

But when the questioning began, it was clear that the marijuana menace had not touched upon the Washington solons too strongly:

MR. DINGELL: I want to be certain what this is. Is this the same weed that grows wild in some of our Western States which is sometimes called the loco weed?

MR. ANSLINGER: No, sir; that is another family.

MR. DINGELL: That is also a harmful drug-producing weed, is it not?

MR. ANSLINGER: Not to my knowledge; it is not used by humans.

CHAIRMAN DOUGHTON: In what particular sections does this weed grow wild?

MR. ANSLINGER: In almost every State in the Union today.

MR. REED: What you are describing is a plant which has a rather large flower?

MR. ANSLINGER: No, sir; a very small flower.

After that discouraging exchange, Anslinger got right into the meat of the issue, his gore report. He trotted out all the familiar cases, titillating the congressmen. But then he abruptly changed the subject and, in a revealing moment, attempted to differentiate the marijuana and opiate habits.

MR. ANSLINGER: This drug is not being used by those who have been using heroin and morphine. It is being used by a different class, by a much younger group of people. The age of the morphine and heroin addict is increasing all the time, whereas the marihuana smoker is quite young.

MR. DINGELL: I am just wondering whether the marihuana addict graduates into a heroin, an opium or a cocaine user.

MR. ANSLINGER: No, sir; I have not heard of a case of that kind. I think it is an entirely different class. The marihuana addict does not go in that direction.

MR. DINGELL: And the hardened narcotic user does not fall back on marihuana?

MR. ANSLINGER: No, sir; he would not touch that.

We shall see how in a space of fifteen years Anslinger will completely contradict himself, maintaining that the devil weed leads directly to the big H. At this point, however, the Commissioner was not making a case for marijuana's harmlessness as much as pointing out the horrifying specter of a completely new menace that his poor, understaffed, underbudgeted department had to combat.

Anslinger coped with a few feeble questions from the congressmen and submitted a few statements for the record, among them Baskette's aforementioned "Spanish-speaking degenerate" letter, Gomila's article, and Stanley's "Developer of Criminals." Wednesday's hearings opened with more documents entered—letters urging passage of the bill from Anslinger's army units. Then, Dr. Munch took the witness stand.

Munch began by recounting his ten years' experience with the Food and Drug Administration and his background in toxicology and pharmacology. But from his opening statement, Munch began to talk in advanced Casey Stengelese, losing most of the committee with each elaborate circle he circumscribed:

DR. MUNCH: In connection with my studies of cannabis, or marihuana, I have followed its effects on animals and also, so far as possible, its effect upon humans. I find that the doses which are capable of producing effects must be very nearly poisonous doses; that is to say, small doses have little effect. The effect is directed first at the hind brain, or cerebellum, leading to a disturbance of the equilibrium, so that a man will go temporarily into a state resembling alcoholism. Larger doses tend to depress the heart. Continuous use will tend to cause the degeneration of one part of the brain, that part that is useful for higher or psychic reasoning, or the memory. . . . Those are the disturbing and harmful effects that follow continued exposure to marihuana. . . . Animals which show a particular susceptibility, that is, which show a response to a given dose, when they begin to show it will acquire a tolerance. We have to give larger doses as the animals are used over a period of 6 months or a year. This means that the animal is becoming habituated, and finally the animal must be discarded because it is no longer serviceable.

MR. MCCORMACK: We are more concerned with human beings than with animals. Of course I realize that those experiments are necessary and valuable, because so far as the effect is concerned, they have a significance also. But we would like to have whatever evidence you have as to the conditions existing in the country, as to what the effect is upon human beings. Not that we are not concerned about the animals, but the important matter before us concerns the use of this drug by human beings.

As the questioning dragged on, Munch revealed his limited knowledge of the historical uses of marijuana. In response to a query about the medical uses of cannabis, he noted:

> In the early days it was used in cases of sleeplessness and to make your last moments on earth less painful when you were dying from tetanus or rabies. There may be other uses, but I have not found them.

After a while, the congressmen began to lead Munch on, in a desperate attempt to focus the discussion:

Mr. McCormack: I take it that the effect is different upon different persons.

Dr. Munch: Yes, sir.

Mr. McCormack: There is no question but what this is a drug, is there?

Dr. Munch: None at all.

Mr. McCormack: There is no dispute about that?

Dr. Munch: No.

Mr. McCormack: Is it a harmful drug?

Dr. Munch: Any drug that produces the degeneration of the brain is harmful. Yes; it is.

Mr. McCormack: I agree with you on that, but I want to ask you these questions and have your answers for the record, because they will assist us in passing upon the legislation.

Dr. Munch: I have said it is a harmful drug.

Mr. McCormack: In some cases does it not bring about extreme inertia?

Dr. Munch: Yes; it does.

Mr. McCormack: And in other cases it causes violent irritability?

Dr. Munch: Yes, sir.

Mr. McCormack: And those results lead to a disintegration of personality, do they not?

Dr. Munch: Yes, sir.

Mr. McCormack: That is really the net result of the use of that drug, no matter what other effects there may be; its continued use means the disintegration of the personality of the person who uses it?

Dr. Munch: Yes; that is true.

Mr. McCormack: Can you give us any idea as to the period of continued use that occurs before this disintegration takes place?

Dr. Munch: I can only speak from my knowledge of animals. In some animals we see the effect after about 3 months, while in others it requires more than a year when they are given the same dose.

Mr. McCormack: Are there not some animals on which it reacted, as I understand it, in a manner similar to its reaction on human beings? Is that right?

DR. MUNCH: Yes, sir.

MR. MCCORMACK: Have you experimented upon any animals whose reaction to this drug would be similar to that of human beings?

DR. MUNCH: The reason we use dogs is because the reaction of dogs to this drug closely resembles the reaction of human beings.

MR. MCCORMACK: And the continued use of it, as you have observed the reaction on dogs, has resulted in the disintegration of the personality?

DR. MUNCH: Yes. So far as I can tell, not being a dog psychologist, the effects will develop in from 3 months to a year.

This of course would be the strongest scientific evidence the committee would hear during the course of the hearings. After Wollner testified briefly, the committee heard from Dr. D. E. Buckingham, a government veterinarian for the District of Columbia. The depth of his insight into this topic was evidenced in the first few minutes of his testimony:

DR. BUCKINGHAM: Because of the immense amount of damage that this drug does, I would like to go on record as voting against the use of it by veterinarians in the District of Columbia. Unfortunately, I have not read the bill, but with reference to its use by veterinarians, I believe that the entire profession in the District would be behind me in vetoing its use in veterinary practice.

Once again, the questioning was sharp and insightful:

MR. BOEHNE: Is there any evidence to show that this plant is used by larger animals in nature? Will animals, whether wild or domestic, use it in their native state as a forage plant, or do they reject it?

DR. BUCKINGHAM: This is a foreign drug, but I am not aware of animals' using it like they do loco weed on the western range. Would that be a parallel?

MR. BOEHNE: Yes. Where it is scattered around through its use as bird seed and grows along the fences, would a grazing cow eat it?

DR. BUCKINGHAM: No, sir. They might by mistake.

Mr. Boehne: Would they reject it?

Dr. Buckingham: I believe they would.

Mr. Boehne: Naturally, they would not prefer to eat it.

Dr. Buckingham: Yes, sir. Of course, animals eat a number of plants that are of no benefit to them. As they graze, animals will leave aside noxious weeds which might possibly be put in this same category.

And that was the extent of the case the Department made for its bill. Anslinger with some horror stories; Munch, a pharmacologist making inferences about human behavior based on experiments with dogs, experiments which he admitted he was not qualified to interpret. The paucity of substance in the government's arguments is amazing. In fact, it was not until the hostile witnesses appeared before the committee that the substance of the issue was revealed. First up was Ralph Lozier, the general counsel for the National Institute of Oilseed Products. This was a trade association of about twenty firms who utilized hempseed oil in such various products as paint, soap and linoleum, and who, under the provisions of the bill, would suddenly be regulated by the Bureau of Narcotics in the Department of Treasury.

Lozier began by going on record supporting the portion of the bill that dealt with limiting and suppressing the use of marijuana as a drug. However, he waxed eloquently in opposing the regulation, under this bill, of the entire hempseed oil industry:

> Respectable authorities tell us that in the Orient at least 200,000,000 people use this drug; and when we take into consideration that for hundreds, yes, thousands of years, practically that number of people have been using this drug, it is significant that in Asia and elsewhere in the Orient, where poverty stalks abroad on every hand and where they draw on all the plant resources which a bountiful nature has given that domain—it is a significant fact that none of those 200,000,000 people has ever, since the dawn of civilization, been found using the seed of this plant or using the oil as a drug. Now if there were any deleterious properties or principles in the seed or oil, it is reasonable to suppose that these Orientals who have been reaching out in their poverty for something that would satisfy their morbid appetite, would have discovered it. . . . If the committee please, the hemp seed, or the seed of the *Cannabis sativa L.*, is used in all the Oriental nations and also in a part of Russia as food. It is grown in their fields and used as oatmeal. Millions of people

> every day are using hemp seed in the Orient as food. They have been doing that for many generations, especially in periods of famines. . . . The point I make is this, that this bill is too all-inclusive. This bill is a world-encircling measure. This bill brings the activities, the crushing of this great industry, under the supervision of a bureau, which may mean its suppression. Last year there was imported into the U.S. 62,813,000 pounds of hemp seed; in 1935 there was imported 116,000,000 pounds. . . .

Lozier was objecting to both the fees required for the licensing process and the supervision in the form of reports that would be generated. He ran into trouble, though, in convincing the aroused congressmen that these imported seeds did not carry with them the blueprints for the destruction of Western civilization.

However, by the next morning, Hester reported that an agreement had been reached in private session whereby the hempseed industry agreed to pay the occupational tax if the definition of marijuana was changed to eliminate the oil made from the seeds and the meal and cake made from the crushed seeds. Friday's session featured the next great industry threatened by this measure, the birdseed industry. Raymond G. Scarlett began his testimony by regretting that only two representatives of the seed industry could appear, since their trade association was in session in Chicago. However, his plight soon became apparent:

Mr. Scarlett: We handle a considerable quantity of hempseed annually for use in pigeon feeds. . . . We have not been able to find any seed that will take its place. If you substitute anything for the hemp, it has a tendency to change the character of the squabs produced; and if we were deprived of the use of hempseed, it would affect all of the pigeon producers in the United States, of which I understand there are upwards of 40,000.

Chairman Doughton: Does that seed have the same effect on pigeons as the drug has on individuals?

Mr. Scarlett: I have never noticed it. It has a tendency to bring back the feathers and improve the birds. We are not interested in spreading marihuana, or anything like that. We do not want to be drug peddlers. But it has occurred to us that if we could sterilize the seed there would be no possibility of the plant's being produced from the seeds that the pigeons might throw on the ground.

But what a bombshell Scarlett just threw—the idea of sterilizing the birdseed to keep both the Treasury men and the birds happy. It was a compromise that found its way into the final draft of the bill.

But with further questioning, Mr. Disney, one of the congressmen, continued to remain confused with respect to the difference between field hemp and marijuana. Hester came to the rescue, repeating that marijuana was just a colloquial Mexican term for the flowered top and leaves of the hemp plant. Disney was not satisfied and referred to his copy of the bill, then raised a new issue.

MR. DISNEY: I notice that in section 1, at the beginning of the bill, in subdivision (c) it says that the producer is one—"who (1) plants, grows, cultivates or in any way facilitates the natural growth of marihuana, (2) harvests and transfers or makes use of marihuana; or (3) fails to destroy marihuana within 10 days after notice that such marihuana is growing upon the land under his control." To what extent do you expect to go along that line, where it is an ordinary weed?

MR. HESTER: The person on whose land the plant was growing wild would be notified by the Treasury Department that he had this plant growing on his land, and if he did not destroy the weed, he would become a producer under the bill and subject to the tax. He would not be committing a crime if he failed to cut it and would merely have to pay a tax.

MR. LEWIS: Suppose he is not raising it for the market.

MR. HESTER: If a person cultivates it, he would be producing it; he would become a producer under the bill.

MR. LEWIS: Without raising it for the market?

MR. HESTER: That is right. That is the only way it can be handled, I believe. Since this plant will grow wild, a person might evade the occupational tax on producers by stating to the internal revenue agent that the plant was growing wild.

MR. LEWIS: You mean if he goes out and digs it up as a weed?

MR. HESTER: No; if you have a farm and it is growing on your farm wild, and the Government agent sees it growing there, and they notify you what it is, then you are required to destroy that.

If you do not do it, then you become a producer and subject to the occupational tax.

Mr. Lewis: How widely distributed is it as a weed?

Mr. Hester: Mr. Anslinger said it will grow in practically all of the States wild.

Chairman Doughton: I would like to know about the process of destroying it, if it grows wild on a man's farm. I have had considerable experience in trying to destroy weeds, and it requires a lot of expense. Who would defray the expense required in fighting and destroying that weed?

Mr. Hester: This is the thing to remember, that if he did not destroy it, he would simply become a producer under this bill and have to pay a small occupational tax, and the Government would know it is there. He doesn't have to destroy it if he does not want to, but if he does not, he pays a small occupational tax.

Mr. Lewis: How much?

Mr. Hester: $25 a year.

Mr. Reed: I know something about farming, although I am not familiar with the manner in which this plant spreads. I know that we have tried on our farms to keep out certain weeds, but we could not do it because the expense is too great. You will have a revolution on your hands if, as you say, this plant grows generally throughout the country and you try to charge the farmers a tax of $25, as you said.

It was clearly rough going for Hester. Despite the New Deal attitude that government had a responsibility in extending itself over areas of our citizens' lives that were formerly sacrosanct, Hester was imposing a burden on one of the traditional symbols of American free enterprise and rugged individualism—the American farmer. And worse yet, he was raising the specter of a G-man in the cornfields, snooping around for concealed wild hemp. For the first time in the hearings, the Department was on the defensive:

Mr. Hester: It does not seem to me to be an undue hardship to put a small occupational tax on a person who has this growing wild on his land. The Government could get no information whatsoever from him otherwise. It is the only way the Government could get any information as to where this is growing wild.

Mr. Reed: But the next step is to destroy this weed?

Mr. Hester: Not necessarily to destroy it, but so that the

Government will know where it is. There is no provision in the bill that requires them to destroy it. It says to the farmer, if you do not destroy it within 10 days, you will have to qualify as a producer and pay a small occupational tax.

MR. REED: What is the Government going to do then, put a man there to watch it?

MR. HESTER: No.

MR. REED: How will it stamp it out?

MR. HESTER: In the final analysis, if the man, the farmer, does not want to pay the small occupational tax, he will have to destroy it himself, or Congress will have to make an appropriation for the Department of Agriculture which will permit them to send people throughout the country to stamp it out.

The discussion wore on with Reed pressing the case of the small farmer combating a burgeoning menace beyond his control. The issue was not resolved in session, but by the time the bill passed the House and was presented to the Senate, the occupational tax had been lowered to five dollars and the third clause in the producer's section had been deleted, taking the burden of removal off the overworked farmer's hands. But the real challenger to the bill was to come the following Tuesday morning, May 4, when Dr. William C. Woodward of the American Medical Association would testify as a hostile witness to H.R. 6385.

Woodward was a strange rebel. He was both a doctor and a lawyer, and before he became the legislative counsel of the American Medical Association, he was the health officer of the District of Columbia for twenty-five years, then the Health Commissioner of Boston from 1918 to 1922, when he went to work for the AMA. He enjoyed less than cordial relations with Anslinger, as his response to the Commissioner's marijuana questionnaire showed, perhaps because of the aftermath of the Harrison Act, where thousands of doctors were arrested and intimidated by the Prohibition Unit, Narcotics Division.

Woodward made clear from the outset that he would be a hostile witness:

> Mr. Chairman and gentlemen. It is with great regret that I find myself in opposition to any measure that is proposed by the Government, and particularly in opposition to any measure that has been proposed by the Secretary of the Treasury for the purpose of suppressing traffic in narcotics. I cooperated with Hamilton Wright

in drafting the Harrison Narcotic Act. I have been more or less in touch with the narcotic situation since that time. During the past two years I have visited the Bureau of Narcotics probably ten or more times. Unfortunately, I had no knowledge that such a bill as this was proposed until after it had been introduced.

After submitting some editorial matter from the *AMA Journal* for the record, Woodward, moving into his critique of the bill, maintained that the medicinal use of cannabis was in no way responsible for this marijuana menace:

In all that you have heard here thus far, no mention has been made of any excessive use of the drug by any doctor or its excessive distribution by any pharmacist. And yet the burden of this bill is placed heavily on the doctors and pharmacists of the country; and I may say very heavily, most heavily, possibly of all, on the farmers of the country. . . . The medicinal use [of Cannabis] has greatly decreased. The drug is very seldom used. That is partially because of the uncertainty of the effects of the drug. . . . To say, however, as has been proposed here, that the use of the drug should be prevented by a prohibitive tax, loses sight of the fact that future investigation may show that there are substantial medical uses for cannabis.

After citing a few studies that admit the utility of cannabis preparations as sedatives and antispasmodics, and point to the use of cannabis as a valuable adjunct to psychoanalysis, Woodward unleashed a most articulate, scathing attack on the flimsy evidence that Anslinger and company presented in the first few days of hearings:

That there is a certain amount of narcotic addiction of an objectionable character no one will deny. The newspapers have called attention to it so prominently that there must be some grounds for their statements. It has surprised me, however, that the facts on which these statements have been based have not been brought before this committee by competent primary evidence. We are referring to newspaper publications concerning the prevalence of marihuana addiction. We are told that the use of marihuana causes crime.

But yet no one has been produced from the Bureau of Prisons to show the number of prisoners who have been found addicted to the marihuana habit. An informal inquiry shows that the Bureau of Prisons has no evidence on that point.

You have been told that schoolchildren are great users of marihuana cigarettes. No one has been summoned from the Children's Bureau to show the nature and extent of the habit, among children.

Inquiry of the Children's Bureau shows that they have had no occasion to investigate it and know nothing particularly of it.

Inquiry of the Office of Education—and they certainly should know something of the prevalence of the habit among the schoolchildren of the country, if there is a prevalent habit—indicated that they have had no occasion to investigate and know nothing of it.

Moreover, there is in the Treasury Department itself, the Public Health Service, with its Division of Mental Hygiene. The Division of Mental Hygiene was, in the first place, the Division of Narcotics. It was converted into the Division of Mental Hygiene, I think, about 1930. That particular Bureau has control at the present time of the narcotics farms that were created about 1929 or 1930 and came into operation a few years later. No one has been summoned from that Bureau to give evidence on that point.

Informal inquiry by me indicates that they have had no record of any marihuana or Cannabis addicts who have ever been committed to those farms.

The Bureau of the Public Health Service also has a division of pharmacology. If you desire evidence as to the pharmacology of Cannabis, that obviously is the place where you can get direct and primary evidence, rather than the indirect hearsay evidence.

Woodward, however, did not argue that cannabis should not be controlled. He felt that the Bureau of Narcotics was mandated by the United States Code, title 21, section 198, to work directly with the states "in the suppression of the abuse of narcotic drugs . . . and to that end he [the Secretary of the Treasury] is authorized (1) to cooperate in the drafting of such legislation as may be needed . . . and (2) to arrange for the exchange of information concerning the use and abuse of narcotic drugs in said States and for cooperation in the institution and persecution of cases in the courts of the United States and before the licensing boards and courts of the several states." So Woodward laid the blame on the Treasury Department for not acting since 1930 on this menace.

After questioning whether the use of marijuana constituted a "menace," Woodward went on to critique the shotgun features of the bill:

That means that every potential owner of land in the United States is a potential and maybe an unwitting producer of marihuana. If the weed springs up on his land without his knowledge, he may have to go out and cut it, on notice. . . . Incidentally, at this point, there is one provision in the section that I have just read that I feel confident may have escaped the notice of the Secretary of the

> Treasury when he recommended the introduction of this bill: because under the section that I have just read anyone who makes use of marihuana is a producer. As a producer, he must be taxed, but he apparently has the right to pay that tax and obtain the drug as a matter of course. Reduced to its last analysis that means that any addict that can afford to raise the tax can go in and register as a producer and can then obtain such of the drug as he wants on order forms, for his own use. That, it seems to me, must be clearly an oversight.
>
> Coming back now to the question of State laws, I think admittedly they are weak. They have laws. But if the Federal Government, instead of proposing a law as is here proposed, will cooperate effectively with the States in the suppression, not only of marihuana addiction, but of opium and cocaine addiction, we shall get better results.

Hardly revolutionary critiques. Woodward, so far, apart from embarrassing the Committee with respect to the shoddy testimony that was scheduled, really was quite moderate in his attacks on the bill. From the point of view of a doctor, he was merely mouthing the AMA line that has held steadfast to this day: Big government out of medical affairs. The Marihuana Tax Act was viewed as another encroachment into the sacrosanct free enterprise world of medicine. That doctors should have to register, pay one dollar a year in taxes, and then keep copious records on a drug that was rarely used was the height of absurdity to Woodward.

But Woodward did offer glimpses of an ideology that was heretical to Commissioner Anslinger and his Bureau, especially in the years to come. For one, Woodward left open the question of the medical uses of marijuana. Anslinger, of course, was convinced there were none. But worse yet, Woodward, near the end of his testimony, offered an ideological scheme that would be diametrically opposed to the course that Anslinger's Bureau would take with respect to drug addicts. Woodward saw drug addicts as sick people, patients in need of treatment. Anslinger viewed the same people as fiends, the narcotics merely amplifying existent evil character structures. For Woodward one solution to the problem is education. Anslinger would opt for electrocution.

Immediately after this opening statement, the committee members, as one, pounced on the good doctor. They challenged his credentials; they accused him of misrepresenting the AMA position; then even engaged in some New Deal–baiting, accusing him of obstructing social progress.

The more Woodward was grilled, the more the heresies tumbled out of his mouth. He suggested that any increase in the marijuana habit was a result of "newspaper exploitation of the habit," a suggestion that did not sit well with the committee. And, finally, after many hours of testimony—testimony that lasted more than three times longer than Anslinger's—Woodward was dismissed without so much as a thank-you.

At the Senate hearings on July 12, 1937, the Clinton and Anslinger show resumed. Anslinger had updated his gore report. The senators were even more naïve about the plant than the congressmen had been, and their questions revealed an ignorance of the subject that was almost amusing. During his brief testimony, Anslinger circulated the photograph of the dead New Jersey murder victim, whose mutilated face had caused even the hardened coroner to turn away. One by one, the august senators perused the battered black face:

MR. ANSLINGER: We have many cases of this kind.

SENATOR BROWN: It affects them that way?

MR. ANSLINGER: Yes.

SENATOR DAVIS: [viewing the photograph] Was there in this case a blood or skin disease caused by marihuana?

MR. ANSLINGER: No; this is a photograph of the murdered man, Senator. It shows the fury of the murderer.

SENATOR BROWN: That is terrible.

MR. ANSLINGER: That is one of the worst cases that has come to my attention . . .

After a bit more cross-examination in which Anslinger repeated his House testimony, one senator finally had the presence to ask what the implications of the bill would be in terms of dollars and cents:

SENATOR BROWN: Will this entail any considerable increase in personnel for the Department?

MR. HESTER: No, I do not think so.

MR. ANSLINGER: No, sir.

So, after testimony from two hemp growers who succeeded in reducing the tax on producers from five dollars to one dollar, the hearings were concluded. Mr. Woodward did not even bother to appear in person, but sent a perfunctory letter opposing the measure for the record.

committees reported the bill favorably and on June 10, , the bill came to the House floor. And it was clear from the debate that the prevailing attitude toward it was one of ignorance and nonchalance:

MR. SNELL: What is this bill?

MR. RAYBURN: It has something to do with something that is called marihuana. I believe it is a narcotic of some kind.

MR. FRED M. VINSON: Marihuana is the same as hashish.

When the bill was voted on four days later, the act passed without a roll call after less than two pages of debate.

Upon passage, it received even less public attention. Most major newspapers made no mention of the new bill's passing Congress. Yet by the end of the summer, President Roosevelt would sign the bill, and on September 1, 1937, the Marihuana Tax Act would go into effect—the first federal legislation prohibiting the unregulated traffic in marijuana.

Yet Anslinger must have certainly had mixed feelings about the law's passage. It is clear from a study of the Bureau's files that he consistently fought against this federal legislation, for pragmatic as well as ideological reasons. In an interview in 1970 he claimed to have doubted the constitutionality of such a measure at that time and felt that Oliphant's proposed bill was "ridiculous." Even after the decision was made by the Treasury Department to submit it to Congress, Anslinger claimed that he did not believe it would pass.

But why such opposition? For one, he probably felt that regulating the marijuana traffic would be impossible due to the incredible proliferation of the weed—a position that his agent in New Orleans had taken. He also always felt that heroin was far more dangerous than marijuana. And since the new marijuana legislation would not mean a bigger budget for the Bureau, as Tipton had promised the senators, Anslinger would reap no financial remuneration for his hard-pressed Bureau, who would be saddled with the difficult job of enforcing this measure.

But Anslinger was a good soldier. Just as he had done in the early thirties to secure the passage of the Uniform State Narcotics Law, the Commissioner put on a splendid show for the unenlightened congressmen. He plotted out a campaign that would be the envy of any bleeding-heart liberal on Madison

Avenue. Placements of the Bureau's line on marijuana were made in numerous national magazines and newspapers; speeches were made; radio broadcasts were transmitted.

And in all these messages, Anslinger appealed to the people of the United States to assist him in the tremendous work that had to be done. He presaged this strategy in his July *American Magazine* article, which was obviously written well before the hearings had been held. Of the forthcoming law, he warned:

> The passage of such a law, however, should not be the signal for the public to lean back, fold its hands, and decide that all danger is over. America now faces a condition in which a new, although ancient, narcotic has come to live next door to us, a narcotic that does not have to be smuggled into this country. This means a job of unceasing watchfulness by every police department and by every public-spirited civic organization.
>
> In Los Angeles, Calif., a youth was walking along a downtown street after inhaling a marihuana cigarette. For many addicts, merely a portion of a "reefer" is enough to induce intoxication. Suddenly, for no reason, he decided that someone had threatened to kill him and that his life at that very moment was in danger. Wildly he looked about him. The only person in sight was an aged bootblack. Drug-crazed nerve centers conjured the innocent old shoe-shiner into a destroying monster. Mad with fright, the addict hurried to his room and got a gun. He killed the old man, and then, later, babbled his grief over what had been wanton, uncontrolled murder.
>
> "I thought someone was after me," he said. "That's the only reason I did it. I had never seen the old fellow before. Something just told me to kill him!"
>
> That's marihuana!

That's marijuana according to Anslinger. But the *American* article, along with the others, seemed to have struck a responsive chord in an America that four years earlier had still been banning alcohol. Letters came to the Bureau from all over America expressing amazement and horror at this new menace that the media was showcasing. Typical of the responses was this missive from a young lad in Richmond, Virginia:

> Dear Sir:
>
> I have recently read your article on marijuana and I would love to give my time and energy in the fight against this assassin of youth. Being a youth myself I am in hopes of being able, in some way, to

help. I am writing this letter to offer my life, if it could be used, for my fellows.

Please, may I help?

Anslinger replied:

I appreciate your offer of assistance as I realize that it is inspired by the highest of motives. Our agents are all under the Civil Service and the examinations are held from time to time. Your local Civil Service secretary can supply you with further information.

So, in the wake of the bill's passing Congress, an intensive campaign was waged publicizing this new national menace and enlarging the corps of Anslinger's Army. However, Anslinger would soon be confronted with some problems as a result of his excessive zeal to warn the public of the assassin-at-large. For one, he would be faced with the dilemma that in order to justify the bill and his Bureau's relations with respect to the weed, marijuana must remain defined as a menace or an epidemic. At the same time, a too hysterical approach would lead people to believe that the Bureau's efforts at combating this problem were ineffective.

Additionally, as was noted earlier, there was a sticky problem with relation to marijuana and crime. The courts were just beginning to see the first "marihuana defenses," cases where the defense contended that it was the weed itself that caused the criminal behavior. In this view, "normal" people are transformed into deviants by virtue of their use of this noxious drug. But, in the wake of the passage of the Marihuana Tax Act, Anslinger did not seem to be giving these problems much thought. However, there was one commentator, an M.D. named Henry Smith Williams, who in 1938 published *Drug Addicts Are Human Beings* and, in an amazingly prophetic statement, commented on the Tax Act passed the previous year:

So, a Marihuana Tax bill was introduced and presently enacted as Federal law. And the foundation was thus laid for a racket that should quite eclipse even the billion-dollar illicit drug industry that the Harrison Act (as misinterpreted) developed and fostered. For the new drug has qualities that put it in a class by itself.

For example: Marihuana, despite its high-sounding name, is merely a product of the familiar hemp plant—an agricultural product to which (according to statements made before the Congres-

> sional committee) upward of 10,000 acres of land in the United States are devoted. . . .
>
> Racketeers who developed a billion-dollar illicit drug industry, using opium that had to be smuggled into the country, should have no difficulty at all in developing a five-billion-dollar racket with marihuana—provided only that the press can be induced to stimulate curiosity by giving the drug publicity.

Of course Williams was right. By 1978 government estimates claimed the illicit marijuana industry was grossing $5 billion a year. Most observers felt these figures were tremendously understated. But Williams would attain no distinction for his foresight. As a reformer, a humanist, in the drug abuse field, he was also many years ahead of his time. For in 1936 the Federal Bureau of Narcotics, led by Harry Jacob Anslinger, had waged war against the World Narcotics Research Foundation, a West Coast–based organization that Williams and his physician brother E. H. Williams founded. E.H. was harassed and ultimately arrested and convicted for operating a narcotics clinic in Los Angeles and, through a technical mistake by his lawyer, lost his chance for appeal.

The arrest and prosecution of such an esteemed citizen (E.H. was a prolific author, was listed in *Who's Who,* and was an associate editor of the *Encyclopaedia Britannica*) should come as no surprise to Anslinger-watchers. The Commissioner was never flexible enough to brook dissent within or without his ranks, and vendettas against his opponents were a common occurrence during his thirty-two-year tenure at the Bureau. However, before 1937 his opponents were limited to a few liberal, humanist doctors who tried to propagate the ridiculous notion that drug addicts were sick people in need of care. But with the advent of the new Tax Act, a whole new category of American citizens was added to Anslinger's enemy list. These were young and old, black and brown and white, city dwellers and country bumpkins. They had one thing in common though; they all smoked reefer and enjoyed it, which to the Calvinist Commissioner was as much a sin as the commission of the act itself.

CHAPTER 6:
The Mighty Mezz and the Brooklyn Kid

Despite the claims of the Bureau of Narcotics and the resultant dissemination of these ideas in the mass-circulation sensationalistic press of the day, the marijuana culture in the United States in the 1920s and 1930s was a small deviant culture. There was never any hard evidence that reefer smoking had become widespread among schoolchildren anytime during the thirties; rather we find that the diffusion of marijuana use remained with a number of subcultures. Sailors, jazzmen, circus people, entertainers, gangsters, the odd cowboy, along with the blacks and the Mexicans—the first "heads" in America were the night people, the beautiful losers, the early existentialists. And from the beginning, marijuana became of more than routine significance in their lives. A native mythology grew up around the weed, similar to the mythologies that surrounded its use for thousands of years in Asia.

But this was an American mythos; and as such it is noted for its pragmatic, utilitarian qualities. Marijuana was never really linked to a religious context at first; rather it was seen as a psychic equalizer—a substance that would confer status and dignity on an outsider while at the same time providing the user with a sensual treat that could allay the heaviest of depressions.

It wasn't surprising then that of all the groups that adopted, utilized and ritualized the drug, the jazz musicians did the most to proselytize it, too. Musicians have always been a deviant subculture in American life, and early progenitors of the jazz sounds that would rule the music scene by the late forties were little short of outcasts in the early twenties. Of course, part of the prerequisites to being great musicians was the obligatory suffering and oppression; and of that, jazz musicians, especially the black ones, had their fill. And marijuana seemed to be the great equalizer, a substance that could unlock sensual treasure troves to the initiated without even informing the squares that something strange was going on. Perhaps it was the indetectable qualities of the experience (apart from the pungent smoke and the reddened eyes) that provided a further impetus for the ritualization of the marijuana culture. At any rate, a subculture grew up around the weed itself, complete with a glossary of names, expressions, signs and—later—clothes and paraphernalia. And, of course, after the federal regulation and the correspondent publicity, this grass subculture became all the more secretive, insular, furtive, and sometimes less fun.

Because if marijuana was any one thing to the wide array of groups that smoked it throughout our history, it was fun. A great escape, a sensual tool, an ecstatic holy herb, a medium for the politics of joy—whatever its guises, it always made its devotees feel good.

And one combination that couldn't be beat was marijuana and music. Oh, how many countless thousands of hippies from the Haight to Second Avenue transcended their egos and vibrated in harmony with the Great Force and Jerry Garcia's E-string while under the influence. And before them, the bopsters and Krupa's drums or the cats and Satch's trumpet? No, grass got intertwined with sounds early on, and it was the musicians who got to it first and turned on their audiences.

And the most legendary cat who ever blew both horn and reefer was Milton "Mezz" Mezzrow. Mezzrow was a Jewish kid from Chicago who got in with the "wrong" crowd early on, learned to blow some sax, and spent the rest of his seventy-three years obsessed with riffs and reefer. He grew up in Capone's Chicago, and was immediately attracted to black culture, ultimately becoming one of the first whites to pass (even marrying a black woman on the second go-around), settling down in Harlem, New York City. By the late thirties, Mezz had become a household word in Harlem's head households, purveying a brand of muta that could not be beat. Mezz's complete colorful career is documented in his autobiography *Really the Blues*, written with Bernard Wolfe and first published in 1946.

Around 1923 in Chicago, at the Martinique Club where he was playing a gig, Mezzrow was first turned on by a jockey who had scored some of the potent "golden-leaf" that was coming into

New Orleans—to the terror of Messrs. Gomila and Stanley. After being coached in the technique of smoking the joint, Mezzrow readied to play. He wrote:

> After I finished the weed I went back to the bandstand. Everything seemed normal and I began to play as usual. I passed a stick of gage around for the other boys to smoke, and we started a set.
>
> The first thing I noticed was that I began to hear my saxophone as though it were inside my head, but I couldn't hear much of the band in back of me. . . . I found I was slurring much better and putting just the right feeling into my phrases—I was really coming on. . . . I felt like I could go on playing for years without running out of ideas and energy. There wasn't any struggle; it was all made-to-order and suddenly there wasn't a sour note, or a discord in the world that could bother me. I began to feel very happy and sure of myself. With my loaded horn I could take on all the fist-swinging, evil things in the world and bring them together in perfect harmony, spreading peace and joy and relaxation to all the keyed-up and punchy people everywhere. I began to preach my millenniums on my horn, leading all the sinners on to glory.

Mezzrow became a confirmed head after that first experience in Chicago, and, as such, developed an ideology that justified its use and even laid claim to a higher moral standard. Muta was a benevolent substance, as opposed to alcohol, the predominant intoxicant. And this perspective led to a stance of demystification with respect to Anslinger's line:

> Every one of us that smoked the stuff came to the conclusion that it wasn't habit-forming and couldn't be called a narcotic. We found out that at one time the government had discussed it as a drug and tried to include it in the Harrison Anti-Narcotic Act but never could dig up any scientific reason for it. There being no law against muta then, we used to roll our cigarettes right out in the open and light up like you would on a Camel or Chesterfield. To us a muggle wasn't any more dangerous or habit-forming than those other great American vices, the five-cent coke and the ice cream cone, only it gave you more kicks for your money.
>
> Us vipers began to know that we had a gang of things in common; we ate like starved cannibals who finally latch on to a missionary, and we laughed a whole lot and lazed around in an easygoing way, and we all decided that the muta had some aphrodisiac qualities, too, which didn't run us away from it. All the puffed-up strutting little people we saw around, jogging their self-important way along so chesty and chumpy, plotting and scheming and getting more wrinkled and jumpy all the time, made us all howl, they struck us so weird. Not that we got rowdy and rough about it. We were on another plane in another sphere compared to the musicians who

were bottle babies, always hitting the jug and then coming up brawling after they got loaded. We liked things to be easy and relaxed, mellow and mild, not loud or loutish, and the scowling chin-out tension of the lush-hounds with their false courage didn't appeal to us.

Besides, the lushies didn't even play good music—their tones became hard and evil, not natural, soft and soulful—and anything that messed up the music instead of sending it on its way was out with us. We members of the viper school were for making music that was real foxy, all lit up with inspiration and her mammy. The juice guzzlers went sour fast on their instruments, then turned grimy because it preyed on their minds. . . .

By 1929 Mezzrow had moved from the Midwest to New York City, and had immediately set up shop in Harlem, which at that time was the breeding ground for jazz musicians and other practitioners of the night life. He began running with Louis Armstrong, who with his unique scatting style was the hottest jazz vocalist around. Armstrong and Mezzrow defined a whole style for the young jazz devotees in Harlem, a style that encompassed music, language, dress, and, of course, choice of intoxicant. They were "vipers"—they had their own way of talking, walking and—with it—their own affirmative identity:

All the raggedy kids, especially those who became vipers, were so inspired with self-respect after digging how neat and natty Louis was, they started to dress up real good, and took pride in it too, because if Louis did it it must be right. The slogan in our circle of vipers became, *Light up and be somebody.*

One day Mezzrow chanced on some old friends who turned him on to a Mexican connection, and the new gold-leaf hit Harlem like a storm. The saxophonist slowly found himself turning into a reefer man instead of a reed man;

Overnight I was the most popular man in Harlem. New words came into being to meet the situation: the mezz and the mighty mezz, referring, I blush to say, to me and to the tea both; mezzroll, to describe the kind of fat, well-packed and clean cigarette I use to roll . . . ; the hard-cuttin' mezz and the righteous bush. Some of those phrases really found a permanent place in Harlemese, and even crept out to color American slang in general.

In fact, a whole new language was adopted by the vipers, a secret inner city code that served to both mystify squares and solidify the sometime tenuous relationships between marginal men. Mezzrow recounts a typical scene, selling grass under the Tree of Hope, his corner territory.

First Cat: Hey there, Poppa Mezz, is you anywhere?

Me: Man, I'm down with it, stickin' like a honky.

First Cat: Lay a trey on me, ole man.

Me: Got to do it, slot. (pointing to a man standing in front of Big John's ginmill) Gun the snatcher on your left raise—the head mixer laid a bundle his ways, he's posin' back like crime sure pays.

First Cat: Father grab him, I ain't paying him no rabbit. Jim, this jive you got is a gasser; I'm going up to my dommy and dig that new mess Pops laid down from Okeh. I hear he riffed back on Zackly. Pick you up at The Track when the kitchen mechanics romp.

Fortunately, Mezzrow provides a translation.

First Cat: Hello, Mezz, have you got any marijuana?

Me: Plenty, old man, my pockets are full as a factory hand's on payday.

First Cat: Let me have three cigarettes [fifty cents' worth].

Me: I sure will, slowmouth. [A private interracial joke suggesting a mouth as big and as avaricious as the coin slot in a vending machine, always looking for something to put in it.] (pointing to a man standing in front of Big John's ginmill) Look at the detective on your left—the head bartender slipped him some hush money, and he's swaggering around as if crime does pay.

First Cat: I hope he croaks; I'm not paying him even a tiny bit of mind. [Literally, "father grab him" suggests that the Lord ought to snatch the man and haul him away; and when you don't pay a man no rabbit, you're not paying him any more attention than would a rabbit's butt as it disappears hurriedly over the fence.] Friend, this marijuana of yours is terrific; I'm going home and listen to that new record Louis Armstrong made for the Okeh company. I hear he did some wonderful playing and singing on the number "Exactly Like You." See you at the Savoy Ballroom on Thursday. [That is, the maids' night off, when all the domestic workers will be dancing there.]

Mezzrow became an established figure on that street corner known variously as the Reefer King, the Link Between the Races, the Philosopher, the Mezz, Poppa Mezz, Mother Mezz, Pop's Boy, the White Mayor of Harlem, the Man That Hipped the World, and the Man with the Righteous Bush. But his dealing was typical of the early marijuana trade—it was more proselytizing than mercenary activity. Mezzrow didn't sell weed like Fuller brushes; it was more like a family affair; if you were a friend or a friend of a friend, you could cop, often even if you didn't have all the cash up front. And even the other dealers didn't consider themselves in a competitive situation. Mezzrow recalls how the other peddlers would tell their customers, "This may not be as good as the mezz, but it's pretty close to it. Ain't no more reefer after the mezz." In fact, the other dealers were all customers of Mezz's when it came to their personal stash.

As the reefer scene burgeoned in the early thirties, Mezzrow turned down many overtures, from organized crime and others, to expand his herbal business. In April 1933 he even visited the midtown offices of a big radio booker who was intent on seeing Mezzrow to put together a mixed band. Or so the Mezz thought. No sooner had he sat down in the office, than the booker took out some color slides—all microscopic blowups of different varieties of weed in full color! The agent was convinced, scientifically, that Mezz had the best gage in town and that millions could be made by financing his brand throughout the country. Milton politely refused.

Mezzrow, of course, was one of the first whites to make the Harlem scene, but by the early 1930s more and more whites were sojourning uptown to pick up on the good music, the fine dancing, the tasty ribs, and the righteous bush. The scene was centered around the Savoy Ballroom at 141st and Lenox, where early arrivers could gain entrance for twenty cents. The Savoy had at least one jumping band each night; and, by the night's end, one could go to urinate and get a contact high from the heavy marijuana mist. And when the Savoy shut its doors at 4:00 A.M. or so, the vipers all retired to tea pads, which were slightly less elegant versions of the 1883 hashish houses—apartments in Harlem that featured colored lights, big Wurlitzers stocked with the latest sides, and reefer at fifty cents a pop.

Kaiser's was the most famous of the tea pads. It was in a sub-sub-subbasement, accessible only after navigating through the cellars of several other buildings. It was dimly lit, mostly in red and blue, and featured three rooms where people could gather and do their own thing or one huge central room with easy chairs and the inevitable jukebox.

After Kaiser's ran its course, the next spot was a pad run by an ambitious black gal from North Carolina who could neither read nor write but who knew green from blue. She did a tremendous business in weed, oftentimes employing young white girls up from the Village to sit all day and roll slim, well-tailored joints. For their troubles, the girls would get all the grass they could smoke. The entrepreneur was smart enough to invest some of her illicit earnings and today owns apartment houses and storefronts all along 125th Street.

But any apartment could be turned into a tea pad, and many were, if only for a night or two to scrape up some dough for the rent. This, of course, became the famous institutionalized Harlem "rent party," where sale of weed was often the difference between staying and eviction. And if the rent parties or Kaiser's didn't provide enough variety, there was always the unnamed tea pad that really provided ambience along with the muta. It was located in the rear of a funeral parlor, and all the heads had to pay their respects before paying for their reefer in the back.

Although the jazz cats in Harlem would wax eloquently on the virtues of reefer as opposed to demon alcohol, there were no real attempts to proselytize weed outside of their immediate circles. No forays into the Bronx or Brooklyn, no traveling salesman numbers. Part of their scene's charm and power was its exclusivity. So, naturally, the Bronx and Brooklyn came to them. By the late 1930s, it wasn't unusual to see Jewish working-class kids from Prospect Park hanging around the Savoy, digging the music and looking to score. One of those early would-be vipers was Bernie Brightman.

Today Bernie lives in a nice renovated brownstone overlooking Prospect Park in Brooklyn. He's a charming, good-humored graying goateed hipster who, at the ripe age of fifty-three, chucked his middle-class businessman's trip and went back to his reefer roots to establish STASH Records. Starting with an album called *Reefer Songs*, an anthology of vintage marijuana ditties from the jazz era, Brightman has gone on to produce six grass collections, along with a gay album, a woman's jazz set, and a slew of fascinating collector's material anthologies.*

Sloman traveled out to Brooklyn to obtain the aural documents of the rarely recognized jazz marijuana culture and to chat with Bernie, one of the first white recruits to that culture. They sat in Bernie's office, surrounded by thousands of jazz albums and tapes, jazz memorabilia, record mailers, and other STASH material, sipping tea, chatting about the tea scene.

"How did you get into the whole marijuana record business?" the reporter queried.

"I was in real estate," Brightman replied in slow, measured tones. "I was trying to find a new identity. I had come out of selling a large business and losing a million dollars. I was going through a whole crazy number; my whole family was fucked up at that time. My marriage was fucked up. Here I was in my early fifties facing that kind of shit. So I went from having an awful lot of money to really starting to scuffle. It was a heavy trip. I had been doing real estate for about two and a half years. Then a very, very old friend of mine, who later turned sour on me, came to me a few years ago and said, 'Why don't we do a record on all the good pot things? All the good pot songs we know?' So I said, 'Great; how much will it cost?' He figured a grand, and I said, 'Let's do it.' It wound up costing a little more than a thousand. We did that first album, *Reefer Songs*, and I used all my experience in terms of promoting it, selling it, and so forth. It did extremely well. We sold a lot of it in six months, but then his wife got bugged 'cause I was getting too much publicity; he didn't do anything to promote it; I was doing all the work, financing it and everything else. He came over and wanted me to sell out. Finally, I made a deal with him and bought him out. Today he's an enemy. An ex-hipster. Goes to work every day, sits in a machine, and sews furs. Jealous, envious. Probably saying, 'That son of a bitch stole my business from me.' "

"I guess the best place to start in terms of the early pot scene is with your own experiences. When did you first get turned on?"

* The entire catalog can be had from STASH Records, P.O. Box 390, Brooklyn, N.Y. 11215. It is well worth the price of a postcard since the distribution of these classics, unfortunately, is spotty.

"Firstly, you have to remember that for a white person who was sixteen years of age during the Depression, people of your generation have no idea of what the economics of the Depression were all about," Brightman gently lectures. "We're talking about a time in American life when you went out when you got out of high school, and you made eight dollars a week on the job. So you had to find the social kind of life you lived was different. Very different from today. I got into dancing at an early age. This was the era of swing. Benny Goodman at the Paramount. The step that followed when you were into that was to start listening, if you were sharp and tuned into jazz and some of the black bands of the time."

"This is about what year?"

"We're talking about 1937."

"Which is the year the Marihuana Tax Act was enacted." Sloman plays scholar.

"Right. Which was an interesting year for many reasons. My step into becoming a viper was the fact that I heard you could get into this place called the Savoy Ballroom up at 141st and Lenox for twenty cents if you got there before eight o'clock. Now, a nickel carfare from Brooklyn—subways were a nickel then—and you got into the Savoy for twenty cents. There were two live jumping bands every Saturday night. All the lindy hoppers would be there early."

"You went alone?"

"I went with another friend, never alone. Walked from the subway into the Savoy, and there was this guy who became my partner in STASH; I knew him from my neighborhood as a guy who played tenor, and I played alto sax. He said, 'Wanna smoke some reefer?' and I said, 'Why not?' I knew nothing about it; I'd never heard of it."

"Never?" Sloman seemed incredulous. "None of the myths? None of the newspaper stories?"

"Never heard of it. There was never a newspaper story in those days about it. Nothing about it. So he says, 'All right, gimme a quarter.' He brings us two joints. So we go into the bathroom of the Savoy, and we each smoke a joint. I get stoned out of my fucking head. I had never been high before; I was ready to buy a small bottle of wine or something like that just to get with it. So we smoked these two joints, and I come out and I'm having the greatest time of my life. I found out later on that he bought three joints for the quarter and kept one for himself.

He was entitled. He was the connection. I wasn't upset about it; I just started going to the Savoy every Saturday night and buying my own shit. On the corner right before you hit the Savoy, there were these two cats named Mickey and Crappy who sold pot. They were partners."

"White? Black?"

"Black. That was a black corner. Crappy just died last year in the VA hospital. He owned that corner for the rest of his life. Later he became the numbers man on that corner. He also opened a check cashing place when he retired from numbers, but that was Crappy's corner for the rest of his life. I'm close to Crappy—his name was Clarence—because I was tight with his sister and we almost got into a marital situation; but he was coming from a sort of middle-class black family, and they didn't want her to get too tight with a white guy—which was a shock to me. In my political naïveté, I thought that would be the greatest thing in the whole world. So there were two sides to Crappy's life. There was Clarence, the son of a guy who worked for the post office up on Sugar Hill; and there was Crappy, who sold shit on 141st and Lenox with Mickey, his partner."

"How many whites were going up there?"

"Saturday night there were a lot of whites. A lot of white women. A lot of them dug on the black cats. Saturday night at the Savoy was a happy, happy night. Black people really teach you how to enjoy life on Saturday night when you've been slaving all week long in the garment district, schlepping, and freight elevators; but you knew that Saturday night we were all gonna hang loose and have a ball. It wasn't too expensive. It was a really marvelous culture to get into for a poor kid because it brought some joy to your life. Then, too, there was the status involved. The guys who became smokers—vipers—who went back to their neighborhoods now became the hipsters. You were the guys who knew what sharp peg clothing was like, who wore the big three-inch hats, long jackets, big knotted ties. You were already getting into a little different status than the average guy."

"I want to ask you about this whole viper mythology. What else went with it—other than knowing the right music, the right clothes?"

"The right clothes, knowing the right music. A certain kind of language. A different language than the average person used."

"Which came from black culture . . ." Sloman interrupted.

"Which came from black culture and jazz culture. Generally speaking, it was being hip to life a little bit differently than the average square was. Starting to get into seeing life a little differently that resulted in changes of consciousness within your own head."

"In what way?"

"Most of the guys that I knew were really not prejudiced—the white guys—as a result of being up at the Savoy. Many of them, I'd say, were the early nonprejudiced people just as in the jazz world the white musicians were probably the earliest non-prejudiced whites in the country. It was a positive thing in that respect, even though some of the vipers, the so-called hipsters, were such schmucks, looking at them in retrospect. They were total schmucks, totally unaware of what many other things were about. Many of them didn't take the lesson of consciousness and carry it into creating a better lifestyle for themselves. Many of them were too programmed. They became victims of economics. Instead of trying to take that consciousness and make their lives a little better for themselves.

"I knew guys that got into the music business and tried to rip off the black culture and the jazz scene. I knew guys who got into lifestyles of not really enjoying what you were supposed to be made aware of through the change of consciousness. But when it came to the prejudice number, I must give them credit that they were not in that place."

"Was there a notion that you were an outlaw then?" Sloman was still probing for traces of Anslinger-consciousness.

"Never felt anything illegal about it." Bernie shrugged. "Never felt criminal. I would many times walk around the city—this was in '38 and '39. My friends and I would be smoking a joint and the cop would be ten, twelve feet in front of us. We'd know it was cool 'cause the cop didn't know what reefer was. He didn't know what the smell was. There was no problem. We'd go to dances, we'd go to functions, we'd go to sit in different clubs in the Village—and smoke. We used to go to dances on Sunday night in Brighton Beach, and we'd send one little guy named Powder Puff—he was the errand boy. He'd go up to Harlem for a Sunday, and, I swear to God, there would be fifty guys lined up. He'd come back with enough grass—we all chipped in—and fifty guys would be passing joints. Fifty guys! Can you imagine that kind of scene in 1939?"

"These are mostly middle-class Jewish kids?"

"Mostly working class. A few middle-class kids in the scene, but not too many. Largely Jewish. Coney Island cats, Brownsville cats. They had cellar clubs, boardwalk clubs. You belonged to clubs. There was a very heavy club in Coney Island called Alteos. Guys like Joe Heller were part of a younger group that came up after the senior Alteos. A lot of very prestigious people from today's art world have graduated from some of these places. These were social clubs. You'd meet, come in with a girl, listen to music, smoke if you were into smoking."

"What percentage of your friends smoked?" the sociologist in Sloman asked.

"In '37 maybe I knew about nine people that were smoking. By the time 1939 came around, there must've been sixty, seventy people smoking in the neighborhood, even guys that preached against it to me turned on."

"What would the guys that preached against it say?"

"Bad for you. They were afraid of it. Bad for the health. Bad for the head. Make you crazy."

"Sounds like the Jewish mother syndrome. Right after the Tax Bill passed was when that whole wave of Anslinger publicity got started up. Those stories about the kid that killed his family with an ax . . ."

"There really wasn't all that much in New York," Bernie interrupted. "New York was too hep to the scene. New York was the Apple. You could lay that stuff down in the Midwest or in Texas and Oklahoma, but who was gonna pay that much attention to that stuff in New York? They didn't waste their time here. Last I heard, Anslinger had made his deals with the liquor companies and the drug companies. He had made his private deal with them that he was gonna pursue this course of action, and they were glad about it."

"So you started early, at sixteen. What was it like? Was it just a Saturday night thing?"

"It started off being a Saturday night thing, and then we started smoking while we worked in the garment center. We'd meet in little alleys on our lunch hour, and we'd trade and see who had the best pot, who copped the best pot during the weekend. There was a whole number that went down in terms of getting high during lunch hour. My friends would sometimes meet me and I'd meet a couple of these cats from Coney Island who worked in my area, and there was a lot of cutting that went on between the two groups. We'd be a foursome, and conversationally a lot of 'capping' would go on—that's the expression we used. Little expressions that went down. It was an interesting kind of experience because the rest of the afternoon you're working stoned; it's a different world you're looking at. But it wasn't too prevalent. Very few people. It was certainly not stylish like coke is today."

"When you were doing it, it was like a secret society almost," Sloman wondered. "Even today, the way you talk about vipers has that grand mythology."

"Well, it seemed to be a special kind of club, and it was nice to be a part of it. We didn't have that much else in our lives going. Being poor is kind of dull."

"When did you first start going to the tea pads?"

"Within a year of the Savoy. It was a question of what you could afford to do after the Savoy on that particular Saturday night. Some people went down to the Apollo to catch the midnight show. Sometimes we'd go down to a Chinese restaurant on 47th Street where a lot of the vipers would go."

"You'd get the munchies?"

"Yeah, big munchies." Bernie smiled. "We weren't hip at that point to ribs, but that became a thing years later. Tea pads were opened up for me because I met an older black woman who liked me. She became my old lady for a while. We would go someplace after the Savoy that wasn't expensive where we could sit and have atmosphere and music, smoke, feel romantic, get romantic, whatever. It was a very, very big part of the Harlem scene, just as house rent parties were. People did various things to pay the rent—talk about evictions going down. It was very convenient for someone who was trying to raise some bread to put in some nice dim lights on Saturday night and have some reefer and music up there."

"What was the first tea pad experience like for you?"

"It was a marvelous experience; I felt grown up. A very sexual kind of feeling, too. After all, you're seventeen years old, going into this kind of atmosphere, and you're going to get stoned on top of it, or you are stoned before you come in. You're ready for any kind of experience. You're ready for the Queen of Sheba to come out and seduce you. There were times on Saturday nights, when we had some money, where we'd go out looking for dollar prostitutes. Horny kids. Didn't have any way of getting laid in those days. Jewish girls weren't putting out."

"Yeah, I know those stories." Sloman empathized completely.

"That led into some wild experiences," Brightman continued. "Had some hectic nights in Harlem, which basically was a very relaxed place to be 'cause nobody was going to discourage the money that was coming into Harlem in those Depression years. There was no uptightness of white-black, that sort of thing. But you could get into some nasty situations with prostitution. I've seen naked guys running in the streets late at night with women with knives in their hands and razors in their hands chasing them. That kind of shit. Hairy things happening. Of course we graduated after a while from buying joints to buying ounces; that led to a whole different thing."

"When did that start?"

"I think I must have been about seventeen and a half or so. I heard about a connection named Emerson, and I started copping good grass from him. I think we originally paid six dollars an ounce. Since none of us wanted to take it home—very few of us had privacy in working-class houses. You slept in a bed with your brother. You didn't have private chests. Where were you going to keep this shit? Where you gonna hide it? What we started doing, since there were three people involved in buying an ounce, two dollars apiece—on a low budget, that was a hunk of money. What we would do was to go to a cheap hotel for a buck, and we'd spend all night cleaning, rolling, dividing it up, so that way we could fill a pack of cigarettes with each one's share of the joints we had. We'd go back to the neighborhood, and we'd deal off enough of it to pay for what our costs were. So it became a production process in the hotel. One guy would clean, one guy would stuff, and one guy would tuck. Tucking was a very important thing. You had to tuck it nice so you could open it up with your fingernail easily."

"Tuck what?" Sloman lost the drift.

"Tuck the joint. There was a Mezz tuck. Let me explain what a Mezz tuck is like. It's a tuck where you use a flat matchstick, and you close it so that all you have to do when you want to open a joint is take two fingers and open it up easily. We rolled up joints. We rolled up all the grass. We'd buy paper—Bambu. Weren't that many places that sold Bambu in those days. Where do you buy Bambu? There weren't any head shops in those days. You had to go to a place on 14th Street, a Spanish place, a Spanish grocery store. That's where we got our papers."

"The scene was mostly centered around Harlem to cop?"

"Originally Harlem. It spread out; when I came back from World War II it was all over."

"Was there any heat from the cops?"

"Never heard of anyone being busted until I was in the army, and guys started getting busted while I was away. Oh, Mezzrow got busted. I never met him, but I knew who he was. He was a legend."

"A role model?"

"No, except for the fact he used to smoke opium. I always wanted to smoke opium. So what we used to do was follow Chinese guys who looked like they were high on the subway and see where they went. We spent hours following Chinese guys just to see if we could find an opium den. We never did, though. Mezzrow was something else, though. All that shit in his book is true; he was an ethical dealer, never wanted to commercialize."

"When did you split for the army?"

"I left right after Pearl Harbor," Bernie remembered aloud, "and I got stationed all over the country. Certain places were very good for copping; I was surprised. I copped real good in Kansas, New Orleans, Florida. I was surprised that I got it in Kansas. I think it was domestic shit. 'Cause the army was growing hemp for the wartime effort, and I think they were playing around with the marijuana farms. I knew cats on duty on some of those farms who were always able to cop. When I came back from the army, I found very young kids into smack. That threw me."

"Did people believe that marijuana led to heroin?" Sloman remembered that Anslinger propagated that line by the early 1950s.

"I don't think a lot of these people came into it through grass, like your sixties people got into acid. I think there's a whole different story here. The people I met when I got back from the army who got into smack went right into smack. They didn't fuck around with marijuana. Whereas in the sixties the whole mythology about marijuana had built up, and as a result of being lied to by authorities on the grass thing, a lot of kids felt that if they lied to them there, they must have lied about the rest of the shit. It wasn't true of the post–World War II crop I saw. They went right into smack as their first choice."

"How had the grass scene changed when you got back?"

"I got back in late '45, and the change was tremendous. It

wasn't just grass anymore. Now we're getting into hash, which didn't exist for us before the war. By some screwy good luck, I managed to score a kilo of hash for $200. It was unbelievably good. One poke shit. We all had water pipes; we built our own with stuff from the drugstores. Usually it was an older viper who had been on the scene for many years, smoking for ten, twenty years already, who laid some of that stuff on us younger people."

"So you're talking about guys who were smoking from 1910?" Sloman was intrigued, trying to plug the holes in his chronology of smoking.

"Absolutely. Guys who had been around circuses, carnivals. Some of these cats, don't forget, were into cocaine back in those days. Racetrack people. All kinds of people around the track were very educated in drugs from way back. River people. I'm talking about the Mississippi when riverboats plied their trade. I'm sure reefer went up the river just the way music went up the river. The entertainment business in America goes back a long, long ways. Cats who worked around it, whether it be tent shows or whatever. I think probably, as cocaine got a little more difficult to obtain and opium got a little more difficult to obtain, with the new federal laws around 1914, a lot of people got into smoking grass."

Bernie interrupted the narrative to bring out some munchies, Brooklyn-style. Sloman devoured a bagel and lox, sipped a glass of tea, and listened to the narrative.

"You know, there was a small group of us who got politically conscious due, in some sense, to the grass. There was an interaction between us: I turned a particular friend on to grass, and he became a viper; and at the same time he turned me on to politics or literature or classical music, museums, parks, zoos, things like that. Some people didn't have the good fortune to have that kind of input into their lives. All they ever stayed with was jazz and grass, which wasn't the worst thing in the world. For a few of us grass changed our lives in a very important way. But the average guy I knew from those years, today still smokes grass Saturday night or when he comes home from work. Still puts on the same music he listened to in those days—Lester Young and Count Basie. But they're not much into Beethoven, Mozart or literature or museums."

"What about your parents?" Sloman suddenly flashed. "Did they ever find out back in the forties?"

"Are you kidding?" Bernie smiled mischievously. "My parents were my stash when I came back from the army. I lived on East 9th Street between B and C, one of those seventeen-and-a-half-dollar apartments. Those were the early days, the end of '45, '46, when I got hold of this fantastic hash. It was called light green. And everyone started coming, trying to rob my apartment, looking for the stash. Which is an interesting story about a bunch of people involved in smoking over the years. Some of the characters who always looked for people's stashes to rob them. I knew some guys who have really pulled some shit. They robbed Emerson's stash, our first connection in Harlem. They'd sometimes send two guys in to make a buy. One guy would be in a place, maybe three or four flights upstairs, where he could watch where Emerson went out and what part of the hall he kept his stash. They finally found it later and copped it.

"Now I had such fantastic hash that guys—I mean—you smoked a toke. One toke on the water pipe. They were selling the hash on Coney Island in these old bungalows in a water pipe. They put one poke in the pipe, and they sold it for fifty cents. That's how great the shit was, and you were glad to get it. Every week someone was busting into my apartment. There was nothing there to rob, though; I was keeping my stash in my old army duffle bag in my parents' house in Brooklyn. I would just take a little bit of it so I wouldn't get ripped off; I had half a key, and it lasted over three years."

"Your parents never found out? You never told them?" Sloman seemed surprised.

"Why should I tell them?" Bernie shrugged. "It was foreign to them. What would it mean to my parents to know that I smoked marijuana?"

"So what happened after you got back from the army?"

"Let me preface with this—what happened about 1940, a year before I went into the army. The big change was that they no longer let you smoke grass in the toilets in the Savoy Ballroom. In '37–'38 they let you smoke openly in the toilet; you could drink a pint bottle, and nobody stopped you. By 1940 they had bouncers you had to respect; they could kick the shit out of you. The smoking was becoming a little too public. They were worried about their licensing. You either had to go into the telephone booth, or you did it under a table somewhere, that kind of thing. You could still smoke in certain clubs in the Village.

When I came back from the army, the most shocking thing was how many people were into smack. Then people began to use Bennie strips. You could get Benzedrine inhalers, open it up, take the inhaler strip out, put it in any kind of drink, and you'd do an all-night session of talking. Talk your head off, and screw up your stomach."

"Did you go to school when you got back?"

"I went to college for a while and collected checks. It was called the 52-20 Club. If you were a veteran, you could get twenty dollars a week for fifty-two weeks. So I collected that for fifty-two weeks. First I went to City College, then NYU. For a year. Then I got into the airline business with three other cats. Nonscheduled airlines. I went down to Florida, where I set up a branch with another guy. Met all the Florida vipers."

"Were they different?"

"They had to be extremely cautious. One of the gals that was smoking with us—her husband was a policeman with the Miami Police Department. So she taught us to be very careful down there. They were more hostile about the fact that people who smoked grass were usually more partial to blacks. You gotta realize blacks had to have a pass to be in Miami Beach after dark around 1948. So we had to be careful. There were people with smack, though, down there. All kinds of drug people. Everyone thought I was a big dealer. They thought the airline thing was just a front for bringing in shit. That's what my wife told me after we got married. She thought I was a big number with drugs. Bringing it in by airplane."

"You woulda been one of the first pioneers." Sloman smiled.

"That's true." Brightman shook his head ruefully and got up to clear away Sloman's plate. "I was just a poor schnook though. I shoulda done it."

CHAPTER 7:
The Bureau Retreats

Although the passage of the Marihuana Tax Act of 1937 did little to deter Bernie Brightman from schlepping up to Harlem to hit the tea pads, the legislation did effectively end the medicinal cannabis market. Due to the licensing regulations, most wholesale dealers refused to distribute the drug after the act passed. In a letter to Anslinger in response to the Commissioner's query, J. T. Huffman of Manito, Illinois, one of the largest dealers in cannabis, noted:

> I have decided to discontinue the collection and sale of the herb owing to the fact that it has been placed in the narcotic list by both State and Federal laws. I have no cannabis . . . and have not made any collection this season as practically all of the manufacturers and dealers whom I have done business with have decided to discontinue the use and sale of this herb.

On the letterhead, where he listed the products he distributed, Huffman had emphatically crossed out "American Cannabis"!

But if the bill had a significant effect on the future of marijuana as a medicine (a few years after its passage, cannabis would be dropped from the *U.S. Pharmacopaeia*, at Anslinger's urging), its effect on the Bureau of Narcotics was less than medicinal. In 1937 Anslinger was operating on a $1,275,000 budget, an amount that would be slashed by $8,000 in the two years to come.

Anslinger, as we have seen, had always resisted federal legislation on marijuana; but by October 1, 1937, he was faced with enforcing a new law prohibiting certain transfers of the substance with no additional funds to carry out the task. What was worse, as the New Orleans field agent had predicted, marijuana was everywhere; and, thanks largely to the tremendous PR job the Commissioner was doing, the lay public was becoming increasingly aware of it and the insidious menace it represented to wholesome Americans.

That there would be a problem in enforcing this law was seen in a memo Chicago District Supervisor of Bureau of Narcotics Mrs. Elizabeth Bass sent to the Commissioner on March 12, 1937:

> In reply to your letter . . . I beg to state that we have here, of course, no organized campaign on Marihuana, but I have been interested in the subject about three years and have taken every pain to inform myself on the entire subject . . . and I have accepted every invitation to speak on the matter that I could. . . .
>
> We have all assisted the local officers in the destruction of such fields, and where evidence of cultivation was present we have helped them make the cases against the offenders.
>
> The most important missionary work that I have done in the matter has been in the education of sheriffs, deputy sheriffs, chiefs of police, etc., in the regions outside the large cities. They are universally, until they have such education from us, entirely ignorant on the whole subject. We have spent much time and money in the propaganda against the use of Marihuana cigarettes and in the instruction of local officers and in making speeches at various points. I have not, of course, been able to include any of these expenses in my Form 1012, as these matters are not covered by the Harrison Narcotic Law and its amendments.

Mrs. Bass would have no relief after the new Federal Act went into effect, for no additional funds were earmarked for the enforcement of the marijuana law. Without the funds to seriously go after marijuana violators and with the knowledge that to fight the widespread weed would be a losing concern, Anslinger relied on a strict punitive application of the law in the courts. From the onset, he wasn't disappointed.

The first cases under the Marihuana Tax Act were heard in the court of U.S. District Judge J. Foster Symes, in Denver, Colorado, on October 8, 1937. Under the watchful eye of the Commissioner, who was seated in the courtroom, Judge Symes threw the book at the first two offenders. He gave Samuel Caldwell, fifty-eight, an admitted peddler, a four-year term in Leavenworth and a $1,000 fine. He sentenced Moses Baca, twenty-six, a confessed user, to eighteen months in Leavenworth. Which would seem to be a nice arrangement, since Caldwell was Baca's connection.

But the sentences were a departure for Denver, since prior to the Act, peddlers would get, at most, sixty days in the county jail for marijuana sales. And, to underscore the new policies, Symes made a short speech from the bench:

> I consider marihuana the worst of all narcotics—far worse than the use of morphine or cocaine. Under its influence men become beasts, just as was the case with Baca. Marihuana destroys life itself. I have no sympathy with those who sell this weed. In future [*sic*] I will impose the heaviest penalties. The government is going to enforce this new law to the letter.

This case was a milestone in a number of respects. One, it paved the way for a strict enforcement of the new law, with the most stringent penalties meted out. Second, it was typical of the cases that would be brought—one peddler dealing a few cigarettes to a willing user.

Anslinger was tickled pink by the outcome, praising the D.A.s, lauding the judge's comments, and putting his own two cents in for the willing press. "These men have shown the way to other district attorneys throughout the nation. Marijuana has become our greatest problem. . . . It is on the increase. But we will enforce the new law to the very letter."

Make that small letter. From October 1, 1937, the day the Act went into effect, until the year's end, the fearless agents of Anslinger made 369 seizures, consisting of 229 kilograms of bulk marijuana and 2,852 illicit cigarettes. Hardly the big time. In fact, by December 14, 1937, Anslinger was moved to issue a confidential memo to all his district supervisors:

> The Bureau has noted that a great many marihuana cases of a comparatively minor type are being reported.
>
> Thus far the courts have shown a very good attitude with respect to the disposition of marihuana cases and we do not wish to bring about a reaction by congesting court calendars with cases of a petty type. It is realized that necessarily some cases of this sort will be developed, but it is believed that in a great number of cases if more strenuous efforts were made to ascertain sources of supply, cases which could command more respect in the courts would be developed.
>
> Please give this matter your earnest attention.

A revelatory memo! Here was the Commissioner, a scant two months after the long-awaited federal legislation against the "worst of all narcotics" (in his own words), ordering his agents off the marijuana case! And that, in fact, was what he was doing. The notion of developing larger cases, commanding more "respect in the courts," was a canard, for there was no large centralized organized traffic in marijuana at this point. It seems more likely that Anslinger was being a realist in calling off the troops before the battle was hardly joined. For an understaffed, underpaid, undercover army was no match for a scrawny, over-publicized, much maligned plant which, true to its nature as a weed, positively thrived on such abuse.

So 1937, the year of the great Act, also signaled the year of the great Retrenchment. And Anslinger, always the strategist, would open (or close, to be precise) several fronts simultaneously in this new action. To his credit, the Commissioner never deviated from his line that marijuana was a noxious drug, still dangerous, still worthy of prohibition. However, cognizant that the Bureau would never be able to control the weed in the manner that the advance publicity would warrant, Anslinger began to retract some of the wilder claims that he had made with respect to its deleterious effects and, at the same time, began a major campaign of harassment aimed at the marijuana crusaders to his right.

For, by the mid-1930s, there emerged on the scene a curious by-product of the Bureau-generated publicity—the Marijuana Ministers. They were gentlemen—some of the cloth, all of the hemp—who, in the name of Our Lord Savior Jesus Christ (with thanks to Our Commissioner Harry Anslinger), would crisscross this great land of ours, armed only with the Word that Jesus stays off the grass. Having such a high moral authority in their corner, the Marijuana Ministers were a fearless lot, at times even consorting with the emissaries of the devil, the practitioners of the reefer trade, in an attempt to "know thine enemy." Their ideology often propelled them even to the right of Anslinger, for instance, when they condemned even the socially sanctioned recreational drugs like alcohol and tobacco. But their moral fervor also allowed them a perspective on the drug menace that Anslinger would never be able to share. Because they viewed marijuana addicts as fallen sinners, it followed that these unfortunates were weak people who needed help. It was not far from this position to suggest that addicts were worthy of medical attention. In Anslinger's church, this last statement was tantamount to heresy.

Starting in late 1937, the Bureau went after these marijuana crusaders who had taken, in Anslinger's eyes, an excessive position on the issue.

In Michigan Reverend Robert James Devine was peddling his anti-marijuana tracts, "The Menace of Marihuana" and "The Moloch of Marihuana," at twenty-five cents a crack, which infuriated the Commissioner. In 1939 Anslinger sent his field agents out to "cover" the reverend's lectures on the evils of the weed. Anslinger then reported to Gaston, his superior in Treasury: "As this religious booklet was marked 25¢ per copy, wouldn't it be proper to say that as the booklet is to be sold (probably cost him 1¢ per copy) we cannot assist him?" Gaston replied, "Absolutely." Anslinger then discredited Devine in a letter to a top official of the National Woman's Christian Temperance Union, pointing out that Devine's ". . . material was very sensational and contained several glaring inaccuracies."

But the full vent of the Commissioner's wrath was saved for one Earle Albert Rowell. Rowell had been on the drug circuit since 1925, lecturing on the evils of narcotics under the aegis of the California White Cross, a church-based temperance activist group. With his son Robert, Rowell scoured the country, gathering data for his books and lecturing before entranced church groups. The Rowells published three books: *Battling the Wolves of Society—: The Narcotics Evil; The Dope Adventures of David Dare;* and their masterpiece, *On the Trail of Marihuana—The Weed of Madness.*

Rowell became a foe of Anslinger's with his first book, *Battling the Wolves of Society*, where he opines that addicts deserve medical treatment and not prison terms. In fact, Rowell took an extremely avant-garde position for such a fundamentalist; namely, that perhaps it was better that unfortunate addicts have access to drugs rather than run amuck in society in an attempt to satisfy their craving.

At any rate, by their third book the Rowells were the object of scrutiny by Anslinger. And in a time when he desired to desensationalize the marijuana issue, *On the Trail of Marihuana* was as volatile as a thin reefer in the hands of a cornfed midwestern schoolchild.

The book opened with a tragic car crash—four youths dead, one mangled. Of course the copilot was the weed, deceiving the naïve youths into thinking that they were crawling when they were really doing eighty miles per hour. After that, every cherished marijuana myth was trotted out, in Rowell's "You-Are-There" pulp dime-novel style. Rowell's prose was a deep, lurid purple; in the world of reefer fiction, he out-Anslingered Anslinger. Which probably contributed to his woes:

> When a person smokes a marihuana cigarette, he may become a calm philosopher, a merry reveler, a cruel murderer, or a mad insensate. The results are as varied as human nature. There is absolutely no foretelling the effect on any one individual. Marijuana is, indeed, the unknown quantity in narcotic drugs. . . .
>
> We now know that marihuana—
>
> 1. Destroys will power, making a jellyfish of the user. He cannot say no.
> 2. Eliminates the line between right and wrong, and substitutes one's own warped desires of the base suggestions of others as the standard of right.
> 3. Above all, causes crime; fills the victim with an irrepressible urge to violence.
> 4. Incites to revolting immoralities, including rape and murder.
> 5. Causes many accidents, both industrial and automobile.
> 6. Ruins careers forever.
> 7. Causes insanity as its specialty.
> 8. EITHER IN SELF-DEFENSE OR AS A MEANS OF REVENUE, USERS MAKE SMOKERS OF OTHERS, THUS PERPETUATING THE EVIL.

And Rowell was no armchair alarmist; he and his son stalked the wild weed in open fields, crowded cities, slimy tamale joints, even in Tampa, Florida, to investigate the fabled Licata massacre—something that Anslinger had never deigned. Rowell's report was fascinating:

> On our tour of the states, we arrived in Tampa a few months after this horrible crime took place. The police and district attorney's staff who worked on the case told us the entire terrible and fantastic story, and took us to the house where the crime had been enacted.
>
> The police confided to us also that the father, who had been murdered, was by no means blameless, for he had been making these cigarettes, and having his son Victor peddle them to the students at the high school he attended. In time, Victor sampled his own product. Then came the quintuple murder. Thus the father, who had sown the wind, reaped the whirlwind.
>
> This crime struck home to the hearts and minds of the inhabitants of Florida the terrific potency of marihuana. Many months later we found the memory of this atrocity to be very vivid; the whole state had become marihuana conscious.

Rowell repeated the charges that marijuana was a "killer drug," and he relied heavily on Anslinger's gore list for exemplars. In fact, to the crusader, marijuana was more pernicious than alcohol, and even morphine! Rowell realized that thousands of Americans around the turn of the century had been users of patent medicines that contained the opiates and had unwillingly become addicts by the time federal legislation cut off their supply, forcing them to deal with the underworld:

> There are thousands of fine men and women who have been innocently addicted to morphine, and who, so long as they can obtain enough of the drug to keep them "comfortable," show no marked evidence of degeneration. While the drug attacks mind and body, it is the desperation to which the victim is driven by the pains of drug privation that hastens moral degeneration.

For Rowell the opiates were dangerous because the user becomes frenzied only when he is deprived of his drug. But the marijuanist is far more dangerous because he might do anything while under the influence of the drug:

> The marihuana user, freed from the restraint of gravitation, bumps his head against the sky. Street lights become orangoutangs with eyes of fire. Huge slimy snakes crawl through small cracks in the sidewalk, and prehistoric monsters, intent on his destruction, emerge from keyholes, and pursue him down the street. He feels squirrels walking over his back, while he is being pelted by some unseen enemy with lightning bolts. He will thrill you with the most plausible accounts of desperados who lurk in the doorway ahead, waiting with long, sharp knives to pounce on him and carve him to pieces. . .
>
> Not only are moral inhibitions removed and the Ten Commandments abolished in the mind of the confirmed marihuana user, but a positive conviction is added that it is right to steal, commit rape, and murder, and that it is actually wrong not to do these horrible things.

But what set Rowell apart from Anslinger was his theory on the progression from marijuana to harder drugs. Anslinger, of course, scoffed at such ideas during his testimony before the House in 1937. Rowell, however, not only saw marijuana as a percursor to heroin, he quite correctly argued that most marijuana smokers start out with the dread nicotine! And Rowell was also heretical in pinning the marijuana traffic to organized crime, as part of their dope master plan to enslave the youth of the country:

> Slowly, insidiously, for over three hundred years, Lady Nicotine was setting the stage for a grand climax. The long years of tobacco using were but an introduction to and a training for marihuana use. Tobacco, which was first smoked in a pipe, then as a cigar, and at last as a cigarette, demanded more and more of itself until its supposed pleasure palled, and some of the tobacco victims looked about for something stronger. Tobacco was no longer potent enough.
>
> They cast about for something new and more powerful. A few heard that the Mexicans had a new kind of tobacco with a "thrill" in it. They found it much stronger than tobacco, and recommended it to others. The cult spread like wildfire. No close-knit dope ring was pushing it. In fact, for once, here was a vice, a narcotic, whose use was nationwide before dope peddlers woke up. At first they looked upon it as a rival drug, then discovered it to be the habit of an entirely new group of persons they had never succeeded in reaching with their dope before; but now, with marihuana as the monitor, they saw in it, for the first time, the means of making dope users of millions of boys and girls.

But worse than this startling revelation was Rowell's assertion that police officials were doing nothing to stop the burgeoning marijuana traffic. Everywhere they went, he complained, they were met with ignorance or indifference on the part of the officials. The Rowells were forced to eradicate the weed themselves, and oftentimes they would lead a large weed-hunting expedition, good Christians all, taking action to stop the scourge.

As for the Marihuana Tax Act, Rowell felt that it had a pernicious effect on law enforcement.

> Now that there is a Federal law, we find both city and state officials quite willing, even anxious, to wash their hands of the whole matter and let Uncle Sam do it all. But when it takes 20,000 men to police New York City, how can we expect 300 Federal narcotic officials to police the whole United States and its possessions? . . . The seriousness of the whole situation demands that the drug no longer be shrouded in mystery; that a campaign of education concerning its noxious effects be instituted especially among those who are its main victims—the youth. . . . Meanwhile marihuana peddling goes merrily on, and will continue to flourish until you and you and you decide that it is a personal matter—a life-and-death threat demanding your immediate, resolute and unwearied attack against an enemy too deadly to trifle with.

Anslinger, needless to say, did not look too kindly upon these theories. He was already on record that marijuana use did not lead to the opiates. By 1938 he was concerned with reducing the publicity surrounding marijuana. In fact, on April 11, 1938, Anslinger fired off a letter to H. C. Williams, the Acting District Supervisor in Texas:

> Referring to your letter dated April 6, 1938, you will please, in a tactful way, decline to present the radio talks on marihuana anytime in the near future.
>
> For your information, our present policy is to discourage undue emphasis on Marihuana for the reason that in some sections of the country recently, press reports have been so exaggerated that interest in the subject has become almost "hysterical" and we are therefore trying to mold public opinion along more conservative and saner lines.
>
> Please refuse the invitations diplomatically.

It didn't take long for Anslinger to move against Rowell. Even though he was dissuaded by close friends from paying too much attention to Rowell, who was dismissed by them as a harmless zealot, Anslinger mounted what can only be called a dirty-tricks campaign against the crusader. According to Rowell's account, published in sociologist Alfred R. Lindesmith's *The Addict and the Law,* the harassment campaign began in 1938 in Wayne, Pennsylvania. Rowell was arrested and threatened with prosecution by Bureau of Narcotics agents for possessing an opium pipe that contained scrapings of opium and other small quantities of narcotics. Of course these drugs had been furnished Rowell by local police authorities in his educational campaign and were used during the lectures.

The charges were never followed up, but the Bureau broadcast that he had been arrested, and accused him of profiteering on his anti-narcotics campaign. In Evanston, Illinois, according to Rowell, he was threatened with prosecution for failure to pay an amusement tax. He also claimed to have been followed and watched on his speaking tour by narcotics agents.

In addition, derogatory information concerning him was circulated to opinion leaders in the areas where the Rowells were to have spoken, causing cancellations in some cases. These cancellations themselves were then written up and circulated by narcotics officials to further discredit Rowell. All in all, a campaign worthy of the Watergaters—some forty years earlier! The harassment was successful. Rowell and son disappeared from view by the early forties, and the Bureau once again cornered the marijuana publicity market.

However, Anslinger had another problem that resulted from the marijuana backlash, and that was the newly discovered marijuana insanity plea. As early as 1936, in the brutal murder case in New Jersey that Anslinger was prone to immortalize, the defense had raised the logical assertion that since marijuana was said to destroy men's wills and make jellyfish of them, then the hapless smokers who committed crimes while under the influence were really not responsible for these actions.

The prosecutors in that New Jersey case admitted that the brutality of the murder was accounted for by the narcotic; however, they argued that the defendant's intellect had not been totally prostrated by the drug. The judge agreed with the prosecution, and the marijuana defense fell.

However, after the 1937 Act a large number of defendants throughout the country resurrected the marijuana insanity plea, in some cases aided indirectly by the Bureau of Narcotics. And once again, a pivotal figure in this chapter of the marijuana story was Dr. James A. Munch, of saliva-test fame.

Munch had maintained his close association with the Bureau after his testimony at the 1937 Tax Act hearings. He was a consultant to the Bureau and had received grants to do further studies in the pharmacology of marijuana at Temple University, where he was a professor.

In February 1938 he was approached by the lawyers representing Mrs. Ethel "Bunny" Sohl, a twenty-year-old tomboy daughter of a Newark, New Jersey, policeman who was to stand trial that month for the fatal shooting of a Newark bus driver. Munch was asked to appear at the trial as a marijuana expert, and, after gaining the approval of the Philadelphia office of the Bureau of Narcotics, he agreed to testify.

During the trial, the defense established the fact that Bunny had been a user of "marijuana cigarettes," which "made wrong things seem right," according to the girl. "The smokes made me forget all about the pain in my head," Bunny testified, referring to the pain she had suffered since an automobile accident four years prior to the incident. Bunny was introduced to the weed by her husband, who was now serving time for check forgery.

The defense trotted out Bunny's family in an attempt to establish the marijuana defense. Her grandmother, mother and father all took the stand and testified to the young girl's "queerness." But it was Munch's testimony that would be the main factor in saving Bunny Sohl and her companion in crime from the electric chair. In a banner headline, "Court Admits 'Loco Weed' as Defense for Bunny," the Newark *Ledger* reported Munch's testimony prominently:

> Hope for escape from the electric chair was held out yesterday to Bunny Sohl when the State lost a move to bar an expert's testimony on her plea that doped cigarettes led her to robbery and a slaying.
>
> Dr. James E. Munch, Temple University physiologist, who has stalked the secrets of marihuana by smoking it himself, took the stand in defense of the 20-year-old blonde and told the jury of a delirious dream world he found when he puffed a "reefer". . . .
>
> Described by the defense as the country's foremost authority on marihuana, Dr. Munch, a small, nervous man spellbound an incredulous county court audience with his revelation of the "happiness and joy" that came when he inhaled a "Mexican weed" to "lose all conception of time and space."
>
> "I passed into an ink bottle," the narcotic expert began without preliminaries, talking in precise jerks like an animated textbook. His flashing black eyes danced over the jurors. "I peeked over the edge and I wrote a book," he said. "I was in the same bottle for 200 years." He smiled politely, puffed an imaginary smoke ring through his lips, and flicked his fingers over his knees like a pianist rippling a keyboard. Spectators tittered. Attendants bellowed, "Quiet, please!" The doctor looked around him like a man waking up in a strange place and continued the tale of the nightmare he had on a "Mexican weed."
>
> "In the same bottle 200 years," he explained. "After that I flew out." He sighed and smiled again. "I flew around the world a few times." Then the dream was over. "I was back in my chair. I looked at my clock. I had been gone fifteen minutes". . . .
>
> "Space vanishes," the doctor explained in his discussion of the "weed." "You can walk across the ocean. You can jump from here to the Panama Canal. Things you do seem to be the things you should do. The weakling feels he can fight a prizefighter."
>
> Effects he said were "delightful, horrible, gruesome, unusual and bizarre." He termed these stages "being high." He said: "Individuals at this stage will be forced to commit robberies." Prosecutor William A. Wachenfeld objected to the doctor's "romancing," and the remark on robberies was stricken from the record.
>
> Before he finished, the doctor told of marihuana murderers, and of two addicts who "attempted to drive an automobile at a high rate of speed over a road that didn't exist out in a desert in a gully."

The jury, obviously fascinated by Munch's story, returned a verdict of guilty and recommended life imprisonment rather than the chair for the two wayward youths. However, the verdict was greeted with dismay by many editorialists who feared that reefers would be refuge for many a criminal to come.

Despite the local publicity, the *Sohl* case did not make much of a stir outside New Jersey. However, a few months later, Munch once again testified as a defense "expert," this time in a case in New York City. Arthur Friedman, twenty-one, was one of five youths charged with the fatal shooting of Detective Michael J. Foley in a restaurant holdup. On April 7, 1938, Munch journeyed down from Temple and repeated his fantastic story, this time for the Big Apple jurors. The *New York Post* heralded his tale with a banner headline: PROF FLIES HIGH AND CRASHES, ALL ON WINGS OF MARIHUANA—*After "200 Years at Bottom of Ink Bottle," Expert Testifies at Murder Trial.*

This time the reaction from Washington was swift. Two days later Anslinger fired off a letter to his New York District Supervisor:

> What I would like to know is whether it was definitely established that the boy smoked the drug before the crime. Possibly the District Attorney can give you some information on this point. I am very anxious to know whether Dr. Munch, in spite of my admonition, proceeded with his testimony before he was absolutely certain that the drug had been used. I want this information so that we may be able to determine our future relations with Dr. Munch.

On April 12, in a file record of a telephone call from a narcotics investigator to the District Supervisor, it was reported:

> . . . Dr. Munch got on the stand and put up a perfect defense for this man who murdered the cop and the two district attorneys are very sore about it. They think Munch is a representative of the Bureau of Narcotics and wonder why the Commissioner sent him up there. . . . The two DAs say that Dr. Munch recited his testimony like a parrot and they are informed it is the same, word for word, as the testimony he gave in the Sohl case in Philadelphia. They say he spoke as though he worked with the Commissioner.

Two days later Anslinger wrote Munch. He warned his pot-smoking colleague that the marijuana defense was rapidly spreading as an "afterthought" on the part of shrewd defense counselors. "We have reliable information that the word is being passed along through the young underworld to 'blame it on the weed' when tried for a crime."

Anslinger ended by requesting that in the future Munch refrain from testifying for the defense in criminal cases, and, to underscore the message, sent a letter the same day to the District Supervisor in Philadelphia, requesting him to personally express his displeasure to Munch.

The broadsides worked. Munch was positively repentant in a six-page letter he wrote to Anslinger explaining his testimony at the two trials. He made certain not to convey the impression that he worked for the Bureau, Munch maintained, and he had noted that his studies of marijuana were scientific, not the frivolous thrill-seeking of a dilettante:

> I pointed out . . . that I had made some studies of marihuana action on animals, on myself, and had observed the effects on a number of Mexicans. However, I did not want to lend myself to the establishment of "marihuana" as a defense for any moron who might desire to commit any sort of crime, then blame it on the action of the drug and escape the proper penalty of the law. . . .

Apparently it was not enough, for on April 26, Anslinger wrote a three-page letter to the New York District Supervisor, to be circulated, in which he angrily rebutted six statements that Munch had made during his testimony in the *Friedman* case.

Anslinger contradicted Munch's testimony in detail, not only to determine how the Bureau would deal in their future relations with the pharmacologist, but also "for future reference in case Dr. Munch is again employed by defense counsel in New York or elsewhere. . . ." So, by the spring of 1938, the Commissioner was beginning to reap the harvest of '37. After all, if that Deadly Green Goddess was really the assassin of youth, then it was only logical that youthful users who committed mayhem were themselves victims of extenuating circumstances, since that dread Marijuana was the source of their frenzy.

And so the gore file was temporarily shelved, the 8 x 10 glossies of the victim of that brutal New Jersey murder—the one with the skull that resembled a rotten pomegranate—were filed under "Pulp—Bloody," and in 1938 the Bureau had realized that "no general rule could be evolved" with respect to the relationship between marijuana and crime, since the "physiological effects of marihuana are variable." And so did Anslinger's theories vary, a direct function of bureaucratic need.

March 3, 1978. Six o'clock in the evening. Sloman was in Washington, where he had just put in a solid week of eight to five in the Drug Enforcement Agency library, poring over the old files of the Bureau of Narcotics. The next day he would travel to Baltimore, stopping there to interview an anti-marijuana modern-day crusader before he would return home to New York. But this Friday night he had stayed in Washington to see his beloved New York Rangers pick up an easy two points against the hapless Washington Capitals. Except that a slight whitening in the morning had threatened ticket sales enough for the Caps' front office to arbitrarily postpone the ice hockey game.

Sloman was pissed. The buses were running, there was no snow on the roads, and, what was worse, he was stuck another night in Washington with nothing to do. But on a whim he picked up the phone and dialed a number in suburban Maryland. Five rings later Dr. James Munch answered.

"Dr. Munch"—Sloman was flabbergasted to be talking to the man whose testimony in 1937 had helped to shape our drug history—"I'm finishing a book on the social history of marijuana . . ."

"I don't know nothing about it except I've only been at it about thirty years." It was the same voice Sloman had read about—the barking exuberance, bordering on the edge of mania.

"I've been going through all the documents and one of the things that intrigued me was all the stuff right after the act was passed. The insanity question—the testimony. Was that a legitimate defense at that time?"

"Absolutely," Munch squealed.

"You testified at the Arthur Friedman trial . . ."

Munch interrupted. "You talking about 1935?"

"1938, I think," Sloman said politely.

"Anslinger did the legal work; I did the scientific work, checking out the background of marijuana." Munch was off and running. "For that I have then and later got in touch with Scotland Yard, the French, the Turkish, the Belgian, the African, the Indian—representatives from all countries in which marijuana has been studied. From that I testified that there was no legitimate medicinal use for marijuana at that time. And I'm not at all sure I've changed my mind on that. However, I did claim, based on that experience, and on my own observations, and on cultivating material and checking it, that both the male and female plants had activity."

"You were the first one to say that," Sloman marveled.

"Only the female had been working before. Also, that long-continued use will cause irreversible brain damage. I know that has been argued both ways ever since, but the most recent reports I have seen confirm that excessive use—which is not defined; it just means too much—will cause definite brain damage. Irreversible. That's about my story."

"You testified at those famous 1937 hearings. What was it like?"

"Representative Doughtee [*sic*] of North Carolina, as I remember, was the man in charge of that particular work. And I worked with Harry Anslinger for some years before, had permission to raise the material and study it, which we did, growing it myself and checking it, trying it only once, which was enough for me—"

"That was a great paragraph you wrote about being at the bottom of an ink bottle for 200 years," Sloman laughed.

Munch chuckled. "That's right, that was me."

"So you actually smoked once?"

"Yeah, I was curious, being a pharmacologist, and thought I'd try it once and see what it was all about before I let anybody else fool with it, and I found out that . . . well, you got the picture what happened to me there. Frankly, I've forgotten most of the details since then, but that's all right. Now, what happened was that when we started originally, cannabinol was supposed to be the active ingredient. But Wollner and I, working with Anslinger and Joe Levine and the people at Treasury, showed that cannabinol is not the only active ingredient. THC came much later. The general story is that there was a great variation in the potency of all the materials then on the market; so we arranged for Quimby to go down to Mississippi and grow various brands and various seeds down there for a dependable uniform source of material to be used by all research workers. And that is done, as you probably already know. And that made a constant reference instead of varying all over the map, as it had done before."

"Would you say at that time, say around the time of the hearings, that there was tremendous public awareness of marijuana?"

"Not in the United States. In England and in India, yes, and they were taking steps then to check the use of it. We followed the British and the Indians in that regard."

"But at that time, basically, we're talking about an American public that was pretty unaware of it and a Congress that really wasn't that sophisticated with respect to . . ."

Munch cut Sloman off. "That's right. It was being grown commercially in only one place in the United States, and that was down in Florence, South Carolina; so I went down and looked at the growing there and got some of the materials that I used in my studies for Harry Anslinger."

"Now what about the illicit . . ."

Again the doctor jumped in. "Very little at that time."

"How about the stories like the *Licata* case and linking it with violence at that time?"

"That was mainly among Mexicans or people who were able to get the material smuggled out across the border from Mexico. Most of the crime committed in the early days—like the chap down in Florida who killed the hotel clerk, and the other chap who killed his parents—was by Mexicans who had gotten some of the material brought up from Maheekow."

"Could you infer, as they did, causal relationships between smoking marijuana and the commission of crimes?"

"Yes, I wrote a paper on that which you may happen to have, since it was published. I published three of them in the *Bulletin of Narcotics*."

Sloman remembered that article, which was virtually a replay of Anslinger's gore parade, reprinted some thirty years later! "What about the Friedman trial?" Sloman was getting impatient. "Now at a certain point Anslinger didn't want to allow that kind of defense testimony for an insanity plea."

"Well, what happened was that after the law was passed, a certain number of chaps felt happy to violate the law. Remember Prohibition? Well, same story. Since this had become illegal, they thought they had to try it. Now to do that, they did their best to tear down not only my testimony but also that of Anslinger himself." It was clear that Munch had misunderstood which testimony Sloman was referring to, but there was no stopping the pharmacological cannonball. "We were, Anslinger was a member of this United Nations narcotic outfit, remember, for years and years and years, and a lot of my information I got firsthand from Harry, much of it unpublished. Naturally. On the harm and the dangers and all that sort of thing. But I contacted the various pharmacologists, toxicologists; the commission found that there was no dependable reliance on a use for the material in human medicine at that time. I mean at the time of the hearings."

"But how about a case like the *Friedman* case, where this guy claimed that he was insane temporarily because he had smoked marijuana and went out and shot . . . I think it was a cop." Sloman swung back to the subject.

"What happened was, a number of those cases which I included, I reviewed the reports made to Anslinger by our field agents at the Bureau of Narcotics; and the paper I wrote had to do with the checking by the Bureau of Narcotics people on the authenticity of the material used and the definite relationship between its use and the crime that was being reported. So that most of the information in there was checked and double-checked by the Federal Bureau of Narcotics."

Somehow Munch had strayed back to his 1966 article. Sloman made one final attempt to get some data on the *Friedman* case.

"But I remember that I read a memo Anslinger had written where, in fact, he stated that he didn't want people associated with the Bureau to testify for the defense in these cases because he felt that these kids were just copping a plea . . ."

"I got sucked in on one of those in Elizabeth, New Jersey," Munch recalled ruefully. "I guess you've heard about that. I was reluctant to go, but Harry said to go on up and try it out because they needed a legal precedent. So I went, not because I was interested, but because Harry was. That was Bunny Sohl and somebody else—I've forgotten who. But you're familiar with that.

"They were found guilty and were both sent to prison. What happened was that they'd been smoking marijuana, and they held up and shot a bus driver and got something like five or six dollars out of his money bag. But we did a good job on it, I guess. I ran about three days on the witness stand for it, anyway. The main thing I remember was that they asked me a purely hypothetical question that was one hour long, and they asked me, did I want it repeated, and I said no, they didn't need to. So the judge thanked me for that. But my testimony was, if these girls had in fact, in truth, been smoking marijuana, then their conduct in shooting the bus driver and stealing money would be entirely in accord with what I would expect. They were found guilty, sent to prison for twenty years or something, and later let out."

"I'm trying to get some kind of sense of what sort of guy Anslinger was. I've talked to some people who worked with him in the old Bureau, but you had a long-term relationship with him. What kind of person was he?"

"Well, I found it good, because what had happened originally, I had shown that the injection of the saliva or urine of racehorses into the mice would cause definite symptoms in the mice within five minutes." Annddd he's off. "That was one of my pets. Now the result was, Harry was much interested in that, and that's when I got acquainted with him—because of the doping of racehorses all over the country. So I developed the so-called mouse test—the biological test. The net result of that test on a few thousand horses was that if the horse had been given any improper medication within twenty-four hours, I could guess 90 percent of the time what the medication had been. I was wrong once in a while. But I was right 100 percent in saying the horse had been doped or had not been doped.

"Now that was important, for when they're using a product like cocaine, for example, it decomposes in the body of the horse and is not present as cocaine; so a chemist would not spot that. But my mice show characteristic reactions of a cocaine derivative. So we built a mobile laboratory for the Maryland Racing Commission, and I had my associates come to Maryland, Boston, New Hampshire, Illinois, the state of Washington, and a good many other places. The chemists didn't like me because I'd be taking money out of their pockets. They got twenty-five dollars an assay; it took them three days to run one to find out what was there. Whereas, we went right out to the race tracks, got the sample directly from the saliva in the barns, and tested immediately. And so we knew within five minutes."

"So that was the first time you had come in contact with Anslinger?"

"That's right. At that time we found that the smaller race tracks were busy using amphetamine and other things of that sort, and that about seven out of eight horses were being doped."

"That was a famous thing for him," Sloman recollected. "I remember going through Anslinger's archives, and he had at least twenty magazine articles about that thing with the horses. How did you get on to the marijuana research?"

"Well, at that, Doughtee [*sic*] made an approach to Harry Anslinger while we were doing the mouse-testing on racehorses, and Harry asked me to sit in with a chap named Wollner, who was a chemist for the Treasury and advisor to the Secretary of the Treasury, and other chemists, to see what I could do from the pharmacological standpoint. So Harry invited me in because I'd been a saliva-test horsepert, to get in on the marijuana deal. Long story, you see."

"What kind of person was he?" Sloman tried anew.

"Very lovely. He had been in charge of alcohol tax before, and then they brought him in after the war. Now he'd been an ambassador to Venezuela and several foreign countries—very lovely person to work with, a little strict once in a while. He had to be."

"Strict in what way?" Sloman perked up.

"The law said this and now we're going to try to stick to the law. If there are going to be any exceptions, I want to know about them. Ordinarily, if the law said this, we're going to conform to the law, because Congress passed a law and we think we ought to enforce it. He trained a number of chaps to succeed him. George Cunningham died. George White was out in California—he didn't want to come east—so we got a chap who lives on Hampshire Avenue—I'll think of his name in a minute; that's right, Giordano. He came in when Anslinger retired; then politics reared its ugly head and Giordano got out. And now, of course, I'm not commenting on what the situation is; I'm just keeping my mouth shut."

"I really admire the fact that before you got into the whole subject you tried it once." Sloman admired Munch's spirit of adventure in the thirties. "Do you know if anybody at the Bureau ever tried it?"

"I can't answer that. I think probably some of them did, but they never formally reported it to me. They might have reported it either to Harry or to Giordano."

"He never did it himself—Anslinger?" Sloman prodded.

"Not as far as I know. No, he didn't believe in that."

"He's a kind of straight and narrow guy?"

"Very much."

"So, are you still active?" Sloman changed the subject.

"Well, I'm a semiretired insultant." Munch cracked. "What I mean by that is, I'm retained by drug companies from time to time; right now I'm being retained by some lawyers in connection with medical malpractice suits."

"Have you kept up your interest in marijuana?"

"Well, there have been no marijuana cases that have retained me lately; everybody knows I've been opposed to the legalization of it, and I guess that's probably one reason I haven't been called in."

"What's your feeling about . . . HEW puts out statistics that say 25 million Americans smoke marijuana regularly . . ."

Munch scoffed. "That's from Du Pont and his crowd. I haven't checked up on them . . ."

"I told those figures to one of Anslinger's old lieutenants and he said, 'Boy, that really scares me; I don't like to hear that.' "

"I know; well, none of us do." Munch shuddered.

"Do you still think marijuana is such a dangerous drug?"

"Yes. In overdose."

"Well, what's . . ."

"Overdose would vary with the individual involved, because in some cases, one cigarette could be an overdose, and in others, they might smoke half a dozen and still not show any effects."

"How about the theory in the fifties that marijuana was the first step toward using other drugs—eventually heroin?"

"Well, it was all right in the fifties. I don't think it has any standing now though," Munch admitted. "A lot of those earlier theories were just good theories, and we had to try and explain them somehow. The same way that we now have about a million high school girls who are pregnant every year. Now if you . . . why do they want to get pregnant?"

Sloman was stumped. "I don't know. What's your theory?"

Munch chuckled. "I don't know. There's no relation to marijuana. Now don't get me on that."

"But those marijuana figures are staggering and if you do a little research into the historical ways marijuana has been used . . ." Sloman began to lecture, but was cut off by the pharmacologist, who was shouting to someone in the room.

"Just a minute—your stuff is boiling; your stuff is boiling! I have to stop and get my dinner here. I'm sorry, I didn't get your name."

"Larry Sloman," the reporter answered.

"Well, if I can be of any help, I'll be glad to hear from you, and if you publish something, I'd be glad to get a copy of it;

anything else you want, you just drop me a note, okay, Harry?"

Larry agreed and hung up the phone, and started thinking about how he was going to spend Friday night in Washington.

But if Anslinger was moving, as early as 1937, to defuse marijuana as a social issue, there was one area where he would still collect case histories, compile charts, and maintain that marijuana was a menace. That, of course, occurred during his yearly visit to the Appropriations Hearings, where the budget of the Bureau had to be justified. As late as the December 1936 hearings for the 1938 budget, Anslinger was still lauding the states' handling of the problem. However, at the first meeting after the Tax Act was passed, which ironically fell on December 14, 1937—the same day Anslinger circulated that memo calling for a reduction in the number of "petty" marijuana cases brought up—he ruefully noted the additional burden marijuana enforcement meant to his Bureau.

MR. LUDLOW: We are making vigorous efforts to hold down these bills. Do you think you could get on with less?

MR. ANSLINGER: We took on the administration of the marihuana law and did not get any increase for that purpose. The way we are running, we may have to request a deficiency of $100,000 at the end of the year; but I sincerely hope that you will not see me here for a deficit. Beginning the first of the year, Mr. Chairman, I shall control all travel out of Washington. That is a hard job. I have to do that to make up some of this money. We went ahead at high speed and broke up 10 big distributing rings, and now we find ourselves in the hole financially.

MR. LUDLOW: You have to find some way to recoup?

MR. ANSLINGER: Yes; and keep the enforcement of the Marihuana Act going. Not a dollar has been appropriated in connection with enforcement of the marihuana law. We have taken on the work in connection with the Marihuana Act in addition to our other duties.

The next year, on January 23, 1939, Anslinger again appeared to testify about the proposed 1940 budget. Again marijuana was the Commissioner's whipping boy, and this time he stressed the large eradication program that the Bureau had undertaken.

MR. ANSLINGER: I have my first report to make to you gentlemen on this subject since the passage of the act. Since the passage of the act, we have arrested, roughly, 1,000 traffickers. We have had to go into the traffic at the expense of traffic in other drugs because there was no added appropriation to take care of this work. We had to absorb it with our other duties. I would like to have this statement, showing the destruction of marihuana throughout the United States, made a part of the record. It amounts to 26,000 tons throughout the country. [A two-page table listing state, city and county eradications was inserted.]

However, during cross-examination, Anslinger was almost temperate in his discussion on marijuana, in line with his new policy to downplay the sensationalism surrounding the drug.

Mr. Ludlow: About how many cigarettes is it necessary to smoke to become an addict, if that is known?

Mr. Anslinger: I do not know whether there is such a thing as a marihuana addict. We do not know whether they become addicted to it. It seems that they can quit after they have smoked 1 or 100 marihuana cigarettes. The effect upon the individual is difficult to determine, but we think that the effect of only one cigarette may possibly cause permanent damage.

Mr. Ludlow: You would not call marihuana a habit-forming drug?

Mr. Anslinger: No, sir; it is generally agreed that marihuana is not a habit-forming drug. There have been a few cases wherein the withdrawal of the drug has produced symptoms similar to those produced by heroin and morphine, but those cases are few. In other cases men have smoked marihuana from 10 to 20 years and yet fail to show any ill effects. On the other hand, we know cases where people have smoked only a few cigarettes and, as a result, became mentally deranged.

It was obviously incredibly difficult for Anslinger to restrain his bloodlust and talk dispassionately about the former assassin of youth. In fact, every few years the old Anslinger would momentarily re-emerge, and the shark would bite with those pearly whites. In the 1940 "Traffic in Opium" report, an annual PR tome which was designed as much for the Appropriations Committee as anyone, Anslinger dipped once more into the gore bucket and showcased the case of Eleutero Gonzalez.

> The murders and suicide described in the following cases are typical of the crimes associated with marihuana:
>
> Near Del Rio, Tex., on September 11, 1940, one Eleutero Gonzalez allegedly while under the influence of marihuana, shot to death two women and then committed suicide in a manner which indicated that he was bereft of all reasoning. A description of the crimes was contained in the Sheriffs' Association of Texas Magazine for September 1940, excerpts of which are quoted:
>
> ". . . The Gonzalez case was one of the most brutal that Del Rio has seen in many years. . . . The young women were shot to death. . . . The killer, probably maddened in the realization of the magnitude and horribleness of his crime . . . literally sliced himself to bits about the abdomen, around the heart and throat. . . ."
>
> It was the opinion of the law enforcement officers that Gonzalez was under the influence of marihuana at the time of the double murder and suicide. They also believed that he had previously used marihuana. A handful of marihuana was found in Gonzalez' room after the tragedy. It was the opinion of the doctor who saw Gonzalez just before he died, that no one could have mutilated himself as Gonzalez was mutilated, unless he was unable to feel "shock" and the only thing he knew that would produce such a condition, to such a degree, is marihuana. . . . Indications were that Gonzalez had wandered around in the fields for hours after the killing and after his self-mutilation.

But for the most part Anslinger managed to suppress his fetish and instead came armed, year in and year out, with figures of arrests, kilograms seized, fields eradicated, etc. And always it was the marijuana problem, no longer deranged killers or debauched youth but fields and fields and fields of old, carelessly sown birdseed that matured into potential troublestalks, that Anslinger used as a shield to keep his appropriations from being slashed.

MR. LUDLOW: Do you need all of this money that they are recommending in the Budget, or do you think you could permit a little cut in it without any embarrassment?

MR. ANSLINGER: Well, I would not want to work with much less than we have. We have the traffic pretty well under control.

MR. LUDLOW: And you would like to keep it under control?

MR. ANSLINGER: Yes, sir; we would like to keep it under control. We still have a very substantial marihuana problem.

But the marijuana problem seemed to be a public relations problem. Anslinger's dilemma was that he needed an identifiable social type, *i.e.*, dope fiend, crazed mass-murderer, deranged youth, who could summon up all the latent Calvinistic tendencies in the American populace and move them to action against the problem. However, as his 1937 experience showed, this new villain should not be too horrifying or a new panic would sweep the country and demand better enforcement of the laws. Clearly, murderous Mexicans were passé and fallow fields of abandoned hemp just were not cutting it. But, beginning in 1938, Anslinger was starting to receive reports from the sticks about a new phenomenon surrounding marijuana use. A new social group was taking to the drug, cohorts who were basically retreatist in their orientation to society, not very aggressive as individuals, and obsessed with a dedication to their craft that made them easy prey for a public relations–minded enforcer. They were fun-loving, hedonistic, naïve sorts, and their openness made them tall targets for systematic infiltration by agents with the intent of creating a crime situation where no victim could be identified. By 1945 Anslinger and his crew had their new enemies. Only this time the murderers were jazz musicians, and their weapons were their horns.

CHAPTER 8:
Marijuana Finds a Voice

Among other things, marijuana was said to enhance one's auditory acuity, and likely recipients of that effect would be jazz musicians. The drug had long been known to the musical world, and it was only natural that the musicians who used it would begin writing songs about their experiences. Although a bit less eloquent and elegiac than the French poets who sang hashish's praises in the mid-1850s, the reefer songs were fascinating expressions of the role marijuana played in musician culture—a role that changed, as we shall see, as marijuana became the object of repressive laws governing its use.

The earliest songs glamorized a new social hero: the reefer man, the cat in the know who made the rounds of Harlem nightclubs delivering his load of joy to the droves eager to get high and forget about their worldly travails. The early songs were whimsical and hyperbolic, but were taken at face value by government agents who were anxious to attribute the most bizarre effects to the drug. So, when Cab Calloway, in 1932, sang "The Reefer Man," Anslinger and his cronies started a new case file.

> Man, what's the matter with that cat there?
> (Must be full o' reefer)
> Full of reefers? (Yeah, man)
> You mean that cat's high? (Sailin')
> Sailin'? (Lightly) Git away from here!
> Man, is that the reefer man?
> I believe he's losing his mind
> Oh, have you ever met that funny reefer man?
> Oh, have you ever met that funny reefer man?
> If he says he swam to China: He sell you South Carolina
> Then you know you're talking to that reefer man.

Have you ever met the funny reefer man?
Have you ever met the funny reefer man?
If he says he walks the ocean
Every time he takes the notion
Then you know you're talking to the reefer man.

Have you ever met a funny reefer man?
Have you ever met a funny reefer man?
If he takes a sudden mania
Wants to give you Pennsylvania
Then you know you're talking to the reefer man. . . .

While it is unclear whether the reefer man was a dealer or just a consumer (and the distinction is not that crucial, since from the beginning participants in the marijuana culture have often shared some of their stash at cost), there were soon songs that lionized a new subcultural hero—the reefer dealer. In November 1932 Cab Calloway immortalized "The Man from Harlem":

It was up at Mike's the other night
There was really quite a sight
Gather round folks while I give you all the lowdown
(It's a mess, too)
Tables were filled with gaudy frails
Chewing on their fingernails
They were waiting for the Man from Harlem
Drinks were served six bits a throw
Things were moving kinda slow
Everybody's nerves were getting jumpy:
All at once the room was still
Men forgot all about their bill
Who should enter but the Man from Harlem
Everybody rolled their eyes
Women started heaving sighs
Someone hollered, "Music, lights and gin"
Everybody cleared a space
They had big broad smiles on every face
How they all loved to see the Man from Harlem
When he started in to step
He filled everyone with plenty pep
He twist and squirm, it was just a dirty shame
Everyone was in a daze
Women watched him with amaze
Everyone said she'll have the Man from Harlem
Looked over in the corner, there was a couple of frails
And they sure did look kinda low
Another cat walked up and said to the Man from Harlem:

> "Go over there and see what's the matter with them girls."
> They said, "I'm kinda low." He said, "I got just what you need
> C'mon sisters, light up on these weeds and get high and
> forget about everything."

From the start marijuana was seen as a recreational drug, capable of making a poor "frail" throw off his troubles and "forget about everything." Many of the references to marijuana may have passed the uninitiated ear, but by the end of 1935, the reefer sensibility was even beginning to invade traditional Tin Pan Alley music. Jimmie Lunceford and his Orchestra covered "My Blue Heaven" in December of that year, but heaven seemed just a little bit higher in this version:

> Just Molly and me, baby makes three
> Stuff sits there 'n it's mellow in my—
> Mellow in my blue heaven.

By 1936, as the nation became more cognizant of marijuana use as a "social problem," the music culture began to refer to its use more obliquely. Andy Kirk and his Twelve Clouds of Joy bemoan the fate of a tea pad latecomer, referring to marijuana as "jive," one of the more colorful entries in the viper lexicon.

> The latest craze, the country's rage is jive, jive, jive
> This modern treat makes life complete, jive, jive, jive
> All the jive is gone, all the jive is gone
> I'm sorry, gate, but you got here late
> All the jive is gone
> All the jive is gone, all the jive is gone
> So come on in, drink some gin
> All the jive is gone.

But the most moving statement of the social function of marijuana for the lower-class user was "When I Get Low, I Get High," recorded in April 1936 by Chick Webb and his Orchestra and featuring the young Ella Fitzgerald's vocal:

> My fur coat's poor and Lord ain't it cold
> But I'm not gonna holler, 'cause I still got a dollar
> And when I get low, oh oh oh oh oh I get high
> My man walked out, now you know that ain't right
> Well, he better watch out if I meet him tonight
> I said when I get low, oh oh oh oh oh I get high

All this hard luck in this town has found me
Nobody knows how trouble goes round and round me
Oh oh oh oh
I'm all alone with no one to pet me
But old rocking chair is never gonna get me
'Cause when I get low, oh oh oh oh I get high.

Certainly the image of the weed smoker as portrayed in these songs is diametrically opposed to the Bureau's conception of the homicidal, mentally impaired fiend. Marijuana was viewed as a mild intoxicant in these songs, a convenient, cheap way to escape from the day-to-day troubles of the lower- and working-class member. It was seen as a playful, whimsical drug, and the lyrics and the bouncing swing music underscored that frivolity. However, the irony and the whimsy were lost on the officials who began to quote these songs as if they were gospel. In Anslinger's July 1937 "Assassin of Youth" piece, the Commissioner quoted Cab Calloway's "Reefer Man," and then painted "the real picture of the reefer man," not "some funny fellow who, should he take the notion, could walk across the ocean," but a wanton, motiveless murderer!!

The Marihuana Tax Act had a visible effect on the music culture, as seen through the songs. The references to marijuana became more muted, the argot more obscure, and the attitude toward the drug itself much more critical. Just four days after the law went into effect, Georgia White sang "The Stuff Is Here," but it was no longer a cause for public celebration.

Close the window and lock the door
Take the rug up off the floor
Hey, hey, let's all get gay
The stuff is here.

By 1938 marijuana was still being alluded to, but more and more obliquely. Cootie Williams and his Rug Cutters, a name that was itself probably deemed worthy of investigation, managed to sneak a reefer reference into their campy rendition of "Old Man River":

You and me, we sweat and strain
Body all weary and racked with pain
Toting the barge, liftin up the bale
Smoke a little tea and sing Oh sol o mio!

But marijuana was not always viewed uncritically, even by its devotees. By the 1940s a few songs emerged where the notion of the cost of using reefer was advanced. Lil Green exhibits this self-consciousness in her 1941 rendition of "Knocking Myself Out," but it's clear that to the protagonist in the song, the rewards of intoxication outweigh the eventual cost of the habit.

Lissen, girls and boys, I got one stick
Give me a match and let's take a whiff quick
I'm gonna knock myself out
Yes, I'm gonna kill myself
I'm gonna knock myself out
Gradually by degrees. . . .
I use to didn't blow gage, drink nothing of the kind
But my man quit me, and that changed my mind
That's why I knock myself out . . .
I know to blow this jive, it's a sin and a shame
But it's the only thing ease my heart about my man
Is when I knock myself out. . . .

In 1945 the Barney Bigard Sextet recorded one of the first anti-marijuana songs, "Sweet Marihuana Brown." Here the heroine, who is as much the weed itself as the viper Brown, proves to be most bittersweet after more than a passing acquaintance.

Boy, she's really frantic, the wildest chick in town
She blows her gage, flies in a rage
Sweet Marihuana Brown
In her victory garden the seeds grow all around
She plants, you dig, she's flipped her wig
Sweet Marihuana Brown
She don't know where she's going, she don't care where she's been
But every time you take her out, she's bound to take you in.
Boy, that gal means trouble, you ought to put her down
Get hep, take care, look out, beware of Sweet Marihuana Brown.

But most of the jazz musicians still courted Miss Brown, although in a more circumspect fashion. One consequence of the Tax Act was to make the marijuana subculture more furtive, more ritualized. By virtue of its prohibition, reefer was seen to be more attractive, a weed powerful enough to move legislators and bureaucrats to action. If anything, smoking marijuana became more romantic to most on the scene; however, its illegal status dictated a less casual attitude toward its use. As early as December 1938, Buster Bailey and his Rhythm Busters were celebrating the weed in "Light Up," yet at the same time, cautioning their fellow vipers:

> Light up, I know how you feel,
> You find what I mean in any old field,
> Now get your gig going,
> I'll say that's the thing,
> Don't let that man getcha,
> Just puff on your cig and blow those smoke rings.

So a new social type was added to the viper's mythology: the G-man, the government agent who could bust a hundred vipers in a single collar. C. P. Johnson and his band spoke for a multitude of muggle-heads in 1945 when they told the sad saga of the day the "G-Man Got the T-Man."

> I stopped by Joe's the other night and all of the cats looked beat
> And no one sounded me to say, "Zeke, are you all reet?"
> Now I never really knew the reason
> That the cats all looked so square
> But now I'm hip and I dig it, because jive is in the air
> Cats can't buy their jive at night
> So now they hurry home, since the G-Man got the T-Man and gone
> They have to drink their lush and stagger
> Even though they know it's wrong
> Cause the G-Man got the T-Man and gone
> Boy, one night when the joint was jumping and a knock came at the door
> In stepped a man with a shiny badge and a brand-new forty-four
> They've arrested my connection
> And I can't find any more
> 'Cause the G-Man got the T-Man and gone.

By the late forties all direct references to marijuana had disappeared, and the few remaining musicians who sang about the weed were more coy than ever in making reference to it. Julia Lee, backed by her Boyfriends, had some other vegetable on her mind when she sang her popular "Spinach Song."

> Spinach has Vitamins A, B and D
> But spinach never appealed to me
> But one day while having dinner with a guy
> I decided to give it a try
> I didn't like it the first time, it was so new to me
> I didn't like it the first time, I was so young, you see

I used to run away from the stuff
But now somehow I can't get enough
I didn't like it the first time but oh, how it grew on me.

The song had one unanticipated consequence. Although spinach sales remained the same, a case file was started on a young sailor named Popeye, who was rumored to be engaged in trafficking. After a short investigation the matter was dropped, and Popeye's file was destroyed.

After an investigation of the *modus operandi* of Anslinger and his crowd, that last item is almost believable. Although it is doubtful that narcotics agents were posted at the docks on the watch for reefer men trying to "walk across the ocean every time [they] got the notion," Anslinger seemed to take almost every other whimsy expressed in the reefer songs at face value. And, being the master at public relations that he was, by 1940 the time was right for another great marijuana crusade. And here was a ready-made enemy: an alien subculture of kooks, strange musicians with bizarre habits, who played late into the night, partied well into the morning, slept smack into the afternoon. Refugees from the American Protestant Ethic, flaunting their new-fashioned (and fashionable) morality with every hot lick of their licorice sticks and every tinkle of their ivories. The story of the forties with respect to marijuana is the story of the prosecution and assassination of the Marquis de Swing, as performed by the agents of the Bureau of Narcotics and their extremely handy adjunct, the informer man.

CHAPTER 9:
The Jazz Musicians' Pogrom

One reason why we appreciated pot, as y'all calls it now, was the warmth it always brought forth from the other person—especially the ones that lit up a good stick of that shuzzit or gage. As we always used to say, gage is more of a medicine than a dope. But with all the riggermaroo going on, no one can do anything about it. After all, the vipers during my heydays are all way up in age—too old to suffer those drastic penalties. So we had to put it down. But if we all get as old as Methuselah, our memories will always be of lots of beauty and warmth from gage. Well, that was my life and I don't feel ashamed at all. Mary Warner, honey, you sure was good and I enjoyed you "heep much." But the price got a little too high to pay (law-wise). At first you was a misdemeanor. But as the years rolled on, you lost your misdo and got meanor and meanor (jailhousely speaking). Soooo, bye-bye, Dearest, I'll have to put you down.

—From *Louie Armstrong*
by Max Jones and John Chilton
Little, Brown & Co., 1971

By 1949 it was clear to Anslinger and his right-hand honcho Malachi Harney that it was impossible to enforce the drug laws, since drug transactions are victimless crimes (unless of course we consider the drug user to be his own victim). That is to say, nobody in the exchange is about to report any other active parties to the authorities. So Harney developed a brilliant idea. The Bureau would use informants, some getting as much as $2,000 a crack to grease their tongues, and suddenly the Bureau's arm could reach into every roach-infested, dank corner of any ghetto in the country. The informants were extremely versatile; besides reporting on transactions that had already gone down, they could, of course, instigate exchanges, as in: "Hey, Jack, could you get me a trey of reefer? I got the bread." When the deal went down, Uncle Sam was there to collect the tax—and more.

So the informants opened a whole new world to Anslinger, who was saddled with a small force of only three-hundred-odd agents at the time, and the Commissioner went for the scheme whole hog. Using money from a special fund of $160,000, the sawbucks flew onto the streets and data began to be gathered on Anslinger's new enemies. Armed with a new weapon—the much-needed federal legislation—and no real threat to engulf, the bureaucrat did the next best thing: he bought his way into a culture that, by its very nature, he had despised from the start, and tried to silence it by arresting its members for their usage of an herb. This was a story that would be repeated again in the sixties, although on a much larger scale. However, as we have seen, Anslinger was doomed to failure. Perhaps it was the resilience of the weed culture (again we must recall that weeds thrive on abuse), perhaps it was the ultimate failure of any program in moral entrepreneurship. But it might just have been due to the ineptness of a Bureau that demonstrated its effectiveness in the early thirties by the fact that an agent was sent out on the trail of a supposed peddler who was found to have been two years dead. Perhaps some future researcher will, after all, discover a file labeled "Popeye, a/k/a 'Sailor Man.' "

> The subject, a fair piano player, crashed the keys and began a series of wild melodies and vulgar variations that sounded like the jungles in the dead of night. It has been said that a marihuana smoker originated swing music. That does not indict such music, but indicates that the musical mind is far from the notes in front of him.

More unpublished Anslinger. Beginning in the early 1930s the Commissioner began a file that would later be known as the "Marijuana and Musicians" file. Each time a marijuana case involved a member of the musical fraternity, special note would be made of it, and before long a huge dossier had been compiled. Sensing a chapter in some future book, Anslinger waxed eloquently on scrap paper:

> Music hath charms, but not this music. It hails the drug. The well-informed would just as soon hear a song about sitting in the pleasant shade of the hood of a cobra. Some of the songs are: "Reefer Man," "Smoking Reefers," "Chant of the Weeds," "Send in the Viper," "Muggles," "Vipers Moan," and "Texas Tea Party." . . . When Cab Calloway renders his interpretation of Marawanna [*sic*], the rumba without words, it may sound like a mass of discords to most of us, but to many of those who are listening and possibly to Cab himself, this brings to mind the delightful dreams lived under the spell of Marihuana (the rage that is sweeping Sleepy Town from coast to coast). And when some Harlem nightclub entertainer flashes pearly teeth while extolling that "Reefer Man," it may seem like a lot of nonsense to us, but to him and many of his theatrical brothers, both white and black, that "Reefer Man" is just about as real and important as the milkman to the average American family. For the Reefer Man supplies them with their Reefers, the cigarettes made of Marihuana.

The battle between the Bureau and the jazz world first surfaced in February 1938, when two Mexicans were arrested in Minneapolis and charged with violation of the Tax Act by growing and distributing $5,000 worth of marijuana. The arrest prompted a statement by Joseph Bell, District Supervisor for the Bureau, linking swing music, the big apple dance, and jam sessions to the increase in the usage of the drug. "The tempo of present-day music and the big apple dance and these jam sessions seem to do something to the nerves," the G-man told the *Minneapolis Tribune*. "As a result, use of marihuana is on the increase. Not only is it being used by dance band musicians, but by boys and girls who listen and dance to these bands. They seem to think they need a stimulant for their nerves."

Sidney Berman, the editor of *The Orchestra World*, a music magazine, immediately fired off a letter to the Bureau complaining: "This is a rather serious charge against the popular orchestra field, which we represent, and we would appreciate further clarification on the subject. Naturally we are not interested in promoting crime, and if we can be useful in bringing this matter out into the open in our field, we are more than glad to throw our columns open to you."

After a short investigation it was determined that it was not Mr. Bell who had made the statements, but one of the Mexicans arrested, during a newspaper interview while he was being detained in the Bureau's Minneapolis offices. However, Bell did further confirm the new "menace" and wrote both

Anslinger and Berman: "This person [the Mexican] stated that the use of Marihuana is quite prevalent among musicians, particularly so-called 'jazz bands,' because, under the influence of the drug, they seem to acquire a certain talent which they do not ordinarily possess. In the words of the individual I mention, they 'get hot.' "

The Bureau's desire to investigate the use of marijuana by musicians was hampered by its inability to find agents who could penetrate the netherworld of the jazz player. This deficiency led to such harebrained capers as the Herbert Napka matter. Napka was a Deputy Clerk of Courts in Sandusky, Ohio, who at one time had headed a small band that played the small-town cabaret circuit in the Midwest. While traveling that circuit, Napka claimed to have observed much muggles-smoking among both musicians and patrons. Napka's short-lived musical career ended when he was fined $100 by the Federation of Musicians for not complying with regulations.

In December 1938, anxious to resume his musical career after clerking for two years, Herbert visited the District Supervisor of the Bureau and reported his experience in observing marijuana users. He also claimed to have knowledge that the weed was being sold "promiscuously," both to nightclub patrons and to schoolchildren. And he also came armed with a plan. Herbert was desirous of organizing an orchestra of twelve members called the "Weed Hounds" to tour the country, playing every rickety, cheap cabaret, buying marijuana at each stop, locating the sources of supply for the Bureau. He asked the G-man for a $350 advance, claiming that once the band hit the road, they could sustain themselves. There was one more requirement, namely, that the Bureau arrange with the Federation of Musicians that there would be no interference with his band playing wherever he wished.

The District Supervisor, in submitting his report to Anslinger, was duly skeptical.

> I told him that as soon as the Government would contact the Federation of Musicians in his behalf, it would be a direct tipoff that he was connected with us; and, so far as the $350 was concerned, I told him I was not sure that the Government would approve same. . . . No doubt Mr. Napka is sincere in wanting to start the band to assist in the eradication of marihuana, but the motive back of it is that he would like to get back as a band leader and use the Government to intercede with the Federation of Musicians as a means of raising himself to "big time," as he calls it.

The supervisor submitted Herbert's proposition, but there is no further mention in the files of a band named "Weed Hounds" touring the country, while doing comparative shopping.

But by 1941 the link between marijuana and swing music, propagated by a lurid press, was strong enough to evoke a response from *The Keynote,* the monthly publication of the Detroit Federation of Musicians. In a front-page editorial in the January-February 1941 issue, the president and secretary-treasurer of the union went on record with a promise to weed out any musicians found guilty of using the weed.

MARIJUANA—A SCOURGE

Marijuana—weed—grass—tea—reefers—call it anything you like—is classed by law and by effect in the same category as narcotics. For some reason or other—and no matter how it hurts, let's face it—the comparatively few musicians who are addicted to its use have gained for the entire music profession a reputation among law enforcement officers, and to some extent among the general public, that is most unsavory, and every day bring disgrace and worse to the good reputation of the great majority who do not use it. Marijuana causes far more than mere moral degeneration—it breaks down the mentality of its slaves. Some of the so-called "jazz hounds" who think that their talents show off the best when "high" should take a trip to Eloise Hospital and see the wrecked human beings there, jibbering idiots who likewise used to think it was fun to be taken out of the world of reality into a false sense of super-being. Now they can't think at all! The responsible heads of your organization are determined to do their utmost to stamp out this most vicious practice—Detroit Musicians are no worse than those of other cities, and the problem is one which must be faced by every local union and by our National organization. This condition is so serious that your Board of Directors has taken drastic action to curb it by adopting the following regulation:

Any member found guilty of the use of Marijuana, or on proof that a member uses same, such member shall immediately be expelled from membership.

Anslinger immediately jumped into the fray, ordering his Detroit agents to investigate the local music scene. It was determined that the resolution had been mostly precautionary; however, a subsequent arrest revealed a large reefer ring that catered to the needs of the touring bands visiting Detroit.

A few weeks later the *Los Angeles Daily News* revealed that the two local musicians who had been killed in a car crash were found to have had marijuana cigarettes in their pockets. Again Sidney Berman was on the alert, asking Anslinger for any developments in the case, since his magazine was "vitally interested." Anslinger wrote back that he was unable to comment on pending cases; however, in a note attached to an interoffice memo on the subject, he stated: "Because of the fact that musicians appear to be among the principal users of marijuana, a sharp quote may serve to jolt these people on the dangers of the use of this weed."

Anslinger got the quote he wanted and more, only it was written by a staff member of *Down Beat*, the prestigious jazz publication. In its January 15, 1943, issue, reporter Mike Levin, writing under a banner headline "Tea Scandal Stirs Musicdom," reluctantly reported an escapade involving well-known entertainers, musicians, soldiers and Lady Reefer. The details themselves, in retrospect, seem fairly tame: some big-name band members and a few nightclub entertainers got caught with some soldiers in one of the entertainer's midtown hotel room, which was serving as a makeshift "reefer parlor." But what was more interesting was the way *Down Beat* played the story. The piece was prefaced with an editorial sidebar:

> (The editors of *Down Beat* don't like to print this story. We've killed several like this in previous months, believing that they could cause only harm and aid no one. Parts of this story, which we previously suppressed, we were not only given permission to use by the army, but unofficially requested to do so. The facts, from unimpeachable sources, are given below for reasons you will find on our editorial page.)

After no more than 100 words outlining the case, Levin's article turned into a general diatribe against the weed smokers in the musicians' ranks.

> This is one of the sorriest messes that we've seen. Immediately after the story broke originally, the *Beat*'s New York office was deluged with requests for information. . . . At first our attitude was "we don't know a thing"; but when the big news weeklies began checking, we started thinking. And when one of the leaders concerned called up in a panic lest his band be ruined by adverse publicity as being a bunch of "teahounds," we knew some action was in order. . . . We know that there are musicians who smoke tea. . . . We know that there is a select clique that has been working in the top bands for years who do it, and we know that they are going to get it in the neck if they aren't careful. And if the business as a whole isn't careful, it is going to take a bad rap along with them. Once more the

old bogies are going to be floating around. "Musician" is going to be synonymous with "weed hound." The business neither deserves nor can stand a national campaign of this sort. . . . The Narcotic Bureau has the names and facts concerning many of the musicians who use tea. They aren't as interested in jailing these men as they are in finding out the sources of supply and the selling agents. We can only suggest to anyone who uses the stuff: STOP IT NOW, BEFORE YOU GET YOURSELF AND YOUR FRIENDS IN A POTFULL OF TROUBLE! We can only suggest to the AFM that it pass a ruling calling for instant expulsion of anyone caught using tea. . . .

So, with the enemy's own house organ behind the Commissioner's campaign, Anslinger made 1943 the year of a concerted Bureau attack on the music teaheads. On July 2, 1943, Malachi Harney wrote a memo to Anslinger outlining the campaign.

I talked to ——— on the telephone today about the "boogie-woogie" bands and marihuana tie-up and I said we thought it might be about time to give the matter some real attention. ——— said he thought he could get an informer or two who would be able to work in these musical circles and that he would start on this right away. I told ——— that I thought he should build up probably 20 or 30 cases before he made any arrests.

Anslinger apparently approved; he penciled in: "They should be made in various districts."

At first the going was rough for the G-men. Unable to infiltrate the jazz demimonde, the agents were sad to report their initial failures to Anslinger. On August 9 the Chicago District Supervisor wrote Harry:

I am sorry to report that we have made no cases involving musicians, and do not have any preliminary purchases where musicians are involved. However, I have instructed the agents to make this a matter for special endeavor, and I hope to be able to report some progress in the near future.

Harney received a similar memo a week later from the Ohio-Michigan district noting that "we have had several cases started here, but unfortunately arrests had to be made," ruining any chance of a well-orchestrated nationwide sweep.

By September Anslinger was still craving publicity and desirous of a national roundup that could catapult the Bureau back on the front pages. On September 7, 1943, he sent a confidential letter to his San Francisco District Supervisor that read:

> Because of the increasing volume of reports indicating that many musicians of the "swing band" type are responsible for the spread of the marihuana smoking vice, I should like you to give the problem some special attention in your district. If possible, I should like you to develop a number of cases in which arrests would be withheld so as to synchronize those with arrests to be made in other districts. Please let me know what are the possibilities along this line in your district.

Four days later the Commissioner received a confidential reply:

> Reference is had to your letter of September 7, 1943, regarding the development of marihuana cases against musicians of the "swing band" type, and the synchronizing of arrests with those to be made in other districts. You are perhaps aware that musicians who are marihuana smokers do not ordinarily engage in selling marihuana. They are generally on the receiving end. Doubtless some distribution is made to other members of the band who are users of marihuana. This being so, the only cases that are likely to be made against them are possession cases. Ordinarily in developing a case of that nature, the arrest is made when the person is found in possession, but regardless of this, I shall endeavor to have my agents do their best to build up some cases with a view of making arrests that can be synchronized with those in other districts.

One reason Anslinger was so intent on rounding up the jazz community was the perception that musicians were dodging the draft via the marijuana "addiction" route. Working in close cooperation with the Selective Service System, Anslinger developed a number of cases where one's rejection for marijuana addiction became grounds for investigation by the Bureau. In March 1944 a drummer with the NBC Studio orchestra was arrested for smoking marijuana in the NBC washroom. After his arrest he implicated other band members in a futile attempt to get his job back. He first came to the attention of the Bureau, however, in a communication from the Selective Service. A memo attached to his file noted:

> ———'s name was furnished to us by the Induction authorities as rejected because of drug addiction. He is a musician, and stated that anyone wearing a bow tie and carrying a musician's case would be regarded by marihuana peddlers as potential purchasers at places frequented by musicians.

By December 1944 Anslinger was still stymied by the close-knit jazz community, and the added fillip of musicians avoiding serving their country by being classified 4-F for indulgence in their vice was more than the bureaucrat could bear. On December 19 he wrote his New York District Supervisor:

> I have in mind such cases as that of ——— who was the subject of your letter to the Bureau dated December 6, 1944. Not only is this man not in the Army where he belongs, but he brazenly tells us that he is able to maintain an almost constant supply of marihuana. I am transmitting a schedule prepared in the file room here which shows some of the musicians (and their orchestral connections) who have been rejected by the military as marihuana users. I wish you would study this and give me any suggestions which you may have for dealing with the law violations upon which these men appear to be capitalizing.

Two months later the District Supervisor replied in a letter that highlights the difficulty that agents encountered in developing reliable informants to aid in the musical pogrom the Commissioner so fervently desired:

> . . . It has been found that musicians, as a class, associate mostly with co-workers and members of the theatrical profession. There is also a feeling of helpfulness displayed by them towards one another due to the fact that some of them go along for many years before reaching a high paid status in the profession, and after doing so fail to remain in that status. They also have periods of unemployment which particularly affects the low-paid members. Due to the aforementioned, it is difficult to induce an active and well-acquainted musician to inform on members of his profession and it should also be taken into consideration that the Musicians' Unions control all of their employment and an informant might possibly risk expulsion from the Union in some manner or other.
>
> This office has attempted, and is still doing so, to develop confidential informants among musicians and our efforts have not been successful enough to secure information leading to the popular musicians, some of whom are mentioned in the list attached to the Bureau letter. With reference to the aforementioned list, one of the men mentioned, as you know, ——— was arrested in New York, New York, on March 8, 1944, by agents of this office, and one marihuana cigarette found in his possession was seized. . . . This man, at the time of his arrest, was employed as a drummer by the National Broadcasting Company Studio Orchestra in this city at a salary of $120.00 per week, and a member of the American Federation of Musicians. The facts as to his arrest were communicated to the National Broadcasting Corporation at New York City, and on April 12, 1944, ——— musician's contractor and conductor of the aforementioned orchestra, discharged him. The loss of his position hurt him very much and he attempted to have this office intercede for him with ——— which, of course, was not done.

> With further reference to ——— you are advised that after his arrest, he stated that members of the National Broadcasting Company Studio Orchestra smoked marihuana cigarettes in the washrooms of the National Broadcasting Corporation in this city. This information was also communicated to the Corporation and a Free-Lance Script Writer's pass was issued to an agent of this office to enable him to visit the washrooms used by the orchestra at any hour. The assistance of the Protective Department of the Corporation was also secured and numerous investigations were made and no evidence found that marihuana was being smoked as alleged.

The list referred to in these communications had names of many of the most prominent musicians of the time, including Thelonious Monk. Anslinger also developed a second list, designating the orchestras which the marijuana rejectees were affiliated with. So, even though these groups did not have any documented connection with marijuana, band members associated with the following celebrities were on file in the Bureau: Louis Armstrong, Les Brown, Count Basie, Cab Calloway, Jimmy Dorsey, Duke Ellington, Dizzy Gillespie, Lionel Hampton, Andre Kostelanetz, the Milton Berle show, the Coca-Cola program, Jackie Gleason, and the Kate Smith program.

Typical of the hearsay nature of this drive are the following excerpts from Correspondence Reference Forms of the Bureau from 1948 and 1949, all on file in duplicate in the Washington office:

> Defendant is a colored man in Camden, Texas, born ——— is 5′8″ tall, 165 lbs., black complexion, black hair, black eyes. He has scars on left forehead, and tattoo of a dagger and the word ——— on his right forearm. He is a musician and plays the trumpet in small "hot bands." He has a very large mouth and thick lips, which earned him his name of ———. He is a marihuana smoker.

> Refers to Memorandum Report relative to the visit of Mr. ——— of Minnesota, who reported the activities of his two daughters with negro musicians. ——— stated that the girls had lived good and normal lives until within the past few months. It was further stated that his two daughters would be picked up by two negro members of the ——— Orchestra and they would all go to the ———, known as a resort for "jamb fests" and then would go to a residential address and would not come out until three or four o'clock in the morning. ——— suspicioned that his daughters were using marihuana. Upon investigation the following negroes were listed as members of the Orchestra: —————. Should be a matter of investigation.

By 1948 it was clear that Anslinger's campaign had hardly come to fruition. Several famous musicians, including drummer Gene Krupa, had been arrested and jailed on possession charges, but the Bureau was never able to orchestrate the massive roundup it had desired. But on August 3, 1948, the campaign against the weed got an unexpected boost when Robert Mitchum, then thirty-one and a rising young screen idol, was arrested in Laurel Canyon, along with three others, on a felony narcotics charge, possession, and conspiracy to possess marijuana.

Both Anslinger and Mitchum thought the arrest would end the actor's budding career; in fact, at his booking, Mitchum answered "Former actor" when asked his occupation. Confronted by a horde of reporters, he glumly said, "Sure, I've been using the stuff since I was a kid. I guess it's all over now. I'm ruined. This is the bitter end." But a few minutes later he did a strange about-face and claimed the arrest was a "frame-up."

Mitchum immediately hired the hottest lawyer in Hollywood, Jerry Geisler, who had sprung Errol Flynn from statutory rape charges and had successfully defended Charlie Chaplin from a Mann Act violation. Geisler succeeded in getting Mitchum's trial postponed until January 1949.

Anslinger immediately sought to make hay out of both the Krupa and Mitchum busts. In an unpublished essay, "Marihuana and Musicians," the Commissioner reminisced on the Krupa affair:

> Gene Krupa, famed drum-beating swing bandleader, who is idolized by thousands of minors throughout the country, and starred in the motion pictures GEORGE WHITE'S SCANDALS and TO BEAT THE BAND, served a 90-day sentence for violation of the marihuana laws.
>
> During one of Krupa's engagements at the Hollywood Palladium and the Los Angeles Orpheum Theatre, we received information which resulted in his arrest later in San Fransciso for possession of marihuana, and contributing to juvenile delinquency by sending his 17-year-old valet to his hotel room for "reefers" (marihuana). Krupa was found guilty and sentenced to 90 days in jail and fined $500. He was later found guilty of using this minor in the unlawful transportation of narcotics and was sentenced to imprisonment for a period of 1 to 6 years, but the conviction was later reversed on appeal. . . .
>
> The remaining engagements of the band in Detroit were canceled and the band was booted out of its Detroit hotel room after (other) members were arrested on narcotic charges. Three thousand

> youthful "zoot-suiters" decked out in their weird costumes, had mobbed the RKO-Downtown Theatre at 5 a.m. to await the opening of Krupa's show at 11 A.M. It took a special squad of policemen to keep order. Truant officers, dispatched by the Board of Education, weeded out 50 absentees and sent them back to school, and harried parents appeared to claim their missing offspring. . . .
>
> After Krupa's conviction on the marihuana law violations, it was reported in a newspaper column that "Gene Krupa's well-wishers are setting up a $100,000 fund for a public relations buildup, so that Krupa's career won't be ruined by his present difficulties."

Ah! The envy just drooled out of the Commissioner's mouth on that last paragraph. What he could do with $100,000 for his own public campaigns! Krupa, of course, rebounded nicely from his arrest, as did Mitchum, to everyone's surprise. A scant month after the bust, Mitchum's new movie was released, and it did boffo at the box office. Which prompted a classic J'accuse by that venerable gossip Earl Wilson, who, in his nationally syndicated column, took a poke at Mitchum and the jazzmen.

COLUMNIST TAKES A PUNCH AT TEA-SMOKING MUSICIANS

> New York, Sept. 29—Ah swayuh (as they say down South) I'm getting to be a reformer! Today I'm going to beat up that Marijuana Mob—the Reefer Rats. I asked a fellow whether reefers are still freely sold here. He went to a likely source—a swing musician, in the Fifties somewhere. "Seen Mr. Alexander?" he asked the musician. "Mr. Alexander" is sort of a password for "tea." "How many?" said the musician. He was as shy as a Broadway billboard. "Half a dozen sticks." "Is that all?" The musician was disappointed at meeting such a picayunish user. He brought six of the thin, roll-your-owns out and collected six dollars. It seems to me that Petrillo or somebody ought to clean up this despicable swing musician's mess, which has a livery stable smell. Marijuana and musicians lately seem to go together like ham and eggs. A few musicians are just plain scum, with the morals of a procurer, and they besmirch the decent musicians, who outnumber them by far.
>
> But nothing'll happen; nobody cares much. Nobody cares much about anything. Bob Mitchum thought he was washed up, but he didn't appreciate his public's curiosity. Gangs of goggle-eyed goofs busted their britches to gape at him in his new film, and they howled hilariously when in one scene he asked for a cigarette. The wages of sin is a hit picture! Musicians are, however, the worst reefer users, and I deplore the moronic efforts to convince us that marijuana is no more harmful than a cubeb. . . .
>
> . . . the whole swing music business is so entranced with reefers that it keeps echoing that the La Guardia Report in 1945 said that

reefers aren't habit-forming. *Down Beat* seems as happy printing it as a cab driver who's just knocked down a pedestrian. I'll take the more recent opinion of Colonel Garland Williams, head of U.S. narcotics enforcement.

"Reefers *are* habit-forming. All perverts may not be marijuana smokers, but practically all marijuana smokers are perverted," he says. Nice people, these music bums who light up. But don't take my word for it.

Three weeks ago I wrote that Mitchum had kicked away his career. Looks like he's given it a shot in the arm, if you'll pardon the expression. Congratulations, Bob! When'll I ever learn that Americans don't care what movie stars do—as long as they make it spicy?

On January 10, 1949, Mitchum was found guilty of the lesser charge of conspiracy. On February 9 he submitted the following written plea for probation:

My first use of marijuana was an isolated instance in 1936 when I was working in Toledo. I had no further contact with it until about 1947, at a time when I was working very hard. During 1947 and 1948 I occasionally used marijuana when in the company of people who used it. I was never a confirmed smoker of marijuana and never purchased marijuana for use by myself. The only explanation I have for the use of marijuana is the fact that when you are in the company of people who use it, it is easier to go along with them than not to.

The only effect that I ever noticed from smoking marijuana was a sort of mild sedative, a release of tension when I was overworking. It never made me boisterous or quarrelsome. If anything, it calmed me and reduced my activity. I have never used any other drug. My attitude with respect to the future use of marijuana is that I will not use marijuana at any time whatsoever.

His pleas notwithstanding, Mitchum was sentenced to a year in jail, which was then suspended. The actor was placed on two years' probation, with the condition that the first sixty days be spent in jail. However, the following September the D.A. announced that the case had been reopened to determine if the entire episode had been engineered by extortionists. And on January 31, 1951, with almost no publicity, the court quietly ruled that the verdict of guilty be set aside, a plea of not guilty entered, and that the complaint be dismissed. Mitchum's exoneration was never publicized by his studio, by himself, or by Harry Anslinger.

Anslinger, perhaps, had been too busy still searching for reefer-smoking musicians. In October 1948 he had attempted to revive his campaign against the jazz musicians by enlisting the aid of the unions. In a memo to a subordinate, Anslinger noted:

> I think it is time to prepare a letter to Petrillo (President, American Federation of Musicians) requesting that consideration be given to canceling the union membership of drug addict musicians and musicians convicted of violating the narcotic laws.

The draft letter met the Commissioner's approval, and he sent it for approval to his superior, Under Secretary Foley. It read:

> Arrests involving a certain type of musician in marihuana cases are on the increase. The following few of many cases are cited as examples: [names deleted] As you know, some of these musicians acquire followings among juveniles. We are all familiar with the type of hero worship in which the juvenile is a slavish imitator of the things, good or bad, which are done by the object of his admiration.
>
> In my opinion there is a real juvenile delinquency threat in the marihuana antics of these persons. We, of course, are using all of the limited law enforcement facilities at our command.
>
> I am bringing this situation to your attention because I feel that you might suggest ways in which your organization could assist in eliminating the antisocial activities of this segment of the musician's profession. Hoping that you can assist us in suppressing this abuse, I am
>
> Cordially yours,
> H. J. Anslinger

The draft letter came back with a simple comment on it: "Mr. Foley disapproves."

"The worst group we had there were the jazz musicians. And I wouldn't tell you what proportion of them were marijuana users, but it was more than half. In those days."

Sloman still had the talkative Dr. Munch on the phone, and he was determined to get Munch's views on Anslinger's jazz musician crusade. The reporter knew that Munch was aware of the jazz scene; after all, he hung around race tracks and blew some weed himself.

"Yeah, but why would he want to go after them?" Sloman wondered.

"Because the chief effect, as far as they were concerned, is that it lengthens the sense of time, and therefore they could get more grace beats into their music than they could if they simply followed a written copy." Munch had completely lost Sloman, right out of the gate. "In other words, if you're a musician, you're going to play the thing the way it's printed on a sheet. But if you're using marijuana, you're going to work in about twice as much music in between the first note and the second note. That's what made jazz musicians. The idea that they could jazz things up, liven them up, you see."

Sloman felt his head spinning. He felt that he had been at the bottom of an ink well for 200 years. With a Herculean effort he managed the next question. "So what's wrong with that? I mean, I still don't see why Anslinger went after those people?"

"They were spreading it around as sources, because they were looked up to by a good many of the teen-agers as being idols."

"Oh, I see," Sloman lied.

"In other words, their example must be all right or the jazz musicians wouldn't do it. Teen-agers, who were no different then than they are today, thought that if they did it, then it was all right for us to do it. What we're trying to do is not so much to grab individual teen-agers as to go after the source from which it has been obtained. I told you that before."

"Were the musicians actively promoting the use of marijuana?"

"Not directly," Munch admitted. "At least most of them didn't. But the fact was that youngsters found out they were using, so therefore they decided they were going to use."

"They wanted to try it, like imitation, huh?"

"Yeah. Teen-agers. Peer stuff." Munch dismissed the subject.

"I've talked to some of the counsels from the old Bureau, and they thought that the marijuana thing was used as a political thing by Anslinger. In other words, to get more appropriations. . . ."

"No," Munch protested, "he was generally interested in the welfare of the people. He was the same way on cocaine, he was the same way on heroin . . ."

"I bet he was," Sloman interrupted. "I bet he was."

Despite the setback in the Petrillo affair, Anslinger pressed on with his crusade. On March 1, 1949, he testified before the Ways and Means Appropriations Committee in regards to the

1950 Budget and took the opportunity to link the jazz world to the marijuana traffic and to use the issue to protect his projected budget from the parsimonious congressmen.

MR. FERNANDEZ: Then I take it there is more widespread use of it (marihuana) in the past 2 years than there was before the war.

DR. ANSLINGER: [The title was conferred by the House stenographer] I think the traffic has increased in marihuana, and unfortunately particularly among the young people. We have been running into a lot of traffic among these jazz musicians, and I am not speaking about the good musicians, but the jazz type. In one place down here in North Carolina we arrested a whole orchestra, everybody in the orchestra. In Chicago we have arrested some rather prominent jazz musicians; and in New York. It is pretty widespread. The musicians ought to do something about it. I have asked them to do something to see if they can't clean their own house a bit. And we have seized sources of supply from these musicians at different times. We have not made the progress with the marihuana traffic that has been made otherwise. You will notice, however, that in violations reported, our cases year after year seem to be about the same.

The public outcry was immediate. Picking up on the distinction between good musicians and the jazz type, scores of letters and protests came into the Treasury. Typical of them was this broadside from a Spokane newspaperman, addressed to Secretary of Treasury John Snyder:

> I would like to commend your man Anslinger on his efforts to curb the marijuana traffic. However, if the level of his intelligence is exemplified by his remark that is underlined in the inclosed [*sic*] clipping, he will not be very successful in his present line of work or any other undertaking. It takes a stupid man to relegate all jazz musicians to mediocrity when some of them are recognized by scholars as great creators.

Down Beat, in their next issue, made the Commissioner's quote the subject of their lead editorial.

> HOW TO DRAW A GENERALIZATION
>
> One musician in Massachusetts, another in California, and several from scattered points in between clipped and sent to *Down Beat* the

> news story released by Associated Press and United Press early in March quoting H. J. Anslinger, narcotics commissioner in Washington, D.C., as follows:
>
> "I'm not talking [*sic*] about the good musicians but the jazz type."
>
> Oh brother! . . . According to this worthy gent, there are just two kinds of musicians, good musicians and jazz musicians. How can you tell them apart? The jazz musicians are the ones who smoke marijuana.
>
> How confused can you get? . . . The bad time given to musicians by the daily press in the general run of things is serious enough. But when a government official in a report to congress divides them arbitrarily into two groups, "good" and "jazz," it is going a little too far.

The complete editorial was clipped and sent to Anslinger by Under Secretary Williams, but the Commissioner weathered the storm once again. After all, if he could get away with "ginger-colored nigger," this latest imbroglio was nothing more than a tempest in a teapot. Three years later Harry was at it again, with a scheme that would have the Department of State cancel the passports of musicians who had ever been involved in court proceedings relating to reefer. Thelonious Monk was one of the musicians singled out for scrutiny in Europe, where newspapers were blaming American jazzmen for the influx of the marijuana habit. However, cooler heads at Treasury prevailed, and Anslinger's latest scheme was rejected as too vague.

Anslinger, though, was not without his allies within the jazz world. In 1950 Cab Calloway, who had made his reputation singing about the exotic dope scene in such classics as "Minnie the Moocher" and "Have You Seen That Reefer Man?," wrote a scathing article for *Ebony* magazine entitled "Is Dope Killing Our Musicians?" The Commissioner was quick to make reference to the piece in every forum he could find, as an example of the dread within the musical community toward the use of narcotics. But the significant story was that the jazz world had fought the Bureau to a draw. If Anslinger had had his druthers (and about $500,000 a year more in appropriations), America might have seen a massive roundup of jazz musicians in the forties, with long, severe sentences meted out as deterrents for these wanton violators of the Tax Act.

However, that was not the case. The Commissioner was checked by the top brass in the Treasury Department, foiling his furthest-out schemes. But certainly the shrewdness of the jazzmen themselves was a factor. For the reefer cats were aware of their outcast status; in fact, they seemed to relish it. They had created a self-contained culture, and squares like Anslinger were no match for the gates. This brash disdain for the square world's imperatives was nowhere demonstrated more clearly than in the conduct of Fats Waller, the great jazz pianist.

As a part of the war effort, Waller was asked to make a recording for the Armed Forces radio. Because of the vinyl shortage, albums weren't pressed during World War II, but several thousand pressings of the Armed Forces radio "V-Discs" were distributed to all the bases overseas. So, sixteen days after Anslinger's edict to try to synchronize massive "swing band" arrests, Waller chose to record for posterity (and our boys overseas) the classic reefer song "If You're a Viper." He prefaced it with a scatlike introduction:

> Hey, cats, it's four o'clock in the mornin'. I just left the V-Disc studio. Here we are in Harlem. Everybody's here but the police. 'N they'll be here any minute. It's high time, so catch this song. Here 'tis:
>
> Dreamed about a reefer five foot long
> Mighty mezz but not too strong
> You'll be high but not for long
> If you're a viper
> I'm the king of everything
> Gagota Gagota Gagota Gagota be high before I swing
> Let the bells ring: ding dong ding
> If you're a viper
> Say you know you're high when your throat gets dry
> Mmmmm! Everything's dandy! Shbbbshtbbshb ah yes
> You run down to the candy store,
> Bust your conk on peppermint candy
> Then you know your little brown body's sent
> You don't give a darn if you don't pay rent
> 'Cause the sky's high—soo 'm I—Yes, Yes
> I vipe a bit. Well, I'm gonna vipe a bit on the eighty-eight now
> [piano solo]
> O stop it, darlin' I didn't know you cared
> That's enough, now; wait a minute, wait a minute
> Wait a minute! Let me dream now [sigh]
> That's a killer, Yes, baby, better nix out on the sidelines
> My wife's here tonight, she don't vipe either
> Eh? No git away! Are you kidding? Oh, dear . . .
> Say you know you're high? Yes, I know I'm high
> 'Cause everything is fine and dandy

Yes, going down to the candy store—mmm
Get me wrigglies on some peppermint candy
I love it I love it I love it! Yes, baby, but my body's sent
I ain't worried 'bout no rent; get away from me, you huzzy!
Yeah! Sky's high 'n' so 'm I 'n' gonna lay down and relax
Oh dear, oh dear—Mamma!

The gumshoes at the Bureau and the Army brass let that one slip right by them, but the guys in the barracks caught the drift, especially those stationed in the Philippines, where the weed was said to be excellent.

CHAPTER 10:
The Little Flower Meets the Swedish Angel

In addition to orchestrating action against the jazz musicians, who posed a threat to America's youth by their example of the recreational use of marijuana, with the only side effect being contorted faces during solos, and against the fundamentalist marijuana sensationalists, who, in their fervor to denounce the drug, left the Bureau vulnerable to charges of shoddy enforcement, Anslinger protected his conception of marijuana from the ravages of scientific assault. The Bureau never sponsored any impartial investigation into the effects of cannabis on humans, and any studies that deviated from the Bureau line were met with a rigorous campaign of denunciation.

In 1938, with the Tax Act freshly passed, it was clear that little was still known about the now illicit substance. Another marijuana conference was held, presided over by the Commissioner, on December 5, 1938, and again many pharmacologists, agronomists, chemists, and a psychiatrist convened to outline their state of knowledge with respect to the drug.

Which was pretty nil. The conferees were still uncertain about the active principal in marijuana and were much concerned about the inability to attain standard doses for research purposes. In addition, a few of the panelists had connections to the almost defunct hemp industry and were concerned about the bad name the marijuana law had given to their livelihood.

Anslinger himself seemed concerned, not that these industries were threatened, but that a large amount of commercial hemp harvested in 1934 was still on the ground.

> It is giving us a great deal of difficulty. The farmers up in Minnesota in some of the sections have been subjected to various promotion schemes. Due to the existence of stacks of the old 1934 and 1935

> crops of harvested hemp in Southern Minnesota, which is a menace to society in that it has been used by traffickers, we have arrested a gang who took a truckload of this Marihuana into New York. I will say that the farmers up there have been cooperating with us 100%. If they see anybody around that section who looks like a trafficker, they bring out their old shotguns, and he is soon disposed of. We have very little trouble from the farmers up there.

But the only real substantive discussion occurred when Dr. Walter Bromberg, the senior psychiatrist at Bellevue Hospital in New York, presented his findings with respect to marijuana and crime, findings which did not please Mr. Anslinger. Bromberg began by outlining his experiences as a member of the Psychiatric Clinic of the Court of General Sessions in New York. He saw two types of marijuana reaction: acute intoxication (marijuana psychosis), which could last from hours to several days; and toxic psychosis, either toxic or functional psychosis, in which marijuana initiates underlying psychosis.

Bromberg also reported that marijuana provided a stimulus for sexual interest as part of a general aesthetic enhancement of objects in the environment. Sexual fantasies and illusions were seen to increase. Bromberg also reported that the user would speak more rapidly, as part of the general speeded-up physical motility, and he would perceive himself as "witty, even brilliant; his ideas flow quickly and words come readily to the tongue." Bromberg also noted that the smoker finds it "pleasant to be with others and to impart his experiences to them. . . . It is felt that this need for a social setting is a reaction to an inner anxiety arising from the threat of bodily destruction implied in somatic illusions induced by Marihuana."

But Bromberg first stirred up controversy when he bemoaned the difficulty in obtaining subjects on which to do marijuana research.

> It is remarkable how much anxiety is developed when one looks for experimental subjects among laymen. The drug is popularly supposed to release aggressive and sexual impulses beyond the point of control; it is also regarded as being habit-forming. The legendary history and social connotation of hashish smoking may help to develop in those who have had no experience with the drug a series of anxieties masking sexual fantasies and aggressive impulses. This has gone almost to the point of mass hysteria. Some public officials are unwilling to allow the use of Marihuana cigarettes for experimental purposes on the ground that it may be "immoral," tending to foster the development of drug addiction among the public.

Bromberg then went on to review case studies where the different marijuana reactions were found. However, he was careful to note that aside from the direct "toxic" effect of the drug, the personality of the user played a tremendous role in the ensuing psychotic state. In fact, he allowed that "one is apt to overestimate the place of marihuana in the causation of a psychotic picture." Bromberg even went further, suggesting that in some cases marijuana use was a healthy attempt to cope with a developing functional psychosis.

> Often Cannabis intoxication represents a stage in the incipiency of a psychosis. The patient who is developing a functional psychosis strives in the incipient stage to overcome the unconsciously perceived difficulties. In this sense Marihuana usage represents a healthy reactive tendency, even though the mechanism may be unknown to the patient.

Obviously the psychiatric jargon was too much for Anslinger to follow, for not once during Bromberg's monologue did he lodge a complaint.

However, after a lunch recess, the fireworks began. Bromberg began by arguing, in response to a question from Mr. Herwick from the Food and Drug Administration, that marijuana did not cause physiological addiction; rather, it seemed to induce a hedonistic addiction, namely, "addiction of pleasure-loving, and in that category comes smoking and colorful music and things of that nature."

But the greatest heresy occurred when Bromberg, using the data he had gathered from the court, argued that there was no real relationship between marijuana and crime:

> In considering all the Marihuana cases in both General Sessions and Special Sessions courts, a total of 212 convictions, it is an impressive fact that only 30 offenders had been arrested before for drug charges. This does not argue very strongly for Marihuana as a drug that initiates criminal careers. . . . The writer believes it highly desirable and important that a Commission be appointed to examine the matter scientifically. . . . The most that one can say on the basis of ascertainable facts is that prolonged Marihuana usage constitutes a "sensual" addiction, in that the user wishes to experience again and again the ecstatic feelings which the drug produces. . . . Then we took the cases of the Marihuana users and tried to break them down. It indicates that no murderers were found among this group of 67, not one murder committed in these six or seven years by a

> Marihuana user. There were no sex cases among these 67. We have, however, seven hundred odd sex cases, from first-degree rape down to exhibitionism, and in the course of the six or seven years, not one of them was a Marihuana user, according to history or physical examination.

This data must have been too much for Anslinger to bear. But Bromberg went further and, in so doing, attacked the very foundation on which the Anslingerian Marijuana Edifice rested, the Gore File. Apparently Bromberg had actually had the temerity to double-check one of the Commissioner's pet marijuana-induced mutilations, a crime so heinous that Anslinger willingly circulated it to many authors to serve as an infamous exemplar. Bromberg was charitable in his refutation:

> There is one other point which I would like to mention and that is the case of a man named Ogden who is reported among others in Mr. Merrill's paper as having been an addict. I saw him and spent some time with him. He was a psychopathic individual; I think he had been in the State hospital at Lexington, and had had several other arrests. But nothing in his history indicated Marihuana. In other words, the newspaper accounts must be discounted. The fact of the matter was that he had not even been a drug addict, but a homosexualist. The offender was murdered by him and shoved into a trunk. I do not know whether he disarticulated his arms or not, but he sent the trunk to the express station, and they saw blood oozing out of it, and picked him up. He told the story rather frankly. It was a horrible crime. I think Marihuana was innocent of that. I am sure of that, because I have been able to check that very carefully.

At this point Anslinger could take no more:

> We have observed two cases of sex crimes where we have been able to prove the connection with Marihuana. A boy named Perez, in Baltimore, raped a ten-year-old girl, and of course he blamed it on Marihuana. It so happened that just a year before that, Perez had been picked up by the Baltimore Police for the sale of 2,500 grains of Cannabis, and got three months in jail. This sex offense happened the following year. And there is another case down in Corpus Christi that we have been able to establish, where an oil worker with a good reputation obtained and smoked a cigarette, after which he raped his young daughter. These are two cases that I know of in which we have proof.

Having started on this impressionistic data to combat Bromberg's results, there was no stopping the conferees. Even Dr.

Matchett, the chief chemist of the Bureau of Narcotics, had an anecdote:

DR. MATCHETT: One of the Internal Revenue officials, formerly in Texas, had told us that down there persons use alcohol and Marihuana together, and where they were very wild, it took four or five officers to bring a man in. He attributed that to the combined effect rather than the effect of either one.

MR. SMITH: Still, there is a good deal of fancy on the part of some officers whose experience with Marihuana is new. I have had some experience with one or two sheriffs. I know of one who recently employed the services of two other sheriffs and four deputy sheriffs to secure the arrest of a farmer on a farm where the material was growing. Any youngster 18 or 19 years old could have gone there and done it alone. This was because of the first experience of those officers with it. I think the men were anxious to capitalize on the possible publicity which might attend the arrest. So that sometimes you run up against that problem, where they report that it is necessary for a number of them to subdue an individual. That may be an effort to make it appear a more serious type of crime. So that I think that we have to put our tongues in our cheeks as to this also.

DR. MATCHETT: This story came from Deputy Commissioner Berkshire of the Alcohol Tax Unit.

Anslinger then brought up the associated use of marijuana and heroin. At the hearings for the Tax Act the year before, he had unequivocally stated that marijuana users do not graduate to the opiates. Now, in 1938, he still held that position, although, as we shall see, he will conveniently shift ten years later and link the two drugs. After a few minutes of discussion, wherein Bromberg supported Anslinger's notion that marijuana users did not go on to heroin, Wollner asked Bromberg a methodological question about the crime statistics and the use of drugs:

MR. WOLLNER: I wonder how much can be deduced from the present figures in the matter of crime, in view of the fact that these figures represent a static picture, whereas the entire Marihuana picture, as far as I know, is on an upcurve. Have you noticed any tendencies that are not static over a period of years, Dr. Bromberg?

DR. BROMBERG: That is a very good question, because the whole thing depends on the relationship between the two. But I have been in contact with the court for about five years, and the number of Marihuana peddlers has not increased, but the number of Marihuana users we do not know about.

MR. WOLLNER: In what order, would you say?

DR. BROMBERG: It is impossible to say. These are only approximations, I admit. It all depends on the police activities. They make a drive, and the figures go up. They forget about it, and there are no figures.

COMMISSIONER ANSLINGER: Are there any questions as to this phase of the problem? I must say that we are still sort of groping as to a lot of these questions.

Although Anslinger moved quickly to cut off Bromberg, it was evident that there were a few participants who did not share the Bureau's perspective on the marijuana issue. Aside from Bromberg, the most prominent dissenter on the panel was Dr. Lawrence Kolb, head of the Division of Mental Hygiene in the Public Health Service, and the man responsible for the federal narcotics hospitals in Lexington, Kentucky. Kolb, though silent during the time his superiors in Treasury were drafting the Tax Act bill, had lately expressed doubts about the Bureau's position on the drug. He refuted the notion that marijuana was addicting, noting that a user deprived of the drug would merely display a "hankering" for it. He also argued against a causal explanation of crime via marijuana. Although a latecomer to the meeting, he was not at all shy when Commissioner Anslinger called on him to report:

MR. SMITH: I would like to ask Dr. Bromberg, or anybody else who has had experience, as to the likelihood of development of perversion. Has anybody had any experience on that?

COMMISSIONER ANSLINGER: Dr. Kolb, have you run into anything on that?

DR. KOLB: No, sir.

COMMISSIONER ANSLINGER: How many of these users have you in Lexington?

DR. KOLB: There are about one hundred patients who have used it occasionally, but they are mostly opium and heroin users. About twenty-five have used nothing but Marihuana alone. But, just as Dr. Bromberg has stated, they use it occasionally, just to see if it is another drug that they need.

COMMISSIONER ANSLINGER: Are these Marihuana users, as such, a younger group than your opium smokers?

DR. KOLB: Most of the time. For instance, we had a man from Puerto Rico, about fifty years old, who had been a judge, and who said it was a political plot that he should get four years. I do not know how politics came into it. He said, "Well, they are trying to get rid of me." He never had any criminal record. That seemed to be a rather strong sentence for users.

COMMISSIONER ANSLINGER: We have noticed the tendency in Puerto Rico, even with heroin users, to give them five years for use only.

DR. KOLB: Yes, they give them a very severe sentence. The district attorney wrote me and wanted to take it up with Judge Cooper. I told him that from the standpoint of rehabilitation, it was a rather harmful matter to put a man in prison for four years. He is liable to learn a lot of things in prison and then go out and hate society and use them against society. It is my idea that users should get one year, and especially the fellow who does not have a criminal record.

COMMISSIONER ANSLINGER: I do not think the courts here are being too severe.

Wollner, to the apparent dismay of the Commissioner, continued the line of inquiry:

MR. WOLLNER: I am going to ask an awfully unfair question. What percentage of these people would have been in jail if they had not smoked Marihuana?

DR. KOLB: Well, very few of them.

MR. WOLLNER: They would not have been in jail?

DR. KOLB: That applies to a great many users of drugs.

After a few more minutes of rambling discourse, Anslinger cut off the conversation, noting that "we seem to have covered the sociological phases, so far as we are able to." He then presented Mr. Wollner, who reported on the chemical phases, where, according to Anslinger, "most of the spadework has got to be done anyway."

However, Wollner, in his opening statement, noted the inadequacy of the chemical data also. "I should certainly be within the reasonable bounds of correctness when I guess that ninety percent of the stuff that has been written on the chemical end of Cannabis is absolutely wrong, and of the other ten percent, at least two-thirds of it is of no consequence." Given this paucity of data, both sociological and scientific, one would have thought that Anslinger would welcome serious investigation into the problem. However, the Commissioner was just as quick to nix any scientific research on humans (Munch's dogs remained fair game for the Green Goddess, however) as he was to ignore Bromberg's earlier request for a commission to study the marijuana issue.

DR. MUNCH: Doctor, here is one other thought, and that is that we have not been picking on any of the prisoners lately.

COMMISSIONER ANSLINGER: Doctor, we are not dealing with the same problem as opium, where we can take the addict to a hospital in Lexington and go through all of the experiments. There is a little danger that this drug might affect a man permanently. He might do something which we may be sorry for later. I think that must be given serious thought.

While Anslinger apparently still considered Munch somewhat suspect after the ink bottle imbroglio, this rationale to deny any scientific tests of marijuana on humans was used throughout Anslinger's thirty-two-year tenure at the Bureau of Narcotics. By draping a blanket over the subject, Anslinger quite neatly accomplished two distinct goals. First, he was able to propagate his own creative theories on marijuana with little resistance (and whenever he encountered resistance, the Bureau waged a most unscientific counterattack, as we shall see). And second, by thwarting researchers, whom he denied the proper permission to obtain and possess the drug for experiment's sake, he was able to resist any movement for change in the marijuana laws, since so little was known about the subject.

It must be noted that Anslinger held dearly to his own theories about marijuana, despite evidence to the contrary that was collected by his own Bureau! Since the Tax Act, the Bureau, endeavoring to do a little sociological research, distributed marijuana questionnaires to persons arrested under the new legislation. On June 8, 1938, in a memo to Assistant Secretary of Treasury Gibbons, Will Wood, the Acting Commissioner of Narcotics, revealed the results of an examination of forty cases, people who had been arrested by the Bureau for marijuana use:

> . . . 36 individuals stated that they were definitely affected by smoking marihuana; 2 stated that they received no effect from marihuana smoking; and 2 stated that there was little or no effect from the use of this drug. . . . The symptoms which these people describe seem to be somewhat similar to intoxication from alcohol.

A pretty benign conclusion, especially when one examines the questionnaire itself. After asking simple demographic information, the questionnaire takes a twist on the second page, where the queries seem to be a bit leading with respect to antisocial activities connected with the use of the substance. After asking whether the user has noted any permanent bad effects, "Either physical or mental," the questionnaire ends on an open-ended note:

> 18a. The *U.S. Pharmacopaeia* standardized the drug by the physiological assay on dogs. This test is based on the degree of incoordination produced in dogs. After the dog is used for a period of time, the detrimental effect of the drug on the brain demonstrates itself. The dog must be destroyed. What effect has this drug on your brain?

While transmitting data that suggests the relative benignness of marijuana to his superiors by memoranda, Anslinger, at the same time, kept up the Bureau's line, albeit a bit toned down from the thirties, in the popular press and in trade journals. In October 1941, writing in "Law Enforcement," the Missouri police officers' house organ, it was "Shark Fin" Anslinger back in town:

> Do I overstate the case when I say that a more terrible enemy to society than a mad dog is innocently growing up in every community, perhaps, in Missouri? It is the Marihuana weed, within whose leaves and flowers lurks a poison that turns man into a wild beast, destroys his mind, his will, his morals, and his soul. What will Missourians do about it? Not get terrified and angered as they do when a mad dog breaks loose among them. They can visualize the mad dog—they cannot visualize the assassin wrapped up in the flower of a towering weed. And until they see something, they have no picture to guide and stimulate their thought and action.

Apparently without vast legions of brain-addled, vacant-eyed, giggling marijuanists parading aimlessly through the streets of Missouri, Anslinger was having a tough time getting cooperation for his weed-eradication programs.

One year later the Commissioner was dealt another blow, this time not from public apathy, but from a scientific study that appeared in the prestigious *American Journal of Psychiatry.* It was entitled "The Psychiatric Aspects of Marijuana Intoxication," and it was a harbinger from the team of scientists working in New York that would produce what would later be known euphemistically as the "La Guardia Report," the most exhaustive study of marijuana done in the United States up to that time.

The report originated in September 1938, when, faced with a public aroused by the flammable newspaper reports of marijuana horrors, "The Little Flower," New York City's Mayor Fiorello La Guardia, decided to appoint a blue-ribbon panel to study the phenomenon. He went to the prestigious New York Academy of Medicine, and a panel of thirty-one eminent physicians, psychiatrists, clinical psychologists, pharmacologists, chemists and sociologists undertook a scientific study, ultilizing both sociological fieldwork methods and controlled clinical experiments.

The first findings to leak out were contained in the *American Journal of Psychiatry* paper of September 1942, written by two practicing psychiatrists, Dr. Samuel Allentuck and Dr. Karl Bowman, both members of the Mayor's Committee. In that article the authors reported the results of research done on seventy-seven patients at Welfare Island. They concluded that a characteristic marijuana psychosis did not exist, that the drug "will not produce a psychosis *de novo* in a well-integrated, stable person." Marijuana was seen as a mild euphoriant, utilized "for the purpose of producing sensations comparable to those produced by alcohol," a finding that should have been no surprise to the Commissioner, since his own questionnaire study had revealed that.

The article went on to debunk a few more cherished Bureau myths, but, more importantly, it ended with an appeal for more research, with an eye on marijuana's possible medicinal role:

> Marihuana, like alcohol, does not alter the basic personality, but, by relaxing inhibitions, may permit antisocial tendencies formerly sup-

pressed to come to the fore. Marihuana does not of itself give rise to antisocial behavior. There is no evidence to suggest that the continued use of marihuana is a steppingstone to the use of opiates. Prolonged use of the drug does not lead to physical, mental, or moral degeneration, nor have we observed any permanent deleterious effects from its continued use. Quite the contrary, marihuana and its derivatives and allied synthetics have potentially valuable therapeutic applications which merit future investigation.

Anslinger was quick to counterattack. In the January 16, 1943, issue of the *Journal of the American Medical Association*, he replied to both the Allentuck and Bowman article and a supporting editorial that appeared in the sister publication of *Journal of the American Medical Association* in December 1942. Anslinger's long letter contained a string of quotes from supposedly scientific sources documenting the fact that marijuana produces mental disorders and physical deterioration. That done, he also deplored the conclusions of Allentuck and Bowman:

. . . It is very unfortunate that Drs. Allentuck and Bowman should have stated so unqualifiedly that use of marihuana does not lead to physical, mental, or moral degeneration and that no permanent deleterious effects from its continued use were observed. I am aware, of course, that the *American Journal of Psychiatry* and the *Journal of the American Medical Association* are published for a select professional group of readers who will understand the statement for what it was, that is, a scientific statement that certain phenomena were not observed in the study of a small group drawn from a prison population. More undiscriminating readers are perhaps likely to interpret the statement as the final word of the medical profession. Also, there may well be some unsavory persons engaged in the illicit marihuana trade who will make use of the statement in pushing their dangerous traffic.

As if that were not enough, the same year another attack on the Bureau's theories came in the form of an editorial in *Military Surgeon*, written by Colonel J. M. Pholen. Pholen reviewed the experiences among the soldiers in Panama with respect to marijuana-smoking and concluded:

There is no hesitancy in saying that the reputation of marijuana as a troublemaker in the Panama Department was due to its association with alcohol, which, upon investigation, was always found the prime agent. . . . It is the writer's considered opinion that the smoking of

> the leaves, flowers and seeds of *Cannabis sativa* is no more harmful than the smoking of tobacco, or mullein or sumac leaves, or any of the other plants that have been used for this purpose. There appears to be the occasional individual who, having smoked this plant, prefers its mild exhilaration to that of tobacco, but they are most exceptional. Ordinarily, after the first curiosity is satisfied, tobacco is much preferred. It is further considered that the legislation in relation to marihuana was ill-advised, that it branded as a menace and a crime a matter of trivial importance. It is understood that this legislation is furthermore a serious detriment to the development of a hemp fiber industry in this country. Finally, it is hoped that no witch hunt will be instituted in the military services over a problem that does not exist.

But in 1944 the largest threat to Anslinger's hegemony over public conceptions of marijuana occurred when the long-delayed "La Guardia Report" was finally issued. The report itself was alleged to have been the target of a campaign of suppression by the Bureau, and its publication came some six years after the scientific committee was convened. Be that as it may, the report was a bombshell, exploding the Anslingerian myths of the grave menace of marijuana.

The sociological study, which had the full cooperation and actual assistance of the New York City Police Department, came to thirteen conclusions with respect to the marijuana traffic in New York City:

> 1—Marihuana is used extensively in the Borough of Manhattan, but the problem is not as acute as it is reported to be in other sections of the United States.
> 2—The introduction of marihuana into this area is recent as compared with other localities.
> 3—The cost of marihuana is low and therefore within the purchasing power of most persons.
> 4—The distribution and use of marihuana is centered in Harlem.
> 5—The majority of marihuana smokers are Negroes and Latin Americans.
> 6—The consensus among marihuana smokers is that the use of the drug creates a definite feeling of adequacy.
> 7—The practice of smoking marihuana does not lead to addiction in the medical sense of the word.
> 8—The sale and distribution of marihuana is not under the control of any single organized group.
> 9—The use of marihuana does not lead to morphine or heroin or cocaine addiction, and no effort is made to create a market for these narcotics by stimulating the practice of marihuana-smoking.

10—Marihuana is not the determining factor in the commission of major crimes.
11—Marihuana-smoking is not widespread among schoolchildren.
12—Juvenile delinquency is not associated with the practice of smoking marihuana.
13—The publicity concerning the catastrophic effects of marihuana-smoking in New York City is unfounded.

Every cherished Bureau canon—poof!—up in smoke! And that last conclusion—surely Anslinger must have taken personal affront at such a thinly veiled attack on his PR skills. To make matters worse, the clinical studies also came up benign—and this consisted of studies made with marijuana extract supplied by Treasury's Wollner! For example, Florence Halpern, in her study of the emotional reactions of and general personality structure of marijuana users, concluded:

1—Under the influence of marihuana the basic personality structure of the individual does not change, but some of the more superficial aspects of his behavior show alteration.
2—With the use of marihuana the individual experiences increased feelings of relaxation, disinhibition, and self-confidence.
3—The new feeling of self-confidence induced by the drug expresses itself primarily through oral rather than through physical activity. There is some indication of a diminution in physical activity.
4—The disinhibition which results from the use of marihuana releases what is latent in the individual's thoughts and emotions, but doesn't evoke responses which would be totally alien to him in his undrugged state.
5—Marihuana not only releases pleasant reactions, but also feelings of anxiety.
6—Individuals with a limited capacity for effective experience and who have difficulty in making social contacts are more likely to resort to marihuana than those more capable of outgoing responses.

Still a far cry from ax murderers, homicidal infant rapists, and demented schoolchildren! The Bureau immediately set out to discredit the Report, marshaling the correct-thinking remnants of Anslinger's Army—the women's clubs, the religious groups, the right-wing press. Also, Anslinger traded on his newfound alliance with the AMA, who, in gratitude for the curtailment of arrests of doctors for narcotics violations under the Anslinger regime, were willing to play footsie with the Commissioner on the marijuana issue.

So it was no surprise to see a rebuttal editorial to the Mayor's Committee Report in the April 28, 1945, issue of the *Journal of the American Medical Association.* In fact, many observers credit the most unscientific prose to the pen of the Commissioner himself.

MARIHUANA PROBLEMS

For many years medical scientists have considered cannabis a dangerous drug. Nevertheless, a book called *Marihuana Problems,* by the New York City Mayor's Committee on Marihuana, submits an analysis by seventeen doctors of tests on 77 prisoners and, on this narrow and thoroughly unscientific foundation, draws sweeping and inadequate conclusions which minimize the harmfulness of marihuana. Already the book has done harm. One investigator has described some tearful parents who brought their 16-year-old son to a physician after he had been detected in the act of smoking marihuana. A noticeable mental deterioration had been evident for some time, even to their lay minds. The boy said he had read an account of the La Guardia Committee Report and that this was his justification for using marihuana. He read in *Down Beat,* a musical journal, an analysis of this report under the caption "Light Up, Gates, Report Finds 'Tea' a Good Kick."

A criminal lawyer for marihuana drug peddlers had already used the La Guardia Report as a basis to have defendants set free by the court.

The value of the conclusions is destroyed by the fact that the experiments were conducted on 77 confined criminals. Prisoners were obliged to be content with the quantities of drug administered. Antisocial behavior could not have been noticed, as they were prisoners. At liberty, some of them would have given free rein to their inclinations and would probably not have stopped at the dose producing "the pleasurable principle." A recent tragedy, the case of the hotel bellboy who killed a federal guard in Oklahoma City while under the influence of marihuana, is more eloquent testimony concerning the dangers of the drug. . . .

The book states unqualifiedly to the public that the use of this narcotic does not lead to physical, mental, or moral degeneration and that permanent deleterious effects from its continued use were not observed on 77 prisoners. This statement has already done great damage to the cause of law enforcement. Public officials will do well to disregard this unscientific, uncritical study, and continue to regard marihuana as a menace wherever it is purveyed.

But if this editorial attempted to be temperate in its criticism, the Bureau inspired other attacks on the report in trade journals, the *Union Signal, Clubwoman News,* and other periodicals that were scathing. Typical of these was a review of the report in the *Connecticut State Medical Journal*, which questioned why the report was even published, in light of the criticisms by Anslinger and Bouquet of the earlier Bowman and Allentuck article:

> The insistence of those who wrote the book in giving unwarranted conclusions, in spite of convincing evidence to the contrary, may remind one of the persistence of a narcotic addict in explaining to a physician the reason why a narcotic is needed to alleviate symptoms. For example, one addict in Connecticut had a habit of putting on a heavy brace around her neck when going to a doctor's office for prescriptions to convince the doctor that she actually had need for narcotics.

As time passed it became clear that the Bureau's position with respect to marijuana was becoming more and more untenable. No longer could there be any talk of an epidemic, because the arrests over the years seemed to hover between 1,000 and 1,500. The La Guardia Report and the work of Bromberg and, to some degree, Kolb served to put Anslinger on the defensive. Suddenly a new paradigm for looking at marijuana was emerging, one formulated by the most respected professionals in the country, the Academy of Medicine, among others.

In the thirties Anslinger's theories about marijuana had been disseminated to a mass audience by the Hearst papers' sensationalistic stories and by independently produced Hollywood movies such as *Reefer Madness* (originally titled *Tell Your Children*), *Assassin of Youth*, and *Marihuana, Weed with Roots in Hell*. Similarly, when the competition checked in with their version, bowdlerized accounts appeared in mass circulation papers. Such was the case when Dr. J. D. Reichard, former Medical Director of the Public Health Service Hospital in Lexington, Kentucky, defected from the Bureau line in 1946. Reichard, who had retired, wrote an article for *Federal Probation* magazine entitled "Some Myths About Marihuana." And one by one he demolished Anslinger's arguments and validated the insurgents' views.

Although he concluded, somewhat moralistically, that the use of marijuana was harmful in that it develops the "habit of escaping all discomfort and all unpleasantness by the use of some substance," his specific critiques of the crime, insanity, and addictive theses were well taken and, in fact, were the subject of several columns by nationally syndicated columnists in early 1947.

But Anslinger was too preoccupied to be concerned with Reichard's defection. For 1947 was the year that a Bureau-sanctioned film, *To the Ends of the Earth*, was released, amid great hoopla. The film, which starred Dick Powell as one of Anslinger's fearless G-men, even featured the Commissioner himself in a cameo, signing a treaty at "Long Island, home of the United Nations." Though Powell tracked down opium smugglers on three continents and won the heroine in the end, the film was no smash, falling far short of rival Bureaucrat J. Edgar Hoover's *The FBI Story*, starring Jimmy Stewart. But filming his story only whetted the Commissioner's appetite, and for the next few years much of his time would be devoted to hassling over movie contracts, pilots and book contracts. On August 19, 1948, Anslinger wrote Reg Kauffman, a longtime close friend, who was editor of a right-wing Bangor, Maine, newspaper, to express his dissatisfaction with *To the Ends of the Earth* and his determination to propagate his fervently held beliefs to a large audience:

> Thoughts-while-shaving sometimes blossom into big fields. Somewhere in the back of my head I have had a hazy idea as to what to do about some of the material which I have catalogued mentally and some which I have accumulated in paper form.
>
> Quite recently the experience that I had with producer Jay Richard Kennedy, who brought out the film *To the Ends of the Earth*, has given me another slant. I talked to him for half an hour, and within a month he was back with a script in which he turned my conversation into a two-and-a-half-million-dollar production. I am quite sure that he and his associates have handsomely cashed in on the picture. . . .
>
> . . . Another recent picture with which I am familiar was developed from a plot. The picture went over big, was made very cheaply, and has already netted the producers some million and a half.
>
> Don't think that my judgment is being warped by these dollar signs, or that I have sold out ideas for money. . . .
>
> I am giving you this to consider along with your thoughts-while-shaving idea, because with your great writing ability I think you have been on the wrong side of the racket, both insofar as monetary consideration is concerned and in putting something over to the public. One of the directors of RKO recently informed me that they were so short on stories that they didn't know where to turn. I have in mind about ten thrillers that could be done from experiences

> other than narcotics which would make some of this current fiction you see on the screen look like ham and eggs.

With Anslinger actively stalking the studios, things at the Bureau slowed down a bit. So slow that when a furor developed later that year over drugs that would later cause tremendous damage—barbiturates—Anslinger refused to move at all. He rejected as out of hand any governmental interference on the barbiturate issue and his less-government, right-wing stance won the plaudits of the editors at the *Oklahoma City Times*, who, in October 1948, opined:

> A WELL-DESERVED REBUKE
>
> It is hardly news when a bureaucrat seeks new powers and bigger worlds to conquer with the help of an expanded budget. But when one rejects an opportunity to ask for a larger club, it definitely becomes news of page one variety. Harry J. Anslinger, U.S. narcotics commissioner, made such news Thursday. He made it by flatly telling the nation's retail druggists, in an address to them at Atlantic City, that any control of barbiturates (commonly known as sleeping pills) was a purely local concern. He flatly rejected a proposed bill to put the sleeping pill in the "same control compartment" with morphine. His rejection was more than news, too. It was a well-deserved rebuke to a group of businessmen. Too many businessmen rant over the cost of government and then run to the same government asking it to solve their own problems. Most druggists and medical men agree the sleeping pill business is badly overdone. But if they are so minded, they can police the sleeping pellet pretty thoroughly themselves without help (or hindrance) from another costly agency of government.

While some businessmen were rebuked by Anslinger's position, another small group, the barbiturate manufacturers, were overjoyed. For the next eight years, at least, Anslinger would unalterably oppose any legislation trying to control barbiturates, whose horribly addictive properties were just being discovered. As late as October 1955, Anslinger was testifying before Congress that barbiturate control was a medical, not a police, problem. "I would prefer to see the barbiturate problem remain a medical problem and see if the doctors cannot keep this stuff in the bottle and control it in that way," Anslinger told the Boggs hearings, "rather than to suddenly make it a police problem. I think we would probably be as popular as the Prohibition Bureau if this thing went into effect."

But the prohibition on marijuana was another story. There was no great reefer industry to contend with, and apparently the Bureau's popularity among Mexicans, jazz musicians, gangsters, show biz folk and Negroes was of no concern to Anslinger. While he saw no reason to deny the average hardworking white American his nightly potion to induce REM-less sleep, he was still concerned, after all these years, with preventing a small minority from obtaining and using a natural tranquilizer that would color their dreams a soft green.

But by 1949 a new approach was needed for the marijuana problem. The old line had been discredited by the empirical world, and although the myths died hard, the Commissioner was in need of a new bugaboo, a latter-day Licata on which the archetypal fears of the nation could focus. And it was the empirical world that provided him with the raw stuff from which the great myth could be woven, and then presented to a public ripe for another demon.

For by the late forties another opiate had raised its ugly head, its use especially common among the soldiers home from the war. Heroin—the big H—was turning up all over, even in Harlem among the cats who mocked those on the hip and preferred the weed over the opium pipe. Heroin was the next big drug, and what better way to breathe a little life into the marijuana menace than to link it to the deadly scourge that was the key in the master plan the cunning Japs and Red Chinese had devised to take over the American way of life? Anslinger apparently truly held this paranoid world view; he was convinced that smack was some sinister Oriental fifth column rendering our stronghearted men helpless, with broken arms and broken spirits.

So it was just a hop, skip and jump from that empirical world to connect heroin to marijuana. After all, didn't all heroin addicts start out by smoking the deadly weed? Wasn't it true that the weed lost its magic, leaving the hapless hedonist only the ooze at the end of the needle with which to attain his twisted, numbed nirvana?

Of course the answer was no, but that didn't bother the Commissioner. With the same unalterable logic, one could argue that alcohol, or milk, or even breast-feeding, led to heroin addiction. But marijuana in 1949 was still sufficiently exotic and possessed of a demonic mythology that the marijuana-heroin linkup was not only plausible, but eminently possible. So it should come as no surprise that in the 1949 edition of the Bureau house organ "Traffic in Opium and Other Dangerous Drugs," Anslinger unveiled his latest PR coup:

> The Bureau has noticed during the past few years an alarming increase in the number of young persons, those in their teens and early twenties, arrested for violation of the Federal marihuana and narcotics laws in New York, Chicago, and San Francisco. . . . There has also been an increasing number of these young narcotics offenders who admit starting the use of narcotics with marihuana, then after a short while changing to the more powerful narcotics such as heroin, morphine, and cocaine.

No matter that this position directly contradicted Anslinger's own sworn testimony before the 1937 hearings, where he was eager to portray the marihuanists as a *new* social group representing a new, more insidious menace. No, this marijuana-leads-directly-to-heroin theory would serve the Commissioner extremely well for the next twenty-odd years, providing the fuel for the maintenance of the fiend mythology.

CHAPTER 11:
Allen Ginsberg Versus the Moloch Bureau

Marijuana was clearly used as a recreational drug by the jazz culture; a substance that could enhance the senses, allay the troubles of the workaday world, and induce a situation where the paramount concern was to have fun. By the end of the forties, however, a new group of young white intellectually inclined jazz devotees began experimenting with the drug and, with their clinical studies, reaped different fruit from the flowering tops. They were aware of the European tradition of hashish use, and they saw in the drug a fantastic device for altering their state of consciousness. More in the spirit of Ludlow rather than Mezzrow, they would experiment with the weed and then write elegiac verses, although in some cases, as in Kerouac's *Mexico City Blues*, they wrote their marijuana-drenched verses structured like jazz riffs, that one 242 choruses long. They would later become known as the beat writers, and Allen Ginsberg would become their most famous, and some would say most elegant, spokesperson.

So Sloman traveled over to Ginsberg's tenement apartment on the Lower East Side to pick up the thread that was left at Bernie Brightman's in Brooklyn. Ginsberg was one who could take the tale right up to the present. He had been through the hipster/beatnik scene, the flower-power hippie trip, and had emerged into the seventies as a credible social critic, amassing treasure troves of data files on such diverse issues as the CIA smuggling of opiates, Gnostic consciousness, and the plutonium cartels. Besides, Sloman had always loved the poster of Ginsberg that was sold in the mid-sixties, the one where he was wearing a huge placard at an early marijuana demonstration, like some bearded, horn-rimmed rent-a-vagrant advertising three-dollar haircuts, a styrofoam cup of coffee gingerly held aloft, with a light snow topping his almost bald pate like white laurel leaves. The sign, crudely hand-lettered, read "Pot Is Fun," and the sly, sheepish—no, elfish—grin on Ginsberg's face was testimony to that.

So Sloman sat down with the poet in the back workroom of his flat and, surrounded by books, documents, newspaper clippings, things to be filed, letters to be answered, and a phone that would ring at least ten times an hour, the two traced the weed's roots further.

"It was in 1945 or 1946 that I first had grass," Ginsberg remembered in a slow, scholarly, measured voice. "I was hanging around Times Square then with Burroughs and Kerouac, and Burroughs had run into a drug scene and knew Herbert Huncke. Burroughs writes about that at great length in *Junkie*, and Kerouac's first novels, *Vanity of Duluoz* and *Town and the City*, will have pictures of the Times Square hustler, junk, marijuana, Benzedrine scene of the mid- and late forties. I remember grass was hard to get then. Dr. Kinsey was around. We were all being part of his statistics. Huncke lived for a long while around Times Square, around Bickford's which was the great intellectual or drug-meeting center. That's where I met Dr. Kinsey."

"Did it come out of the jazz tradition . . . ?" Sloman started to ask.

"No," Allen interrupted, "it was a mixed tradition." They scanned a flow chart that the sociologist Ned Polsky had prepared on the historical diffusion of marijuana in the United States. "Aha!" Ginsberg found his family tree. "Here. I'm picking up this story among criminals, prostitutes, musicians, movie people, circus and legit theater people, 42nd Street, Times Square, 1945."

"What about the literary tradition? Ludlow, Baudelaire?"

The poet nodded. "That was in the books. So when we ran into the Times Square use of grass, we assumed the Times Square people were some sort of Gnostic Illuminati descendants of the street people you might have seen in *Children of Paradise* or from Cocteau's movies. Actually, I got my first grass from Puerto Rican seamen. I was in New Orleans; I was on a ship. I had heard a lot about grass."

"What had you heard about it?"

"Just that it was grass." Allen smiled. "I didn't know what it was. I heard that it got you high. I had already had Benzedrine; I had already had morphine and heroin before I had grass. Morphine and heroin led me to grass! I had found those quite delightful, taken in moderation, so I figured that grass must be awfully nice too, and not habit-forming like everybody told me. Despite the government propaganda."

"Was that propaganda salient to you?"

"When they had a narcotics bust, they would just say that they had seized drugs or narcotics, and there wouldn't be any account in the newspapers as to whether it was marijuana or cocaine or heroin. They obfuscated everything, and even the news reporters were snowed and just reported that dope was seized. So the common person, like my father or Lionel Trilling, whether a sophisticated intellectual or a high school teacher, thought that all narcotics were the same, and that all were habit-forming, and that all users would become dope fiends—the image they had of dope fiends was probably from Chaplin's *Easy Street.* That's the guy with the dark-shadowed eyes and the giant needle who slumps over and gives himself a big fix, then all of a sudden jumps up and rapes the pretty heroine, and Chaplin comes in and beats him over the head with a giant stick. So nobody knew what narcotics were and nobody knew the distinction.

"And one of the big discoveries for me was that there weren't narcotics, there was this grass, which was an herb, and morphine and opiates, all completely separate substances with separate effects. At that point I was eager to try it. I had just finished reading Rimbaud's *Season in Hell,* the alchemy of the word *Illuminations.* "Now is the time of the hashishins," the famous phrase. Anyway, I scored some grass from this sailor at 105th Street, right near Central Park. This guy had his family there; it was amazing how open and trusting he was. It was a family domestic scene; his mamma was there, his brother-in-law. They sent his brother-in-law to get the box of twenty dollars' worth of grass. So I had the honor of bringing back the first box full of grass to Kerouac and Burroughs in my own community at Columbia University.

"They already had had some experience. I was younger, naïve from New Jersey, but Burroughs had had some in the thirties and Jack had probably smoked some hanging around Mitten's and the jazz subculture: Lester Young, Charlie Parker, Thelonious Monk."

"What was your reaction the first time?" Sloman envisioned a Ludlow-mystical trip.

"The first time I got high, not the first time I smoked, but the first time I appreciated it, stands out in my mind like a red-letter day in my life. I was with a Columbia friend, Walter Adams, and he had this car, so we started driving around Broadway and 91st Street, and we got lost. We didn't know north from south from west, which direction was which, and all of a sudden we were in a universe of blinking lights and automobiles going up and down the streets very slowly and traffic jams and people walking between the cars, cops with whistles, people walking dogs, and restaurants and strange-looking streets in the middle of this giant megalopolis. I forgot it was New York. I was in the middle of the universe, with all this activity going on like in some kind of vast robot city inhabited by human beings also." He paused to chuckle, then dug right back into the narrative.

"So we finally got the car turned in the right direction, finally figured where Broadway was. A block from my house and I couldn't figure out which direction to go. I got a little scared, wondering if this was what it did to your sense of time and space. So we finally got the car put away, and we went into a corner restaurant and sat down at a round table in a brightly lighted old-fashioned ice cream parlor. It was old-fashioned, but modern style with formica tables. I sat down and ordered a black and white sundae, and this great plate came up. A huge, round, beautiful, creamy, white ice cream and this giant dishful, this great mound of snowlike ice cream, but absolutely sweet and pure and clean and bright, and some thick, great-tasting, hot (almost steaming) chocolate syrup on top of it which, when touching the cold ice cream, formed a kind of hard chewy candy. And I remember putting a spoon into it and putting it into my mouth and saying what an *amazing* taste it had. I had never really appreciated what an outstanding invention a black and white ice cream sundae was—and how cheap it was, too! How giant and filling it was, but also what an amazing contrast of the hot chocolate and moist, cool ice cream, and I was really fascinated by the whole ice cream culture.

"Then halfway through I realized the whole place was swaying back and forth, and the lights were dazzling. The sky was infinitely extensive and spacious, the plate-glass windows of the restaurant showed people walking back and forth with their dogs, smiling and chattering or weeping. And it was a grand moment of synchronicity; everything was joyful and gay, and it was the first and only ice cream sundae I've ever enjoyed in my life; everything else has been anticlimax." They both laughed at that.

"There was one month when I was first smoking grass once or twice a week on elegant and selected special occasions, and it made the whole universe swing. I was then studying Cézanne, and I made an arrangement to see some water colors stored at the Museum of Modern Art. So I took a couple of sticks of grass before the show, sat down and smoked it in the garden . . ."

"Didn't anyone know what you were doing?" Sloman questioned.

"In those days nobody knew the smell of grass. It smelled like those cigarettes they had for asthma. And when I saw the Cézannes, I discerned his use of space, understanding his use of hot colors advancing and cold colors receding. "Eyeball kicks" I called it in *Howl*—optical consciousness. Smoking marijuana made me more aware of that sensory illusion you get when you look out through your eyeballs and see a two-dimensional optical field; normally it looks three-dimensional, but if you rest your eyes in space, you can also see it as two-dimensional and you realize it's kind of an illusion. Maya, maya sensory space. Cézanne was very conscious of that optical space, and the marijuana had sensitized me to that precise awareness or mindfulness, and so I'll always thank it for leading me to the paintings, into modern optics, the same eyeball experiments that led into cubism or through Paul Klee into the magic squares.

"So it was a beginning of the exploration of the senses, which actually is the first scratchings of the Buddhist meditation exercises we would learn. In Buddhist meditations you sit, actually observing how the senses operate, and explore the wall of the senses: sight, smell, sound, taste, touch and mind. Marijuana catalyzed the same kind of observation without the Buddhist terminology or discipline. I began to realize 'the eye altering alters all' that's Blake, and taste sensation, taste buds, gave me a sensation of enormous awe of the space I was in. Which in the years ahead would lead to fear and trembling in awe of the enormity I was in, both taking the drug or altering the mind and, at the same time, being in the universe. In fact, there was a time about 1949 when I found it difficult to smoke because it had such a strong effect of fear and trembling . . ."

"But it was existential, not like paranoia . . ."

"A great deal of paranoia," Ginsberg corrected. "It was connected with my exploring the unknown, the illegal unknown. There was this trip laid on it that there were dope fiends. Anybody who had that altered consciousness was sort of a fiend. That was the *official* terminology and conception. Now a fiend—that's a very strange category of human being. Even the Nazis didn't have fiends; they had Jews, but they didn't have human beings who were actual fiends. What is a fiend?" Ginsberg leaped up and grabbed a massive unabridged dictionary from the wall, then shuffled to the "F" section.

"It's a horrific category, indicating some kind of strange reality, or almost science-fiction distortion of reality. It has a very funny association. Let's see the origin of the word. Hmmm—fiend. 1. Satan; the Devil. Any evil spirit. A diabolically cruel or wicked person. So it had to do with the devil and with the diabolic. So it's a kind of Catholic concept of some unremediable extreme evil, fixed, eternal evil. The origin is from the Icelandic—to hate. Ohhh. Well, okay, so that was dope fiends; that means the Narcotics Department was cultivating—were using—a word which has as its root the word 'hatred.' One who smoked marijuana in the forties would naturally be affected by this giant official government propaganda, which was reproduced in every media at great length."

"And done with a tremendous amount of support from the religious community," Sloman added.

"And in the medical community and the newspaper community and the Veterans' Organizations, and the Woman's Christian Temperance Union. But here was this notion of a satanic hatred which was imposed on the activity of smoking this herb. Naturally it was internalized by anyone who smoked in the sense it was part of the set and setting of the experience. In 1947, walking on the Columbia campus after having smoked a little grass, I knew I was the only person in that entire several acres of 20,000 intelligent scholars who was in this particular state of consciousness. Naturally I wondered if I were some kind of a satanic fiend, some hateful satanic aberration of consciousness, to be the only one who had smoked this strange preparation, which was very illegal and which was considered a heavy thing that you might be sent to jail for and be shamed and mocked forever by the English Department or the French Department, especially. So it was like being part of a cosmic conspiracy or Gnostic conspiracy to resurrect a lost art or a lost knowledge or a lost consciousness. One was very aware of all that, but at the same time, being human, naturally doubting one's role. Is this the right thing to do? Have I made a pact with the devil? What's going on here?"

"That didn't seem to bother the earlier subcultural users," Sloman observed.

"They had some traditions, though. But a white Jewish fellow from Jersey picking up on it in Times Square and going to look at Cézanne. In a way it was a great opportunity. It was an open field, what would happen to you; except for the fiend thing, there was no real social wisdom. When you got high, you could look at Cézanne or have an ice cream sundae or be in the universe with an awesome, spacious presence—vibe. I would make 1948 the great year, the great Rubicon year of consciousness in America, that goes through beat, hippie, zippy, Yippie, to the sixties to White House administrative assistant nowadays. A whole new consciousness that began like an exploration of the mind. Natural visionary experiences and the beginnings of natural breakthroughs without drugs. Gary Snyder, myself, Robert Duncan, and others."

"Did you use grass besides being a device to reorient the senses? Did you actually write about it, or on it?"

"There's an early poem I have"—Allen sprang up again and scampered back with a slim volume, *Empty Mirror*—"called 'Marihuana Notation' which is a perfect and explicit account of how it alters the consciousness. Anyway, it goes:

How sick I am
That thought always comes to me with horror
Is it this strange for everybody?
But such fugitive feelings have always been my métier
Baudelaire, yet he had great, joyful moments staring into space
Looking into the middle distance, contemplating his image in eternity
They were his moments of identity
It's solitude that produces these thoughts
It is December almost
They are singing Christmas Carols in front of the department stores down the block on 14th Street.

So the typical marijuana switch from some abstract, spun-out, spaced-out, historic, conceptual trip and, all of a sudden, focusing on a very specific, concrete, realistic, in-this-world objective. So the interest of this poem was the switch from all this daydreaming intellect into a concrete objective, coming back to myself, coming back to the actual place, to the sound of Christmas carols. This carries within it many of the seeds you were talking about, the traditional French literary, except that it was December almost; it wasn't Paris, visions of hashish, and correspondences by the ocean in blue space, it was New York streets seen very clearly.

"Although there wasn't a great deal of influence of marijuana on the writing, there was influence with respect to the sensory appreciation of arts like music, particularly the Bach music, and painting. I would consciously get high and go to the museum to look at specific paintings, so actually our original use was for aesthetic study, aesthetic perception, deepening it. I was somewhat disappointed later on, when the counterculture developed the use of grass for party purposes rather than for study purposes. I always thought that was the wrong direction, that grass should be used with mindful attentiveness, rather than just for kicks—that's silly. In fact, that's probably where Kerouac and others began separating themselves as artists from the hippie-dippy movement, so to speak. That aspect of the hippie movement was hippie-dippy, you know: 'Let's get high.' 'Cause it was ridiculous just to get high to do nothing. To get high and look at something, yes."

"I remember talking to Jack's brother-in-law Nicky at his bar in Lowell, and he told me that Jack's mother was always suspicious of you," Sloman recalled. "She thought you were the one who turned her son into a marijuana addict."

"She hated all his friends." Ginsberg stroked his graying beard. "Jack did a lot of writing on grass. *Mexico City Blues*—he used grass deliberately in that, which is very important, because it was a very influential book on me, Snyder, McClure, and other poets. Dylan, too. Dylan said he had his mind blown by it in 1959. Jack was living in Mexico then, and he told me he used to get up every morning, take a cup of black coffee, smoke a huge joint, and then sit around for half an hour and write anything that was in his mind. Completely disassociated."

"*Mexico City Blues* is great; almost like a fusion of three cultural strains going on here," Sloman enthused, "the Jazz thing, the European Baudelairian thing, and the sacramental Buddhist area."

"Look at this one"—Ginsberg was off and reading—"That sense I had of being the only one high at Columbia or the only American high on grass in Mexico City. 'And I am only an Apache/Smoking hashi/In old Cabashy/By the lamp.' So he's up in Mexico City on a roof at night writing these funny little poems, thinking about the great normal middle-class America."

"Was that whole self-image of the outlaw, the fiend, accepted?"

"No, he's kidding you. But there is the internalization of the official brainwash image."

"Well, one of the things that was said in the sixties was 'We smoke grass and we're outlaws,' and it was tied in to a whole set of social activities which you know are compatible with that view of being an outlaw. It seems like the genesis of it was the forties, when, like you said, you were a white Jewish kid, affected by that imagery . . ."

"Look, here's something very important," Ginsberg interrupted. "The public image of propaganda and official reality of the dope fiend, and marijuana leading directly to the madhouse and out of this world, extraordinary evil-filled hatred, and Satan. That was accepted by very sophisticated people like Lionel Trilling or Mark Van Doren at Columbia, who had never had any experience with black culture or marijuana. Aside from a small group of aesthetic *cognoscenti* like Gertrude Stein and Bryan Gison, Paul Bowles, the regular square culture people like *Saturday Review*, *Reader's Digest*, or anybody we call cultured, *Partisan Review*, they didn't have any idea of the black culture.

"When I smoked grass I suddenly realized how amazing it was that on the evidence of my own senses, which I did not doubt, here was a very mild stimulator of perception that led me into all sorts of awes and cosmic vibrations and appreciations of Cézanne and Renaissance paintings and color and tastes. It had something to do with the augmentation of the senses, the refreshment of senses or the exploration of modes of consciousness. And here was this great government plot to suppress it and make it seem as if it were something diabolic, satanic, full of hatred and fiendishness and madness, and so the difference between the official story and the personal consciousness I experienced catalyzed a complete reexamination of all my consciousness in every direction.

"In relation to the state, in relation to the media, in relation to teachers, high school mythology, in relation to patriotic mythology, government. It was the first time I ever had solid evidence in my own body that there was a difference between reality as I saw it myself and reality as it was described officially by the state, the government, the police and the media. And from then on I realized that marijuana was going to be an enormous political catalyst, because anybody who got high would immediately see through the official hallucination that had been laid down and would begin questioning, 'What is this war? What is the military budget?' "

"So the political implications of smoking came real early?"

"Oh, yeah, it was instantaneous. It wasn't just grass. I remember Burroughs, his wife Joan, Kerouac and I sitting on the floor talking, listening to the radio, and I'll never forget hearing Truman come on after Roosevelt's death, and Joan Burroughs was mocking him, saying he sounded like a haberdasher, and how could he run the government? They were always very cynical about the government. So, to a few of us in the forties that experience of marijuana catalyzed a reexamination of all social ideas, because if one law was full of shit and error, then what of all those other laws? And I think that happened in the sixties with the kids. The kids were first opened up, they were square, they believed in the war, and then they smoked some grass and everything was a little funny. The cops were after them, and they began to reexamine everything; they reexamined the war and reexamined capitalism, and I think that was a universal experience."

"Well, how do we get there from the notion of the beats' use of marijuana, which, as the stereotype had it, was retreatist?"

"That was a sterotype that was introduced into circulation by the FBI, the CIA, and the Treasury Department. The notion that marijuana makes you dopey and retreatist and defeatist and all that was a critical notion introduced into modern letters, literary criticism, through the following route. Beginning with Norman Podhoretz's article called 'The Know-Nothing Bohemians,' or some similar article by him or somebody like that, then reinforced by the *Partisan Review*. Podhoretz originally made his reputation ripping off beat energy and attacking

Kerouac and myself; so he introduced that notion and it was picked up and magnified more in the sociological essays in *Encounter* magazine and in the circles around the Congress for Cultural Freedom, then was picked up from them bodily, like trench mouth, and put into *Time* magazine and *Life* magazine and spread nationally. The places where it first surfaced were the intellectual circles that were later connected with the CIA.

"Back in 1961, J. Edgar Hoover, in a speech at some convention at Salt Lake, was quoted in a *New York Daily News* editorial as saying: 'The three biggest threats to America are the Communists, the beatniks and the eggheads.' So I imagine the image of the beatnik and the beatnik's use of dope was deliberately doctored, manufactured and created. People with beards and bugs, dirty and filthy, and bedbugs and cockroaches, and need a shave and need a bath, and ax murderers, violent knife people.

"The people who set the intellectual standards in the fifties, the men of distinction, were the types who would have this kind of feeling and spread it. The people who ran the CIA magazines like *Encounter*, a lot of them were ex-Communists, with some notion of social responsibility and social apocalypse. Then they became frightened of Communism under Stalin, and they started working for the CIA; they turned into cold-war intellectuals and into paranoids, most of them. Then all of a sudden comes up a whole generation of people who are all anarchists, all sort of cheerful about Communism, who think McCarthyism is a big joke, don't take the cold-war Stalinism fight seriously, want to smoke grass and look at Cézanne, and realize that the government is a hallucination run by a bunch of dopes.

"Well, we must be defeatist-retreatist in their eyes; we retreat from reality, daydream and light up. They have grass confused with opium, so we smoke grass and have opium dreams. It comes from that set, a bunch of Jewish and *goyishe* intellectuals who are working in the State Department, who never went down to Harlem, didn't know no nigger, never smoked any grass, didn't shake their ass with jazz, didn't know no jive at all, and so when they saw this kind of nigger life the whites were picking up on, they thought it must be retreatist-defeatist.

"In those days it was like being hit from the side. You couldn't see where it was coming from. Because Kerouac and Burroughs were presenting very intelligent literature I thought—I was too—and the critical reaction was to vulgarize it and to think we were a bunch of violent, knife-wielding juvenile delinquents."

Ginsberg was wired now, the ancient literary feud fueling his passion. He leaped up, grabbed a collection of essays from a shelf, and quickly found Podhoretz's piece.

"Listen:

> Allen Ginsberg wrote a volume of poems which got the San Francisco renaissance off to a screaming start a year or so ago . . . so far everybody's sanity has been spared by the inability of *Naked Lunch* to find a publisher . . .

Can you imagine that? Wait, there's more:

> The notion that to be hopped up is the best of all human conditions lies at the heart of the Beat Generation Ethos . . .

Now this is quite different from what I was describing as the alteration of perceptions."

" 'Hopped up' is such a negative term," Sloman agreed.

"Right! You're asking where that image of beatnik originated. Here it is in Podhoretz's essay, a year or so after *Howl*. Here, listen to this:

> Kerouac's love for Negroes and other dark-skinned people is tied up with primitivism and not with any radical social attitudes. The plain truth is that the primitivism of the beat generation is a cover for an anti-intellectualism so bitter that it makes the ordinary American hatred of it seem positively benign. . . .

He finally calls Kerouac a juvenile delinquent somewhere here. This was the earliest and the largest attack of the beat thing and their use of drugs. Here, he's saying Kerouac wants to kill the intellectuals:

> . . . for the suppressed cry in his books is kill the intellectuals who can talk coherently, kill those who can sit still for five minutes at a time, kill those incomprehensible characters capable of getting seriously involved in a woman, a job or a cause. . . ."

So this was his thing. He took the whole beat thing as an attack on the intellectuals and misunderstood what intellect was and all that. He said it was all solipsism. Now the ideas of this particular essay were then picked up and quoted in *Time* magazine and quoted at various times in *Encounter*, and from there they filtered out into the news media and into the general public's attitude, all from this particular essay.

The afternoon was wearing on, and presently the poet and the reporter were interrupted by the call to dinner. Peter Orlovsky, Allen's longtime companion and friend, and a poet in his own right, had whipped up a succulent fare of pork chops, tofu and salad, and Sloman sat down, along with Allen, Peter, Peter's girlfriend Denise, and Mike, a friend of Allen's. But the phone did not respect the dinner break, and every few minutes Allen would scamper out to the other room to answer it.

During one of these breaks Sloman asked Orlovsky how he had first turned on.

"With Neal, Neal Cassady, in 1954 in San Francisco," Peter recalled in his amiable but somewhat frantically ingenuous delivery. "It was very, very nice. I was aghast; it was hypnotic. I just stood there and drooled."

"No," Sloman scoffed.

"Yeah," Peter protested. "Neal had some pot, and he came in, and this girl was staying there, and I was jealous because Neal just came in and started making out with her. The kitchen floor had dots on the linoleum. So Neal would be sitting on the other end of the table with this girl, and I was going to Junior College then and keeping the house nice and clean and putting out big pots of soup and cleaning the kitchen, so there was a nice kitchen floor. Linoleum. Different-colored dots. Neal was coming in. I was really glad to meet him, because he was full of energy, talking all the time, very high spirits, not a worry in the world, laughing all the time, clowning. No sooner did he come in the door than he started making out with this girl, so I was jealous. So he got me very high, and I shot little arrows in their direction. I could see the arrows going toward Neal, so I went into a stupor. Like I was doing something bad, sort of. I was jealous, and I wasn't talking. I was making this whole horrible scene in my head, so I went into a stupor and couldn't talk, and they didn't know what to do with me. I was drooling at the mouth. Then they finally dragged me into the bedroom and threatened to pour cold water on me. They pulled me onto the floor. They tickled me to get me out of it."

Allen came back in and everyone resumed eating the chops and tofu. Ginsberg grabbed a second pork chop and attacked it with gusto.

"So was that TV show you did in 1961 the first public mention of grass for you?" Sloman wondered.

"There had been some articles, I think, or a few mentions, but only in private conversations. I can remember talking with Neal or Jack or Peter about grass on a bus, and we would lean over and whisper. We were afraid to talk openly. Now you make jokes. The universal fear of dope back then was so great that one would not talk openly—in a bus, for example—as one might cheerfully do now. You couldn't talk about changing the law, much less talk about smoking grass, for fear you'd be arrested."

"Did you know people getting arrested then—in the fifties?"

"Yeah, I knew people getting busted. Huncke. Myself. But what I was trying to describe—that scene in '54, '55—you wouldn't talk openly. What was that feeling?"

Allen directed that last query to Peter.

"It was very lethal"—Peter groped for the right word—"illegal, and the police were always around. We were walking, I think, on First Avenue and Third Street in 1957, and the cops got out of a car and pushed us against the wall and said 'Get in that hallway,' and they searched us; they asked for our ID and stuff."

"It was selective harassment," Allen concurred. "You could be stopped on the street if you had a beard and looked funny, and if you were carrying anything, you could be busted."

"Also the way you answered," Peter noted. "If you came on, you know, and asked, 'Why are you stopping me?'—if you looked at them, they'd pull you into the car and start fooling with your head."

"So nobody carried any marijuana?"

"Well, people carried it, but it was hidden"—Allen finished his chop—"but one was afraid of carrying it. I never could. You'd be afraid to mention it lest someone overhear and call a cop. The pervasive fear of the discovery, the bust, was such that you wouldn't even then talk of it publicly. You would lean over and whisper, maybe, self-consciously, and people would notice you whispering. 'What are you whispering about?' 'Are you Communists?' 'Are you dope fiends?' " The poet shook his head and got up from the table with his empty plate and deposited it in the sink.

"And then you opened your big mouth on TV." Sloman laughed.

"Then I opened my big mouth on TV," Ginsberg affirmed, and the hint of a sly, mischievous grin flickered across his beard and was gone, as furtive as a conversation about grass in the fifties.

Sloman got off the Trailways bus and headed down the block to a fast-foods hamburger stand. He was in Williamsport, Pennsylvania, which was the first pit stop on the way to State College. The reporter was bussing it because it was the least complicated way to get to that small outpost of higher learning, the campus of Pennsylvania State University, where the collected papers of Harry J. Anslinger were stored.

After eating, the handful of passengers filed back into the bus. But Sloman's attention was caught by a new arrival, a sweet-looking teen-ager lugging a heavy Ovation acoustic guitar. She carried her load to the back of the bus and flopped onto a seat.

"Are you going to teach at State College?" she yelled up at Sloman, overhearing his conversation with two of the other passengers. The reporter walked to the back and sat down next to her.

"No, I'm just coming out to do some research for a book I'm writing," he explained. He noticed that she was really young, maybe sixteen, and with her short bowl-cut hair and freckled smile, she could easily pass for a cheerleader.

After a few minutes of chatting she reached into her shoulder bag and pulled out a pipe. "Wanna smoke?" she asked, smiling. "I got some good grass." The suggestion took Sloman aback. Here they were, barreling through the night on the way to Small Town, U.S.A., the former spawning ground of Harry J., the nation's number one Narc, and the first resident Sloman meets—this cherubic little Miss America—whips out her stash before they're out of Williamsport.

"You're doing a book on grass," she said, wide-eyed. "Oh, excellent. I've been partying for two years. It's easy to score around here. I can get myself half an ounce within half an hour at school." She took a deep toke and passed the pipe.

"Do most high school kids in Pennsylvania smoke?" Sloman asked.

"Sure." The girl took another hit and began coughing. "In high school you got heads, hicks and jocks. The heads smoke all the time, most of the jocks get high, and the hicks are dead set against it. They drink. But the stuff we get is excellent. Never dry. A lot of sinsemilla."

"What about your parents?"

"They're divorced," she said casually. "And my mother's cool about it. She lets me party. Sometimes I get her high."

Sloman nodded and accepted one final toke. "What do you do besides party?"

The girl thought for a while and then answered with a rush of teen-age enthusiasm, "Mostly just get high and drink a lot of beer. They go together. We go to lots of frat parties. I play my guitar and sing—been doing that since I was thirteen. I sang at the Pizza Hut, and Highway Pizza, and a couple of steak houses. And I'm on the girls' track team. I was one of the top in the long jump, and I partied the whole time and smoked cigarettes." She giggled. Sloman refused the next bowlful and slumped down into his seat.

"But I'm gonna graduate this year, and I'm glad I'm getting out of the partying environment"—she momentarily got serious—"or I'd become a head. I hope it doesn't hit my little sister till she's fourteen, at least."

Sloman nodded and stared silently out the window, peering at the forlorn Pennsylvania night scenery and thinking about Anslinger and his archives, half stoned in the Belly of the Beast.

CHAPTER 12:
A Gumshoe Remembers Harry

The fifties began very poorly for Harry Anslinger. His budget was less than it had been in 1931, the number of employees at the Bureau was down to an all-time low (280), and the marijuana issue had seemed to recede from the public's consciousness, with a little more than 1,000 violations recorded in 1951. But what was worse, the Commissioner suffered two stunning blows to his literary career. In 1950 MGM rejected the screen rights to his "The Secret of Ghent," a thriller about his early consular days; then, six months later, the *Saturday Evening Post* rejection-slipped a friend's story, "Treasury Dog," the tale of Anslinger's canine agents.

What was worse, there was a new president coming into the White House in 1952, and that meant it was time to crank up the Anslinger Army to secure reappointment for the sometimes controversial Bureau chief. By now Anslinger had the full support of the AMA and the various industries—drug, pharmaceutical—that he was supposed to be regulating, so, after some intensive lobbying by these groups, his reappointment was assured.

Which freed him to continue the more pressing work, work that would be remembered long after the fifties had yielded to the turbulent sixties. For it was in the fifties that the Draconian penalties associated with the drug laws were enacted amid an atmosphere of controlled hysteria. For another casualty of McCarthyism and the rabid anti-Communism of the day were the unfortunate drug addicts, who, in their display of weakness, further alarmed a citizenry that saw the Red Menace behind every lamppost and under every bed. Anslinger was quick to play on those fears, noting in numerous speeches and articles that the source of the crippling opiates in this country was the Red Chinese, who were attempting to infiltrate and weaken our country via the needle.

In the light of this new menace hearings were held in 1951 by the House Ways and Means Committee, hearings that would eventually recommend legislation to shore up the criminal penalties for drug violation. A curious phenomenon developed at the hearings. The Bureau was forced, after all these years, to publicly acquiesce to the views of the respected members of the scientific community with regard to marijuana. Dr. Harris Isbell, who was director of research at the Public Health Service Hospital in Lexington, Kentucky, and a man who traditionally espoused the Bureau line, admitted that many of the old myths were just that. Both in his paper to the House committee and in his testimony before the Kefauver Committee, who held hearings to investigate organized crime that year, Isbell noted the relative innocuous quality to grass-smoking. He testified before the senators:

> Marihuana smokers generally are mildly intoxicated, giggle, laugh, bother no one, and have a good time. They do not stagger or fall, and ordinarily will not attempt to harm anyone. It has not been proved that smoking marihuana leads to crimes of violence or to crimes of a sexual nature. Smoking marihuana has no unpleasant aftereffects, no dependence is developed on the drug, and the practice can easily be stopped at any time. In fact, it is probably easier to stop smoking marihuana cigarettes than tobacco cigarettes.

So the Green Goddess was once again but a paltry weed, a giggle rather than a murder-inducer. However, while it might have lost its power as a Threatening Drug, it was its very weakness that provided the rationale for a new conception which would view it as a steppingstone to the real stuff—the opiates—and, as such, an object once more worthy of much control. Anslinger repeated this position, for the benefit of those congressmen who had neglected to read his 1949 "Traffic in Opium" report, when he testified before the Ways and Means Committee in 1951:

Mr. Boggs: From just what little I saw in that demonstration, I have forgotten the figure Dr. Isbell gave, but my recollection is that only a small percentage of those marihuana cases was anything more than a temporary degree of exhilaration. . . .

MR. ANSLINGER: The danger is this: Over 50 percent of those young addicts started on marihuana-smoking. They started there and graduated to heroin; they took the needle when the thrill of marihuana was gone.

Those hearings resulted in the overwhelming passage of the Boggs Act in 1951, an act which provided uniform penalties for violations of the Narcotic Drugs Import and Export Act and the Marihuana Tax Act, penalties that were:

First offense	2 to 5 years
Second offense	5 to 10 years
Third (and more)	10 to 20 years
Fine	$2,000

When the thrill of those penalties had dulled, the Bureau agitated among the professional groups whose province was drug abuse, and additional hearings were held four years later by a subcommittee of the Senate Judiciary Committee, headed by Senator Price Daniel of Texas. Again Anslinger testified, showcasing the new steppingstone theory, at times before an audience who still wanted to be regaled by tales of reefer madness:

SENATOR DANIEL: Now, do I understand it from you that, while we are discussing marihuana, the real danger there is that the use of marihuana leads many people eventually to the use of heroin and the drugs that do cause them complete addiction; is that true?

MR. ANSLINGER: That is the great problem and our great concern about the use of marihuana; that eventually, if used over a long period, it does lead to heroin addiction. . . .

SENATOR WELKER: Mr. Commissioner, my concluding question with respect to marihuana: Is it or is it not a fact that the marihuana user has been responsible for many of our most sadistic, terrible crimes in this Nation, such as sex slayings, sadistic slayings, and matters of that kind?

MR. ANSLINGER: There have been instances of that, Senator. We have had some rather tragic occurrences by users of marihuana. It does not follow that all crimes can be traced to marihuana. There have been many brutal crimes traced to marihuana, but I would not say that it is the controlling factor in the commission of crimes.

SENATOR WELKER: I will grant you that it is not the controlling factor, but it is a fact that your investigation shows that many of the most sadistic, terrible crimes, solved or unsolved, we can trace directly to the marihuana user?

MR. ANSLINGER: You are correct; in many cases, Senator Welker.

SENATOR WELKER: In other words, it builds up a false sort of feeling on the part of the user so that he has no inhibitions against doing anything; am I correct?

MR. ANSLINGER: He is completely irresponsible.

SENATOR WELKER: Thank you, Commissioner.

Ah! the voice of reason and moderation. The Daniel hearings ultimately yielded the Narcotics Control Act of 1956, which further escalated the penalties and fines and represented the high-water mark of the punitive approach to the drug problem. The states followed the lead of the federal government, both with the Boggs and Daniel bills, and by the end of the fifties marijuana had been integrated into the narcotics legislation of every state. What's more, possession was viewed under the new legislation as evidence of knowingly receiving smuggled marijuana—by now the solons were convinced that the hemp lying around for decades in the fields of Minnesota was lousy stuff—so possession of the drug was considered a felony, and the violator, who by now was still, for the most part, marginally employed blacks, Mexicans, and a few budding beats, was subject to long, stiff jail sentences as punishment for his vice. And every pothead in prison was one less weak link in the American chain of defense that the sly Orientals were eager and anxious to penetrate, like a long, lean, tapered needle puncturing a red, white and blue vein.

By the mid-fifties Anslinger had turned things around for the Bureau. Their appropriations had increased; it was easier to persuade Congress to approve more agents, and he had succeeded in convincing the American public that there was a grave new narcotics problem which could be contained only by a strong punitive approach.

The punishment paradigm was accepted by a majority of the professionals working in the drug abuse field. And when there was dissent, Anslinger moved quickly to eradicate the pockets of resistance. In 1959 Missouri, under the guidance of her young Circuit Attorney, Thomas F. Eagleton, changed the state narcotics law to allow first offenders for possession of drugs the possibility of parole or probation rather than the mandatory sentence of two years in the State Penitentiary that the old law dictated. Anslinger hit the roof. A few days later he announced that the number of agents assigned to Missouri would be cut in half, because, a spokesman for the Bureau told the *St. Louis Globe-Democrat*, "the Commissioner does not like Missouri's new narcotics law."

But Missouri was an exception. It was very rare for a public official to refute Anslinger's theories on the narcotics menace. And the Commissioner, having honed his PR skills during the previous two decades, took every opportunity he could to hit the talk-show circuit, spreading the gospel. Invariably, the host would defer graciously to the imposing looking Commissioner, who by now had lost all his hair, which, along with his incredible bulk, gave one the impression that he was an off-duty wrestler.

However, on September 24, 1957, he ran into a rare instance where an interviewer refused to acquiesce and allow him to spout the Bureau line unchallenged. The interviewer was young, tough John Wingate, and the show was *Nightbeat*, over WABD in Washington, D.C. Wingate had developed a wonderful You-Are-There solemnity to his interviewing, barking out the questions in a clipped cadence that at times seemed to be almost a parody of the "conscientious interviewer."

The show began, predictably enough, with Anslinger turning a question around to talk about "the fight against the living death of the dope user." But after a few minutes into the interview, Wingate interrupted an answer and asked Anslinger a question that nobody had ever had the presence of mind to pose:

WINGATE: Let me ask you this. After all these years, before or after, have you ever, sir, been tempted to take dope?

ANSLINGER: (After a short pause, Anslinger, clearly in shock, managed a nervous chuckle.) Certainly not. I have seen the great tragedy of narcotic addiction. The cases where one marihuana cigarette resulted in murder. Curiosity as to morphine and heroin injections can result in addiction very easily. It would be a very stupid thing to even try.

WINGATE: (with a sly smile in his voice) Not one puff on one marihuana cigarette, sir?

ANSLINGER: (firmly) No!

WINGATE: (moving in for the kill) Okay, what about the enforcement, then, in your service. Is there any rate of casualty there?

ANSLINGER: They never touch it.

WINGATE: Never?

ANSLINGER: Oh, we have maybe one case in ten years where maybe one of the agents happens to fall by the wayside, but that's true in every profession.

Anslinger's archives were a treasure trove. Sloman spent four days poring over the letters, the books, the Bureau files, and especially the magazines. Anslinger was a big pulp fan, and they were all represented here: *True Detective*, *True*, *True Crime*, *True Police Cases*. In fact, the Commissioner had even, on occasion, contributed articles heralding the triumphs of the G-men to these exemplars of sleaze. But even more interesting was Anslinger's own scrapbooks. The archivists had catalogued them into twenty-two volumes, each one crammed full of lurid DRUGS, CRIME, SEX stories. But what was worse, Anslinger had pasted each clipping in and then had made little handwritten scrawls in the blank spots, repeating the most sensational phrases of the story. "Murder!," "Murder!," "Inhaling the Fumes," "Bunch of 'Tea-Hounds' "; the scribbled comments made the scrapbooks read like early *National Enquirer*.

The cataloguing of this vast accumulation of Anslinger's papers fell into the able hands of Ron Phillapelli and Margaret Derrickson. Margaret had done the actual organizing, and she was one person who knew much more than she ever wanted to know about the Commissioner.

"He was a real bureaucrat," Margaret made a sour face as she and Sloman were chatting about Anslinger one afternoon. The reporter had viewed the framed, signed photos of Pete Seeger and Harry Bridges on her wall next to her desk, and he had surmised that she had been a Red-Diaper Baby. The thought of this "Com-symp" cataloguing the old man's papers made him smile.

"He had no ideology," the librarian continued. "He could have been a Nazi or a Commie. He saw it as a publicity thing. But wasn't he a racist! That *Yen* case—with the Chinese guys seducing those innocent white girls into prostitution through the opium—wasn't that too much! I thought that was made up 'cause I first saw it mentioned in one of his pulp articles."

They both laughed. "You know how we got these papers? He called us one day and offered them to us. We never asked for them. But I think I put a curse on him," Margaret ended mysteriously.

"What do you mean?" Sloman leaned in toward the desk.

"I must have put some kind of curse on him"—Margaret was collecting her things, as it was almost noon—"because I was working on the collection, and all of a sudden he dropped dead." With that she laughed heartily and got up to go to lunch.

Sloman was curious as to how Anslinger had been able to generate such support from both political parties over the thirty-odd years of his colorful tenure, gaining reappointment from president to president, from Hoover to Kennedy. From his perusal of Anslinger's papers he had gotten the impression that the Commissioner was a master politician, bestowing whatever favors he controlled on the gatekeepers who could affect his tenure. Each time his appointment came up, Anslinger's elite Army—the hanging judges, the right-wing editors, the reactionary congressmen, the lock-'em-up-and-throw-away-the-key brigade—would surface from the woodwork, beseeching the new President and Secretary of Treasury to keep a strong man on the drug beat.

Among his most vocal supporters were the pharmaceutical captains of industry and the AMA, two of the groups that the Bureau, in theory, helped regulate. In return for the support, Anslinger would go out of his way to perform personal favors for his benefactors. For instance, one drug manufacturer wrote the Commissioner in 1952:

> . . . You mentioned your willingness to commend me to your departmental associates in a way that might expedite in some degree my baggage exam on returning from foreign countries. . . .

Another favorite favor of the Commissioner was to send authentic opium pipes to personages in Congress whom he was courting. This practice had hilarious unanticipated consequences when the recipients acknowledged the gifts:

> Dear Commissioner:
>
> Thanks so much for the opium-smoker's paraphernalia! It is a most interesting outfit, and something with which I was not at all familiar. In fact, I am not sure that I would have been able to guess its use if I had not been told. I am glad to have this curio, and do appreciate your thoughtfulness in presenting it to me.
>
> With kind personal regards, I am
>
> Sincerely,
> J. Edgar Hoover

But surely an authentic opium pipe wouldn't generate the necessary support to maintain Anslinger's position, even if the gummy poppy resin was provided gratis. No, Sloman was intent on getting an insider's view of the Bureau, a firsthand evaluation of Anslinger and his operation. So when a friend offered to introduce him to a former Bureau gumshoe and, later, counsel, the reporter leaped at the chance. A blind meeting was set up at a local bar on Manhattan's east side. Sloman arrived early and waited. And waited. No gumshoe.

"I can't understand it." Howard Diller was shaking his head, swiveling his ample girth back and forth, one leg propped up on his paper-strewn desk. "How could you miss us the other night? Didn't you see the Rolls-Royce parked outside?" It had been a long way from the ten-dollar-a-day per diem to this nicely appointed office towering over Park Avenue. Diller had worked his way up from an undercover agent in the New York office in 1957 to a law degree and a promotion to the legal division of the Bureau. Then, after a stint as a New York state narcotics official, he did the turnaround and went into private practice, defending the very drug dealers that in the late fifties he was so gung-ho on arresting. The result was the Park Avenue office, a beautiful apartment overlooking Central Park, and the silver Rolls parked on the underground lot twenty-two floors below, where Sloman and Diller sat talking about Anslinger.

"I'm interested in learning about Anslinger," the reporter began earnestly.

"I'll give you a lot of insight into Anslinger," Diller said slowly, as if starting a summation. "I suppose there are no more than twenty people in the country living who knew Anslinger.

He was a very private person, and everything he said, he had great confidence was the absolute truth. He was surrounded by some very exciting personalities. They helped to formulate his own opinions. I suppose when he had an opinion, he sought these other persons to bolster it and give credibility to it for Congress.

"You have to understand that in the Congress, we had people from the Bible belt and from the New England States, Baptists from down south and puritans from New England. Like Senator Margaret Chase Smith or Senator Tobey and a host of other people who were all moralists. Anslinger stood for morality.

"He also felt very strongly about the dissemination of information. He was opposed to it. He was opposed to having people in the high school level even get booklets and information about drugs. His position was, contrary to everyone in the Bureau, the more information that was disseminated about drugs, the more people would be inclined to try them.

"He was the supreme boss. He, as I started to say, surrounded himself with some interesting people. He had as chief counsel someone who virtually no one knew—Alfred Tennyson. Tennyson, in appearance, was a spitting image of Lionel Barrymore, in every minor detail. He was an arthritic victim, though, and had an extremely hard time walking. He walked with crutches, very badly mangled. But very tall, very handsome. White hair. Tennyson was a bright man, atypical of those people involved in law enforcement. He made a sensational impression on anybody in Congress or any specialty organization, like the National Association of Pharmaceutical Manufacturers or the American Medical Association. He was the chief legal spokesman for the Bureau, and he spearheaded most of the legislation involving international affairs and matters pertaining to controls of legitimate drug substances.

"Anslinger also surrounded himself with another outstanding personality by the name of Nathan B. Eddy, who was the Commissioner of the National Institute of Health for many years. He was a physician and a pharmacologist, very respected in international health circles.

"Then there was Malachi Harney. He was Anslinger's right-hand man. Very handsome, six feet three inches tall, very refined. Very well educated, a good middle-America type whose background was in law enforcement and who sought to elevate it to the highest possible level. He was very intrigued by the use of informants; it was his belief that with informants, the work of law enforcement could be made very easy.

"So he had, in effect, three alter egos. One in legal with Tennyson, the medical and pharmacological with Dr. Eddy, and the criminologist background with Harney. Wherever he went, he took any one of these three, or all three, and he was well protected. If he had to appear before a subcommittee before the House, he had good people."

It was clear that Diller was prepared to spew forth torrents of this Anslinger-data, as he had instructed his secretary to hold all of his calls. Sloman couldn't have been more pleased, and he allowed counsel to continue uninterrupted.

"There was no Mickey Mouse kind of people with Anslinger. Now he himself in appearance was a grotesquely ugly man. Frightening. He looked like the Swedish Angel—that wrestler. He was about six feet tall, with the biggest head I've ever seen on a person in my life. He was very, very big and very ugly looking and very intimidating, and he was completely bald, as you know. Very large ears. There's some kind of endocrinological problems that people have that make them grotesque looking. He had a few. Very scary.

"He had a disposition about him that used to scare the shit out of people who met him wherever he went. He was like a devilish kind of person. Whenever he came to the office (he was very loyal to his invalid wife, so he would be out for months at a time), word would spread like word of a plague. Everybody had to be on his toes. He would say very little to any of the people. He just looked at you, and he was a scary looking guy. The supreme commander, a bit like General Patton. He had that kind of mystical quality about him and strange manners. I cannot emphasize enough the reverence everyone who worked under him held for him.

"He was well respected in many circles. Many circles thought he was an ass. Where he was respected, you might say where it counted, was in the professional organizations. The AMA held Anslinger up as one of their angels. Since a serious part of that profession has to do with drugs—over the years physicians have found themselves abusively using drugs—so long as Harry Anslinger was Commissioner, there was virtually no federal prosecution of any member of the medical profession."

Sloman finally broke the monologue. "That's quite a counterpoint to the 1914 situation. Thousands of M.D.s were arrested after the Harrison Act."

Diller shrugged. "Forget it. In order for an agent to make an arrest of a doctor, he had to have not only the permission of his superiors, including District Supervisors, but he had to have the approval, in writing, of none other than Harry Anslinger. This assured the doctors of the country that under no circumstances would they ever be federally prosecuted without Mr. Anslinger's approval. In my five years I knew of only one doctor who was prosecuted, and that was a guy in Atlanta who was selling heroin. If a doctor was illicitly dealing in controlled substances to satisfy addiction, the Old Man would take over and say, 'You shouldn't do that.' But no prosecution, no federal investigation. The most that could take place was that the case was referred to the State boards. The most that ever happened realistically was either censure or in some outrageous cases, loss of license for a year or two.

"Take the drug manufacturing business. The profits in controlled substances by the drug manufacturers of this country are enormous. There's probably no more lucrative industry than the drug industry of this country. During the entire Anslinger administration there has never been any investigation or any imposition of controls or inquiry into the high profits of that industry. You couldn't ask too many questions about it, though. He was the boss. There were only three companies, as I recall, that had the right to import opium into the country for the manufacture of opiates. That was French, Kline and King, New York Quinine, and Merck Company. It was a monopoly. Opium was procurable in the Middle East by Merck for maybe five dollars or ten dollars a kilogram; illicitly, of course, it was going for much, much more. The Bureau imposed enforcement on these monopolies, and no one else was permitted to deal with it. And he had a sensational relationship personally with that industry."

"What were the fruits to him?" Sloman wondered.

"I'm not suggesting it was because he was paid off," Diller was quick to reply. "He was such an avatar that he couldn't be interested in it. Very humble life. So, dollar payoffs were of complete disinterest to him. I don't think he could be paid off like one of our recent congressmen with broads. He got paid off in a more interesting, more subtle way. 'Listen, Boss, since you're so good to us, since you've protected us, we are very resourceful. We are very wealthy. Should any difficult piece of legislation come before the Congress that you want enacted, call on us. Should it be anything concerning the illicit distribution of drugs, those people doing it outside our company in competition with us, we'll do anything. We'll help you with your budget. We'll bring all the pressure necessary to ensure your agency functioning undisturbed.' So he had some sensational support from those most important quarters. What he bought with his support of them was their support of him and his theories, which weren't always consistent with the best interests of the country, as we now know. Whatever law he sought to pass, he knew that he could marshal the support of the drug industry."

"Would you say that he was obsessed with power?"

"Oh, he loved it. Absolutely. He was like a Napoleonic guy. I suppose all the aberrations that people who require great power have were all channeled into this man's little brain. Smart, he was not. But shrewd to the extent that he was able to get good, influential people on his team.

"One interesting thing about the man was that he had an arch rival. One wonders how these two men were able to work in a parallel field for over thirty years and not kill each other. The other man was J. Edgar Hoover. They looked alike. Anslinger was bigger, and he hated Hoover. Left alone in a ring, I guess they would have destroyed each other. Each felt that there wasn't enough room for two people like them in the country. Each felt that he had the answers to all the evils of the world. On the one hand, Hoover always felt that it was the Communists and the radicals who would ultimately overthrow this country, and it was his function as an angel of the heavens to save the country from that kind of encroachment. Anslinger said 'You're full of shit! The real disease this country has to worry about is drug addiction.' "

"But Anslinger claims in his book that drug addiction was also the Red Menace . . ." Sloman repeated the theory.

"This was always something that I think one of his advisors had fed him. He himself didn't believe that. That was during the period of time when that was a popular notion—during the McCarthy era. He himself never believed that whole thing. There were Chinese violators, and the truth of the matter was that Chinese opium was popular among some Chinese here—

and among some Jewish gamblers. But the Red thing was a good ingredient to throw in to make it interesting to Congress and to the public.

"But there was another important schism between Hoover and Anslinger, and never the twain shall meet. Anslinger sincerely believed and promoted the concept that in addition to the drug addiction problem, the real menace of this country was organized crime. He defined organized crime as the Mafia. Later, the Cosa Nostra. He also believed that if you were not Italian, you would never really make the big leagues. You could be a damn good criminal with some success, but if you weren't Sicilian, you weren't really in his category. He saw the Italian gangsters infiltrating other areas of activity—unions, industries—and he felt if left to their own way, they would ultimately run this country. A secret government. He had the good fortune of being the Commissioner of an agency that had good strong laws, and, if left to him, he would wipe out organized crime, deal it a death blow, and save the country."

"Who were some of his other enemies?" The reporter wanted a list.

"Hoover was someone he deplored. He had other enemies. His enemies were people who wanted to take a fresh look at the laws. There was a doctor from Staten Island—Ploscowe, I think. There was a man named Rufus King—a lawyer. There was a sociologist—Alfred Lindesmith. Anslinger wanted to throw him in jail. Anslinger would have taken off his left arm as a gesture of devotion if they had ever put that doctor from Staten Island in jail. Also, Anslinger had a real serious hard-on for certain judges that he felt were too lenient. He disliked Judge Edward Weinfeld here in New York with a passion because he had made some negative statements about some men in the Bureau being crooks and dishonest in other ways.

"Anybody that came out with any academic work that would be critical of him, his Bureau, or his philosophy had to go to prison. Or be beheaded. He had no tolerance for disagreement. Anslinger believed very strongly that the best government was one that was a repressive one. That the people were not capable basically of controlling their passions and their needs. That the way to control them in their best interests would be to impose restrictions of one kind or another. The thing that Anslinger concerned himself with a lot was the dissemination of information. He completely disagreed with the free exchange of ideas on the subject. He believed that the free exchange of ideas would result in contamination of the brains of the good people. Therefore, don't disseminate anything negative and you cut it off at the roots. So everything was carefully screened. Everything that came out of the Bureau had his name under it. He had to personally approve everything. And all those who worked for him and knew his line; for example, I was in a position, to a lesser degree, to disseminate information, but it was consistent with the pope's policy. So I was never accused of heresy; I knew exactly what his thinking was. Whoever disagreed was sponsored by the devil in some fashion and really had no business living. I may be harsh, but I think that's accurate."

"Where did the marijuana enforcement fall?" Sloman changed the subject.

"Marijuana by statute had always fallen within the jurisdiction of the Narcotics Bureau. In practice, the Narcotics Bureau, from its inception, was loathe to enforce the marijuana laws. There have been very few marijuana cases in the last forty years on the federal level. That is not to say that Anslinger thought it was good or that it should be legal. On the contrary. Since the agency was small, he felt that priority of the Bureau should be with the hardcore drugs, which were the opiates.

"I was talking before about the La Guardia Report. Fiorello La Guardia was also a moralist and a person who had a great deal of confidence in himself and wanted to do the right thing. When it came to marijuana, La Guardia said: 'What is this all about? You're going to have my policemen go out and lock people up? What is this we're dealing with?' He formed a commission and they submitted a report in the middle forties. When Anslinger heard about the report, he barred anyone from seeing it because he considered it a seditious instrument. Even in my tenure there was one very sophisticated report that was presented by a joint body of the AMA and ABA with respect to some of the laws concerning marijuana and heroin. This ABA-AMA joint report was really sophisticated, professionally done.

"When it came to his attention that the report had some principles and policies and philosophies that were antagonistic to his position, he considered that report as contraband. Not only was it contraband to be disseminated among professional people, political people, and lay people across the country, but it was contraband in the office too. The office had forty copies. One day he walked out of his office and said he wanted the forty copies on his desk and anyone that was caught with a copy, no matter what his position in the Bureau was, would be summarily dismissed. As I recall, thirty-eight or thirty-nine copies turned up, and there was panic as to where the other copies were. I think almost everyone had to submit to lie detector tests and so forth. He was very concerned that the written work which contained matter contradictory to his edict and his philosophy would be disseminated. *And he always prevailed!* He never lost. He prevailed in Congress and in the courts. And, should anybody along the line not go along with the program, they were maligned publicly and in other ways. The Congress always had pockets of senators and representatives who were extremely moralistic and who had our country's interest at heart, if not their civil liberties. They could always look to the Old Man for assistance. They sort of rubbed one another's backs. It worked magnificently. The Old Man always knew that no matter how absurd his policy was, no one was going to have the audacity to give him a hard time.

"The marijuana thing he could never really intellectually justify except to say that in the final analysis, when push came to shove and he was asked, 'Boss, show us scientifically where persons using marijuana screw up; where persons using marijuana are so altered in perception and personality as to present themselves as a clear and present danger to the community,' he would say, 'That might be, but you show me a drug addict and I'll show you a marijuana user. Therefore, since all these drug addicts, the thousands and thousands we've investigated, all started with marijuana, I say to you that if you eliminate marijuana, you eliminate drugs.' Of course we used to kid around in our offices, when we were sure he wasn't around and the place wasn't bugged, that someday the Old Man was going to get wise and see that milk has got to be eliminated, because all people who use drugs, at one time drank milk, and there's a clear pattern that milk users become junkies. It was just ludicrous.

"But he was promotional of his ideas in trying to have the states enforce the marijuana laws, but his men were not authorized to make any big deal on marijuana. The rank and file thought it was a lot of foolishness. No one was really hassled on federal marijuana charges at that time. Until the present day. I didn't have a marijuana case in the office. There was publicity for it; there was promotion to it. But it was just lip service."

"Didn't it help the budget?" Sloman remembered Anslinger's pleas to Congress that the marijuana situation was about to get out of hand.

"Sure. Especially in that period. We've now found the substance that young people are using that will ultimately destroy the country. They're getting off on this crazy weed. As if we weren't plagued enough with the foolishness of Congress repealing the Volstead Act, we have another substance now that's as dangerous as alcohol. He was opposed to alcohol, too."

"What about the rumors that there may have been some alcohol and tobacco interests working out an arrangement with him?" Sloman had been waiting to pop the question.

Diller smiled mischievously. "This is an interesting subject. I have no supporting evidence, just feelings. Prohibition wiped out a really great national industry, and the economy was damaged. Lo and behold, that industry was able to overcome and repeal prohibition laws after a fourteen-year period. They were concerned that after having made this great accomplishment, they would not have another commodity that would be competitive to their industry. The thought at that time was, once the use of marijuana was to become known and its effects realized, persons would find it easier to smoke and gain a feeling of euphoria to one degree or another that was better than alcohol, and that would severely hurt the industry.

"I strongly suspect the Bureau itself was supportive of the alcohol industry, and I think they said, 'Listen, we have to enact legislation.' After all, the 1937 Act was only three years after Prohibition. It's certainly logical that one follows the other. The alcohol industry was concerned with a competing substance, and the Bureau was a natural to enforce it. In reality, the whole thing was a bugaboo and was an instance of our government and one of its agencies being used to protect an industry. We have it in two major businesses, the pharmacological industry and the alcohol industry. I suppose in 1978 those two industries are the most lucrative industries. Production of these little radios and televisions and cars have so much foreign competition, but our drug industry and alcohol industry still flourish."

"How would they, in turn, support his agency?"

"The same way as the pharmaceutical industry did. He came up with some outlandish concepts and they gave him moral support and lobby support in Congress. There was a strong liaison between all these major organizations and the Commissioner's office. They were socially friendly, and they felt they had a home there. This was not an agency of government regulating another private industry, but rather, working in conjunction. It was a very cozy arrangement during my tenure there."

Sloman was still intrigued by Anslinger himself and wanted to try to get some measure of the man. Diller's theories about the alcohol conspiracy seemed too impressionistic, but the lawyer probably had some juicy Anslinger anecdotes, and Sloman was interested in collecting his own gore file. "What was his family like?"

"He had a very close relationship with his wife. She wasn't in the public attention."

"She was a niece of Mellon." Sloman remembered the classic case of nepotism that had elevated Anslinger to the top of the Bureau.

"I never met her. She was never brought forth. He lived well, but on the other hand . . . 99 percent of the Bureau's automobiles were automobiles that had been seized as contraband when they were used in the transportation of drugs. And the agents used them. The way it worked was that the best cars seized went to the supervisors and the bosses. We seized a brand-new Fleetwood Cadillac in our New York office one day —an absolute beauty. It had less than a thousand miles. Eventually we gave that car to Secretary of Treasury Dillon. He was the highest ranking officer in the whole goddamn country pertaining to our business; therefore, he was most entitled to the best car we could seize.

"District Supervisors always drove Cadillacs. Group leaders, who were below, would drive nice Chryslers. The bad agents would drive six-year-old Plymouths. Interestingly, the Old Man was a very strange cat. He would never permit himself to be seen riding in an expensive, so-acquired automobile. He always wanted to drive a Plymouth or a Chevrolet. He never sat in the back—always up front. He didn't want any fanfare. He had a serious job to do, he felt. He didn't want it derailed in any way."

"When did his wife become an invalid?"

"She was an invalid during the late fifties. I didn't know the nature of her illness, but whatever it was, it disabled her from walking. He was so loyal and devoted to her. Carried her wherever he went. He never left her alone. Tears would come to his eyes when he just talked about her. He was loving, warm, affectionate; beyond the call of human duty as a husband to his wife.

"It was a great, great sacrifice that he had to make in that his position in the Bureau was subordinated to the care of his wife during the most serious period of his tenure. Don't forget, this was the time they were discussing the Single Convention on Narcotic Drugs, which was the unification of seven treaties on an international basis with the United Nations. He was with the outstanding country of the world which was promoting this concept. He had to yield. He had to allow subordinates to take over because nothing was more important to him than his absolute devotion to his wife. She couldn't be left alone. He wouldn't trust doctors. I guess the same sick guy that he was in so many other respects evinced itself in this strange and peculiar way."

"He sounds obsessive. What about his son?"

"We know very little about his son. We know very little about anything concerning his private life. He had one son. His private life was very, very private."

"One thing I can't understand is how he could have conned so many people, not only the lay public but the academic community as well, with his ridiculous concepts."

"Aha." Diller raised a legal index finger. "What happened was that Anslinger would come out with a position that was ludicrous, but he would impose on those he surrounded himself with who were credible to do the actual attack. He would select someone like Harney to launch the attack. A man that was articulate and extremely presentable. It wasn't some weird character; he wasn't a 'dese' and 'dose' guy. You wouldn't think he was a nut."

"But he must have been incredibly conservative. When you look at these positions, they're really Byzantine. I mean, did they really believe these positions?"

"That's a good question." Diller smiled paternally. "It is my feeling that the majority of the people Anslinger surrounded himself with did not believe in the position. But because they were part of this cult, it was their responsibility. It would be like a Roman Catholic bishop who in his own conscience believed that some of the concepts of the modern-day church were working against the best interests of the Catholic populace. But, nonetheless, out of respect . . . I knew the guys who were in command of the Registry situation. They would often talk to me and snicker about what they were trying to do. That was true with what they were doing with the statistics. They were the ones who put the statistics into the IBM machines. They were great guys, just affable, gregarious, great guys.

"But they used to get very upset because they felt that someday there was going to be some congressional committee that was going to look into it. They would phony up the statistics. They had IBM machines that were frauds; they were there just to probe; they were doing things scientifically. But when they received the figures, they would chop off a zero or divide by three to come up with the statistics. They would actually lie as to what the input of the machine was. They would say that there were fewer and fewer addicts in the United States, to demonstrate that Anslinger's enforcement was effective, when, in truth, the addict population was continuously increasing. Since Anslinger left the Bureau, it has probably quadrupled across the country. Do you know that in 1960 Anslinger would not acknowledge any more than 40,000 addicts in the country. There's 40,000 addicts in Harlem alone."

"But how could this guy, who was such a paragon of virtue, lie like that?" Sloman asked in half-sincerity.

"He explained it away that he didn't want to panic the country. He didn't want Congress to lose confidence. It's like a doctor telling you to relax, not to smoke or overeat, but what he fails to say is that you might not live two more weeks because your arteries are closing up. When you don't die two weeks later, you ask why he didn't tell you, and he says he didn't want to scare you into a heart attack. That was Anslinger's general attitude. He had his own standards of truthfulness. But always with the end justifying the means. He was protecting the country."

"Did he also lie for PR reasons or for the budget purposes?"

"Anslinger was always concerned with budget. He spent a tremendous amount of energy preparing for the subcommittee hearings. One of the members on the subcommittee of the Ways and Means Committee was a congressman from Paterson, New

Jersey. We had a great deal of respect for him because he was a prominent congressman and he could have knocked the Bureau off. It was as simple as that. The Commissioner was so smart; to placate this man, he set up a little office—a one-man office—in Paterson. Notwithstanding there was no drug addiction or trafficking in Paterson. Just so this congressman could look good. Across the whole country we had only 240 agents, and we're desperately in need of men, and Paterson, New Jersey has an office so this congressman on the Ways and Means Committee could look good. We appeased him. Anslinger was full of those tricks. He was extremely effective at what he sought to accomplish. But always concerned, like General Patton or General MacArthur, that he indeed had a boss. He was always mindful of that. He would never do anything that would disgrace or hold up to public ridicule or in any way impugn the integrity of his bosses."

Sloman laughed derisively. "That's the reason he didn't have mass pogroms of drug addicts."

"Exactly. He always saw fit to attempt to persuade his bosses to go along with him as opposed to bucking or fighting them. There was never any time when there was a spirit of revolution. He was a totally devoted son to his boss. This accounts in great measure for the ability to retain that great power. A very good, strong employee is one who does whatever he does in the name of his bosses. What he did was in the name of the United States."

"Was he that charismatic?"

"Where the Old Man went, a room was illuminated and electrified by his mere presence. His royal highness had arrived. It was not just his physical appearance, but also what he stood for. Chiefs of police, law enforcement heads across the country, everyone would address him in such majestic fashion, like he was a king. He stood for and did things that arch conservative law enforcement officials like Parker from Los Angeles would have given his life to be able to emulate. That's why he and Hoover never got along.

"There was virtually no cooperation to the extent that if the FBI ever had information on trafficking through an informer, they would not divulge it to us. They'd rather have no enforcement of it or no action taken than to give up some of it. Except that some of the men had made friends among FBI agents. My partner had befriended an FBI agent and they were socially friendly, and this FBI agent gave us an informer but swore us to secrecy, because if it ever came out, he would lose his job. That's how serious it was.

"By the way, we had virtually no relationship with any other law enforcement agency. Huey Bowman, who was then head of the Secret Service, and Anslinger were arch enemies. The Alcohol and Tobacco people we regarded as nincompoops. The IRS people were also thought to be incompetent. The only agency we had respect for was Customs, and they were a competing agency. It was like Macy's doing business with Gimbel's. Our bosses wouldn't want us to have anything to do with Customs. So everybody was pretty much pulling in his own direction."

"I'm still a little uncertain about where the marijuana thing falls in." The reporter was still looking for a smoking gun, an easy way to explain the mass of contradictions that was Anslinger.

"Do you have the La Guardia Report?" Diller asked impishly.

"Sure, he tried to suppress that," Sloman shot back.

"He tried to suppress anyone's reports or information that would be contrary to his policy. If push came to shove and he couldn't effectively suppress it in its early stages, he would try to suppress the man, the preparer of the report, as some weirdo. Some person of poor judgment who should be discredited."

"Did he ever cross the line? Did he ever do anything overtly unconstitutional or in really bad taste?" Sloman wanted dirt.

"His men did," Diller replied matter-of-factly. "They were subjects of a million investigations. From my vantage point Anslinger was intolerant of the transgressions of the men. He would never approve of any illegal activity. But he was in an ivory tower, and he was immunized against what was going on."

"What did the men in the field do?" Sloman kept digging.

"Any of the corrupt practices that the men were involved in. Entrapment procedures. Illegal wire-tapping. His policy was that there could be no improprieties in any respect. He religiously believed that, but it wasn't always the case. If it ever came to his attention, it wasn't to be tolerated.

"The great story in this regard is—this is a very exciting story—there was an agent named Anthony Zirilli. An undercover agent who I think has since passed away. Zirilli was his example of a superb undercover man, a person who in a million years you wouldn't take for a law enforcement officer. He looked like a gangster—Anslinger's stereotyped Italian gangster.

"Zirilli was making cases that no one else was able to make. He really infiltrated organized crime and did a fantastic job. He had some connections from his family to the underworld. He knew some card games the underworld figures would play. He was extremely effective in dealing with these people because he was entirely believable and credible. Anslinger loved him; he made a whole bunch of cases.

"Anyway, the Bureau had a policy that you could have no more than two drinks on any tour of duty. In the course of an evening, Zirilli might spend $100 buying drinks for people, and he couldn't put in for that money on what they called a 1012 form. So, on instances where he didn't spend, he exaggerated to make up for the money. He never really did it as a corrupt practice, though.

"He had just completed a big investigation netting several traffickers in one of the southern states. The Commissioner was very pleased. But as I say, there was the suspected padding of his expense account. I suggest to you that it wasn't really padding, but paying back for what he had legitimately expended for the interest of the government. There was no procedure for which he was able to get it by policy.

"Anyway, they called him down to New Orleans as an undercover agent to infiltrate a major organization. They had an informant; it was all set; so he packed his bags and went to New Orleans. He was very enthusiastic. He met with the informant. Then the informant took him to a bar where he met with the major suspect. They negotiated for the purchase of a huge quantity of heroin. Tremendous investigation. He worked on it for a week or two, then the thing just fell apart.

"After he went back to New York, about six weeks later, he got a teletype from Washington that he was wanted in the office of the Commissioner. Zirilli and all the other men thought he was going to be given another award; they had this system where if they did excellent work, they'd get dollar remunerations.

"He got there, and by that time his 1012 had already been prepared and sent in. He was brought into the office of the Commissioner and they introduced him to his 1012 form and asked him if it was accurate. He said 'Yeah.' They asked if he was sure and he said, 'Positive.' They brought in the informant and asked him if he knew this man. 'Yeah, that's my informant.' Turned out he was an agent. Then they brought in the suspect. They asked him to identify the man. He said, 'That's the guy that was supposed to sell me ten kilos of heroin.' They had the man identify himself. He was an undercover agent of the Bureau. The bartender was next. 'Did you ever see this man?' 'Yeah, he was the bartender.' The bartender was an agent.

"It turned out that they kept extremely close tabs on the money that Zirilli spent, and it came to maybe \$35. Zirilli put in for \$150. 'Mr. Zirilli, it is obvious that you lied on your report.' And they took away his shield and his gun. He was defrocked. And forced to sign a voluntary resignation. This was the technique that Anslinger used. He did this to one of his key men."

"What was the reaction of the other agents?"

"They were incensed over it. They couldn't believe that such a thing would take place. They talked about it all the time. In some quarters—I have no gut feeling about it—it was said that certain persons were interested in Zirilli no longer working for the Bureau because of his effectiveness. Some power sought to remove him, since he was really doing a good job."

"Who would that be? Speculate."

"This is all speculation. In that the Bureau at the highest level was met with corruption by some major organized crime figure who got to some major people in the Bureau and said, 'Zirilli's got to go. He's doing too good a job.' I have no personal in-depth feeling as to whether that was the case. But what was indeed truth was that Zirilli was the most effective undercover man in the country."

Sloman smiled. "The way you describe it, it could be no one other than Anslinger."

"Yeah," Diller admitted. "I mean, carrying it to its most remarkable conclusion, if you were in charge of an organized crime family in depth concerned with trafficking in drugs and making millions of dollars, the only thing that could enable you to make a lot of money is that there is a high risk in the business. This eliminates your overwhelming percentage of competition. So if I was in the drug-trafficking industry, what I would want is good strong strict enforcement or else I'd be out of business. Everyone would get into it if there weren't that risk. It was in the interest of the underworld to have an Anslinger, otherwise the price of drugs would never be what it is. The price of opium in those days was twenty-four dollars per pound and a pound of heroin was selling for $15,000. Their profits were so gigantic only because the enforcement was so effective. It could well be that certain powers were indeed in charge. There was really no government effort to eliminate the drug-trafficking business. Never has been."

"That's also very consistent with what has happened on the other side of the coin. Look how Anslinger created a legal monopoly on opium for those three drug companies . . ." Sloman shifted in his seat as darkness fell over the city. They had been talking for a few hours and were the last ones left in the offices.

"This was not known even in Bureau circles," Diller went on, seemingly oblivious to the advancing hour. "Very few men that you'll interview in the Bureau were privy to the controls by the government of the legitimate drug industry. This was always a secret kind of thing that none of us really knew about. In the New York office, where we had, say, a hundred men, we had four men assigned to check up on pharmacists and physicians. Out of those four men, only one or two knew a little about the business. It was all controlled out of Washington by a handful of people."

Diller finally called it quits, but the two men made plans to meet over the weekend to continue the dialogue. So Sloman journeyed that Sunday morning up to Diller's apartment overlooking Central Park. It was a brilliant winter morning with a bright sun cutting through the cool air, and Sloman waited in the lobby for Diller to return from a brief shopping trip. The portly lawyer breezed in, wearing an old gray sweat suit, an oddity in this era of three-striped designer-colored Adidas outfits. "Sorry if I'm late; I was taking breakfast. I eat all my meals out," the counselor apologized, and led the reporter upstairs.

Inside the sparse but nicely furnished apartment Sloman set up his tape recorder, battling Diller's huge dog, who was intent on tasting the microphone. After meeting the lawyer's wife and teen-age daughter, the journalist sat down on the couch and turned on the machine. The dog immediately started barking.

"What I don't understand is, if Anslinger was such a great entrepreneur—leader-type—why was his budget so low all those years?"

Diller crossed his legs and bit into a piece of Danish his wife had placed on the coffee table. "He wanted to keep it low be-

The Marihuana Moloch, as depicted on the cover of Father Robert Devine's widely circulated 1943 pamphlet. *(Fitz Hugh Ludlow Memorial Library)*

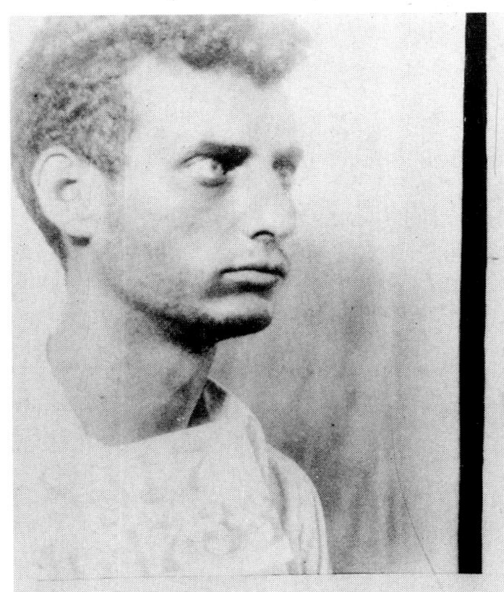

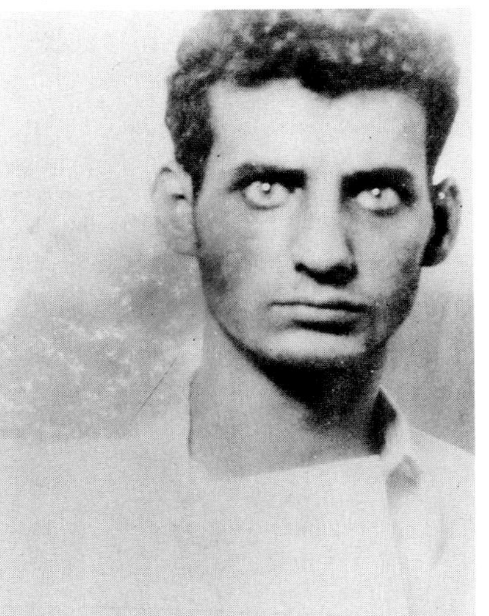

THE MOST HEINOUS CRIME OF 1933

Victor Licata, Tampa, Florida, on October 17, 1933, while under the influence of Marihuana, murdered his Mother, Father, Sister and Two Brothers, WITH AN AXE while they were asleep.

ABOVE: Victor Licata killed his mother, father, and siblings and made headlines when Anslinger linked the murders to being "under the influence" of marijuana. (*Pennsylvania State Historical Society*)

RIGHT: An actual page from the marijuana files of Harry Anslinger. *(Pennsylvania Historical Collections and Labor Archives, Pattee Library, Pennsylvania State University)*

PENN. HISTORICAL COLLECTIONS AND LABOR ARCHIVES. PATTEE LIBRARY PENNSYLVANIA STATE UNIVERSITY UNIVERSITY PARK, PA 16802

Marihuana

Colored students at Univ.of Minn. partying with female students (white) smoking and getting their sympathy with stories of racial persecution. Result pregnancy.

Undercover agent invited to marih.party. Suggestion that everyone take off their pants both male and female. Agent dropped blackjack while disrobing and had to arrest immediately.

Supreme Court. Case in Seattle operator of house of prosti. Must have warrant. Vinson OK but Liberals (frankfurter) wrecking law enforcement with such decisions.

D.C. Court sentences shockingly low. Chf. Justice Law no help. Lowest in country and highest crime ratio. Comparison with Baltimore and other cities, a haven for criminals. D.C. police active and doing all possible.

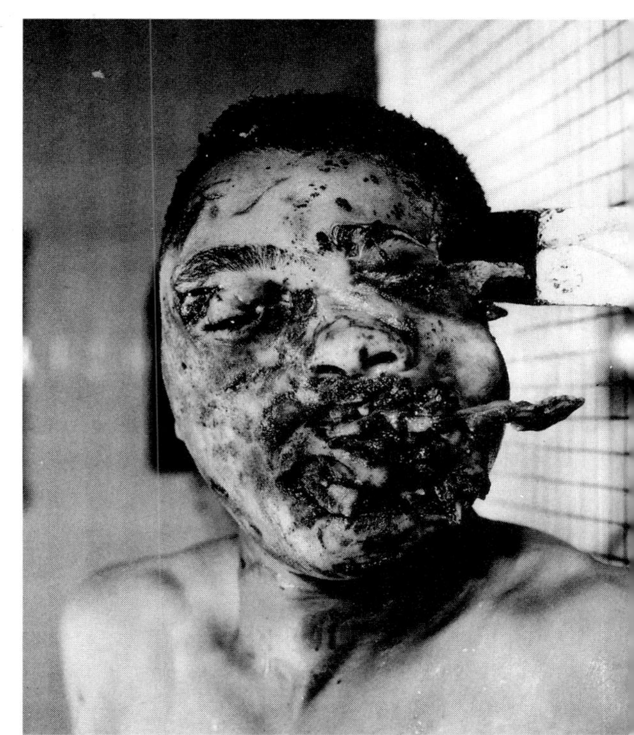

RIGHT: The gore file: This grisly photo of murder victim Thomas Crook, whose killer was allegedly under the influence of marijuana, was widely circulated by Harry Anslinger. (*Pennsylvania State Historical Society*)

BELOW: An intent Anslinger orating at one of his numerous public appearances, at which he impressed upon the United States and the world the necessity for a single convention banning cannabis. (*Pennsylvania State Historical Society*)

Immediately after passage of the federal law in 1937, the Bureau began to battle the killer weed. Here a federal agent poses proudly with his latest seizure, a marijuana plant more than twice his size. (*Pennsylvania State Historical Society*)

TINCTURE OF HIERA PICRA.

Fluid Extract of Canella....................One-and-a-half Ounces.
Aloes....................................One-and-a-half Ounces.
Brandy...................................One Pint.

Dose—One dram, three times a day in amenorrhea.

WINE OF ALOES AND CANELLA.

Socotrine Aloes (rubbed to powder)...........Two Ounces.
Fluid Extract of Canella...................Four Drams.
Sherry Wine.............................Two Pints.

Dose—As a stomachic, one to two drams; as a purgative, half to two ounces.

See Wine of Gentian.

CANNABIS INDICA.

Indian Hemp, Foreign.

The true Cannabis Indica is imported from India. It is cultivated largely in parts of Europe and Asia.

MEDICAL PROPERTIES.

Phrenic, anæsthetic, anti-spasmodic and hypnotic. Unlike opium, it does not constipate the bowels, lessen the appetite, create nausea, produce dryness of the tongue, check pulmonary secretions or produce headache. Used with success in hysteria, chorea, gout, neuralgia, acute and sub-acute rheumatism, tetanus, hydrophobia and the like.

PREPARATIONS.

Fluid Extract..............................Dose, 5 to 10 Drops.
Solid Extract.............................. " 1 to 2 Grains.
Pills......................................Half and One Grain.

TINCTURE OF CANNABIS INDICA.

Fluid Extract.............................Half Ounce.
Diluted Alcohol...........................Twelve Ounces.

Dose—Half to one dram, and gradually increased in *tetanus* every half hour until the paroxysms cease or catalepsy is induced.

DRAUGHT OF CANNABIS INDICA.

Tincture of Cannabis Indica.................Half Dram.
Camphor Mixture...........................One-and-a-half Ounces.

A page from the 1858 catalog of Tilden and Company, who produced the cannabis extract that sent Fitz H. Ludlow on his first trip. *(Fitz Hugh Ludlow Memorial Library)*

The Yippie Brain Trust: Aaron Kay, the famous "pie assassin," and Dana Beal, the Lenin of the marijuana movement, plot their next attack outside Ratner's Bakery in New York City. (*Beverly Cusimano*)

Larry Sloman with William Burroughs in 1983, after finishing his introduction with Sloman, who was then editor-in-chief of *High Times*. (*Ira Colten*)

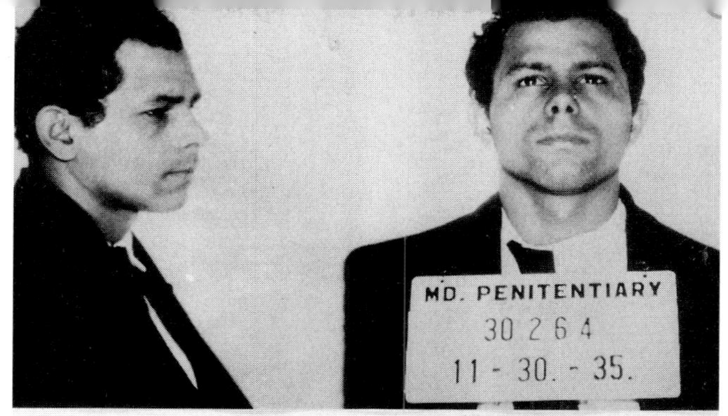

MD. PENITENTIARY
30 2 6 4
11 - 30. - 35.
Augusto Perez, age 22, Puerto Rican seaman,
Convicted Baltimore, Md., rape, carnal knowledge under 14 years. Sentenced to be HANGED. Received Maryland Penetentiary November 22,1935; discharged June 12,1936, HANGED.
Marihuana Addict.

One of many typical photos in Anslinger's files, this mug shot of Augusto Perez boasts a caption that highlights both his Puerto Rican ethnicity and his marijuana use, as well as a rather detailed description of his crime and punishment. (*Pennsylvania State Historical Society*)

Scott Imler confronts Clinton's drug czar, Barry McCaffrey, of the office of national drug control policy in 1997. (*Virginia Lee Hunter*)

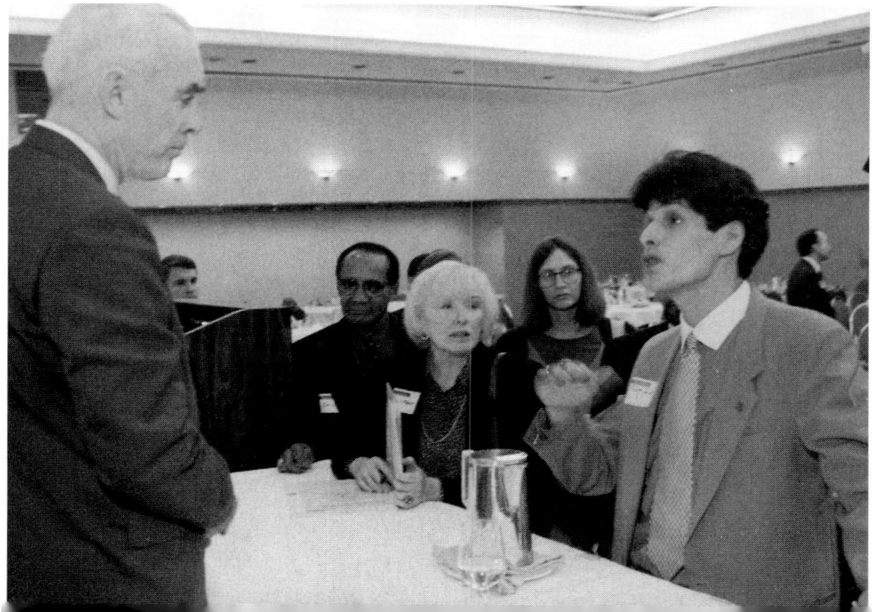

Dennis Peron, the Prince of Pot, stands with demonstrators in 1998. (*Virginia Lee Hunter*)

Jack Herer, father of the hemp movement, also known as "the Hemperor," speaks to a crowd of demonstrators in 1998. (*Virginia Lee Hunter*)

cause he never wanted anyone to knock him out of the box for spending too much money. He was extremely conservative in that respect. His men were not well paid."

"Yet they went ahead and lobbied for the Tax Act in 1937, even knowing it wouldn't add one cent to the budget. It doesn't make too much sense." The reporter seemed perplexed.

"Our conjecture always has been that the alcohol industry was very concerned with having a competitive commodity to deal with. They're the ones that really brought the pressure on the Treasury Department to impose laws against marijuana."

"But was there any evidence of that?" Sloman was still searching for that smoking gun in vain.

"It was only conjecture. It wouldn't be anything that anyone from the liquor industry would make a speech on in the House. That's how Anslinger always dealt. That's how the Bureau always dealt. All subroads. All privately but very effectively."

"Even the guys in the Bureau believed that?"

"Yeah." Diller snuck another piece of Danish. "That's why the men themselves were disenchanted with the whole marijuana thing. They thought they were just being made patsies so the liquor industry could make their millions, and they wanted us to eliminate their competition, which was this other commodity."

"Which, in fact, you were doing." Sloman grabbed some Danish before it all disappeared.

"Absolutely. That was the truth. In the enforcement of the men we would break chops over the illicit use of marijuana, but we would laugh over it, and the men would steal it themselves and often use it and dispose of it."

"No!" Sloman feigned shock.

"Sure. United States attorneys wouldn't accept it as evidence. If it ever got to a jury, they'd feel, here you're talking about a trafficker in death and you're bringing up this foolish marijuana. In reality, the Bureau, notwithstanding its position papers, made very little of this marijuana thing. The men, as a policy matter, were not to make any marijuana cases. In order to justify a marijuana case it had to be a quantity that in 1978 would be a prosecutable case. In other words, 100 pounds or more. These are in my years—1957–61.

"If we made a case, a buy of drugs or a seizure of drugs, a seizure of heroin, and there was five pounds of marijuana, we were not to include it in the report. It was disregarded. He was concerned that someone was liable to get on it. Somebody was liable to say 'What is this all about?' and look into it, become aware that this whole area was ludicrous. He forestalled any real in-depth movement on the part of any group of persons in the country to change the laws, because he wasn't enforcing them. The most he ever did was to encourage the states to enforce them. But he himself and the Bureau never took an interest in the marijuana laws. That was just lip service paid to them."

"And they would keep it?" Sloman was still fixated on all the marijuana that went unreported.

"They would keep it. Sometimes it ended up at a chemist's, but there was never an issue made of it. We used to laugh at it. We would make a street issue over it. If we caught someone in the street, we would toss them. There was no search-and-seizure prohibition against us in New York State, which was one of the thirty states that had no law against search and seizure until the decision of 1961. Up until 1961 you were able to stop anybody you wanted. We had a police state. Federal agents weren't supposed to do that, but we always used city cops to say that they were the ones who did it, when we were really the ones. Prior to 1961 we'd stop somebody on the street, search him, and then take him back to his house and search that. Then we'd call the city cop in, and he was the one who would testify in court that he did it alone."

"In effect, some of the marijuana arrests were being made by federal guys who just turned them over to the city cops?"

"In my career I don't even remember any marijuana cases. They used to have a different numbering system. When you made a marijuana arrest, you would get yourself in trouble, because the supervisor would be displeased because they wanted heroin. You almost had to explain why you did it. Then they wanted to know why you didn't turn it over to the local cops.

"This hands-off policy was also the case with respect to the legitimate inquiries about research with marijuana. The Commissioner's position was that there was no legitimate use for it, so he would never allow any applicants to be recognized. Every so often some university would submit an application to grow some marijuana plants or do a botany experiment on the medicinal uses of marijuana. Anslinger would rely heavily on a man—whose name escapes me—who knew the Commissioner's policy and who would come up with a scientific reason why the application should be denied. A nice old man who played ball and was very credible."

Sloman finished the tea that Mrs. Diller had served, and his mind wandered as the hunger pains in his stomach intensified. The last fifteen minutes or so of the interview had been done under the duress of Diller's huge dog, who, in his playful manner, was sprawling all over the interviewer's lap and punctuating his play with short barks, obscuring his master's replies. Sloman was fascinated at Diller's turnaround, though, and dragged the conversation further into the present.

"When did you first go into private practice?"

"In 1962," Diller explained, peeling the dog off the hapless scribe. "But the defense bar, the lawyers defending drug cases, for example, none of us as a group or individually ever did anything realistically, as far as approaching marijuana laws, to change them. They were great sources of revenue for us. Even the goody-goody lawyers never made an issue of it. They would occasionally scream about it, but they never did anything more than that. They never went to the legislature and said, 'Listen, these laws are absurd.' Now when there is virtually no marijuana enforcement in the city, the lawyers are screaming, 'Bring back those strong marijuana laws.' "

"You're kidding." Sloman was reduced to eating Danish crumbs.

"No, it's money. If you asked the lawyers, they would make the smoking of Kent 100's the first offense, a misdemeanor, and the second offense, a felony. It's good for business. The worst thing that could happen would be the lack of enforcement. Do you know, with the lack of enforcement over gambling laws, there are hundreds of lawyers out of business? Very displeased with that. So the lawyers, my ilk, would love the marijuana busts. The bar is not concerned with what is right and what is wrong. Proprieties. They're concerned with having as much business as possible. If the bar were able to vote secretly in the legislature, they would vote to impose the same penalties on marijuana as on heroin and cocaine. Except they smoke themselves."

"Who are your clients on marijuana charges now?" Sloman wondered.

"We used to have nice middle-class Jewish kids during the sixties, kids whose protest manifestation was the smoking of marijuana. These kids were just generally protesting and stepping out of society a little bit. Not going to school and giving their parents a hard time. That has completely changed. Today we have virtually none of those kids. There was a time when I'd say 30 or 40 percent of the practice involved adolescents. Today I don't think we have a single one of those cases. We're just out of business with them."

"What's changed?" Miraculously, Diller's dog had lost interest in the interview and had sauntered into another room.

"For one thing, the war being over had a salutatory effect. The youth of the country are very, very, very interested in improving their lot: getting a good education, vying to get into the good schools. There has never been such a tremendous demand to get into the better colleges and professional schools. The kids are no longer protesting. They are very pleased with the government's action and reaction to Watergate. It gave them a tremendous boost of confidence to see that even the chief of the country, when he's not doing the right thing, can go. The vice-president, a couple of attorney generals, a Court of Appeals judge, too. The youth have regained remarkable confidence in the system as a result of Watergate."

Diller was clearly enjoying this soapbox. "My experience with youth today—and I love this subject—is diametrically opposite of my experience ten years ago. The kids today, even those who get into a little trouble—they have a gun, or some transgression—are completely different. They're all anxious to work. They're anxious to do well. They're anxious to get ahead. They're anxious to go to school. They don't hate their government. They don't hate policemen. I'm heartened by this, even though my business has dropped."

"But who are your clients now?" Sloman had gotten a little lost in the narrative.

"With respect to marijuana, my clients are mostly men in their twenties and thirties whose careers are bringing up the stuff and who are otherwise legitimate background people of every ethnic group, who are business people dealing in high quantities of marijuana in businesslike fashion. They keep records. They keep books."

"Do they accept arrest as inevitable, as a business setback?"

"They do. They, I'm sure, would be unalterably opposed to any drastic change in the marijuana laws because it would put them out of business. The major traffickers are making oodles and oodles of money, and they hope that sometimes there are busts to keep the price up. I suspect that a group of traffickers, if the downward trend of enforcement of the marijuana laws continues, will go to the legislature and revitalize Anslinger's 1937 article and remind the legislature that it is dangerous and that heavier penalties are needed.

"Look, if you change the laws, the traffickers and the lawyers will be displeased. And the law enforcement people. Law enforcement people have sort of resigned themselves. But not just lawyers will suffer from the decriminalization of marijuana. There are numerous ancillary services, for example: youth counseling, probation officers, judges, hacks in prison—it would be tremendous. We're living in a criminal economy, and decriminalization would hurt so many different people.

"But the courts are not interested in the marijuana cases. The courts have people who are basically into more serious things. The shoplifters, the hundreds of petty types of crime. I had a kid who was intoxicated by alcohol, broke a window in a store, one thing led to another, the cops came, and he beat the cop up. They finally had to beat the shit out of him, and they broke his leg. They held him without bail. He was in Bellevue's prison ward. Finally a month later the case came to court. The kid was in the hospital for a month because he couldn't move his leg. A leg and an arm. It ended up with disorderly conduct and $100 fine. Something more than speeding. Maybe not as much.

"We have an extremely liberal attitude here. The establishment is now after our professional people: lawyers, doctors, judges, policemen, accountants, nursing home operators. They're the ones filling up the penal institutions. That's what the kids are getting such a kick out of. Youthful kids, almost nothing can happen to them. That's why we're losing all this business. Because before, they needed a good lawyer and now a Legal Aid lawyer will do an adequate job. A kid can't go to jail. He has to do something that will take your eyes out."

The anecdote had set Sloman's mind going. He had an uneasiness about the burgeoning marijuana scene, an almost elitist notion that the mass availability of cannabis might not be the best thing for a nation with the emotional maturity that America enjoys. Perhaps he was reading too much Anslinger. Perhaps he was just getting old. But maybe he was right. "Sometimes when I see the statistics on grass, it seems to me that the problem is that there are so many schmucks running around who smoke grass and do other drugs and aren't mature enough. They really seem to abuse it."

"This is the same group, is it not, that also takes alcohol? How many cases have I had—take the *Kelly* case. A handsome seventeen-year-old Irish kid, drinking beer, gets into a confrontation with another kid in Brooklyn where a dance hall is. The other kid is kind of sassy to him, one thing leads to another, the Kelly kid takes out a knife and punctures it into the heart of the other kid and kills him."

Diller had sprung to his feet during this last recital and was pacing the room, resembling a rotund Perry Mason—in a sweat suit. "Fortunately I was able to get probation out of it because he had such an outstanding background and so many people came to his aid." A huge sweet smile swept across Diller's Danished face.

"He got only probation?" Sloman was incredulous.

"Yeah," Diller smiled, half in triumph, half-sheepishly.

"You're a great lawyer," the reporter marveled.

"The thing to do if you get into trouble is to be sure you have some shit in you. There's nothing more a judge wants to hear than, 'Judge, see that horrendous thing that he did. He was so fucked up with alcohol or heroin or methadone that he didn't know what he was doing.' " Diller smiled again.

Sure, Sloman thought cynically, tell Victor Licata that. But all he could say was, "You're a great lawyer."

CHAPTER 13:
Mary Warner Leaves the Ghetto

By the beginning of the sixties the chinks began to show in the Bureau's armor, and it was at the weakest point, marijuana, where reality intruded into the picture. Anslinger's latest position on marijuana was that it was not the horrific causal agent the Bureau made it out to be in the thirties. Rather, it was a substance that invariably would let down its users, because it was too weak to sustain the thrills these debauchees were after. The next step, of course, was heroin.

The weakness in this argument was evident. If it could be shown that marijuana was a relatively benign drug whose use could be moderated, the prohibition rationale would crumble.

But one factor that supported the Bureau's position with respect to the drug was that by 1960 most of the users of marijuana were still nonwhites, and were invariably those at the lowest rung of the socioeconomic ladder. Marijuana was still an exotic substance, linked to crime, violence and the like. Also, the stereotypes that the Bureau fostered went unchallenged, since the user groups had no lobbies, being outside the political process, and had virtually no access to the media.

That changed on February 12, 1961. On that night the Metromedia Network broadcast the John Crosby show. Crosby was a syndicated columnist who hosted a TV talk show, similar to the David Susskind program, but a wee bit more avant-garde, as was evidenced by that night's discussion "Hips and Beats," featuring Allen Ginsberg, Norman Mailer, and anthropologist Ashley Montagu.

That afternoon Mailer and Ginsberg had lunch at a Chinese restaurant, and the poet proposed that they do something interesting that evening, like talk reasonably about the harmlessness of marijuana. Mailer, who had had a bad experience with marijuana, was reluctant; but during the show Ginsberg suddenly changed the subject and brought up grass, relating his experiences with the drug in India and in Tangiers. Mailer then went on to concede that he had had some and it wasn't as bad as all that, and even Ashley Montagu gave a little anthropological background on cannabis use in other cultures. Eventually the talk got around to the marijuana laws, which everyone, including Crosby, thought were too extreme.

The next day there was much reaction. Typical of this was a column in the *Baltimore Sun*, where the TV reviewer was "amazed" to hear "an ardent plea for the legalization of marijuana and the smoking thereof by men, women and children":

> He [Ginsberg] appeared to think that what this country needs is a good 5-cent cigarette composed of *Nicotiana glauca*. It will solve all our problems, he opined. The studio audience, sprinkled with berets, beards, and sandals, mostly seemed to agree.

Reaction came swiftly from another source, the beleaguered Bureau. For the first time opposition views on this issue had been aired on a mass-media outlet by a quasi-respectable source. Anslinger immediately demanded equal time and, over the objections of Crosby, Metromedia granted the Bureau rebuttal time on Crosby's March 5, 1961, show. For the TV exposure Anslinger chose the distinguished Mr. Harney, whose comments cleverly avoided the substantive:

> Even after 40 years of close acquaintance with the problems of the narcotic traffic and narcotic addiction, it was to me a novel experience to find on radio and television an advocate for the use of marihuana—and even by children of any age. This may have shocked and surprised some, which perhaps was one of Mr. Ginsberg's purposes. . . .
>
> Years ago when chemistry was less advanced, the then best test of the potency of cannabis was a biological one. Sometimes dogs were used. The effect of the drug so injured his coordination that the animal had to be destroyed. It shouldn't happen to a dog—much less a human being. It is fortunate for our marihuana smokers that because of our law enforcement program most of these have access in this country to only a very poor quality and potency of the drug. . . . New addictions and new habituations are created in part by people who talk like Mr. Ginsberg, in my opinion. Lest that be considered as only one man's opinion, let me close with this:

> Shortly after the broadcast in question, Mr. Anslinger was talking to a Mexican official who twitted him along this line—"You are always asking us to help you by keeping Mexican marihuana out of your country. But now you have a Mr. Ginsberg advocating it on radio and television."

A strange twit to end on. But it was clear that the Bureau was on the defensive. Crosby, in one of his first syndicated columns after the show, mocked Harney's rebuttal, calling it "a lot of alarmist nonsense concerning pot, about which our Narcotics Bureau knows very little." This was the first televised battle of boo. For the first time the weed had a spokesman for its position, and as the sixties progressed it was a position that would be embraced by a larger and larger segment of the white youth of America. Marijuana would become a vital armament in a burgeoning counterculture that would spring up in the sixties and manifest itself as a full frontal attack on the social and economic institutions of America. Pot would be politicized, its powers embellished, its myth enlarged, its use further ritualized.

As one of the core components of a countercultural perspective, marijuana would enjoy a political association, which it had never had in its almost fifty-year existence as a recreational drug in America. To the Mexicans it was something to take their minds off the drudgery of the beet fields. For the poor blacks it was a similarly endowed recreational drug. The jazzmen used it to enhance their playing, as well as to feed their mystique. The beats saw in it a link to a great literary tradition of Europe. But by the middle of the sixties marijuana had taken on a new meaning for a vast new class of disaffected white middle-class Americans. Writing in *Soul on Ice,* Eldridge Cleaver would see the transformation of the use of marijuana from a furtive, surreptitious rite to an avowed act of insurrection:

> The characteristics of the white rebels which most alarm their elders—the long hair, the new dances, their love for Negro music, their use of marihuana, their mystical attitude toward sex—are also tools of their rebellion. They have turned these tools against the totalitarian fabric of American society—and they mean to change it.

As testimony to Anslinger's political shrewdness, he was aware that this would be the case. Perhaps it was a gut feeling that his karma was catching up with him, perhaps it was the natural thing to do in the face of a new Godless left-wing adversary. At any rate, the authorities moved swiftly to shut off the dissemination of these ideas that would, by the end of the decade, blossom into a flower-loving, pot-smoking alternative culture. And they acted in the only way they knew how. After the Crosby show, the Bureau of Narcotics opened a file on Allen Ginsberg and spent the next few years trying to set him up for a marijuana bust.

But Anslinger would be gone from the front lines of this new battle against the hippies. And his forced retirement from the Bureau in 1962, at the mandatory age of seventy, would be bittersweet in that so much of his work was left undone. The TV series based on his life and exploits, for example. Poor Harry must have spent years negotiating with both TV and movie producers in an attempt to chronicle the fearless exploits of his men, to little avail.

However, the Commissioner did get written into an Armstrong Circle Theatre episode on "Interpol," and the showing occasioned a letter to Anslinger from Frank Reid, a friend who worked with E. R. Squibb and Sons, one of the pharmaceutical concerns that dealt regularly with the Bureau. Reid had two questions for the Commissioner:

> (1) Where did the Commissioner get that full mop of hair?
> (2) How come Frank Reid is with the Narcotic Department?

The reply was pure Anslinger:

> I got the mop for "Interpol" by using Krushchev's banana oil which will put a man in space or on the moon or grow hair on a billiard ball overnight. So, the story of how Frank Reid became one of the gangsters on "Interpol" is quite simple. We have a very nice young Jewish choir boy named George Gaffney on our staff who furnished the technical knowledge for the film. Realizing that "The Untouchables" was under severe attack from the Italian-American societies, it was decided to replace these dago gangsters with Irishmen. The first good Irish name that came to Gaffney's mind was yours—no insinuation meant here. I think if the Irish put their minds to it they could outsmuggle the wops.
>
> An "Interpol" badge is attached with the express provision that you will accept this in lieu of filing suit against "Interpol" for the use of your name.

But this would be one of the last ceremonial gift-givings on the part of Anslinger, for in 1962 he was sent back to Hollidaysburg by John F. Kennedy, who used the mandatory retirement clause as an excuse to excuse the aging Commissioner. In his stead Anslinger bequeathed his Bureau to Henry Giordano, one of his trusted lieutenants. But the Old Man was not powerless, for he still represented the United States on all its international United Nations dealings, a vantage point from which he would be able to gain a last, lingering laugh on all the potheads who were beginning to agitate for a change in the marijuana laws.

And by 1964, incredibly enough, there were the first glimmerings of a pro-pot lobby forming, centered around the bohemian enclave of the Lower East Side in Manhattan. Of course Allen Ginsberg and Peter Orlovsky were among the agitants, and, naturally enough, another addition was made to Ginsberg's Bureau file:

> Reference is made to the recently founded organization "LEMAR" (Legalize Marihuana). According to a newspaper report, this is not a formal organization and it does not have any officers. . . . It was learned recently that these individuals plan on departing for Cuba on Jan. 13, 1965. It is requested that their names be placed on the Customs Suspect List.

A short time later, on February 23, 1965, another Memorandum Report on Ginsberg was filed:

> Reference is made to my Memorandum Report dated Jan. 7, 1965, requesting the names Allen Ginsberg and ——— be placed on the Customs Suspect List. On December 27, 1964, GINSBERG and ——— had marched in front of the Department of Welfare Building, East 9th St. and Avenue C, with signs reading "Smoke Pot, It's Cheaper and Healthier Than Liquor" and "Pot Is a Reality Kick." These individuals are members of an organization called LEMAR (Legalize Marihuana) and their names appear in the files of Interpol.

A month later, on March 12, the file was augmented with a three-page memo outlining Ginsberg's career, including the poet's entry in *Who's Who in America.* The agent also reports visiting Columbia University to make inquiries about Ginsberg's record at school. His name was recognized immediately by those interviewed, and one employee lamented that much of the correspondence from Ginsberg's file had been missing since his graduation, presumably taken by souvenir hunters. The agent concluded:

> From what I have read and heard it would appear that the reported increased and widespread use of marihuana by college students could be attributed in part to the influence of ALLEN GINSBERG and persons of his ilk. It appears that GINSBERG's writings and poetry readings on the many college campuses and avant-garde meeting places have had a strong appeal and have provided a rationale to many college students and persons in intellectual life here and abroad.

The memo ended with a request for the photographs and passport application of Ginsberg, which data was itself duly recorded in a five-page memo in April. In May the FBI got into the act, clipping a story from *Time* magazine that reported on the earlier LEMAR demonstration.

By August of 1965 Ginsberg expressed suspicions that he was about to be set up on marijuana charges. In a letter to his congressman, Charles Joelson, who represented the New Jersey district where Ginsberg's father maintained residence, the poet expressed his fears of entrapment:

> As you may know, I've been active for the last few years in a sort of Fabian reform movement to end the prohibition of marihuana and turn over treatment of junkies (heroin addicts) to the hands of doctors & dismantle the Treas. Dept. Narcotics Bureau. My reasons for this are amiable enough & medically accurate enough but I won't go into that now as it's irrelevant to the present instance. In any case I've gone on radio & TV and argued the case often & occasionally reasonably.
>
> When I came back to NY by plane after 6 months in Prague Moscow London etc on June 30 I was stopped by customs & subjected to detailed intensive search, all my baggage fine tooth combed, the lint out of my pockets sifted for suspicious weed etc, made to undress to my underwear—all the dull humiliations of a Kafkian trial. . . . I'm proposing a change in the law, not smuggling. I resented the situation & thought of complaining—to you, to the NY Times, to God, someone—but was otherwise occupied.
>
> This week I hear from NY that a kid named Jack Martin who was arrested Aug. 4 for possession of pot got a proposition from four Federal Narcotics Agents including the supervisor of the NY Bureau and Agent Bruce Jensen (acting as spokesman) to set me up for an entrapment. Martin apparently said no, I was a poet not a pusher, & they suggested to him that I wouldn't have to be caught with *much* marihuana in my possession & Martin said I was out of

> town anyway. They also apparently threatened to add additional charges to his indictment unless he cooperated.
>
> . . . I should at this point reassure you that I don't trade in drugs, my racket is Poesy, & that to safeguard my public position or Stand on the subject I've kept immaculately & paranoiacally clean the last years. So that if in the next year I am busted it will be some kind of creepy entrapment, probably an outright plant. . . . The Control Habit may be difficult for the police to kick & I suppose that the attempt to set me up is a side-effect of the slow disintoxication syndrome now apparent. . . .

Joelson, of course, forwarded the letter to the Bureau. The Bureau's reply was predictable. In an internal memo discussing the framing of the reply, mention was made that Ginsberg failed to mention in his original letter that he was expelled from Czechoslovakia. It also cites a quote from a noted director of a narcotics clinic in Harlem who told *Time* magazine, in referring to Ginsberg: "They should be picked up by the scruff of their necks, and scrubbed down with Tide and Lestoil." With that option apparently scrapped, the memo ends with:

> 11. GINSBERG states: "I'm not sure what to do to protect myself from the Treasury Department. . . ." It would appear from the letter written by GINSBERG that he is doing nothing more than to set up some form of entrapment defense, prior to and in the event that he should ever be arrested by any City, State, or Federal authorities for violation of the Narcotic Laws.

The Bureau then furnished a response to Congressman Joelson, which ended with a caveat about responding directly to the poet's letter:

> I am enclosing for your information a copy of the recent "Marijuana Newsletter" published by "Lemar." It is respectfully suggested, in view of the facts of this matter, that you do not honor Mr. Ginsberg's comments by a reply. If you do choose to reply, it would not be a surprise to see your letter published in the "Marijuana Newsletter" out of context.

Joelson, however, braved a reply. Although it was never published in the "Marijuana Newsletter," it was not a work without literary merit:

> In reply to your letter of November 30, 1965, I would advise you that I have been in touch with the Bureau of Narcotics and am of the

opinion that nothing has been done in your case that is illegal or inconsistent with law enforcement practices designed to enforce the narcotics laws.

With reference to your remarks that, "We really ought to be done with all this silly shooting" in Vietnam, I believe that although you may have received some acclaim as a poet you lack credentials when it comes to political and international affairs.

Do you really think that if persons having the philosophy of the Viet Cong take over you could possibly survive as a creative writer? Can you believe that you would be allowed to continue to publish your type of work any more than you could have under Hitler?

If you were spared execution or harsh imprisonment, you would be shipped to pick crops, work on an assembly line, or anything else that might please a local commissar.

There may be pros and cons as to our involvement in South Vietnam, but when you dismiss it as "this silly shooting" you show yourself to be as superficial as you are flippant.

More details of the alleged plot to set up Ginsberg surfaced when Jack Martin went on trial in New York on April 13, 1966. The *New York Times*, under a headline, "U.S. Plot to 'Set Up' Ginsberg for Arrest Is Described to Jury," reported testimony by Narcotics Agent Bruce Jensen, who testified that he had asked Martin whether Ginsberg ever possessed or sold narcotics and, in addition, had asked Martin "if he would assist the Bureau of Narcotics as an informant." Although nothing ever came out of this federal intrigue, Ginsberg fared a little worse at the hands of the local magistrates of his home town. In October 1966 he read poetry at the Paterson Y.M.H.A. and, in an off-hand remark, mentioned that he had visited the beautiful Passaic Falls that afternoon. The poet was so impressed by their beauty, he had smoked some marijuana to heighten the experience.

The next day Frank X. Graves, Jr., Paterson's mayor, read the statement in the newspaper and ordered a warrant for Ginsberg's arrest. The next time the poet returned to his home town to read, local police swooped in, and he was charged with smoking marijuana while viewing Passaic Falls. After a short and entertaining trial, the ludicrous charges were of course dropped.

However, by 1966 it was clear that the marijuana laws would be selectively enforced, this time against the new minority group that was so flagrantly using the contraband substance. At the Bureau a campaign was once again set in motion, using the same case history format of the earlier drives against the weed. Even though Anslinger was long gone to the bucolic valley of Hollidaysburg, Pennsylvania, his protégés had learned their lessons well. In a 1966 report entitled "Marihuana Traffic," the case is made of a "dramatic" increase in the total use of marijuana. And the culprits could be found on the college campuses, infecting the nation's youth, once again. After noting a partial list of thirty-one campuses where the marijuana scourge was spreading, a new scapegoat was singled out:

> It is interesting to note a class of individuals who have descended on our institutes of learning, often bringing the drug habit with them. This is a strange breed of beatnik types known as "fringes." These are persons, as the term applies [*sic*], living on the fringe of academic life. They do not attend school but move on and off the campus with the students, tainting them as they go. From Harvard Square to Berkeley, California, these characters are content to become leeches on the academic atmosphere, expounding their theories on changing our nation while daily engaging in the use of drugs and other forms of vice.
>
> The Bureau of Narcotics has in its files heartbreaking stories of the young coed who becomes enmeshed with the beatnik, physically and mentally, supporting him as they go from her monthly allowance.

Though the spirit of Anslinger still informed the work of the Bureau in Washington, the Old Man was far from silent in semiretirement. Never one to miss a good battle against the reefer crowd, Anslinger spread the antidrug gospel every chance he got. Typical of this was his commencement address delivered June 5, 1966, to the budding young citizen-graduates of Saint Francis College in Loretto, Pennsylvania:

> A very great deal of the unrest and trouble being generated on the campuses of United States colleges today can be blamed directly on weak-willed administrators who somehow confuse academic freedom with anarchy. . . . Five years ago the abuse of drugs on the American campus was unheard of. Then, spurred by teachings of ultra-liberal professors, it spread like wildfire. The first real shock came at Oxford where the grandson of former Prime Minister Harold Macmillan died from an overdose of heroin and cocaine. From that time on it appeared all over the world. This has happened (the abuse of drugs) at 16 colleges and universities in this State and 100 throughout the nation. . . . Drugs have killed more people in the world than hydrogen bombs will ever destroy. . . .

> There is considerable slaughter on the highways today due to the driver's being under the influence of marihuana or other drugs. These murderers remain undetected. We are engaged in research to determine whether the driver was using drugs. . . .
>
> You are facing a world where you will need all your senses. Your mind must not be dulled by drugs. You must be alert; completely on guard at all times, not only in the competition of the business world, but in all activities.
>
> Graduates, we beg of you, we beseech you to find some way to destroy the intellectual sanctions which promote free drugs, free love, and other dangerous freedoms. If not checked, these false prophets will put this nation on the road to ruin just as they have done in previous civilizations. . . .
>
> Remain faithful to your beliefs. Trust in yourselves. Believe in your courage and follow where courage bids you go. Place your hand without fear in the hand of the Gentle Guide who will lead you through the winding road which goes uphill all the way. If we be dust, then the whole world is our country and everybody in it our kin. May Divine Providence send you rich blessings in the years ahead.

Though of course we all were dust, it was clear that to Anslinger, some kin were closer than other kin. For at the very time that address was being given, the former commissioner was sewing up a behind-the-scenes move that would banish marijuana from the United States forever, or so the proponents of the Single Convention on Narcotic Drugs hoped. Actually, the Single Convention, which was an international treaty regulating narcotic drugs throughout the world, had been passed originally in 1961. At that time Anslinger had been a prime mover behind the convention; however, a last-minute move to dilute the strength of some of the prohibitions had left a bad taste in the Commissioner's mouth, and the Bureau had recommended that the United States not be a signatory to the treaty.

But with the specter of marijuana and LSD-crazed militants occupying every last "sacred hall" of learning, Anslinger moved to resurrect the treaty and once and for all bind marijuana to stringent international control. On April 27, 1967, Anslinger, along with a deputy assistant Secretary of State and a special assistant to the Secretary of Treasury were the only witnesses before the Senate Foreign Relations Committee. Naturally, all three favored ratification of the long-dormant treaty.

But it was Anslinger who, with characteristic frankness, told the senators the reason for the sudden interest in the pact:

> Another important reason for becoming a party to the 1961 convention is the marijuana problem. . . . Several groups in the United States are loudly agitating to liberalize controls, and, in fact, to legalize its use. In the convention it is very specific that we must prevent its misuse. If the United States becomes a party to the 1961 convention we will be able to use our treaty obligations to resist legalized use of marijuana. This discussion is going on all over the country, in many universities, and in fringe groups, and it is rather disturbing.

Oddly enough, the Foreign Relations Committee heard no witnesses in opposition to the treaty, even though there was no uniform agreement with respect to the regulation of marijuana, even within the government, at this point. Earlier that year the President's Commission on Law Enforcement and Administration of Justice issued its report, "The Challenge of Crime in a Free Society," in which serious doubts were expressed about the severity of the regulations against marijuana. The commission, noting that the marijuana-leads-to-crime-and-heroin theory seemed shoddy, called for an exhaustive study of the use of marijuana under the aegis of the National Institute of Mental Health.

Anslinger's answer was to railroad the Single Convention through the Senate while no one was looking. After the one-day hearing, the treaty passed the Senate by a vote of 84 to 0, without debate, of course. The event was so unremarkable that the *New York Times* didn't even bother to report the passage. But, for the time being at least, Anslinger had the last laugh. Mocked by the hippies, crucified in their underground press, unceremoniously dumped from office by a young, vigorous president who might well have been a weed smoker himself, the bald-domed crusader had his revenge. For even today, in 1978, responsible legislators and prudent administrators point to the Single Convention when explaining why marijuana can never be legalized in America. Citing the *Missouri* v. *Holland* migratory bird case as a precedent, Anslinger's legacy has effectively throttled the dreams of those who would see marijuana dispensed from every corner store, as if they were Kent 100's. The Old Man had scored quite a victory that day in May 1967, and he knew it. "We've got [it] locked up so tightly now, they'll never change the law," he exulted—and so far, he was right.

Sloman was on the phone with Alfred Lindesmith in Bloomington, Indiana. Lindesmith was a longtime foe of Anslinger's, one of the bleeding-heart liberal academics who were always propounding these ridiculous theories that drug addicts need medical care and not incarceration. The Commissioner had moved at various times against Lindesmith, sending agents to his campus at Indiana University, trying to suppress studies and generally foment trouble. The old sociology professor was in his eighties by now, but it was clear to the reporter that he was not at all adverse to reminisce about Anslinger.

"You can't believe what Anslinger says, either, you know," Lindesmith cautioned. "An entrepreneur and a politician like Anslinger is playing a game, and it was perfectly obvious to me when I met him at the White House Conference. I took the subject seriously, I was serious about it when I was doing it, I wasn't playing any goddamn games, and I was afraid at first that Anslinger might have connections with underworld characters and he'd send someone out here and knock me off, which would have been the easiest goddamn thing in the world to do. Okay, now he isn't that type of person; he could have done it easy.

"Okay, now I'm in the White House Conference of 1962 in this big room, and there's a recess, and I wanted to go visit a judge I knew who was in trouble at that time because Anslinger was critical of him because he granted bail to a narcotics offender. So I started off across the room, and lo and behold, suddenly Anslinger is in front of me talking to somebody. And we both had to turn sideways to get past, and he looked at my name tag and said, 'Ah, Doctor Lindesmith,' and he extended his hand, the only words I had ever had with him, and he said, 'You've, uh, you've contributed something to this party.'

" 'Mr. Anslinger,' I said, 'You've made my life very interesting, too.' And he smiled benignly, and it was perfectly obvious to me at that meeting when I met him and Giordano and the other flunkies who had assailed me violently in the smearing way when they wrote that rebuttal on the ABA-AMA report, it was perfectly obvious to me that they were just playing a game. They had no grudge against me; I was just a cipher in the situation, and this was a tactic they used."

While in State College, Sloman had been crashing at the apartment of Bill Cluck, Pennsylvania's twenty-year-old NORML area coordinator. Cluck also happened to run the local head shop, the Lazy J, and he set out to introduce Sloman to State College's leading dopesters.

One morning, after one of those late-night introductions, Sloman and Cluck were talking in the Lazy J.

"I'm young, I'm only twenty," Bill began to reminisce. "I got the education of the sixties in the last two years. It's mind-blowing. I figure I got four or five years to fuck around with doing this NORML stuff, then I can make my million or whatever."

The conversation then turned to the Bellefonte American Legion and the Moose Club, both of which had been raided the previous evening, with the raiding police confiscating slot machines and "other gambling devices," as the news reports put it. However, the chat kept getting interrupted by customer after customer who came in inquiring whether Cluck had any Whippets.

"What are Whippets?" Sloman asked the head-shop entrepreneur and marijuana law reformer.

Bill smiled. "It's just nitrous oxide capsules, but we can't keep them in the store. They line up for blocks when we have these in stock. They help us unload the truck when the nitrous comes in."

"But how does it work?" the reporter wondered.

"Ah, you gotta get a machine. A twenty-dollar pint whipper. It's just like a whipped-cream machine." Cluck turned coy.

"And you sell those, huh?" Sloman almost sneered.

A big cream-eating grin crossed Cluck's face, then he laughed. "Are you crazy? Of course we do."

Following the lead of Ginsberg and Tim Leary and other sources credible to the new generation, the use of marijuana burgeoned during the sixties, especially among white middle-class youth. And for the first time its use became associated with a political position that was inimical to the government. Whereas during the other decades of its utilization in America marijuana served as a purely recreational drug for its devotees, in the sixties the weed took on additional politically charged meaning.

While it was the first time that marijuana became associated with an overtly political stance, *i.e.*, antiwar, antiauthority, from the enforcement point of view, it would not be the first time the marijuana laws could be applied politically. So by the late 1960s, a concerted effort was made to make political arrests by charging the targets with possession of small amounts of marijuana. The classic cases, of course, were the cases of Tim Leary, John Sinclair, Otis Lee Johnson, and Mark Rudd. Four activists, all of different stripe, all arrested in various parts of the country, all receiving outrageous sentences (most over ten years) for possession of minute amounts of grass.

In fact, this idea of making political arrests using marijuana as the violation was institutionalized in 1968 by the Federal Bureau of Investigation as part of a program called "Cointel," a counterintelligence program designed to disrupt the New Left.

The original idea was proposed in a memo from C. D. Brennan to William Sullivan, a high-ranking FBI official. Its goal was clear:

> . . . to expose, disrupt and otherwise neutralize the activities of this group (New Left) and persons connected with it. It is hoped that with this new program their violent and illegal activities may be reduced if not curtailed.

The plan called for a number of "dirty tricks" to be played on the Leftist leadership, including forged letters creating rifts, phony articles planted in friendly media, and "the use of cartoons, photographs, and anonymous letters which will have the effect of ridiculing the New Left."

Additionally, marijuana was seen as a potent tool to disrupt the Leftist opposition:

> Since the use of marijuana and other narcotics is widespread among members of the New Left, you should be alert to opportunities to have them arrested by local authorities on drug charges. Any information concerning the fact that individuals have marijuana or are engaging in a narcotics party should be immediately furnished to local authorities and they should be encouraged to take action.

This strategy would also work against the antiwar coffeehouses that were springing up near every large army base in the United States. Again, marijuana was a convenient entry for the authorities.

> The field was previously advised that New Left groups are attempting to open coffeehouses near military bases in order to influence members of the Armed Forces. Wherever these coffeehouses are, friendly news media should be alerted to them and their purpose. In addition, various drugs, such as marijuana, will probably be utilized by individuals running the coffeehouses or frequenting them. Local law enforcement authorities should be promptly advised whenever you receive an indication that this is being done.

Along with politicos, musicians were once again being busted for possession of marijuana. For the sixties had witnessed a renaissance of the reefer song. Only now the songs were rock and roll anthems as opposed to the sly, whimsical jazz ditties of the thirties. Most everyone, from the Beatles on down, publicly admitted they smoked grass in interviews, and, from the Beatles (except for Ringo) on down, they got popped for possession. Some groups, like the Grateful Dead, even went on to write songs about being arrested for grass, crying all the way to their accountants' offices.

Ofttimes the sentences would be completely disproportionate to the offense. In some states violators charged with simple possession actually received fifty-year jail sentences! Each state had idiosyncratic laws, and within each state the sentences could vary greatly, depending on which judge was trying the case.

But it wasn't always the length of the sentence that told the tale. Sloman had encountered many "horror" stories during his research with respect to the number of years sentenced per joint as one variable. But in many cases the simple arrest process would serve to radically alter the life of the defendant. That was the case of a friend of the reporter's, who'll be called Marvin in this account, lingering testimony to the lifelong implications of his arrest in 1967.

Marvin's story was a common one in the sixties. He was a nice Jewish boy, a credit to his race and religion, enrolled in graduate school in Political Science in 1967 at the University of Wisconsin. He had turned on for the first time in Paris, during a year's stay abroad at the Sorbonne. The first thing he had smoked was some hashish, while enjoying some records in the listening room of the American Embassy.

But it was at Wisconsin that Marvin first started experimenting seriously with drugs. He became a confirmed dope smoker as well as a dabbler in acid and speed. It was the speed that enabled him to flunk his physical, too, along with ten tabs of a migraine drug that had the L and S without the D. And it was after flunking the physical that he decided to go down to Mexico to take in some sun, eat some mushrooms, and cop some gold to bring back to the quasi-commune he was staying in.

In Mexico his intent was to score a few pounds of grass, sell about half, and keep the rest as his group's stash. But once South of the Border he met up with another American who had similar notions, and they decided to combine forces and bring home a payload of thirty kilos, stuffed into the sideboards of Marvin's shiny new Alfa Romeo. Near Acapulco they made a contact, took a cab into the bushes, scored some great grass, and brought it back to their hotel room to clean it and compress it by hand into chunk-size parcels that were then stuffed into the window panels of the car.

"You know, it's really strange"—Marvin was recounting the story to Sloman, sitting in the second-floor living room of his three-story townhouse in Mount Pleasant, an area of Washington, D.C., undergoing a middle-class urban renewal—"I wasn't really aware of what the consequences were. I was really sort of naïve about it. You don't feel there's anything wrong with what you're doing. You think somebody who thinks something's wrong is crazy. In some sense it was exciting to be driving toward the border with thirty kilos of grass secreted in your car. You knew it was illegal. But I wasn't that much into grass as a mystique myself. I liked grass for what it did with my imagination. It helped me to discover for myself that I had this kind of imagination. I had come from a fairly restricted kind of environment."

"Did it have political meaning for you?" Sloman settled deeper into the comfortable couch and scanned the walls of the living room. The room was filled with large plants and attractive macrames and *objets d'art.*

"Afterwards," Marvin recollected. "After I was busted. At that time I was really more interested in discovering who I was, what my capabilities were, doing something different from the expectations of my family or the milieu I grew up in. I was more rebelling against those expectations than any overriding social consciousness. I was interested in getting laid. I was interested in getting stoned."

"So you just wanted to get this shit back into the United States and get high and get laid?"

"Right. I saw it as a very innocent thing to do. I wasn't hurting anybody. Admittedly it was illegal, but I was doing it essentially for other people to have a good time, for myself to have a good time, for myself to make a buck."

"So you packed it into the car . . ."

"Packed it into the car, drove up north, got to Brownsville, Texas, on Christmas Day. Thought that it would be cool going through on Christmas Day, that everybody would be pretty merry. Instead, there wasn't much traffic on Christmas Day, and they had a lot of time to think about who was going through and why did someone want to go through on this holiday, and they stopped us, checked the car real close, and found the dope."

Marvin's narrative was hesitant, full of blank spots. It was obviously painful to even relate the episode that had occurred some eleven years ago. Since the arrest, Marvin had returned to Washington and for the past few years had been working in his father's plumbing subcontracting business. In fact, he was still wearing his tie and sport shirt as he related the story to the reporter.

"You come up to the border station and you anticipate the guy saying, 'Hi. How are you? Go on through.' Instead, he says, 'Hi. How are you? Why don't you get out of the car? Why don't you empty everything out of the car?' That was the first time I felt nervous."

The two smugglers had left the car as the Customs man started pawing through the blankets and trinkets that were there to give the impression of simple tourism. However, the C-man found six seeds on the back floor, found that the windows wouldn't roll down completely, and a few seconds later had the pair under arrest.

"It's so weird. There's nothing you can do. You stand right there and watch them go through the damn thing. You think it's not real. 'What's going on, man? Who are you to look at this stuff?' And the guy just keeps on looking. I started arguing with them. I was screaming that there was nothing wrong with this. That it doesn't hurt anybody. Those kind of arguments. I was screaming, 'It's good for you!' They just said, 'Get into line. Go to that room.' It was like they had heard it all before."

The next thing they knew, the pair was sharing a cell, along with a few other would-be felons in the Brownsville jail. To call it culture shock was quite an understatement. "I started to cry," Marvin remembered. "My first feeling was that they shouldn't separate me from the guy I was with. He was the only one I knew. Going to jail was just so far away from anything I'd ever thought about or conceived. I just didn't know what to do."

"You never thought there was a possibility that if you brought sixty pounds of marijuana into the country, they might pop you?"

Marvin smiled sheepishly. "I never thought of it. Well, I considered it, but blanked it out of my mind as inconceivable. I was naïve. Today I would think of it, obviously. Back then I had never been in trouble. I had never had any relationship to anything that was illegal. I didn't see myself as a character who was a criminal, even though I was bringing marijuana across the border. I didn't see that as a criminal act. Subsequently, people said that was insanity. That I didn't see the consequences of my actions. But I didn't see smoking marijuana as a criminal act. I've never seen it that way and I still don't. It's not a criminal act."

"But there you were."

"There I was. In jail." Marvin shuddered and laughed nervously.

He stayed in jail a week, along with a bunch of Mexicans who knew no English, a few hardened criminals in for rape or murder, and one kindred spirit who was there for bank robbery because he had wanted to give a present to his wife, lacked the do-re-mi, and had robbed a bank. For the middle-class dropout it was still a shock. This was commune city, bunk beds, one overflowed toilet in the middle of the room, beans, coffee and oatmeal for food. A week later his father flew in, arranged bail, and took his errant son back to D.C.

"What was your parents' reaction?" Sloman expected the worst.

"They couldn't believe it," Marvin smiled involuntarily. "Didn't know what to make of it. Their reaction essentially was that I had gone crazy. As far as they were concerned, I was crazy. My mother was ready to commit me."

In lieu of commitment to a psychiatric institution in Saint

Louis, Marvin chose to visit a local Washington Freudian three times a week.

While seeing the shrink, Marvin obtained a job working in a bookstore, establishing a pattern of normality that would come in handy when the trial, which kept getting postponed by Marvin's lawyer, would come up. Finally, about two years after the arrest, Marvin and his family went back to Texas to stand trial before a federal judge. And right away something seemed odd.

"I don't know if there were some shenanigans going on or not, because the attorney said that with a certain amount of money, he could be sure that I wouldn't go to jail. I don't know if he was paying off the judge. I don't know if he had already spoken with the judge and knew what his mind was and was pocketing the money or what." Marvin still shook his head in disbelief.

"How much did it cost?"

"Twenty thousand dollars. For the whole thing. Including the lawyer in Washington. That's a lot of money, I think. I got a seven-year suspended sentence and five years' probation. And a $5,000 fine."

"So it cost you $25,000 in legal fees and fines. How much did the grass cost?"

"That was cheap. That was $80.00 per kilo. My share was $2,400. I lost about $30,000 or $35,000."

"You lost your new sports car."

"Yeah, I lost $35,000 on that deal. That was a business disaster. Bad deal." Marvin chuckled.

But the probation was far worse than the fine. Marvin eventually gave up his bookstore job to attempt a career as a freelance photographer. He was quite good—got a few pictures in *Life* magazine as well as the European weeklies. But he hit a snafu when he had to cover events out of town. Although it was in violation of the terms of his parole, Marvin covered those events anyway. However, his arrest would ultimately come back to haunt him.

"Where it did affect me was when I was trying to become a legitimate photographer and trying to get published in legitimate magazines. There, I couldn't get credentials. I was trying to make contacts with news agencies like Black Star or whatever. I finally got a job to take a picture of something that was going on at the White House. I had been in the White House before when I hooked up with a woman reporter from the *Los Angeles Times* who was doing pieces on Nixon's staff. So I'd go into the White House with her and take pictures of Rosemary Woods or Haldeman or Ziegler. I'd be able to get into the White House as long as I was with her and under her credentials.

"But this one time I got the assignment, I tried to get in by myself, and when you go in, you have to go through the security guards and they ask your name, social security number, and your birthdate. That time they said I just couldn't go in. I asked why, and they just said I couldn't go in. I knew why, but I didn't want to press the issue.

"Meanwhile, that was a first assignment from this New York agency, and I couldn't go in. I was interested in news photography and in Washington, if you're gonna be in news, you have to get credentials."

"So that screwed up your photography career?"

"I thought so. Even if you want to free-lance for *Time* or *Newsweek*, you have to be able to cover all these security things. I couldn't do it."

So Marvin did the next logical thing. He went back to dealing; dealing much more than before he was busted. "I went back to dealing because I still didn't want those things imposed on me. I became more politicized. I became more aware of myself as an individual living in a social context. Where certain people out there set up the rules that are to their own benefit. Before, I was unthinking; I accepted the rules. Then I became aware that those rules benefit certain social groups and try to impose a certain way of living. In a sense I became more distant from what the whole trial experience and what the intention of probation was. Outwardly I was working, but inwardly I wasn't with them. I was still trying to find out what I wanted to do with myself."

What his psychiatrist would call his "antisocial behavior" exhibited itself in other ways during the five years under probation. Along with dealing regularly, Marvin started stealing from retail stores. "I did all kinds of weird things. I got into stealing. I became more rebellious after I got busted. I stole anything, petty theft. Clothing. Supermarkets. I became more paranoid. I just resented the authority. I wanted to fight that authority. That attitude eventually became a political attitude, but at first it was a psychological attitude.

"I stole for two or three years. Petty theft. Defiance. I'd just walk into a store and, if I felt like I wanted something, I'd pick it up and split. I was behaving like a criminal. I *was* a criminal. But I still don't think of myself as a criminal. I wasn't reformed. They didn't get to me. I still don't think of it as a criminal act. Now I've come to understand that smuggling is in a different category than smoking. It's a tax violation. Smuggling is a bigger act. Smoking is just an individual act, smuggling—you're bringing it in for other people."

Marvin finished his probation in 1974 and began settling in to a more conventional lifestyle. He had turned thirty during his term and that, more than anything else, set him to thinking about his future. The job with his father's plumbing subcontracting business gave him a certain amount of autonomy and job security and time to develop his other budding interests, like gourmet cooking, scuba diving and sailing. So here he was in a beautiful renovated townhouse in Mount Pleasant, dating a Washington girl who worked for a private consulting firm, worrying about a second-story ripoff artist who had struck Marvin's house three times, each time taking off with cameras and hi-fi equipment. The big turnaround.

"So, miraculously, you finish your probation and here you are, Mr. Middle-America," Sloman marveled.

"In a certain sense I'm doing what I was brought up to do," Marvin conceded softly.

"Work in your father's business. Take it over. Be a nice Jewish boy." Sloman recited the three commandments.

"Right. Worry about what to buy. Worry about what color sheets to get. All the kind of stuff involved in a normal middle-class life. But also I keep to myself in terms of my own lifestyle: whom I go out with, whom I sleep with, what drugs I take, my attitudes toward government and politics. I still feel alienated from them. I don't think that will ever change. I'll always feel sort of cynical toward government. The less government, the better. The less the government imposes on you, the better. That kind of attitude as a permanent change came about from being busted. Rather than seeing the government as something benevolent, something that helps you, something that you need, you see government as politics, or something that's restrictive or imposing.

"On one side, everything's normal like it's supposed to be. It's a middle-class existence. I know that. I'm not leading any wild kind of life. I go to work every day. Submit bids. I might have gone into photography more. If it were possible for me to get a job in that field, I would probably still be doing it."

"What if you hadn't gotten busted? What if you had made it across that border?"

Marvin paused. "I don't know. I would've sold that dope. Smoked and not worried. Probably done it again. I think I would be less conventional now."

"You look at it and you say, 'Jesus, they busted you.' " Sloman swept a hand out, taking in the room, with its ornaments and plants and coffee table and *Yachting* magazine and gourmet cookbooks. "You served five years' probation, seeing a shrink the whole time, so that theoretically you're becoming adjusted; you went into your father's business, bought a house in an area where the middle class is swarming in to renovate. All the exterior trappings. They succeeded. On one level they succeeded."

Marvin nodded. "I agree."

"Yet there's this whole other level. Another side that's completely alienated."

"They've succeeded in the sense that I'm working"—Marvin was absentmindedly playing with a package of glueless rolling papers—"but they don't succeed in terms of attitude. Respect for them. Patriotic feeling. Nationalism. They've lost that. I don't know what that will mean in the future if there's a lot of people who feel that way."

"Over 2 million people were popped for grass in the last six years," Sloman reminded him.

"Most of them are probably middle-class people. That could be a problem. Dope could be the reason why we didn't want to fight the war in Vietnam. That whole patriotic 'My country, right or wrong' feeling isn't there for me anymore. I can't say, 'I pledge allegiance!' I feel real awkward. I went to a meeting of associated builders and contractors and they started the meeting by saying the Pledge of Allegiance. That was the first time I've had to say it since high school. And I couldn't say it. I couldn't get there."

"The implications of this are staggering, in that they're creating a whole caste of people who are fairly conventional in their lifestyles, but who are totally cynical. Totally alienated. Probably not hesitant to defy authority again."

"But essentially nonviolent people," Marvin cautioned, "which I think is a problem, because they're violent out there. They'll beat you over the head. I don't feel that violence toward the government. I don't want to get into a gunfight with them. Mine is a different kind of defiance than real outward political defiance."

"You still smoke grass?" Sloman wondered, noting the gourmet rolling papers.

"Shit, yeah. Every night. I smoke more now than when I was busted. I still use it to go to sleep. I still like to fantasize with it. I don't mind having hallucinations with it."

"Did you get closer with your family as a result of the bust?"

Marvin smiled. "Not immediately after I was busted. I saw them first as part of the enemy. They saw me as crazy. Years later, five, six, seven years later, we got close. I think it was more a function of my getting older. Even today they still don't accept it. They see that whole period of my life as an aberration."

"To them you're a cured mental patient?"

"Yeah." Marvin shrugged. "I'm healthy again; I'm better now. Their old son again in some ways. They can talk to me again."

"Ever tempted to go back to Mexico?" Sloman smiled.

"No, I haven't been back. I've been to Jamaica and Haiti, though."

"Did you bring back any goodies?"

"I was tempted to, but I didn't do it. I wouldn't smuggle again. I wouldn't smuggle dope."

"What would you smuggle?"

Marvin laughed. "Emeralds from Colombia. I'd think carefully again before doing any kind of smuggling. When I came back from Haiti, every time I'd go through, there was a big book where they checked your name. My name never came up. I don't know who they have in those books, but every time I go through Customs, I worry."

Sloman began wrapping up the interview, as the aroma of Marvin's chicken fricassee wafted upstairs. "Do you regret what happened?"

"No," Marvin shot back, then hesitated. "I regret having been busted. Not reformed. I regret the whole thing. I regret having to go through the paranoia of being busted. That was unpleasant. But I don't regret trying to bring the dope in. I don't regret smoking dope. I don't feel bad about anything."

"You must regret the $35,000," Sloman quipped.

"The $35,000"—Marvin looked pained once more—"that I regret." With that the plumbing subcontractor got up and started downstairs to check on his fricassee.

Throughout the sixties Ginsberg continued his media assault on the antiquated marijuana laws. He did the second-line talk shows; "Never the big one, never on Johnny Carson," the poet remembered. In fact, after one 1971 appearance on Cavett, Arthur Godfrey, who was there to tape Cavett's next show, totally wigged, angrily denouncing "this unnatural bearded freak," and then asked Cavett not to run the show. By this time the Bureau had given up on rebuttals, relying on the inherent conservatism of the interviewers to put Ginsberg's comments in an appropriately derogatory context.

But after Ginsberg's 1966 testimony before the Dodd subcommittee on juvenile delinquency, where the poet urged more studies on hallucinogenics, the media began treating his views with more respect. By then he was a veteran poet, noted author, Guggenheim fellow.

All the while his various governmental agency files thickened. While Ginsberg was never arrested on drug charges, his file suggests that the Bureau paid careful attention to his activities. Sometimes this attention bordered on the voyeuristic, as this 1967 memo showed:

> Subject of Memorandum—Photograph of Allen GINSBERG
>
> 1. On this date, I received a photograph of Allen GINSBERG where he is pictured in an indecent pose. For possible future use, the photograph has been placed in a locked sealed envelope marked "Photograph of Allen GINSBERG—Gen. File: Allen GINSBERG." The locked sealed envelope has been placed in the vault of this office for safekeeping.

Although Ginsberg himself escaped a brush with the narcotics laws, his passion for this issue was fueled by the experiences of many of his closest friends who fell prey to Anslinger and his men. Huncke and Burroughs both ran afoul of the narcotics laws, as did the legendary hero of "On the Road," Neal Cassady.

"Cassady's story was very important," Ginsberg remembered. "It relates to what you were asking about whether the whole rise of the counterculture was involved with grass as well as the war. Around 1946 I gave Neal his first grass, I think. Around Broadway and Amsterdam at 92nd Street. Then he got quite into it. By 1949 and 1950 he was smoking all the time. In the middle of Kerouac's *Visons of Cody*, there's a great on-the-spot transcript of a couple of guys, Neal and Jack, getting high real early and talking about Mezz Mezzrow and the jazz cats. They were talking about a visit Neal and I took from Denver in 1947 to Burroughs' marijuana farm in New Waverly, Texas. Burroughs had left New York and had this farm with Huncke and his wife Joan, and he had a big marijuana garden. Burroughs and Huncke and Neal drove off to New York later and sold the stuff in Times Square.

"Neal got more and more involved in smoking grass. He was sort of a Johnny Appleseed of grass, going around giving grass to everybody in San Francisco. He went on a one-man campaign to turn on everybody in the Bay Area up to 1950. He was well-known by everyone. He was there, and there was this big counterculture. He was the one running around giving grass to everyone and going to Mexico as a railroad man and bringing a whole bunch back. Not to sell, but to give away. He was the big connection for North Beach when North Beach was the big hippie haven. 1957 Beatnik Summer. By 1960 it had spread nationally.

"He became notorious and was known by the police. He was giving it to everybody. He was working on the railroad, too. In fact, he was getting high while he was the main brakeman in the back of the Eisenhower campaign train. He was smoking grass while he was swinging his red brakeman's lantern. He was living on Russian Hill and had to get to work one day and hitched a ride with a couple of guys who took him downtown, and he traded them a stick of pot for the ride. It turned out that they were police. They waited a month or so, then went to him with a warrant and busted him. He was sentenced to five to ten years in jail for one joint. This was 1959. We visited him in San Quentin."

"He lost his Pacific Railroad job, too," Peter added.

"He did two and a half years." Ginsberg almost shouted. "He was one of the early political martyrs. Cassady of all people—he was so nonpolitical—was one of the early political martyrs to the drug law." Ginsberg shook his hairy head.

"He was so happy and full of energy," Orlovsky remembered with a tinge of sadness in his voice.

"He was in two and a half years," Ginsberg continued. "It was an enormous time, right in the middle of his life. It was a criminal thing. That's why I hate the Narcotics Bureau so much. They took this beautiful boy away and put him in jail for two years. This hero. For nothing! The anguish and tragedies the Narcotics Bureau has caused is uncalculable. In California they make 80,000 busts a year and like 60,000 of them are kids."

"Under eighteen. Sixty percent under eighteen," Peter noted.

"Can you imagine 40,000 people being taken from their homes and dragged to jail? And Neal among them. Great people among them. Billie Holiday. But they threw the book at Neal because they knew who he was. The narcs were out to get him," Ginsberg added bitterly.

"So he really changed, huh?" Sloman wondered. "He was kind of carefree and he came out sort of broken?"

Ginsberg shook his head vigorously. "No, he wasn't broken. He came out stronger than ever. Smarter than ever. But the cheerfulness was no longer there. He was a slightly grim person. He never could get another job again that was as good, and it messed up his family. Soon after his bust there was a lot of amphetamine coming on the scene, partly because busting him threw a crimp into grass; it traumatized the grass scene. He continued his lively energetic career with Ken Kesey.

"Neal was an old vet, though. He had had a lot of notoriety as the prototype of 'On the Road.' So people knew who he was. But the reason I have such a grudge against Podhoretz and all the literary people who attacked Kerouac is because, rather than respecting him, by coming on with such a negative attitude to this essentially American optimism and lyricism and making it into a monstrous image, they perhaps unwittingly left it open to a police state mentality to try to bust and persecute literary people who were of that school. Instead of being treated with dignity as a hero, a literary prototype, and a person of energy and artistic interest, Neal was treated as some sort of social monster, and the whole beat thing was treated as a social monsterhood. This left it easy prey.

"When he got busted in 1958, instead of it being a headline in the San Francisco papers that this heroic literary person, friend of Kerouac and myself, had put San Francisco on the map, had been busted and what a shame, instead of being a Sartre-like international scandal, nobody knew and nobody cared. As if it were just another fuck head, dope fiend, beatnik. It was tragic.

"And we were all helpless to do anything. The barrage of beatnikoid imagery sprayed through the media had given the literary scene such a questionable name. First, you had to explain yourself before you could go on. Much less go through history and explain what was wrong with the marijuana laws. So there was Neal, the dope fiend, in San Quentin for two and a half years. Only he knew how unreasonable and irrational the law was. The law, the lawyers, the courts, the police. A giant conspiracy to put him in jail for nothing. Moloch squatting over men's brains."

Ginsberg paused for breath, playing with his beard absent-mindedly. Peter was just silently shaking his head, his long ponytail flailing his back.

Sloman broke the silence. "In effect, what happens after that is the development of a supportive counterculture in which somebody can get busted and *not* think that he's the only one."

"Everybody knew that on a personal level!" Ginsberg shouted, almost in anguish. "On a poetic level. On a literary level. It just hadn't reached the papers."

Of course that was to change in the sixties. And one of the reasons for the rapid increase in the use of marijuana was the shift in the media with regards to the drug. Because more and more journalists began using grass and experiencing firsthand the discrepancy between its effects and the awesome, horrible effects attributed to it by officialdom, more articles took a different view toward the drug itself.

Another great source of media attention was the Draconian penalties that were meted out during the sixties to white, young middle-class Americans. In October 1969 *Life* magazine put pot on its cover and featured a story about a Danville, Virginia, long-distance runner who wound up behind bars serving a twenty-year sentence for transporting three pounds of marijuana.

But even more media scrutiny was centered on celebrity busts, arrests which most often involved the sons and daughters of prominent citizens. Here, even the more conservative elements of the society received no immunity. The list of arrests could have read like a Who's Who: Bebe Rebozo's nephew, Walt Rostow's son, John Steinbeck's son, Spiro Agnew's daughter. In fact, when Robert Kennedy, Jr., and R. Sargent Shriver III were arrested for possession of marijuana on August 8, 1970, Walter Cronkite was moved to note on his nightly news broadcast, "This case is not unusual; more and more parents across the nation find themselves going to court with their children on drug charges. It's becoming an incident of modern living."

But it was not just the youth who were utilizing the drug. In the seventies marijuana broke all the age, class, or racial barriers, and its use became routine among vast new segments. One such group was blue-collar, working-class youth, many of whom received their introduction into the world of marijuana while serving in the armed forces halfway around the world.

Vietnam provided American soldiers with a context in which they could perceive marijuana as a recreational drug, denuded of any political or sociological import. Of course marijuana use among military men was an old tradition in American life from the Philippines to the Canal Zone to India, and it should come as no surprise to find that upwards of 50 percent of the enlisted men in Vietnam admitted to having tried marijuana in a country where potent pot is so available.

But what was so striking about the use of grass in Vietnam was the fact that many of the more conservative and patriotic members of the youth of America were enjoying the same substance that their more radical counterparts back home were crediting with having enlightened them to the immorality of that same war.

Whereas the dissenters at home would associate their use of pot with political and sociological dimensions, marijuana seemed to be used in Vietnam as a coping device. It was this purely recreational use of the drug that would predominate as the seventies moved farther and farther away from the sixties. The veterans who returned to the United States from Vietnam were very much like the Mexicans who migrated to the United States in the early 1900s, working-class people who enjoyed a smoke of marijuana as a diversion from their daily routine. These returning heroes then served as role models for their friends and younger siblings, and marijuana became even more firmly entrenched among the working-class youth.

By the mid-1970s estimates of regular marijuana smokers ran as high as 20 million people, making this cohort a strong closet constituency united by their common predilection for a pleasant change of consciousness. But it seemed that even these numbers did little to change the consciousness of the authorities. Although it was argued that marijuana was not a priority of the Drug Enforcement Agency (the successor to the Bureau of Narcotic and Dangerous Drugs, which superseded the old Bureau of Narcotics), in 1974, 445,600 people were arrested on marijuana violations, the majority of them being young citizens for simple possession.

Of course by now drug enforcement was a big business. When Anslinger left the Bureau to retire to Hollidaysburg, there were 400 agents fighting the battle against drugs. When the Bureau was reorganized under the Justice Department in 1963, their manpower had increased to 2,000. By the mid-1970s, the DEA could boast of having some 10,000 agents scattered throughout the world. And it was more than a little ironic that while thousands of federal and state and local drug enforcement officials were still busting hundreds of thousands of the more than 20 million confirmed potheads, on November 14, 1975, at 1:05 P.M. in a small hospital in Altoona, Pennsylvania, Harry Jacob Anslinger heaved one last sigh and then shrugged off his mortal coil, at last forgetting about traffickers, and killer weeds, and doped racehorses, and his opium pipe collection, at last attaining that peace that he knew deep down in his bones no drug could ever come close to delivering. Although there was no viewing of the body, throughout the country among the cannabis *cognescenti,* thousands of small flames were fired up to mark the occasion.

CHAPTER 14:
A Short Vacation in Hollidaysburg

Sloman finished his research at State College after four days, but he delayed his trip to Washington and the DEA library to travel to Huntington to see someone who had conducted the last interview Harry Anslinger had granted.

Huntington was only thirty miles or so down the road, but there was no public transport to that town. What was worse, Peter, the interviewer, lived in a log cabin about five twisting-dirt-road miles out of the small town. But Sloman was intent on hearing the interview, and somehow by Saturday had persuaded two coeds from State College to drive him down in their car, all expenses paid. So the three packed up the car with beer and contraband and set off that evening.

After three beers, a few pipefuls, and no whippets, the trio finally found the log cabin. Only it wasn't an Abe Lincoln trip; this was a beautiful cabin, complete with wall-to-wall carpeting, nice furniture, and a huge, handsome, wood-burning stove which provided the heat.

The visitors found seats and Peter, who, in his flannels and Pennsylvania Dutch–style beard, reminded Sloman a bit of Lincoln, broke out some beers. It seems that the interview he had with Anslinger was done when he was still a student at Julietta College, a small nearby school. These days Peter was working at a community mental health clinic in a neighboring county.

"I had this guy Greg for a deviance course," Peter remembered, "and I didn't know what to do for a paper, and he said there was this guy down the road that wrote the majority of the drug laws. I didn't know who Harry was or what he was, but he agreed to do an interview for my paper. So I researched him a little bit and saw that he was a pretty heavy dude, and I decided to take a tape recorder along. I went with two other guys to his house. It was on April 21, 1975. He had a nice gold nameplate on his door that said 'Anslinger,' and that sent a chill through me, after reading all about him. He was eighty-two then, short, bald, dark glasses something like yours, turtleneck, sport coat.

"Anyway, he was kinda shaky on his feet, and smaller than he looked in the pictures, kinda shriveled. So I walked in the door and saw a lot of pictures, pictures of him with every president from Hoover to Kennedy, shaking hands. They were hanging all over—James Cagney, John Wayne. He also had a lot of paraphernalia laying around, a set of scales on the table. We talked for thirty minutes with the tape running, then we bull-shitted some more and he took us into the den.

"He had a whole lot of literature there and his books and posters plus a whole huge cabinet full of huge bongs and pipes, nothing like you see in head shops. Something like you'd get in India, Africa. Lots of weapons, too. Guns, machine guns, pearl-handled pistols. I told him he had a real nice gun collection, and he said they were relics of famous crimes.

"We stayed an hour and a half at his house; the other guys really wanted to come along, and they were both pretty tuned up when we pulled in, but I was shaking in my pants. I had been reading about this guy, and from what I understood he was the biggest narc who ever lived. I wasn't gonna fuck around with dope. He'd probably look at my eyes and shoot me. But it didn't matter; as it turned out, he couldn't see anything."

"What was being with him like?" Sloman prodded.

"Wait, I got a question for you," Peter said in his slow, deliberate manner. "The more you research about him, do you think that he believed there was a direct correlation between pot and crime, that pot made you crazy? That if you smoked pot you were an addict and anything could happen to you? Do you believe that he believed that?"

Sloman's answer was a hedge, something to the effect that Anslinger both believed those dictums instinctively and used them for PR purposes. It didn't satisfy Peter.

"I feel that till the end, till I talked to him, Anslinger believed in the direct correlation between smoking pot and going crazy."

"Don't you think it might be that he saw some college students and he decided to give 'em a song and a dance and impress them?" Sloman conjectured.

"Sure it was, but he convinced me." Peter was firm.

"Was he affable? Did you like him at all?" the reporter wondered.

"Oh, yeah, I enjoyed listening to him, but he was very misinformed. But on one hand, at that time, I said to myself, 'What the fuck are you talking about? I been there, buddy, I'm not stupid.' But after I listened to the tape and thought about him and read more, I became convinced that he wasn't bullshitting me at all, that he believed what he was saying. When I came in, I asked him if he had any objections to my recording him, and he said, 'No, I have no fear of tapes.' "

Peter laughed heartily and got up to retrieve the tape. "I listened to this tape at least once a day for a long while." The Anslingerphile flipped the tape to Sloman, who began to put it into the machine. Peter left, and came back with a huge Big Frog Chalice stuffed with marijuana. The pipe made its way around the room as the deep tones of Commissioner Anslinger filled the air:

HARRY: Well, the Supreme Court held that where you have a commodity that is under controversy, and there's a treaty that controls that commodity, uh, say you had a treaty, uh, I think it's *Missouri* vs. *Holland* was the decision rendered by Supreme Court Justice Wendell Holmes. They held that, for instance, migratory birds flew from Canada to Mexico, and the hunters in Missouri were shooting them down, and they put a law through to control it, and the law was hailed unconstitutional because they said that was a matter of states' rights. However, we made a treaty then with Canada and Mexico to protect the migratory birds. Then the hunters went out and shot the birds, and Holland was the U.S. Marshal; he arrested them and that case went to the Superior Court, because without the treaty it was unconstitutional. When they got the treaty, the Supreme Court held, well, now, you have a treaty with other countries to control this commodity, and the Constitution and the laws thereunder, and treaties, are the law of the land. So from that point on our situation in relation to marihuana was analogous to the Supreme Court decision in *Missouri* v. *Holland*.

Now, 108 nations would have to amend it or denounce it. But the United States, Canada and the United Kingdom are the only three countries that are trying to legalize marihuana. Well, this is purely academic, because there's already a Supreme Court decision on it. Either these fellows are talking through their hats or they don't do their night work. If they'd studied the Supreme Court decision in that case, they'd have realized that it couldn't be done. Oh, you can change the law, you can reduce the penalty as they have been doing, but these three nations are the only three countries where legalization is being promoted. All the other countries in the world—there isn't one country in the world that doesn't have laws more severe than ours. In fact, in Africa, where they do have a very severe problem, slaughter on the highway, because here you have a drug where you have no sense of time and distance, and you're driving along the highway at seventy miles per hour, and you think you're going seven miles per hour. And there is slaughter on the highway all over this country, also in Canada, and in the United Kingdom. Now in Africa the natives are so frightened of people who use hashish, which is the same thing as marihuana; there may be fifty different terms for marihuana, but hashish is one of the most prevalent in countries like Egypt, the cradle of civilization, which has a greater hashish-marihuana problem than any country in the world. And they have severe laws.

Now Turkey, they even have the death penalty for possession of marihuana, and there isn't a country in the world that doesn't have very, very strict laws to enforce it. It has been condemned as a dangerous drug by the American Medical Association, by the World Health Organization, and also by the United Nations Commission on Narcotic Drugs. It is one of the worst drugs in relation to the effect on the person's thinking and action. We didn't have any trouble with this drug until 1937, when the states in the Southwest were so up in arms about the crimes, the assaults, the wrecks, killings, murder. . . .

PETER: And they were all directly connected with drug use? They connected all these murders and highway deaths with drug use?

HARRY: They appealed to the federal government for help because, well, there was a lot of interstate traffic; most of the traffic came in from Mexico. In fact, even today most of the marihuana, the viable type, comes in from Mexico. And they have problems there which they have been unable to solve because it's so prevalent.

PETER: What about NORML, the National Organization for the Reform of the Marihuana Laws? They advocate the decriminalization of the penalty, not the legalization. They're in favor of lowering the penalty, and I think they were pretty instrumental in getting a lot of change in Oregon, and in California too.

HARRY: Yeah, I haven't been able to follow them very closely because I can't read anymore and all I get is what I hear on the radio or by telephone from some of my former agents. But I understand that in Oregon, they did have a bad situation there once in Portland, when I was still Commissioner, but I haven't followed too closely, but maybe there it's working, I don't know. I wouldn't be able to tell you.

PETER: In one article the implication was that you thought the marihuana laws were the single, most forceful, laws we had in this country. Do you feel that now you've retired, some of the laws will change?

HARRY: (After a short laugh) I notice that the legislator stays away from it because he knows the women of this country will run him out of office, because they don't want their sons and daughters to be smoking marihuana, but they'll accept it in other countries like India and some of the countries in Africa where it flared up like, like here. The idea of legalization is absolutely out of the question. You're not going to get this government to denounce a treaty to which 108 countries are parties to, particularly since it covers all forms of narcotics. Opium, heroin, morphine, cocaine—which is a very big drug; they haven't tried to legalize that, because there have been some awful things committed in this country by cocaine users.

PETER: I guess part of the reason for the marihuana laws being so tough is the fear of progressing to harder drugs; is that probably a big factor?

HARRY: There is; I had at one time a system whereby I got very quickly the case history of all the teen-agers who were on heroin. And only rarely did I find one who hadn't taken on heroin after starting with marihuana. And I suppose that's still the case today. The progression of getting into the narcotic drug, the progression of one step to the next.

PETER: What about comparing alcohol to marihuana? What's your point of view on that? Given the academic question, is the comparison justified?

HARRY: Well, I tell you, gentlemen, I was also at one time the Assistant Commissioner of Prohibition, and I wasn't a radical. I knew it couldn't work. But they requested me to stay to the end of it until they established the Bureau of Narcotics. But alcohol, after all, doesn't have that prolonged effect that marihuana has. There's where the danger is.

PETER: Are you talking about the incessant use of marihuana, or occasional marihuana users? What's the classification, like hard drinkers?

HARRY: I'm even talking about the man who will use one marihuana cigarette and go out and drive a car and knock things over. A fellow with one or two drinks—it wears off in a couple of hours. Marihuana—that stuff will stay with you for about six hours; you're not going to get away from it. And you don't have that immediate effect. I've investigated it, personally—the case of a young bellboy, smoking marihuana in the hotel, going out and going to the federal building where the army was recruiting and telling the fellow to move aside. They grabbed him, and he grabbed the gun when the guard came in to see what the disturbance was. He got the guard's gun and he killed him. I know that fella had one cigarette, because that's what sort of struck me as peculiar. Here's a boy. He wasn't a drinker, he wasn't a marihuana user; but one of his boyfriends in the hotel induced him to smoke a marihuana, and he went out on the town. He just raised the very devil and then killed someone, and had to go to prison, of course. . . .

PETER: From what I understand, in California the Senate approved the legislation for marihuana reform, but the bill now has to go to the State Assembly.

HARRY: It did? I didn't know that. California they have that, they're so close, adjacent to Mexico across the border. A lot of the stuff they use in New York comes up from California, around that Tijuana area. You'd think Mexicans, with all their trouble, they've got thousands and thousands of cases every year for vicious rapes and assaults. They've never been able to change, 'cause it's so prevalent. They grow most of it. The stuff that used to be grown here was pretty strong. We used to have hemp out in the Midwest that made the best textiles in the world. But the stuff that was grown there during the war when you couldn't get the hemp from Manila, well, it was just grass, that's all. [He laughs.] It had no potency.

Suddenly the tape ran out. The two coeds seemed mesmerized by the dope and the beer and that insistent deep drone that

Harry possessed. The vibration in the room was as thick as the pungent air. Sloman cut it first.

"What was he like after you turned off the tape?"

"We were in a room like this, a very modest house, nicely decorated," Peter was answering a different question. "I didn't see anyone else in the house. I figured he had a housekeeper coming in every day. Someone had to be there to keep an eye on him. When he got out of the chair after the interview, I grabbed him, 'cause he was ready to fall down on the floor. He was pretty shaky. I questioned him about NORML, and he said, 'Who?' He was losing it pretty bad."

"Did he offer you a drink?"

"No. He was very hospitable, though. He greeted us at the door dressed really nice, this turtleneck and plaid jacket. And he shook our hands and for a guy his age spoke really clear. He was really up for an interview. He wouldn't do it in the evenings, though; he said they were bad for him. After I turned off the machine, we went into the den, and I commented on his guns and looked at his books, and he gave me a couple of pamphlets. One was put out by Munch in 1966, listing what a marijuana user looks like: brown fingers, dilated pupils, tends to have zits. He spent a long time going through this box looking for something, but then he said, 'I can't see.' He pulled out this big poster of himself, and he said, 'This is what the hippies up in Greenwich Village think of me.' It was that famous poster of Harry's head, draped with pot leaves. It read, 'Harry J. Anslinger—The Man Who Turned the World Off.' He laughed about that. He seemed to dig our company for a while."

"How did you leave?"

"I think we got pretty satiated with his bullshit. He didn't chase us out. I remember running out of questions. At times feeling 'Fuck it' 'cause he couldn't hear half the things we were saying. He didn't understand some questions, and his responses were always pretty far out, no matter what the question was."

"Did you feel sorry for him?" Sloman finally asked.

"Yeah, I think I did," Peter mused. "He was old; I felt so ambivalent. He was losing it fast, throughout our conversation. You could tell that he was drained. On the other hand, God, it must have been some time when he was peaking on the kind of power he possessed. And now look at him in Hollidaysburg in a small house, flanked by all his guns and scales and pictures . . ."

Peter just trailed off and the room turned eerily quiet, the only sound being the crackling of the logs in the fireplace.

Sloman was excited by the tape, and since he didn't have to be in Washington until Monday, he asked his host to accompany him to Hollidaysburg the next day to try and visit Joseph Leet Anslinger, who was living in Harry's old house. Peter jumped at the offer, and tentative plans were made. The two girls seemed a bit restless by now, so Sloman led the way out. They were accompanied to the car by Peter, who seemed a bit preoccupied.

"Okay!" Peter shouted after them, pausing at the top of the slight incline the girls had just descended. "See you tomorrow. But you know, sometimes when I'm really ripped, off the deep end, sometimes then I think that maybe Harry was right."

Sloman stopped in his tracks and stared back up at Peter. Was this a put-on? If it was, he was a great actor.

"The next time you're ripped and you go off the road into a snowbank, you'll say, 'I believe. Goddamn it, he was right. He was right. He was the Way.' I really believe that sometimes." And with that he waved and disappeared back into the log cabin.

Sloman couldn't get a car the next day, but Peter was so intent on getting Anslinger data that he drove all the way up to State College to pick up the reporter and then backtracked to the Altoona-Hollidaysburg area. It was a briskly beautiful day, a bit cloudy, but invigorating. After a short drive they arrived in Hollidaysburg and immediately stopped at Dave's Dream for a late breakfast.

"Boy, that was fascinating that he started right in talking about the Single Convention when you interviewed him," Sloman marveled. "That must have been the biggest thrill of his life, ramrodding that treaty through. His power was slowly eroding, his critics were getting more and more vocal. Time was proving him to be a shit, and then it all didn't matter. It didn't matter what those weak-kneed bleeding-heart academics thought. They couldn't do shit. It was a treaty. It was the law of the land."

They both attacked their food. "Do you really believe that shit you said last night?" Sloman had to ask.

"Sometimes I believe that Harry was the Way," Peter repeated with a straight face. "I have experienced these revelations in a stoned stupor that 'Jesus Christ, my mind is being ravaged. I can't get anything together.' Maybe he was right in everything he said. Of course, they kind of fade away."

After lunch the two drove to Pine Street and then slowly reconnoitered the street for the magic address. "That's it!" Peter screamed, pointing at a modest looking ranch-style house. "Jesus Christ," he muttered under his breath. They scrambled out of the car and gingerly walked toward the house. "Here's the gold nameplate," Peter hissed, and showed Sloman the treasure. The reporter was bold, though, and he strode up to the porch door and rang the bell. No response.

"I thought I heard someone in there," Peter whispered, and then craned his neck to peek in the window. "It's the same as when I was here. Look, there's all his curios. Jesus, it still looks like a museum."

Meanwhile, Sloman was doing the reporter bit, jotting down the name of the dairy that would come to collect the six empty milk bottles.

But, after ten minutes of knocking and peering and waiting, it was clear that no one was home. Or if they were, they weren't advertising it. So the two trooped back to the car, defeated, until suddenly Sloman came up with a brilliant idea. With Peter in hot pursuit he scurried next door, to a nice art-deco three-story apartment building. After scanning the names on the mailbox, he picked one at random—Mrs. O'Leary—and rang her ground-floor bell. After a few seconds an old woman in curlers opened the door.

"Oh, you're looking for Joseph. He lives next door. Oh, yes, I know him," she answered the reporter without a trace of suspicion. "You're interested in his father, huh? Well, I didn't know him that well, but my deceased husband did. They were both Rotarians. Did you know that Harry built this apartment building? Yes, Mr. Anslinger built this apartment here for an investment. He purchased this land and he built this complex here. You know, I owe my having this apartment to Mr. Anslinger. When he died, his son and his wife moved over to the house next door. But before that, they were living in this apartment."

"What was Mr. Anslinger like?"

"Oh, he was an outstanding man, a very distinguished gentleman. I knew his character and his reputation and he was a great man, but he was just an imposing figure to me. Did he ever talk about his work? Not to me. We didn't socialize with him; my husband had a professional relationship with him, a fraternal one."

"Is he buried in town?" Sloman wondered.

"I don't know." Mrs. O'Leary looked perplexed. "My husband died so soon afterward."

"Did you ever meet his wife?" the reporter pressed on.

"No, his wife was dead." The old woman seemed to hesitate, then leaned conspiratorially toward the pair. "Maybe I shouldn't tell you this, but you're a researcher. Joseph Leet is not Mr. Anslinger's son. He's his wife's son from a former marriage. What I mean is, you will not find any, er, er, Joseph inheriting his father's characteristics. He was adopted by Harry, just a little boy when his mother married. She was a Hollidaysburg girl; her husband died. Mr. Leet died. Joe was not married until late in his life, though. Harry retired in 1962, and that's when Joe came back here."

Mrs. O'Leary's slip was a revelation to the reporter. Throughout his inquiries he had always gotten blank stares from those who knew Anslinger when he had inquired about Harry's son, Joseph Leet Anslinger. It was Sloman's impression that Joseph Leet was deviant in some strange way and that 'Oh, Joseph just didn't seem interested in his father's occupation' seemed too glib an answer to this puzzle. But now the pieces were falling into place. The kid was adopted. Maybe even illegitimate. A whole new vista was opened up to Sloman by this little old lady in curlers and a housecoat.

"What did Joseph do?" he asked casually.

A puzzled look came across Mrs. O'Leary's face. "I don't really know. He was always traveling around; he was hardly ever here. The last I knew of Joseph, he was a drug salesman. He traveled for a drug company."

"Jesus, I should have known!" the reporter shouted involuntarily, and shepherded Peter out the door and eventually in the direction of the cemetery, to stomp for half an hour through knee-high snow looking for a headstone they would never find, leaving poor Mrs. O'Leary standing in her doorway scratching her curlers, convinced that research was far worse on the brain than drugs.

Part 2
Middle-Class Marihuanists

Every new fad, folly or experience, however bizarre, is embraced by people in relation to the manner in which it appeals to their senses or imaginations. If it eventually proves itself to be harmful, uninteresting or foolish, it is dropped by those who are reasonable and have common sense. It is finally embraced by the unstable, emotional, hysterical, degenerate, mentally deficient and vicious classes.

—Harry J. Anslinger—on the historical diffusion of marijuana.

CHAPTER 15:
Smoke, Dolling, Smoke

The trail of marijuana led Sloman out to Bayside, Queens, not far from the neighborhood he grew up in, to have Sunday brunch in the home of his good friend Jeffrey's parents.

The house was a garden apartment nestled in a development adjacent to the Long Island Expressway. Inside, the apartment was furnished like any other middle-aged, middle-class Jewish family's, lots of knick-knacks, a big breakfront full of mementos, old Jews with doleful eyes in gilt-edged frames staring down from the living room walls, eyeing the visitor. The refrigerator, of course, was stuffed to capacity.

But this household boasted something that set it a little bit apart from the surrounding neighbors'. It was the baggie full of Oklahoma homegrown that Jeff's father Abe, sixty-two and a chemical salesman, secreted in his bedroom dresser.

It seemed that Jeff's parents had their first taste of the weed during the 1940s in social clubs in the Bronx, where they grew up. After experimenting occasionally, they never pursued the habit, except on an odd trip to Florida or the Islands. But somehow, as their children grew and progressed into drug experimentation during the sixties, Abe and Lilyan rediscovered the forbidden fruit of their youth, and in the seventies they became confirmed users. It was their story that Sloman was seeking over a Sunday brunch of—what else?—bagels, cream cheese and lox.

Lilyan and Abe had been joined that day, at Sloman's request, by Lilyan's older sister Minnie. Minnie was really responsible for the pot renaissance in these two households, for it was her husband Walter and her children Mindy and Eddie who grew the weed in their backyard, thus playing a key role in the greening of Bayside.

Minnie had obviously taken this interview very seriously, for she was dressed in her best—a nice pantsuit, volumes of pendants and necklaces hanging on her chest, two ball earrings drooping from her ears, some rings for the fingers, and a stunning gold turban atop her head. Lilyan looked sedate in comparison in her black leotard and pants.

Sloman set up his recorder in the dining room, and Jeff and his father discreetly repaired to the den, leaving the two slightly nervous women in the company of the researcher. Lilyan was in the adjoining kitchen, preparing the bagels, as Sloman and Minnie started to chat.

Sloman tried to set Minnie at ease by asking her about her first experience with grass. It was at a party in 1940 in Greenwich Village, and the young Minnie had shared a thin cigarette with her date. It didn't do much for her, and she never even found out what it was called; after all, she had gotten married by 1945 and was too busy for that stuff. So she didn't talk about it or see it or hear about it until the late sixties, when Mindy, her daughter, brought it home.

"How'd you feel about Mindy smoking?" Sloman asked. "Did it upset you? Did you remember your escapades?"

Minnie shook her turban. "I didn't like her smoking, but I knew I wasn't going to stop her. Especially when she was already smoking. She had it in the house and wanted me to. And I thought that I would forever, you know, ban it from the house and not smoke it with her, never. That means I'm joining their league. And I didn't want to do that. Right? But somehow I was overthrown. I couldn't believe it. They won. The demons won." She shook her head and stirred her coffee.

"How did it happen? How did the demons win?" Sloman smiled.

"We passed around a joint and it was strong. At least it affected me that way." Minnie shrugged. "I felt talkative. And this fellow, I didn't like the fellow so much. We never used to talk much. He says, 'Hello, how are you?' very cordial, but I really opened up with him and we became such buddies, with that one stick. We were going someplace to hear some cousins of mine play in a bowling alley. He had this job. So we went out, but I was very talkative. Didn't stop talking for two hours. But fast, rapid. Bubba, bubba, bubba."

"You realized you were talking fast?" Lilyan wondered, from the kitchen.

"Couldn't stop. Usually I don't talk that easily, extemporaneously. But I just talked fast. Or I made mistakes. Maybe in those days I didn't 'cause I think this thing has affected my mind." Minnie giggled nervously. "I want to say 'white,' I say 'black.' If I want to go right, I say I have to go left. You know, I think marijuana did that. I'm afraid."

"Nah," Sloman shrugged it off.

"But I didn't smoke it that much. I used to smoke it once a week thereafter," Minnie concluded.

"But you enjoyed it that first time?" the reporter probed.

"Well, I enjoyed it mostly because it makes me hear better. It intensifies my hearing. When I put my hands down like this and I cover my eyes and my two kids are talking opposite me, ordinarily I can't hear them if they're speaking to each other at the dining room table. I can't hear them because they're talking to each other. They're talking because they don't want me to hear. And I don't hear, period. But I found myself one day after the three of us had taken it, I put my head in my hands, closed my eyes, and I heard every word they said. And I was so amazed, so thrilled. So sharp. I said, 'I love this stuff!' But how can I continue to take this stuff at this rate just to hear? So I say, I will only take it when I go out in company or when I go to the theater.

"In the theater I really don't need it if I have binoculars. I hear well. I can see their lips and how high up I am, especially singing, I hear every word. Because I can connect the two. So I said, 'Well, I just can't go on like this. I'm likely to become an addict.' But I told my ear doctor about it. I go to him for treatment to have my ears cleaned out and stuff. And he said it was true, but he didn't recommend it for that."

"So he told you to stay away from pot?"

"Stay away," Minnie repeated.

"So you didn't listen? You couldn't hear him?" Sloman joked.

"I didn't listen. I could hear beautiful. Not that I hear sharp, like some people say that it affects their musical interpretations. But I just can *hear*." Minnie squealed with delight.

By now the food was ready, and Lilyan brought it into the dining room. Min and Sloman attacked the bagels as Lilyan brought a chair around and joined the conversation.

"So when did you start smoking again?" Sloman managed between mouthfuls.

"After Jeffrey and Rona started. I was very much against

that, of course. I thought it was terrible. And they used to hide it from me. . . ." Lilyan sighed.

"Why were you against it? You smoked in the clubs, you smoked down in Florida . . . ," Sloman remembered.

"What's good for the goose is not always good for the gander," Minnie philosophized.

"Also, I never realized that when they first started smoking, the kids, I never realized that a reefer and pot were the same thing. I smoked reefers as a kid. I thought they were two entirely different types of things. That's why I was always against it." Lilyan reached for a bagel.

"What did you think pot was?" Sloman asked.

"I thought it was something worse. Something that would get you sick. But I was afraid mostly that they shouldn't go on to anything stronger. That something shouldn't happen to them."

"So when did you first start smoking pot again?" Sloman redirected.

"Rona once had some stuff laying in the house, and I found it," Lilyan remembered. "So I said, 'Jesus Christ, I got to see what the hell these kids are so hipped up about.' They were all rolled—I still don't know how to roll—so I found it and I smoked it. No great shakes. The only reason that I objected to myself smoking it was because I had stopped smoking in 1964 and to me it was horrible to start to smoke again. I was afraid, you know, I was going to start smoking cigarettes again because of that. I would get addicted to the taste of the stuff, but then I found out that it wasn't like tobacco at all."

"Did you smoke it alone?" Sloman started on another bagel.

"Yeah," Lilyan gestured. "I was home alone during the day. I didn't smoke a whole cigarette. But I felt good, I felt good. I felt that I wanted to talk to somebody, but there was nobody in the house to talk to. So I put a record on the record player and I started dancing and singing. I was having a great time. And that was it, my first time. I didn't realize till then that it was the same reefer that we smoked when we were kids."

"How do you women get your stuff? Do you buy it?"

They both shook their heads vigorously. "I see they sell it out on the street"—Minnie took the floor—"but I would be afraid to buy it off the street. I see people stopping and buying." She shuddered. "Who knows? They could mix it with sand. God knows what else they could mix it with. Garbage maybe."

"We usually get stuff when my brother's boy Mitchell comes in," Lilyan said.

"He brings in the good stuff," Minnie interjected longingly.

"He leaves a whole bunch with my husband," Lilyan revealed. "Sometimes my husband curses at him, too. 'You have some good pot and you have some bad. Now we want the good.' But he usually leaves quite a bit. This last time he came he had some good stuff, and he and his sister and my husband and I all lit up and smoked two joints and had some time. We had so much fun, ooooh. At 2:30 in the morning, I was making a whole meal. They said. 'Ooh, Aunt Lil, we're hungry.' So I made up a whole batch of French toast and coffee. But their father, my brother, would never do anything like that. He's a doctor, and they'd rather take that yellow pill—what is it they take? Valium. They'd rather take Valium than a couple of drags of a joint. They're stupid."

"I heard you turned on your mother." Sloman remembered the hilarious story Jeff had told him.

Lil's eyes widened. "Yah, momma, may she rest in peace. She was a smoker anyway. So I used to hide the pot in her house, and we used to smoke it in her house, without her knowing it."

"Whadda ya mean, hide it in her house?"

"We used to hide it; I didn't want it to be in my house for my children to see it. So we'd hide a couple of sticks there. She lived in the Bronx. You know, we'd come to visit and we'd smoke it. I remember one time we talked, we sang, and she looked at us and said, 'What are ya smoking there? Schtink-ta, schtink-ta, schtink.' So I said, 'Ma, it's the marijuana that they're talking about.' So she says, 'Let me taste it.' I says, 'Ma, with your head, the way you get dizzy, you don't need it.' 'Let me taste it,' she pouted. I says, 'No!' So I put it down; you know, I'd smoke and leave a little, er . . ."

"Roach," Sloman interjected.

"Right, roach. And she took it by herself. She picked it up and smoked it. She was seventy-two then. I didn't know she did that. And she walked around in her little slippers, and all of a sudden she says, 'Ummmm, I feel so dizzzzy!' I said, 'Ma, what happened?' She said, 'Ummm, how nice! I feel so sexy.' And she rolled over; the way she twisted her body was so adorable. If I only could have captured that on a photograph.

"Then once a bunch of the family went to see Guy Lombardo at the Jones Beach Theatre. It was my husband and I and one of my brother's kids sitting on one side, and my mother and my brother and another kid on the other side. So when we were on the way to the beach, I said, 'Ma, you have to put something on because it gets very cold there.' So she said, 'All right, give me a jacket.' So I went to my closet, and I pulled out a jacket that I hadn't worn in years, and I put it over her shoulders.

"After the first act, during intermission, I got up and walked over to where they were sitting, my mother and my brother. I said, 'Well, Ma, how do you like the show?' She says, 'I got the show right here!' I said, "Whada ya mean you got the show right here?' And I see, *eppis*, by the look on her face, I says, 'Ma, what's the matter?'

"First of all, there was a couple in front of her, a young couple who during the entire first act didn't stop kissing. And they were having a ball with her, because while the first act was on, she got cold and she put the jacket on and she put her hands in the pockets to keep warm. She put her hands in the pockets and she felt cigarettes, so she took them out. I completely forgot there were four joints laying in there. She took a look and she knew already what it was, 'cause she knew what it looked like. So she lit up one and she had a ball. And she drove the couple in front of her crazy. Every time they'd kiss she'd applaud. And when they'd part she'd tap them on the shoulder and say, 'Do it again! It looked so nice!' She had such a good time.

"She was having a ball during the whole show, and after the show she wanted to go down to the dancing and have a dance with her son. I said to my brother, 'Oh boy, she's having a ball on that pot.' So we went dancing—you know, Guy Lombardo plays after the show—and she was dancing with her son. It was the proudest moment. She had such a good time."

During the anecdote, Jeff had entered the room and had gotten absorbed in the story about his grandmother. "Tell Larry about the seders," he urged his mother.

"Which seders?" Minnie looked stumped. "When my Mindy brought the Iranian fellow?"

"There were two seders," Jeff remembered. "One there was this big argument with Cousin Eddie when all the kids got stoned and called you all hypocrites. The other one was when Uncle Walter went upstairs and brought down a handful of pot and he and Daddy started rolling joints and they passed them around the table after the seder."

"Uncle Walter smoked?" Lilyan looked amazed.

"He just supplied it." Minnie knew her husband better. "He didn't like it, yet he would grow it in the backyard. He'd take the plants down, hang them upside down in the attic, take off the leaves, put them in a jar."

"And he never smoked it?" Sloman was puzzled.

"He read books and everything," Jeff grinned.

"He'd put it in jars," Minnie continued, "and I'd say, 'What are you doing? Who are you saving this for?' He'd say, 'The kids.' I says, 'What are you doing? You're corrupting the kids.' He'd say, 'They're gonna go out and buy it anyway, so I'm saving the expense.' If I was going away I'd ask him for some joints and he'd ration them to me. I'd say, 'Why are you so stingy? Give me some more!' " Everyone laughed, and during the commotion Jeff's father Abe slipped into the room. He looked younger than his sixty-two years, and with his wry, cynical manner he served as a perfect foil for the two women.

"Why are you giving Larry such crap?" Abe scoffed as soon as he sat down. "You make things more than they are. You have nothing to give him; you just talk talk talk. Look, Larry, we don't smoke a lot. I never smoked a lot. I smoked a little in high school. I don't have any big stories to tell you; I told you that, Larry."

"What about the cruise?" his wife challenged. "As soon as the boat took off, he found some kids with some pot."

"So a few of us smoked a little pot," Abe scoffed at his wife. "That's all."

"A little pot." Lilyan snickered. "He used to smoke day and night on that ship. Every morning, every afternoon . . ."

"You exaggerate, Lil. You're an exaggerator, and don't talk concerning me because I don't wanna hear exaggerations." Abe grabbed a bagel and bit into it.

"Look, I got two bags from Walter." Minnie rescued the conversation. "Wanna roll one now?"

Abe's face lit up. He grabbed the baggie. "This stuff must be horseshit, Min."

"How do you know it's horseshit?" Minnie seemed hurt.

"Because he grew the other crap there. It was like it wasn't even weed," Abe spat.

"Try the other bag, then," Minnie suggested.

Abe peered into the crumpled-up baggie. "It's all seeds. That's what you got here, a bag of seeds." Jeff's father grabbed the first bag and began pouring the fine powder into a cigarette paper. "This is powder. How the hell is it even gonna stay in the cigarette?"

"It does look very sandy," Min worried. "Try it with a double paper."

"Your husband rations this shit out to you?" Sloman was amazed as the first pungent whiffs of burning hemp crossed the room.

"Now that he took it upstairs and hung it, he rations it." Min took the joint from Abe. "I can't get him to give me some pot."

"What's his fascination with it if he doesn't smoke?" The reporter was still baffled.

"I don't know. Maybe he likes to be a producer."

"Maybe he has delusions of grandeur," Abe piped in, taking a long hit off the joint. "Who knows, maybe he wants to be the pot king?"

"They do call him the clam maven," Minnie remembered. "He loves to dig them."

"Maybe he's selling it on the side," Sloman suggested. "One mature plant can yield quite a bit of grass."

Abe made a face and took the joint from Jeff, who had passed on it each trip around. In the kitchen, his mother was getting dessert ready.

"Walter was afraid," Abe exhaled. "The plant started to stick out in the backyard, so he cut it down."

"Some people talk," Minnie explained to the reporter. "I need the cops behind my house? He pulled it out because our next-door neighbors happened to notice it, the kids next door, and we were watching them look over at it and I told Walter that they recognized it and he said he was gonna take it down. I tried to tell him to leave it because it had such a beautiful bud. The flowers were gonna open up any day." Min shook her head and passed the joint.

After a while, a strange silence fell on the room. Everyone except Jeff was stoned on his ass.

"Do you feel stoned?" Min asked no one in particular.

"Yeah, do you?" Lil, who had visited the room for periodic hits, was back with a plate of Danishes and crumb cake.

"I feel a little tired, a bit of difficulty in speaking." The words were oozing from the usually volatile Min's mouth. "I feel mellow."

"Mellow," Lil's face lit up. "I haven't heard that word for years."

"Remember when we used to go to the old nightclub?" Min began reminiscing, "the Cotton Club, in Harlem."

"You're kidding." Sloman was beside himself. "You used to smoke at the Cotton Club?"

"I didn't know what it was then," Lil remembered. "I used to smoke cigarettes, and I thought the smell we were smelling was from the *schwartzes*."

"*Schwartzes* have that kind of smell, don't they, Lil?" Minnie laughed.

"It was a riot." The room was cracking up. "You used to walk into that club and they must have been smoking, but we'd say, 'Oh, what a stink!' and we actually thought it was the *schwartzes* there."

Everyone dug into the Danishes, and Lil got up to get coffee. Suddenly Sloman broke the silence.

"Sitting around here now, I was thinking, Is this what all that brouhaha was about in the sixties? I mean, is this like the fruits of victory? To have us all sharing a few joints. I mean, grass was such a part of that generation gap thing, that anti-establishment anti-Vietnam trip. Now it seems so co-opted . . ." The words trailed off as the coffee came out.

"There's always a gap between generations." Abe began a speech. "The big gap in this generation was that when we were kids 90 percent of our fathers didn't have hardly what to eat. You were lucky if you had what to eat. Because this was the depression era that I'm talking about. Now our kids never knew from that; that's where the whole generation gap is. It's in the formative years, where in our formative years, we were brought up where a penny was valuable."

"We needed to survive first," Minnie agreed.

"We didn't have the privilege you people have," Lil joined in.

"But I remember even when I was younger, smoking pot, my parents were never very adamant in their opposition to it," Jeff, who had been strangely silent, finally spoke.

"As a mother, my only objection was that they shouldn't get hurt from smoking that stuff and that it shouldn't lead to something worse, that's all." Lil seemed curiously proud. "I didn't realize what smoking pot was at that time. . . ."

"I was afraid something would happen and they would find it on the kids when they were driving and they would be put in jail for that." Minnie shuddered involuntarily. "Now suddenly it's all different."

"With this snowball effect, all these kids starting to come back from Vietnam, all on pot or the hard drugs, the country, the judiciary got more lenient when it came to sentencing," Abe pronounced. "Because more and more kids were getting caught up with it. Well, it was like the wheel started turning and turning and turning, and it's finally gonna wind up where it's gonna be legalized. Reynolds Tobacco and Phillip Morris and all of the others are geared to produce pot already. I guess you know that. They could go into production tomorrow for pot—I read that six months ago."

Everyone seemed talked out and the Danishes were gone, so Min, logical thinker that she is, threw Abe the baggie and he rolled another joint. But no sooner had the thin cigarette begun to make its rounds around the table than Jeff jumped up.

"It smells like shit in here," he screamed, and lunged for the window. "Let's get some goddamn air in the room. That's all you do—every night you foul up the air."

A big smile crept across Abe's face.

"Jesus, what a curious generation gap here," Sloman observed to Min; "Jeff is really pissed off that his parents smoke so much."

"That's some commentary," Minnie sighed as she scoured the plate for the last of the crumb cake.

CHAPTER 16: Amotivational in Suburbia

The thread unraveled. Hot on the heels of his visit to Bayside, where marijuana had made sufficient inroads to be a staple at the seder table, Sloman reunited with his friend Cusimano and Cusimano's wife Beverly, and journeyed up to Croton, a middle-class community in Westchester. They were there to be guests of honor at a party-interview that Sloman's friend Barbara S. was hosting.

Barbara, an amiable, attractive woman in her mid-thirties, managed the career of one of America's most popular schlock artists, a woman whose prints could be had at most department stores across the country. Most of her friends were also young professionals, and besides their similarity in terms of class and occupation, they all shared a common interest in marijuana. They had all turned their back on liquor and had adopted the weed as their recreational drug of choice. Sloman thought it would be fascinating to interview these young, ambitious middle-class potheads, so Barbara used the interview situation as an excuse to party. Barbara would have used almost anything as an excuse to party.

But Sloman had more than just an interview in mind. He was intrigued by one of the arguments that the anti-marijuana legions still used in their attempts to prevent the use of the substance. Basically, they argued that smoking pot leads to something called the "amotivational syndrome." According to this view, marijuana itself causes a certain brain syndrome marked by distortion of perceptions, impairment of judgment, diminished attention span, a difficulty with verbalization, and a loss of thought continuity. The user then becomes apathetic, disoriented and oftentimes depressed—in short, amotivated.

This view had been promulgated most forcefully by Harold Kolansky and William Moore, two Philadelphia psychiatrists who stirred tremendous controversy in the early seventies with a few journal articles outlining this syndrome.

But Sloman had always perceived this issue as a value-laden one. It seemed that the "syndrome" Kolansky and Moore were describing emerged from a set of values that pot smokers in the sixties for the most part shared. When smoking pot was seen as a radical act, as a means of attaining a consciousness that helped one to "see" through the "lies" of the power structure, users exhibited behavior that to a member of the power structure (or one sympathetic to that view) would appear to be amotivational. In other words, to understand this concept, we must define "motivation," and to most of these researchers, "motivation" was any act that would be consistent with attaining status in a competitive, capitalistic society. Conversely, you were "amotivated," and therefore "sick," if you sat around all day smoking pot, listening to music, watching your plants grow, basically having a good time. Having a good time, of course, is not consistent with attaining status in a competitive, capitalistic society.

But tonight, Sloman and the Cusimanos would encounter a new breed of pot smokers, users who would send Kolansky and Moore scurrying back to their couches in an attempt to explain away their presence. Barbara and her friends smoked grass regularly and enjoyed it enormously. However, they also had grandiose ambitions; they wanted to make oodles and oodles of money, garner a tremendous amount of prestige, work very hard at what it was that they did, and enjoy the fruits of their labors through the benefits of a highly developed consumer society. They were the New Hedonists, and their story was what Sloman was after.

Barbara answered the door and ushered the visitors in, introducing them to Eric and Mary, a couple from Manhattan who had arrived early. Eric was a manufacturer of nuts and screws, and Mary, his wife, was a budding interior decorator. They were both in their mid-thirties and well groomed. Cusimano self-consciously touched his torn blue Banlon shirt.

"Here, why don't you start on this?" Ira, Barbara's husband, threw a handful of well-rolled joints onto the coffee table. "There's more after that's finished." In the next room, the children were engaged in loud play.

"Oh god, I want the kids to go to sleep." Mary looked a bit uptight.

"Don't worry." Sloman showed how easy it was to palm a joint.

"No, no," Mary corrected. "I want them to go to sleep before they start smoking all the other things. With the big pipes going around."

Barbara, who had been working on the food in the kitchen, came in. "You know what?" she said in her distinctive nasal tones. "I need a joint myself. I'm really much too straight to be alive. Thank you. Back to my kitchen duties."

But the doorbell interrupted, and Barbara admitted two more couples, all about the same age and all dressed similarly to Barbara and the others present. "Close the door," Barbara was directing traffic, ushering the newcomers in. "Give them joints immediately, please."

"I want to know how I would go about getting my loft into a magazine," Mary had collared the writer, seeking professional counsel. "Last year there were very few, and every time we saw a loft in a magazine, it was a big deal. But now they're all over, so if I don't do it soon I'm never going to get it into a magazine. I'm gonna miss out."

"Talk to the art directors of the magazines," Sloman counseled.

"Mary did a terrific job designing it," Eric broke in. "A lot of sweat. Four years of work. I'd like to get it into something."

Sloman began setting up his recorder, and then he set down the ground rules for the interview. They could talk about anything they wanted; it would be an informal chat. But for the purposes of the transcriber, everyone would in turn at first give his or her name, occupation, age and how many years a smoker. To allay their fears, the participants were allowed to make up names, which about one-quarter of the group chose to do. One by one, they went around the room.

"This is ridiculous," Irma, who chose to be called Petunia, scoffed. "This sounds like we're on David Susskind."

"Do you talk about how it progressed from when you started out, or do you talk about right now?" Barbara worried as she brought in the third variety of dip for the snacks on the coffee table.

"You can do anything. It's open-ended," Sloman reassured her.

"I'll tell you how we started," Ira, who in his fantasies chose Clyde as his nom de pot, began. "For many years when we were younger there was a bunch of people we always went out with. Three or four couples. Constantly. Until we got married and after a while we found they were going out but they weren't asking us. We couldn't imagine what the reasons were. So we finally got them to the house and we asked them point-blank why they were going out and not asking us. They said they'd started smoking marijuana. They knew Barbara was dead set against it."

"I was like really moralistically off the wall about it," Barbara grinned sheepishly.

"Basically because she said it was against the law and she was afraid of getting busted," Ira continued. "After spending a good ten years with all these people, we stopped seeing them. Then we got into a new bunch of friends. It turned out that everybody we met had already smoked pot. I don't even remember who turned us on one night. We didn't even buy. We used to borrow."

"We'd borrow wherever we went." Barbara took a hit and passed a joint, only to find another one coming up on her left.

"Like two cigarettes a week or something," Ira remembered. "Then we started buying half ounces, then ounces, now we're up to three ounces at a time. It's still illegal, but I think that now Barbara finds everybody you speak to smokes marijuana. That's why she smokes constantly. She's a real head." Ira glanced proudly at his wife.

"I start to smoke as soon as I put my ass on the seat of the car when I close the office door," Barbara smiled. "I take out my dollar for the toll and my joint for the ride. As soon as I leave the office I'm shaking. I have even smoked before I went to work. When Ira drives me to work at nine in the morning, he's always smoking, so I smoke. I've done it at least half a dozen times, gone to work stoned. And I did the very biggest and most outrageous thing of my entire career one morning because I was stoned. I got the J. C. Penney's Mother's Day promotion because I was so stoned."

"You mean the idea came to you?" Sloman asked.

"We got it all and we did it. And that was because I went in stoned. But sometimes when I go in stoned I can't get my first telephone call made. I'll be talking to myself. I walked out of my office once on my way someplace and then I got there and said, 'What the hell am I here for?' " Barbara exploded into torrents of laughter, warm, infectious laughter that quickly spread around the semi-stoned room.

"When Barbara smokes she doesn't know what she's doing," Ira patiently explained. "She smoked this afternoon, walked into the bedroom, stood in there looking around, couldn't figure out what she was doing in there, and then realized she had gone in to get dressed. This goes on all the time. She'll start saying something and she'll forget what she was saying."

"I don't exactly like 100 percent of what it does to me," the hostess admitted. "I like 80 percent of what it does."

"What does it do for you?" Sloman inquired as he passed up a joint, to a lingering stare from Irma.

"It makes me understand where I'm at. I think thoughts so clearly and I get so far into myself or whatever I'm thinking about. If I get into a project at work, I get into that project. I mean I'm really into that project. Nothing's left unturned." Barbara smiled proudly.

"Don't you find that it makes your mind more creative?" Fred, the orthodontist, spoke up.

"Is grass accepted in your social circles?" Sloman wondered.

Fred smiled. "Well, we had a party at the house we lived in in Rego Park, before we moved to Connecticut, about eight years ago, and to show you how things were, we had a couple walk out because someone was smoking grass. They wouldn't stay in the same house with anyone smoking. In fact, what's interesting is that there were distinct grass smokers and non–grass smokers and the non–grass smokers sort of went into a separate room and did it hush hush. Nowadays, at every party we've been to in the last few years, provided the hosts are smokers, people who don't smoke will openly mingle with people who do and say, 'I don't smoke,' and it's perfectly accepted."

"Not only that, but the host or hostess will put it out on the table like they used to put out cigarettes," Irma observed.

"But sometimes it's not nice," Barbara glared at her husband. "It's just thrown on the table. But Freddy is known to have powerful stuff." She smiled proudly at her friend.

Carol, who earlier had described herself as a bored housewife, spoke up, "He has them labeled—'Super,' 'Dynamite,' 'Okay.' "

"At his parties you get different containers," Barbara added.

"At Gina and Harvey's house they did it in a classy way. They had one of the girls who was moving around serving the food bring around a tray with joints on it. That was a nice touch," Fred sighed.

"There's no tension between the smokers and the non-smokers?" the reporter queried.

"I know very few people who don't smoke," Irma reported. "And the people who don't, drink a lot, so there's no way you're gonna get a straight crowd around there."

Cusimano, who had been sitting quietly, eating and smoking himself deeper into the couch, piped up. "But don't people feel smoking grass is something that kids do? They sort of outgrow it—mature beyond it."

"But that runs in cycles." Fred had the floor again. "That happened with us. We smoked for a period of time. Certainly every weekend and maybe during the week. Then I guess you became pregnant and I wouldn't let you smoke grass. So I stopped too, and there were periods of time we didn't smoke."

"Boy, that's really nice," Cusimano was impressed.

"I've probably been smoking the longest," Fred continued, accepting a joint, "but yet probably not as much as most people here. I was always a social smoker, so to speak. I wouldn't get up in the morning and take a joint no more than I'd take a shot of Scotch. But that's me. I'm not saying it's wrong to take a joint then."

"What about the afternoon?" Mary wondered. "If you wanted to just lay down and relax?"

Freddy smiled. "And I had no obligations? Hell, yeah, I did it this afternoon."

"Oh, yeah?" Irma suddenly perked up. "I was at work making money and you were at home on the bed smoking a joint?"

"Then I decided to go back to work because I had a lot to do, so I went back to the office," Fred got defensive. "I got a lot accomplished. Paperwork. I didn't work on any patients. That I won't do stoned. I know guys who do. I remember one guy came out of his operatory and said, 'I just did the greatest filling I have ever done in my entire life.' It took him about forty minutes to do it; he could have done it in three. He got off on that filling. The patient probably got the most sensational job he ever had in his life."

"Ira, do you work stoned?"

"I'll come up during the day for three or four hours, and I'll smoke when I come up, but by the time I go down I'm never stoned. I never work on anybody stoned unless it's in the house, one of the kids or Barbara," Ira related.

"We don't care if *they* die," Barbara cracked.

"If I smoke during the day I might get a call and have to go into the office and adjust someone stoned because I have no choice. Sometimes I do better work that way," Ira smiled. "A lot of the practice of chiropractics is the feeling by touch. Bone displacement, just by feeling it. When I'm stoned my fingers are much more sensitive than when I'm not. I'm much more aware of what I'm feeling. I know exactly what's in the body, in the spine, so I know exactly what the bone looks like that I'm working on. But when I'm stoned I can picture the whole back with no skin on it better than when I'm not stoned."

"Yeah, when he gets straight he finds out he's really working on a skeleton," Fred quipped.

By now about ten joints had been consumed, and Ira got up and came back shortly with another handful, scattering them on the coffee table.

"So basically we're talking about a substance that promotes creativity, helps us think better, relaxes us, takes away pain, but the reality is it's still illegal. Do you feel that?" Sloman was sounding more and more like David Susskind.

"There used to be a time when you put the towel by the door," Eric remembered.

"Do any of you smoke in public?" Cusimano was curious. "Outdoors?"

"We did it in a restaurant one night." Carol smiled. "About forty of us at the Ground Round."

"We smoke in movies," her husband Steve added.

"We smoke on the beach and in the car," Ira related.

"Walking through Bloomingdale's—I've seen people do that," Carol recollected. "My sister walks down the street all the time smoking. We were at a bar mitzvah and the people at the next table were stoned."

"And the bar mitzvah boy was stoned," Fred added.

"So basically the fact that it's not legal doesn't seem to deter you?" Sloman summed up.

"It does in one sense to me," Fred objected. "That is when you're traveling. Either out of the city or out of the country. Just the thought that I couldn't bring grass on a vacation where I was specifically going to have a good time really pisses me off.

We brought it anyway, but it scared the shit out of me. So I put it in Irma's purse."

"Do you remember where you put it?" Irma's voice had an edge to it.

"At the bottom of the baby powder that I then put in your purse," Fred smiled.

"My sister rolls joints, maybe twenty of them, then takes sanitary napkins apart, puts them in there, and glues them back together," Carol recalled, blushing a bit.

"That's her stash?" Sloman cracked.

Cusimano quickly changed the subject. "Has grass changed your perceptions? Made you a different person?"

"I think that it would have a tendency to change anybody's life who smoked it as an everyday thing." Barbara got serious for a rare moment. "I have found that it changes my perspective on just so many things that I have become that much more aware. I'm so much more introspective. You start touching yourself. You start getting into your own head. Who the hell ever knew the things that were—I never knew the things that were happening in my head. I had no idea."

"But you're an outgoing person," Fred interrupted. "You smoke grass and you maintain your posture as an outgoing person. Do you think someone who is shy and introverted who smokes grass suddenly as a result . . ."

"You don't know what's going on inside when you're so extroverted," Barbara objected. "I could say things very easily to people, but I had no idea what was going on. It's the first time in my life when I started to smoke that I got in touch with my feelings. 'Cause your head starts to work. You could be in a totally unconscious state sometimes when you're straight. You can go through the day unaware. Grass has changed my whole life. I went in a certain direction. I've taken steps that were bolder than I might have done. I went through all kinds of trips with regard to having to work or not having to work, leaving your children. That's a heavy trip for a person to do. I think smoking is what really made me able to go through with it and understand it and come to terms with it better."

"Those are experiences that are between you and the marijuana as opposed to between you and your best friends?" Sloman probed.

"You know what? It's an experience of me and the marijuana.

But what happens is I'll experience the thought and I have a dear friend who I can speak to and tell it to. And when I say it out loud and she throws it back at me . . . I know I've been through some heavy trips that I might have had to go to a shrink for to talk this stuff out. To get somebody to get it the hell out of me. It works on both levels. You by yourself and you being able to speak more freely."

"What a great concept, a marijuana friend," Sloman marveled.

"You get a chapter," Fred joked, and lit up a joint.

"Many times she gets into bed and she's ready to go to sleep and she turns on the light and starts writing on her pad because she's had an idea," Ira offered, nodding toward his wife.

"What kind of idea? For business?" Sloman posed.

Barbara nodded. "For business."

"What about poems? Stuff like that?"

"Are you kidding?" Barbara shrieked. "I see numbers, prints, colors, subject matter, picture frames. That's all I see, honey."

Everyone cracked up. "I think if you're stoned and you go to sleep you can get more into fantasy," Fred reported.

"Oh, yes." Barbara was beginning to sound like a banshee with the giggles. "Let's get into fantasies! We can talk about what pot does as far as sex goes. Let's touch on sex." Barbara was of one mind. "It's gonna take a fucking genius to make this come out right without being absolutely downright gross. I think that physically your sensation is much sharper. You're so much more aware of it. It becomes much more intense."

"We know about Ira," Fred cracked. "He told us about his fingertips. The joys of being married to a chiropractor."

"That's part of it," Barbara admitted sheepishly. "But getting back to the fantasy thing, not all of them are sexual. I can go on—nobody can do a number like me. I can get myself to be the president of the largest firm, rivaling any in the United States in the art business. And I go through every one of the steps. I don't just get there. I go through how it's going to all happen. Each one of the steps. If I could get organized and backing I could probably do it all. I know every single solitary thing. Yeah. You could go through a whole life like that. Like blueprints."

Sloman was amazed by the intensity of the conversation. Although Barbara and Freddy seemed to dominate the proceedings, every one of the guests sat enraptured and even if merely by nodding seemed to confirm the stories that were being recounted by the others. They had been talking for a few hours now, and except for an occasional break to fetch more marijuana or some wine or soft drinks, nobody had moved from the circle around the coffee table. Inside the kitchen, the hero sandwiches took a back seat to conversation.

"The only time I'm afraid of smoking is when I'm driving," Fred volunteered. "My mind wanders when I'm driving stoned. I didn't smoke coming here until we got off the highway, 'cause then I knew it would be fine. I find my mind wanders. I'm into that third step up to the presidency and I'm on the Bronx River Parkway when I meant to be on the Hutchinson."

"I know," Barbara is squealing again. "I always go to the wrong place because I get into a tape in my mind. I once went to Connecticut. I was in Port Chester, and then I was in Greenwich before I realized I was in the wrong state. I was already into J. C. Penney's second store."

"The only problem I have driving is when coming to a light—I slow down about a block and a half before the light," Ira sighed.

"Steve's driven babysitters right up to their front door." Carol laughed. "I mean literally right to the door."

"Then he pushed down the window with the electric button and rang the doorbell. Never got out of the car," Fred quipped.

"One night the cop stopped him because they saw him leave the area and come back," Carol continued. "He was taking the babysitter home. It's so stupid. But he was stoned; he didn't know what was happening. He kept saying, 'But I wasn't speeding.' All they asked him for was his license, and he kept babbling, 'But I wasn't speeding.' "

"You were going 6 mph—that was the problem," Sloman laughed.

"On the sidewalk in reverse," Fred howled with delight.

"When we get home and I go to take the babysitter home and I'm stoned, the first thought that enters my mind is, Is this girl going to get home alive?" Steve confessed.

"Do you think we're creating this whole generation of babysitters that are going to be deathly afraid of marijuana?" Sloman wondered.

Fred made a face. "They're so stoned they don't know it. I once asked our sitter Ann how much I owed her. She must have been ripped. She said 'I dunno.' I said, 'How many hours did you work?' She said, 'I'm not sure.' 'What time did you come?' 'I think nine.' And I was so stoned I'm figuring a dollar and a half times 11¾ hours, and I said, 'Is five dollars enough?' and she shrugged, 'Yeah.' "

Barbara finished the last of the dip and looked anxiously around. "Do you think we should break for sandwiches now? Everybody's so hungry." Her hunger elicited laughs from the group.

"I want to ask one question," Fred broke in. "You touched on something before. I'd like to know how the other people in this room handle their children with grass."

Carol began laughing. "My mother called from Florida this morning, and the first words out of my six-year-old were, 'Gee, Mommy's been smoking that stuff a lot lately.' "

"We smoke normally in our house, but my son knows the difference between a regular cigarette and pot," Irma reported. "He doesn't associate it with any alteration in our behavior, but he'll come downstairs and tell me, 'Mommy, Daddy's upstairs making you one of those funny cigarettes.' "

"Does he ever ask for one?" Carol wondered. "My daughter asked me for one for show and tell. So my sister rolled her a joint with oregano and she brought it to school for show and tell."

"The teacher smoked it and thought it was the worst grass they ever had," Fred joked.

"Really." Carol slapped him. "She got up in front of her class for show and tell and said, 'This is what my parents smoke. My aunt rolled it for me.' "

"What were the reactions of the kids in school?" Sloman asked.

"Nothing." Carol shrugged. "Most of their parents smoke, so it didn't bother them."

"Would everybody feel comfortable with having a thirteen-year-old son or daughter who smoked?" Sloman asked the next logical question.

"Absolutely not," they all answered in unison.

"I think fifteen seems to be a good age," Fred compromised. "I don't think that junior high kids should be smoking grass. But for high school kids, it's okay. I have kids in my practice come in stoned. And kids tell me they smoke. In fact, I put appliances in a kid's mouth the other day and he said, 'Can I smoke?' and I said, 'It all depends what you're smoking.' I don't notice any degeneracy among them. I do amongst the pill takers. I do amongst the drinkers. And I have juvenile delinquents too. But the average nice kid that's smoking grass . . ."

"That's great." Ira smiled. "They have their own roach holder. They just stick it between the wires."

Everyone howled. "I charge $400 extra for that," Fred deadpanned.

"Larry, should we have a sandwich break now?" Barbara was sounding progressively more desperate.

Cusimano seemed to wake up out of a cannabis stupor and suddenly turned to Carol. "Didn't you describe yourself as a bored housewife when we did the introductions?" Carol managed a nod. "Do you use grass to fight boredom?"

"No, not really," she mused. "The past month I've smoked more than I usually do. That's because Steve wasn't working for a month. I guess part of it was just to relax me. I either smoke or drink wine. It was either one or the other. He did too. That's how we didn't fight for a month. We had to be together all the time. But I try to fight boredom other ways. I go to Bloomingdale's. I do that when I get very bored."

"STOP THE CONVERSATION AND LET'S EAT!" Barbara screamed, and grabbed the tape recorder, shutting it off. She scurried into the kitchen and brought out a huge platter of different types of heroes, along with the standard trimmings. The group descended into the dining room area. One by one, they filled their plates and slowly wound their way back to their places at the coffee table. They tore at the sandwiches with gusto.

"I've done so many funny things stoned." Freddy got whimsical after he had finished his hero. "I could write a book. I was given a job when the orthodontic department of the medical school I went to was getting a visit from a man who was from the certifying board of the association. This man's job, after walking through the clinic, was to determine if the entire program should be certified or not. It's like life or death for the entire department. I was given the job of escorting him around. I didn't know that until that morning.

"At the staff meeting that morning there were fifteen students and thirty or forty faculty members, and the chairman of the department was trying to impress on everybody how important it was to impress this man. He said, 'Fred, here, is going to show him through the clinic.' That was the first I heard of it. I was sitting there, and I was stoned because I had no patients that afternoon. So the whole future of the orthodontic department rested on my stoned shoulders. Someone wondered if he would ask questions of the people as they're working, and the chairman said, 'No, he'll probably just ask Fred some questions.' Just what I needed, right? Someone asked, 'What kind of questions?' and the chairman said, 'Well, he might ask you a question like "What do you know about Sasooni?" ' Sasooni was a man who invented a certain type of angular analysis to measure the bones in the skull. Anyway, the chairman said, 'Stand up, Fred, and pretend I'm the visitor. Doctor, what do you know about Sasooni?' So I looked around, stoned on my ass, and said, 'It goes great with fried rice.' "

"Can I give another sandwich to somebody?" Barbara was drowned out by the laughter. In the background, Barry Manilow was driving Sloman and Cusimano up a wall.

"Do you think it's good from the point of view of the whole society that so many people smoke marijuana?" Sloman had directed the question to the orthodontist.

"Well, I'll tell you something," Fred started slowly. "I really have mixed feelings about it. I met a girl at a party. She lives in the same development we live in, and I really got to know her a bit afterwards. This girl is one of the most up people I've ever seen. So incredibly up that one day I said to her, 'Gail, how often do you smoke?' because it seemed to me that she was always up. She said, 'I don't smoke. I don't even smoke cigarettes.' I couldn't believe that. She was the most stoned-out-of-your-mind person I knew. So high on life. Such exuberance. But all the time. I thought she either had had a prefrontal lobotomy or was taking drugs. Nobody could be that happy all the time. That's the part of it that bothers me. Knowing there's another way.

"Everyone would like to go through life like this girl. Very few people can. In order to rid yourself of whatever your tensions are and really get into whatever you're doing, grass gives you the edge to get that high. So why not? Why not be that high? That high is a great spot. Unfortunately most of us need grass to get there. So from that point of view I don't think it's bad."

"I'm just amazed." Cusimano roused himself once again and stared bleary-eyed at the assemblage. "I'm really flabbergasted.

I thought marijuana use would really decline. I thought it was a passé subject. You know most people have sort of gone beyond. I had no idea of this. God, it's really everywhere." He finished and sort of melted back into the couch.

"I think this is a very important thing to talk about," Barbara tried to raise the issue again. "Mary and I have discussed this before. I agree and sometimes I don't agree. Sometimes you tend to care less about things when you're stoned. Mary feels everything's going to degenerate and things won't get done. She feels society won't be productive. I, on the other hand, feel that what it probably does is it eliminates the anxiety over the idiotic things that go with getting things done, and the dumb things don't get done and the important things do . . ." Barbara's pronouncements were interrupted by Irma and Steven, who were returning after a short trip together to the bathroom. The errant guests were both laughing and sniffling.

"Very unobvious," Barbara howled. "That was really cool. You go to the bathroom together. Everyone's supposed to know that you didn't snort coke."

Irma turned red. "This conversation is much too serious."

"There's a name for what we're talking about." Soloman tried to steer them back to the subject. "It's called the 'amotivational syndrome.' "

Barbara looked impressed. "You mean it's a thing? See, Mary, we're getting an education."

"The idea is that if you smoke enough pot you're not going to give a shit about anything," Sloman summarized.

"Ever?" Irma wished.

"It's true," Barbara looked upset. "Everything's crooked in my house. I laid everything on the table like an animal. You get sloppy. When we talk about productivity, are we talking about all the way from the top level down to the factory worker?"

"Everything. Factory workers, kids in school, the whole fabric of society." Sloman tried to talk over Irma and Steve, who seemed to have lost interest.

"We have to get serious," Barbara lectured them.

"We have to reach a consensus," Sloman continued. "This is a very heavy social issue. We're talking about social policy. We're talking about what sort of culture you want to live in."

"That's too heavy." Irma dismissed it with her hand. "I've had it with very serious. I want to laugh. Why do we have to conduct business now?"

"We're getting up to laugh, but first we have business to do." Barbara sounded like a mother.

"Why?" Irma persisted. "Are we getting paid for this? He's making money on us." She pointed an accusatory finger at the reporter.

"He hasn't made any money yet," Barbara defended her guest.

"He will." Irma was almost getting ugly. "He's gonna have fourteen chapters on us. I want to make money too."

"Actually we can conduct social issues in the kitchen," Barbara said brightly, trying a compromise.

"What's happening here is real endemic. This is where the issue divides," Sloman lectured. "There are people who want to smoke marijuana and think about how it's going to affect their lives, and there are people who want to giggle." He gave Irma a condescending look.

"Right." Mary was sweet in her earnestness. "I think about it too much. I do. I spend too much time thinking about what's happening to the children."

"I think that amotivational behavior certainly does enter into it," Fred admitted. "Which would mean that you would have to have some control. That doesn't mean that it couldn't be controlled."

"One of the first things said here tonight was, 'Boy, wouldn't it be great if for one day everyone in America smoked. What a peaceful place we would have.' I don't know if that's true," Sloman said ruefully. "I don't know."

"With so many people smoking grass today you don't read articles about people smoking it and routinely jumping off the George Washington Bridge," Fred said. "It just doesn't happen. I have never met or witnessed anybody becoming hostile after smoking grass."

"But how many times have you smoked grass with someone who would resolve situations in a hostile manner even if they hadn't smoked grass? To whom hostility and aggression is a plausible reaction?" Sloman wondered.

"I don't smoke grass with the Hell's Angels," Fred shrugged.

"As a rule do you see a lot of middle-class people ever express themselves violently?" Sloman persisted.

"No," Fred admitted. "The people I would be with would never slug it out."

"What about getting paranoid?" Barbara piped in. "Having a

conversation and thinking they're talking about you. How much weight you've gained."

The talk had become disjointed, spurred on by the defection in the ranks of Irma and Steve, plus the cumulative effects of the numerous joints that circulated.

"What about music?" Fred brought a new subject up slowly. "How come I'll buy a record or hear a record and it sucks, it's the worst, I couldn't listen to it, and then one day I'll put it on when I'm stoned and it's the best. From then on in it's the best."

"Give me an example," Sloman said.

"Minnie Ripperton."

Barbara squealed with delight. "Yes, yes. That's the best example in the whole world."

"You know, there are certain things that I think are made for people who are stoned," Fred mentioned. "Black lights. For a while they had these posters and you put the black light on. That was strictly for people who were stoned. If you were straight you couldn't get into that."

"What about water beds?" Barbara brightened. "Water beds stoned are very nice. Oooh." She sighed.

"The Water-pik shower head." Fred smiled. "Certain movies —*2001*, *Star Wars*, visual pictures."

"What else?" Barbara was really getting into the list.

"Haagen Daaz ice cream," Fred cooed.

"Forget it." Barbara dismissed him. "Heavenly hash was made for stoned people."

"Body paints for lovers," Carol chirped. "We bought them, but we've yet to use them."

"That's interesting," Sloman observed. "A lot of the accessories for sensual bodies . . ."

"We got into that when we first started smoking," Barbara was off. "Sexual equipment. You go through all the extra toys."

"E.S.D.—Extra Sensory Devices," Fred laughed.

"This better not be in the book," Barbara got paranoid.

"I think wine too," Fred continued. "The upsurgence of people drinking wine is because of grass. Nobody drinks liquor anymore. We used to go through tons of it at parties. I think the combination of grass and hard alcohol is too potent. Most people can't handle it. It blows you away."

"You get sick, you throw up." Irma rejoined the conversation. "But wine is nice. It's mellow."

"What about Valium?" Sloman wondered. Oddly enough, no one used it regularly. The reporter expressed his amazement.

"I did the best I could," Barbara squealed. "If you wanted some freaks, I could have gotten you a crowd of those too," she howled.

"I take them sometimes to get high," Sloman confessed. "Valium and wine and grass really can get you fucked."

Barbara turned green. "We have to be careful of that F curse," she scolded the reporter. "The kids are still up."

The room got strangely silent. "I can't believe this," Sloman exploded. "Everyone's half ripped out of their mind, stoned, giggling, snorting, howling, and you whisper, 'We have to be careful about that F word.' "

Barbara looked sheepish. "I can't help it. Sometimes when I'm stoned my mother flashes into my mind. That was her talking."

Again everyone was still. It was clear the effects of the pot mitigated against further serious discussion.

"Could you play back one of the tapes you have from about an hour ago?" Ira suddenly requested.

"What's the matter?" Fred asked sardonically. "You lose track of the conversation?"

"If you people are ready, it's almost Goody-Time." Barbara was about to announce the dessert menu.

Sloman had started talking to Freddy about the anti-marijuana crusade that seemed to be making a comeback of sorts. "There's this professor in California who claims that marijuana causes you to urinate in flour bins."

"If it caused you to piss in flower pots I wouldn't be able to survive in my house," Fred laughed, misunderstanding the reporter.

"He'd be walking around with his schlong hanging out from morning to night with an urge to go," Barbara howled.

She got up and went off to the kitchen to prepare the dessert. Fred and Cusimano meanwhile had started a conversation about advertising and dentistry.

"I get around," Fred explained. "I bought a new car in May; I got 19,000 miles on it. I work six days a week, but I like it. It's only temporary; I'm building. I started with one practice in Yonkers. It boomed, so in two months I hired a guy and I don't go there anymore. I pay him top dollar. Later we'll enter into a percentage, because I want him to have the incentive to continue doing top work. As soon as one of my other offices gets busy, I'll put him in there too."

"Why doesn't he just go into it for himself?" Cusimano wonders.

"Where's he gonna get his patients? He can advertise, but that won't bring that many people in. What I do is look for endorsements. PR. When the PBA sends out a letter to five thousand members recommending me, it's got a lot more clout to it than an ad in the *Daily News*. The percentage of returns is much higher."

It was almost a quarter to one, and they had been talking for hours. The grass made it seem longer.

"I think we really answered that question of before," Cusimano struggled for the strength to get the words out. "Look, you're an ambitious entrepreneur. He's a real ambitious entrepreneur. Barbara's a real high-powered ambitious person—she fantasizes about her clients' prints. And you've got one of the biggest scams in dentistry going. It's great. Pretty soon you won't have to look at a tooth."

"Yeah." Fred smiled. "I can keep one practice as a hobby."

Barbara interrupted the conversation. "I want you to all get ready," she announced in her high-pitched siren of a stoned voice. "This is a great pot house to be in. It's the greatest place to be stoned, because come about one o'clock, when you're getting your chocolate frenzy, I've got all the stuff to go with it. Okay. We'll start with hot apple pie right out of the oven."

The entire room ooohed and ahhhed as one.

"Then we'll go into a chocolate-covered marble cake. There's going to be chocolate Sealtest all-natural ice cream with very large chips in it."

"She did a study one year," Irma boasted. "She tested all the ice creams for the largest chips, and Sealtest won."

Barbara smiled proudly.

"Yeah, but the best ice cream in the world is Bassett's," Sloman smirked.

Barbara looked horrified. "You mean I missed an entire ice cream company?" she moaned.

"Bassett's is from Philadelphia," the journalist explained. "It's the greatest ice cream when you're stoned. It's handmade; they make it with three times the cream."

Barbara looked mesmerized. "Did you shut off the tape recorder yet?" There was a plea in her voice.

"No, why?" Sloman asked.

"I wanted to know if it was party time yet," the young executive whined. Sensing defeat, Sloman relented. "Yeah, it's party time."

"Okay, gang," Barbara squealed with delight. "We got hot fudge and sprinkles on the table, the ice cream's beginning to melt; better dig in."

And like kids at a birthday party, the adults jockeyed for position around the dining room table. Cusimano put a body block on Sloman, nearly knocking him into the hot fudge. Fred broke into the line and innocently made his sundae backwards. A proud smile crept across Barbara's face as she surveyed the scene. Sloman, his sundae finally made, came up next to her.

"This was a great party. We got a lot accomplished. These people are great," he gushed.

In the corner, about five of the guests were hitting on Cusimano for some free public relations advice.

"When I die I want to be buried in the chocolate batter at Carvel's," Barbara noted, oblivious to what Sloman had said.

"You should go live in Hershey, Pennsylvania." The reporter smiled.

But Barbara was still in her munchies reverie. "And I want them to spill in hot fudge," she said, a smile slowly creeping across her shitfaced face, "instead of closing the coffin." And then she was gone, slowly making her way toward the table, to patiently wait her turn at the chocolate goodies.

CHAPTER 17:
A Dealer's Lament

Having established that millions of people in America smoke marijuana illicitly, it's clear that not everyone is as lucky as Jeff's father, who has a nephew who keeps him in Oklahoman homegrown. Some people, like Barbara and her friends, have tastes that run to the more exotic and potent varieties of weed. And where there's a demand, you usually encounter a supplier.

With marijuana, it is fair to say that most users are also dealers. Typically a person may purchase a few ounces at a time and then sell some of the surplus, usually at cost, to a friend. During the sixties, that ethic became almost institutionalized, and many large transfers of grass yielded only small profits. The dealer was more proselytizer than businessman.

But in the seventies, pot has become a commodity. No longer a sacred substance, it is viewed as a cash crop by the peasants who grow it in the Third World, by the smugglers who fly or boat or drive it across the border, by the unloaders who unload the cargo, by the truckers who drive it to all points west, north and east of where it is weighed and crated. So, it is only natural that the dealers who advance the money to purchase large quantities of contraband should expect a sizable return on their investment. And this they get.

Sloman, in the spirit of that great investigative journalist Earle Albert Rowell, wanted to talk to a typical dealer. He was interested in the notion that marijuana dealers had become almost indistinguishable from legitimate businessmen, and he was interested in the way they would account for engaging in behavior that was illegal, given that the sixties "smash the state" dictum was inoperative.

A friend of a friend of a friend who knew a young dealer in the

Boston area promised to approach him. A few days later Sloman received a strange letter in the mail. It bore the return address of an engine oil company in Los Angeles, California, yet the letter had been postmarked Cambridge, Massachusetts. What's more, the envelope had clearly been used before; it had been slit open and taped at the top, and a new label had been affixed over the old one, which was heavily inked out.

The letter itself was brief:

> Mr. Sloman:
>
> An acquaintance of mine, Mark ———, mentioned that you are in the process of compiling notes for a book. Mark feels that I have some experiences which you might consider informative and useful. I would be glad to talk to you, provided my anonymity remains preserved, of course. If you are interested, supply Mark with a telephone number at which I can call you collect, and a name by which you will recognize the caller.

Prudent procedures, Sloman thought, and he contacted Mark. A week later, he received a collect call from the newly named Mr. Roche, who was more than willing to talk to the reporter so that he could have "something tangible to show my grandchildren when they ask me what I did." A few weeks later, a meeting was arranged at Ken's Pub, a jock bar on Boylston Street in Boston.

Sloman arrived a little early and waited for Mr. Roche at the bar, which was fairly packed due to the NFL Division Championship Game just getting started. But Sloman couldn't get into the game, because every time a likely looking Roche would enter, he would attempt some nonverbal gesture to indicate that he was the researcher. After a few embarrassing false leads, the reporter was glad that the rendezvous was taking place in a jock bar and not a gay bar.

But finally a medium-height thin kid strode in, wearing an orange down vest, a tan CPO shirt, and a BMW T shirt. "Mr. Roche, I presume." Sloman was certain, and the two men repaired to a table at the rear of the dark bar. Over hamburgers, they swapped résumés and found that they had fairly similar backgrounds. Both were Jewish, middle-class, sensitive and basically shy. But while Sloman had only dabbled in drugs during college, Roche, who at twenty-two was seven years younger, had had a good deal of experience with drugs ranging from LSD to heroin. At sixteen, he was already selling LSD to his classmates in high school. From there it was a small step indeed to becoming a big marijuana dealer on campus at his small liberal arts college in New England.

For Roche, dealing grew out of his fascination with the drugs themselves. One thing that he admired about the hippie dealers who had supplied him with acid during high school was their high standards and quality control. Another thing that solidified his commitment to the drug scene was a trip to Jamaica early in his college days. The fact that he could observe people who lived with grass as an integral part of their lives, smoking it all day without growing breasts, made a strong impression on the young entrepreneur. And when, during his first year in college, he ran into some seniors who turned him on to black hash and pointed out that the little white streaks were not opium but merely mold, the education of a dealer was complete.

But early on in his budding career, a crisis occurred. His father, who owned a small business with an income which, when combined with that from his mother's own small business, totaled around $150,000 a year, found out his secret.

"At that time I was thinking about buying a new car," Roche remembered, sipping from his gin and tonic, "and I had stopped home for some reason. I was in my room, measuring out some lines of coke to keep me up so I could go drop off about ten pounds of pot, when my father knocked at my door. So I put the coke away and invited him in to talk. I was about eighteen at the time, and he said, 'I want to know if you have been selling drugs at school.' I just looked at him and asked, 'What gives you that impression?' He said he had it from inside sources, and I asked him to tell me his sources and I might be willing to talk about it. I was pretty cunning, and I got it out of him that it was a girl in one of my classes whom I had been in conflict with for a long time. Somehow it had come up in her therapy, and her psychiatrist, the jerk, went and told my father.

"Well, I admitted that I was, and I told him that I was doing it to get a car, that I never touch anything but grass and I only middled it from one person to another. I held it for as little time as possible, just marking it up. I approached it in a businesslike intellectual style and fashion, and realized the risks and minimized them whenever possible."

"You were only following in your father's footsteps." Sloman polished off the remains of his Tom Collins.

"He understood it, but more, he admired it," Roche remembered, "to the point where he said, 'Don't worry, I won't tell your mother.' And to this day he has my trust in these things. I told him again, too; I forget why. Oh yeah, I proceeded to total that car two months after I bought it, two blocks away from my parents' house. I wasn't even that stoned; I was just driving recklessly and having fun and I had forty Quaaludes under the front seat. I just rammed a telephone pole, a tree and another car. I got out and hid the Quaaludes before the police came.

"I decided it was time to keep a low profile, so I bought a little economy car, and a year later I had the economy car stolen. In fact, I did it myself. I backed it into a wall, then drove it straight forward into a wall so there was body damage, then I drove it to a very large parking mall and started ripping out all the ignition wires. I knew they would find it that night, and they did.

"Then I went to buy a new car. And my parents thought I would be replacing it with another $1,000 economy car. But I went ahead and found another BMW, and they couldn't figure out how I could afford it, especially since I was paying my own tuition and rent on my apartment."

"How much did you make dealing grass?" Sloman wondered.

"Let's see, my freshman year I made about $1,200. My sophomore year I made $3,700, my junior year about $20,000, and $25,000 my senior year. Doing one or two deals a year."

"All this just middling?"

"Essentially." Roche tried to keep a straight face, but then broke out laughing. "No, no, you believed it too! That's what I told him. Actually it's all middling unless you import it yourself, but I resent that term when you don't have a client for your contraband."

"What was your clientele like?" Sloman finished off his hamburger.

"It's hard to say." Roche smiled. "I detect two questions there. Who is smoking it and who is buying it? They're not necessarily one and the same, when a guy buys ten pounds. I sold a considerable amount around the campus, and I can safely say that there were times when the entire campus was smoking my grass. I swear, if I had it to do over again, I know now how to do it. I would spend a year each at about six different schools. The only way to start is to get yourself set up at colleges."

"Like a campus rep?" Sloman laughed.

"I know one guy who had made about $2.5 million at my age. He just started young, and he developed connections at schools around the country. He had people like me, the one main man, the undergraduate, who also had other side connections. So this guy who was going to school in Louisiana had connections in Atlanta, Philadelphia, New York, Chicago, Boston, Detroit and a couple on the West Coast. That's what I would do, because I realized I was peaking, reaching the saturation level of my local environment too soon."

"That kid made $2.5 million on campuses?" Sloman was shocked.

"He was incredible." Roche smiled involuntarily, his eyes twinkling behind his aviator wire-rimmed glasses. "He was a six-year medical student at Tulane in his first or second year. But he was more into partying than school. His father was an orthopedic surgeon and wanted him to be a doctor. Then the kid met this older guy—let's call him Charlie—a guy around forty, who asked him if he wanted to make the big time. He needed someone to groom into this business. He got into a lot of things—Quaaludes from the Dominican Republic, limousines filled with pot, hash and coke over the border from Mexico, stuff like that.

"Anyway, all good things must come to an end, and he almost got busted. They were setting up one final deal where Charlie would make $1.2 million, the kid would make $650,000, and another guy $400,000. They had three boats coming in from South America, two from Colombia with pot, and one from Bolivia with coke. By some freak chance, one of the boats got busted and the captain talked.

"About the same time the boats were coming in, my friend was in New York City, and he got busted for snorting coke in a car. They connected him to the boat, and they realized they had some leverage on him and put the kid to the screws. They had the kid, but they couldn't find Charlie, so they put him through absolute hell for a year and a half—trials, hearings, grand juries—and all they wanted was Charlie. This is the way the DEA works. They thought it was one guy responsible for the distribution in the country.

"In the meantime, my friend had stashes of cash all over the country in safe-deposit boxes. So he told the attorneys, one of whom was a former New York City Councilman, and his father to go to Brownsville, Texas, which is the only place you can get a safe-deposit box without registering it either by name or by social security number. All you needed was a key. No matter who you are, if you have the key, you can get in. So they went down there and brought back $2 million cash in large suitcases, and the father got so pissed off he sort of disowned the kid."

"Why was the father pissed? His son was a self-made millionaire," Sloman reasoned.

"But he didn't need it," Roche emphasized. "The father was too. And the grandmother had millions in trust for the kid when he turned twenty-one. So the father turned his back on the kid, and the attorneys wouldn't give him any of the money because the IRS was following him, so he had to wait on tables! He was broke for a long time; the law firm was holding his money.

"Finally, after three years, the DEA couldn't make a case, mainly because they couldn't find anyone to corroborate the stories. People who might have been able to were given $25,000 each and sent on long vacations. So after the IRS gave up too, the attorneys started to legitimate the cash. Between January 1 and the middle of last year, they took $100,000 and invested in one of Secretariat's foals, bought an apartment complex in Aspen, three jewel mines in Brazil, a solar energy plant in Canada, and municipal bonds.

"Here's where the corruption comes into it. The guy who had been sitting on the New York City Council had tremendous political connections, and he had someone in all the metro centers, bondsmen who were predating the bonds back to the fifties, saying they were purchased then and would mature now. But the bond office in Atlanta was being monitored, and all of a sudden they saw $100,000 worth of bond traffic go through in one day, cash, and were dubious as to what had gone on. So they investigated and found this kid's name.

"At the same time, the kid got busted in a small town in New York with a pound of Hawaiian pot that I had just sold him. So his name again appeared in court. And despite the fact that the judge had been paid, an assistant D.A. from New York City came up and asked for a postponement to develop a case. Things started spiraling, and they tied him in with what had happened four years ago and they found out about the bonds in Atlanta and then all the shit hit the fan.

"The attorneys took him out of that town, and they found a remote place for him with bodyguards. He wasn't allowed to make any calls anymore. I couldn't get in touch with him, and I haven't heard from him since. He had told me he would leave the country if it looked like the roof was falling in. He said he had over a million dollars stashed away in Swiss banks. When he went to Brazil to buy those jewel mines, he got in touch with Charlie; they hadn't seen each other since the bust. Charlie had had his face redone, was living in an expensive house, and looked good. So the kid told me that rather than take the rap that's what he would do. And I haven't heard from him since."

Roche finished the long monologue and slumped back into his chair. He took a long hit off his second gin and tonic.

"I don't understand." Sloman shook his head. "Why did he fool around with that Hawaiian grass?"

Roche smiled. "His lawyers weren't giving him enough cash to spend, that's the only reason. When I met him he was on vacation and he was wild. He had spent everything he had. He was hedonistic—any pleasure he indulged. He was very frustrated. His problem was his father gave him endless shit, and the kid was never going to make enough out of himself until he was the most important person in the world. He was always wheeling and dealing. At the time I met him and for the six months that followed, he was always traveling. One of ten days maybe he'd stay at home. He was in Montreal, Arizona, California, South America. All business trips, trying to legitimize cash and feeling important.

"He was preparing to move to Aspen, to live. He bought a house there. But in the meantime, things were accelerating. His girlfriend was graduating from school this spring in upstate New York, and he had to hang around with her. She was the only thing he still had. His parents had kissed him off. He didn't have any friends, 'cause when you get to have that much money how can you have friends? 'Cause they can't do anything you can do.

"So he needed money. And he enjoyed putting things together, making things happen. He and I share many similar attitudes—the enjoyment of flying down to put together a deal where in ten minutes you can make thousands. No scruples, or ethics or morals. You make as much as you can possibly make. So you're sitting with a wad of bills, and then you go out and spend it. You think you're having fun doing that."

"How typical is that?" Sloman wondered. As Roche pondered the question, the reporter noticed that the tables around them were beginning to fill up as the afternoon drew to a close.

"Very. I should get on to my more intimate knowledge. That was a very meaningful story to me, though. He is the only kid I ever met that got introduced into the business as young as I did and had been more successful than myself. There were few people who got into it, let alone people who succeeded, who shared stories and good times and had similar interests. Everyone else was either much older or noticeably disturbed, unhappy, frustrated. Or else they were like legally blind. There was some sadness about it. That's the thing—none of them are happy. Out of all the people who make all the money, none of them are happy. Which comes down to my philosophy."

The dealer paused and took a sip of his drink. Sloman cautiously peered at the couple to their right, who seemed oblivious of their discussion. "It's easy money," Roche resumed. "And people call it easy for very good reasons. It's very easy to make, and you think you're having a great time until you get caught and then you have to pay the consequences. It's very easy to make money gambling, or off prostitution, or with drugs, or stealing off old ladies, or fraud, or computer crimes, or any of those things. It's much harder to do it legitimately; when you do it legit, you have to face things like responsibilities, obligations. You can't just escape; you have to motivate yourself. That's what people want to get away from—these supercapable people, smart, the ones who are dealing all over the country.

"They could have promising legitimate futures if they wanted to. For the most part I could tell they all had parents who pushed them like mad. They had parents they could never quite please or satisfy. For one reason or another, they just felt frustrated. They thought they would show them if they drove in a Mercedes Benz, or lived in a house on the ocean, or went away for five weeks in the winter time or ten weeks in the summer, or had a beautiful bombshell of a wife who used to be a whore. These roles, images. It's always greener on the other side. They're afraid to do it themselves. They're all unhappy. It's not the dope hero that has been portrayed in *High Times*."

Roche trailed off, and Sloman realized that the interview was turning into therapy of sorts. It was clear that Roche was a private person, all the more private due to his line of work. Sloman was part priest, part psychotherapist. And the gin and tonics didn't hurt either.

"The only achievement was putting things together," the dealer remembered sadly. "That's why people never stagnate in the business. As soon as you put one together, you realize that you have achieved at a certain level. But that isn't enough, because the whole reason you went into it in the first place was because what you were doing was not enough. You either have to climb the ladder or get out of it. That's why people keep taking more risks, getting deeper involved. They need that greater sense of achievement out of what they are doing."

"What if it were legal?" Sloman added a confounding variable.

Roche made a face. "That would screw up things royally. Because of the way that the people that grow it negotiate with the people who buy it right now. One overwhelming feeling I have about the whole business is that it is incredibly easy. So much easier than people are willing to understand or realize. Putting together your own pot deal is so easy. Most of it comes from Colombia—I'm talking about high-grade pot, not the shit that people are smoking all over the country. Most people do smoke terrible pot. I rarely ever smoke other people's pot. It's usually not worth smoking.

"It's easy to get pot out of Colombia. Let me tell you how illegitimate the Colombian government is. Since I spoke to you on the phone, the people I have been in business with for the past two years did another deal where my best friend, the closest to me out of the network, actually went down on a boat and came back. He was on an eighty-foot shrimp boat, and they got to Colombia and they were supposed to make radio contact. And the captain couldn't find the place to make contact. They missed the deadline for making radio contact and had to come back home. That's the way things always happen. It always gets fucked up.

"So he came back and got another captain, and this one was supposed to be very good, and they set out again. They made their radio contact, and they were supposed to stay fifteen miles offshore, out of visible range but close enough to move in quickly if they had to. In this case, the money had already been brought down and paid, $500,000. And what they got in return for that money was 35,000 pounds of pot. They were supposed to get 50,000 pounds, but no one told my friend that two days later he would get another 15,000.

"He loaded up forty cayugas, Colombian canoes, three and a half miles offshore, paddling them through the ocean, big waves, with sharks swimming all around. They had paid off the Colombian Coast Guard, so they had two Coast Guard boats guarding them, making sure no other boats came near. That's how corrupt they are down there. The only time they had trouble down there was about a year ago, when the head of the Colombian DEA, an American agent, was assassinated. That presented a lot of hassles. It seems he wouldn't take a bribe so they got him out of the way. So the only way someone could get that position was if they would be cool and cooperate.

"Anyway, this particular boat came into Louisiana, and there's only one spot in the whole trip that's dangerous. When is this book coming out?" Roche suddenly asked.

"Next year about this time." Sloman was somewhat taken aback.

"Okay," Roche continued. "It's called the Verrazano Straits. It's the southern tip of Mexico. It takes about twelve hours to get through the straits, and it's where the American Coast Guard patrols, and it's the only access into the Gulf of Mexico coming from South America. See, they don't patrol the shorelines. They bust you at the access routes. That's why you have to study the charts. You have to understand how to beat the enemy, where they patrol.

"The next step is to find a good place to land the boat and unload. You usually rent land under some guise, oceanographic research, whatever. They hire a crew of people at around three dollars or five dollars per pound to unload it onto trailer trucks. In this deal, 35,000 pounds arrived and 6,000 pounds got wet on the way in, so they dumped that and had 29,000 pounds left. They usually end up renting a farm house in a remote area and bring the pot there to look at it and weigh it. It all comes in bales, trash-compacted. So they put it on tremendous scales and get a digital read-out instantly."

"What about the 6,000 pounds wasted?" Sloman backtracked. "Is that anticipated?"

"This particular gig has been in operation for years, so the $500,000 is just like an installment. They keep sending money, and they keep growing pot for them. It's an ongoing thing. Anyway, the guy who put the deal together, who went with the boat, was supposed to get a salary, either $100,000 or $150,000. That was my friend. Now he had a choice of taking it in pot or in cash. If he took pot, he stood to make a lot more. So he got several hundred pounds, and it was all terrible garbage," Roche spat.

"Why?" Sloman asked.

"He doesn't smoke." The dealer laughed. "He just does coke and drinks Scotch. He doesn't touch marijuana. He doesn't understand it. The pot he got just sucks. It's terrible garbage, immature, leafy. But you never can tell. Sometimes it varies tremendously within one shipment, because it comes from different farms."

"How easy is it to make contact initially in Colombia?"

"Usually you contact Americans who live there. They go down there with the express purpose of putting together deals and stay there. Another thing to understand is the economy of the countries where all the deals come from—they're all starving! Even the poorest, most unknowledgeable pauper in the street will find the people to put you in touch with. Sometimes that might work out. It might be one twelve- or fifteen-year-old who just wants to stay alive and be able to eat who knows the right person to get in touch with. They have communication networks in the tribes and villages. It's the way they subsist. Look what happened on that last deal. A whole village came out to bring out those 35,000 pounds in cayugas. A whole village! Kids, mothers, fathers, and not one of them smokes pot! None! It's just the way they live. They think those crazy Americans, ho, ho, ha, ha."

"I don't understand." Sloman was puzzled. "Doesn't anyone taste this stuff before it's bought? How can you buy 35,000 pounds of Colombian that's shit?"

Roche smiled benignly. "When you talk about pot at the ton level, you're just talking about any commodity. Grade A, B, C, like eggs, large, medium, small. No matter how shitty the pot, they sell it. Someone eventually buys that stuff, but not me. And not my clientele—not the young doctors, lawyers or young professors who are the best clientele. They're the ones with plenty of cash to spend on what they feel is good times."

"Okay, getting back to the deal, now we want to distribute it." Sloman returned to the scenario.

"Okay, it's all arranged before the boat comes in. There are all these small campers and trucks waiting. Usually, the general location is very mysterious. You go into a bar like Ken's Pub, and you walk in with your palms up and someone will greet you, take the keys to your car, and while you are sitting down and having dinner, they will have it loaded and returned to you, and you can leave from there and never know where it came from.

Trust. It's all trust. I have never known anyone to sample anywhere along the line. The business as I know it is all based on trust. I didn't have capital to buy these large quantities of pot; I never paid cash up front. I paid when I collected it. That's the way most of the business still operates."

"Were you ever scared?" Sloman was beginning to feel the effects of the Tom Collinses and of sitting in the same chair for a few hours in the back of a dimly lit jock bar.

Roche laughed at the question, then paused for what seemed like ages. "I was always scared around large quantities of pot. You always think the worst whenever you're surrounded by a ton of pot. Everyone's on edge. Plus everyone is coked out or stoned. Coke goes with a dealer's way of life. They can all afford it, so they're always doing it. Every time I was around a major deal, I wound up getting turned on, and it was always affecting my state of mind. When you do coke, you get naturally paranoid. I always felt that I would be the unlucky one there at the wrong time and get busted. That was frightening."

"Ever get busted? Any close encounters?" Sloman wondered.

"Never." Roche was proud. "Never close."

"Never even stopped for traffic violations . . ."

"Well, I had a trunk full of pot, a hundred pounds or so, and I got stopped for speeding. I gave them a complete set of false I.D.s. But he didn't search the car because I think I'm an intelligent type of person who commands a certain kind of respect with whoever deals with me. And this was a guy who knew I wasn't some moron who had stolen a car, who was drunk. I wasn't harried and distressed. I was normal and I said, 'How fast was I going? No kidding? How'd you tell? Where were you?' My I.D. was for someone who was deceased."

"Were you shitting?" Sloman couldn't imagine staying calm.

Roche allowed a smile. "I was going nuts! I didn't know if he had figured out that I.D. yet. But that's standard operating procedure. Always, when you pay for airplane tickets or rental cars. It was a legitimate driver's license that I had gotten from someone who sells them. Two hundred and fifty dollars. A hundred dollars for a social security number. Five hundred dollars for a passport. That's real easy to get."

Roche paused and finished off his fourth drink. Suddenly a look of surprise flashed into his eyes, and a girl came up to the table and greeted him warmly. He said, "Excuse me," and got up and followed her back to her table. A few minutes later he was back.

"An old customer," he said apologetically, and signaled the waitress for another drink. "Putting together one of these deals is so easy," he reiterated. "But you have to know what the enemy, the cops, are doing to try and catch you. That's sometimes the most difficult and troublesome thing to get. You see the cops as enemies or schmucks. But the greatest part of the whole thing is getting away with it. Not spending the money, not making the money, just getting away with it. It's just a caper. Feeling that sense of achievement."

"Did you conceive of yourself as having some sort of social responsibility?" Sloman rememberd the sixties dealers and their almost altruistic desires to turn on the world.

"I always felt a certain degree of pride while I was at school that so many people were smoking my drugs and enjoying them," Roche said deliberately, almost incredulously. "One year I kept records, I kept books. That year I sold different kinds of pot, hash, black beauties and Quaaludes, and I wanted to know the exact quantity that I sold, that I bought, from whom, when and to whom. From that I got the total gross margin and the total net margin, the difference being what I personally consumed." A smile played across his face. "It was often a net loss.

"People loved me. That's one thing about being a dealer. It's illusionary because you think that people really like you. They don't like you, they like your drugs. You're like any other merchant who has what they want. It's a buying public, and they want what you got." Roche seemed bitter. "You get calls from people, or they stop by your house late at night. They want to hang out with you because you turned them on to good mushrooms. They used to always hang out at my apartment. It's part of the dealer mystique to encourage people to stop by."

"Like the BMOC," Sloman chuckled.

"BMOC used to be one of my favorite expressions," Roche admitted with a smile. "I believed in that, and I understood that one of the reasons I was doing it was that I enjoyed the popularity. I didn't believe that there was any part of my personality that would naturally attract people to me as a friend. It was what I had to offer them as a drug dealer, and it bothered me. It makes you feel somewhat used."

"How'd you cope with that?"

Roche thought a few seconds. "I would rationalize that by

saying no matter how I was treated, how incredible or false these friendships were, regardless, it was thanks to them that I just bought my new car or new stereo or went on vacation or paid tuition. As you may have already guessed, I think my parents pushed me a lot when I was younger and I resisted being a good student. I was scared too much of failing, for fear that would mean maybe that they wouldn't love me as much. The standard stuff. That's what probably motivated me to get involved in the first place."

Roche trailed off and played with his drink. It was getting darker by the minute, and the noise level was intensifying. Sloman felt as though he were in the middle of some strange encounter session.

"What about girlfriends?" the reporter wondered. "Can you have some sort of normal life?"

"That wasn't much of a problem," Roche revealed. "Most of the time I found girls loved the excitement, the money. One thing they loved to do was count the money. Counting the money was a big chore at those levels." He laughed heartily. "The girls loved it. When you're counting piles, it kills your hands, they get numb, you can't move them after a while. Like in half-million-dollar deals! Usually you have to count things twice. The girls loved that." His laugh was almost a giggle, and Sloman was reminded how young he still was.

"Weren't you afraid in those transactions?"

A sly smile crossed his face. "You're leading to the rip-off. I got ripped off twice. It's inevitable. Everyone that deals gets ripped off. Everyone. Either you get ripped off in a discreet way, with someone telling you you only gave them so much, or what they got wasn't what they were told, or why did you put it in their trust they didn't touch it. Or you get ripped off at gunpoint—you go to meet someone who's supposed to sell you a hundred pounds in a parking lot and you wind up being confronted with total strangers with masks on and guns who say, 'Turn it over.'

"Once a guy owed me $5,400 after a $15,000 deal, and I went to the people I purchased it from and they gave me sort of an allowance because I had been ripped. And it seemed that the guy that ripped me off for the $5,400 was involved with one of the more notorious families in New York City. He was training dogs for porno films, something like that. Anyway, the people that sold me the pot sent some people to see the people he was working for, and they said they didn't realize the kid was in so much trouble. So they suggested getting rid of him—they'd pay my debt and pay these other guys to take care of him. So the guys representing me said they'd call their creditor, and one morning they called me and woke me up and said, 'You can get paid off tomorrow. All you gotta do is say "Let the kid die." ' And I said, 'No way! No way!' I don't care if people thought I was a fool. Let them think what they want. So I'll starve for a while, or I just won't be able to go to Jamaica next year. But it wasn't worth seeing someone die."

"How typical was that?"

"Most people just wind up taking a loss." Roche shrugged. "In this case the reason I was getting assistance was that some very good people liked me very much. They looked at me like a little brother. This was the guy that made a couple million. He said his friend Charlie used to have a professional collect money. This guy was a professional assassin, thug, killer, collector, six feet six inches tall, 250 pounds, good with guns, attractive, neat. The CIA used to use this guy as a mercenary.

"A guy once owed Charlie ten grand for a long time. So they got together in a barroom like this—Charlie, the kid, the guy who owed the money, and the collector. Charlie was telling the guy, 'My friend here doesn't like to see me owed money. Show him how upset you get.' And the collector took his glass and took a huge bite out it, then spit it out at the guy. Needless to say, the guy showed up hours later with the ten grand in cash."

Roche was playing with his glass, and Sloman noticed how delicate his hands were, almost feminine. The hands of a great pianist, Sloman could imagine the kid's mother saying years ago.

"That turned me off when they called me up and said that that guy's life was in my hands for $5,400. But the reason I stayed involved with this organization was that I wanted to drive." Roche smiled sheepishly. "I wanted to drive the trucks up when the pot came in. I had the opportunity to do it once, but I turned it down 'cause I was scared. But in one trip you can bring in a ton and a quarter, that's 2,500 pounds at ten dollars per pound, that's $25,000 for a ride that takes less than a day."

"But you don't look like a truck driver," Sloman protested, thinking that Roche resembled a science fair winner a lot more.

"So you get a haircut, put on a funny little cap, wear sunglasses and a white T shirt, and you're fine." The dealer shrugged. "The only reason I never got to do it was because these people liked me too much."

"Where do they get the drivers?"

"Usually friends, never professionals. When you're a dealer you're talking about making and spending tremendous amounts of cash which can only be spent on one type of leisure item. You can't go out and buy a $100,000 home and pay for it in cash. Some government agency will always ask you where you got the money, and you'll get busted. You end up hanging around exclusively with drug dealers or the people who leech off you or just nice people who you turn on to whatever drug is around. Or you subsidize a vacation for one, 'cause if you want to be able to enjoy yourself you gotta make sure they get some money too or else you have no friends. So you let them drive a truck or unload a boat. You want to get people involved so they'll be your friend, keep you company. The whole thing is sad.

"After this one deal, a guy was telling me, 'You know, there's something I realized.' He said, 'It has been a great awakening for me and I feel I'm a better person for it. This summer I dumped my old girlfriend and got married, and I learned that all those people I hung around with on their yachts in Florida or their estates up here, running away on all those vacations, they're all unhappy!' I was looking at this guy, and he was telling me this while he was paying the bill in cash for his $15,000 Mercedes, meeting a girl and marrying her in four days, considering buying a $150,000 home. It seemed slightly inconsistent, but even he was acknowledging it. He said he'd been involved with it for six years, and in those six years he made about $350,000 and pissed it all away. And you know how much of that went for coke? A lot! He spent about $20,000 on coke this summer alone."

"What does grass mean to you now?" Sloman remembered how his own experience of music had changed after he had been privy to the backstage side of that world. "I mean, isn't it a little demystified now that you routinely handle hundreds of tons?"

Roche wasted no time in answering. "In February I acquired a supply of pot that could conceivably last me for a lifetime. It was the best pot I had seen since I had started smoking. I got fifteen pounds of gold pot in one lump cube, which was what I had left from a 130-pound deal. I kept it for my stash. It meant that I no longer had to look around for good marijuana. I always had my own lifetime supply, I could get high as often as I wanted on pot that was of the highest possible quality. So that removed some of the mystique about it, the fanfare of purchasing it, trying it, sitting down in dealers' houses and checking it out, seeing if you're getting high. 'Are you high? I'm high, you high?' That stuff.

"I understand now that smoking isn't going to solve any problems. It won't give me any answers. For me it's a way of relaxing, or escaping. I find it difficult to concentrate when I smoke. I can't focus my thoughts on one thing for a sustained period of time, which means if there's something bothering me, I can't dwell on that problem because my mind is running off.

"Also, when you first start smoking your gut reaction is it's against the law. Some people don't smoke for that reason; some people don't jaywalk either. It's a mentality. I learned early that it's easy to beat the law if you want to. That's why they call it easy money."

"How is it so easy?"

Roche smiled ironically. "It's really easy to beat the law in life. That knowledge has put me in a position where I am frustrated again. I have learned that the grass is no longer so green on the other side." The dealer chuckled at his own pun. "The money's not buying me happiness, and the lifestyle's not buying me happiness."

Just then Sloman noticed that a familiar song was playing in the background, the lyrics floating over the din of the early-evening crowd. It was Dylan, singing, "But I would not feel so all alone/Everybody must get stoned." And for the first time Sloman really felt the desperation in Dylan's voice, as his very words were mocked by the bittersweet Salvation Army horns. Roche was listening too, and then he leaned in over the table toward Sloman.

"It comes down to the fact that the people who get involved on the smoking level or the dealing level are all frustrated to some degree. Life just isn't enough for them without it. I would maintain that the people who use it use it to avoid something else, to avoid reality or the unpleasantness of life. That's a statement I would make about users. Those who deal in it are just frustrated and unfulfilled. I have talked to a couple of psychologists about smokers, and they all concur that marijuana inhibits the growth of the mind. That you can't mature, grow or develop emotionally or intellectually with continued and repeated use of marijuana."

"But isn't that a bit of a biased sample?" the sociologist argued. "Don't they base those statements on patients who have come to them presenting problems?"

"I agree with them, though," Roche shrugged. "Maybe conservative elements have perpetuated the whole idea. Maybe I've become ultraconservative after doing this. It's funny—the people that I was originally exposed to were from the sixties, original acid freaks, and that whole mentality was so different. There's been such a big changing of the guard. Now pot is just another commodity rather than a sacred substance. Those hippie dealers were content with themselves; they didn't care about materialism."

"What kind of person do you think you would have been if you hadn't been a marijuana smoker?" Sloman asked the standard question, but somehow it seemed to fit so well here.

Roche hesitated. "Obviously I would be a lot taller," he joked, then got serious. "If I had never smoked marijuana, I would probably be in law or medical school right now, quite honestly. I feel that whatever motivated me to smoke marijuana motivated me to become disinterested in school. I'll probably go back and get a business degree in a couple of years, then probably get a job with some large corporation, hopefully working in South America, and establish something again."

Sloman had fallen for the bit, but there was something about the way Roche said it that suggested that he was only half-joking. "I always have the vision of being put in the right place at the right time and capitalizing on it. I really feel that the way to start out is to get a legitimate basis, get something sound and credible . . ."

"Can't you exorcise this demon?" It was a confession scene again.

"I can't get this out of my system," Roche almost whined. "Out of my mind. I'm telling ya, there's nothing like it. It's excitement."

"Do you ever try to gamble?" Sloman felt like a social worker.

"I hate it," Roche pouted. "It's dumb. You don't have any control over the odds. At least when you deal you can feel that you are masterminding it. It's like committing the perfect murder just to see if you can get away with it. I don't need the money, I really don't."

"So why do it?" Sloman, the Jewish mother.

Roche smiled. "I suppose that deep down psychologically I still feel unfulfilled. Maybe I'll find fulfillment . . ."

"You know you won't." Sloman was almost screaming. "C'mon!"

"You gotta understand, some people adopt an attitude of day-to-day life, life should be enjoyed today regardless of what tomorrow brings. It's a cultural thing. I believe in that somewhat . . ."

"Bullshit," the superego across the table roared. "You'd feel guilty!"

Roche laughed nervously. "I guess I would. Well, I can dream." He sighed. "But I feel pretty comfortable with myself now. I felt for a while that I was fooling around, not serious about school or anything. Then I started dealing, and then I got into that pretty heavily, and the consumption that went along with it. At one point, I said not only am I jeopardizing my life by getting involved on the wrong side of the law, but I'm jeopardizing my health, from a sanity point of view, with the drugs I was consuming. So I'm in one of my nonsmoking periods now. I used to be an advocate of smoking every day, but now I stop for a couple of weeks. I do it in spurts now. I do it to clean out my system."

"Do you envision going to law school some day?" The guidance counselor took the floor.

"Yes, very much so." Roche seemed earnest. "In fact, I still think that the best possible position to deal from is that of an attorney. You get the best contacts. I can't help it." Roche giggled. "Like I said, there is such an excitement element to it. I loved flying all over the country, and I would always rationalize the air fare, saying I could get that back by selling an extra few pounds. I flew all over. Actually I flew a lot of shuttles, but I liked the longer flights, the whole image."

"What did you wear?" Sloman sipped his Tom Collins.

"I always dressed well. Three-piece suits, briefcase. Images. It's greener on the other side. I couldn't hack doing it legitimately, though. It's the greatest trip to stop at a red light and look at the guy next to me and realize that he has no idea that I have $50,000 cash sitting in a little bag on the floor, or flying in a plane with that much money or contraband.

"It's like the first time you come into contact with a large quantity of contraband in a room. It's such a strange feeling. On the one hand you feel good to be trusted by others. Also a sense of pride that you're gonna get away with something to beat the other side, the opposition, the enemy, the law. But at the same time, it's like a dialectic. You say to yourself what power you have here, that if you just made a couple of phone calls, it could bust the whole thing. Tens of thousands, maybe even millions, of dollars' worth of contraband, and people busted so the network crumbles. People wouldn't be smoking or popping or tripping for a long, long time. That's a weird feeling, a sense of power, of respect."

"You can't find any substitute gratifications?"

"I used to think that there were no other substitutes." Roche began fidgeting more with his ice cubes. "I used to think that it was too hard or took too long. Oh, okay, so I could work hard now and graduate magna cum laude, go to law school, pass the bar. Then maybe get my own practice. Then maybe land a few big cases, and win them. Then maybe by the time I'm thirty-four or forty, with a bombshell of a wife and two little brats, living in suburbia with 1.7 Chevrolets or a Cadillac, then I will feel happy. But I just didn't want to wait. I wanted instant gratification. At eighteen, I felt like I was somewhat accomplished when I bought my first BMW; that was a big symbol to me."

"The picture you paint of the others involved is just so grisly, the way it's gone down."

"They're all unhappy." Roche pulled the last word out like spaghetti. "A lot of them get busted, or they turn into junkies, or they spend all their money, or they marry girls or go out with those that just want a sugar daddy to hang out with and pay all the bills. They are real victims."

Roche leaned over the table and whispered conspiratorially, "But I was clever. I patronized them. I gave them the feeling that they were great, they were so smart and together, and I developed a sense of trust. It was mostly bullshit. I always felt sorry for them. I always felt I would be the one who would show them how it should be done. But I got out of it because I felt the risks were exceeding the benefits. It was a rational decision, but

I will never forget the feeling of excitement, the adrenalin."

Roche leaned back wearily. "What would you compare it to?" Sloman was fascinated by the aphrodisiac qualities of the thrill.

"Nothing." Roche was certain. "Nothing. First of all, I was busy, busy, busy, busy. It was always difficult meeting time schedules, drops to make and driving to do, testing, trying, weighing and measuring, and then counting cash, deliveries, picking up more pot, waiting for phone calls, making phone calls from only pay phones and with special numbers and codes and middlemen. It was always a busy life. Sometimes you would wait for days at a time in some motel room, waiting for someone to show up or call.

"And then, when it happened, it was like everybody else, all these peons, were just going about their normal lives, totally unaware. That was the most amazing thing about the whole trip. That people were so unaware. People like you, the girl behind the bar, the guy driving the cab, they could be deceived so easily. That's what I got off on a lot. I never told many people what I did. So I wasn't one of those people who needed to expound on my accomplishments to feel gratification or happiness or satisfaction. I got it more internally, I guess."

"Incredible." Sloman was feeling the effects of the drinks and the talk. "That sounds like you were the Invisible Man."

"That's my vision of power, I guess." Roche smiled ironically. "I put this deal together, and it's my word that makes a $100,000 transaction like that. But the funny thing was that I lived by myself in a sense. No one could share this with me. Not even the girlfriends. All they were were girls who wanted to go out for a good time. They never really understood how much time and effort it took on my part. How much planning I put into it to make it work just the way I wanted it to work. If it didn't work that way, I would be pissed."

"It sounds like something that was really lonely . . ." Sloman trailed off.

"Precisely." Roche smiled. "Very lonely. But I really feel that I approached it with zeal, integrity, sincerity, responsibility, the way I wasn't approaching the real world because I couldn't—I was afraid of rejection or failure or whatever it was. I was inhibited too easily, and I was too serious, maybe."

"But isn't this a greater test? I could see this being a much greater achievement than succeeding in the real world."

Roche laughed, again a bit derisively. "Maybe we have different perspectives. I still maintain that it is easy money. Now if you want to make money, you have to like borrow it, you have to get credit, get everything organized, do the paperwork. I was cutting through all the bullshit. Maybe it was harder, but I disliked the bullshit."

"But you had to transcend a lot." Sloman recalled his own solidly middle-class weaning. "You could always have copped out and done something legitimately at a lower level than, say, doctor or lawyer. Like CPA. But you did stuff that violated all the values and mores that say that people like you don't break the law. Man, when I was demonstrating in the sixties against the war, the first and last thing my father would say to me was 'Don't get arrested; you'll ruin your future.' "

"I heard the same things," Roche remembered. "But you have to understand the mentality of the dealers. They are above the law. Most criminals seriously don't believe there is much chance of their getting caught. I really believed that. There was part of me that said I was outsmarting them. I would pull up next to a cop on the road with pot in the car and sort of smile, or light up a joint in a bus station, or smoke walking by a policeman. Sometimes I would go out of my way when I was dealing to make it more dangerous. To increase the risk. Like I'd run a light, get into a chase with cops with a trunkful of pot. They didn't know where I was going; they could never find me. Or like that time I gave the cop false identification. I was only augmenting the situation, making it worse. It was that feeling of being above the law and smirking. Although it wasn't much of a challenge to beat your average schmuck cop." Roche laughed heartily. "But that's the spontaneous feeling you get."

"But yet you say you used to shit in your pants around a ton of pot?"

"But I didn't shit in my pants the way some do." Roche got defensive. "I like to race my car now, and I shit in my pants when I am driving on a track at 100 mph and death is real close. I enjoy it, I love it, and I have learned how to be in control. It's been a hobby for about a year."

"Do you see that as some sort of methadone maintenance program for dealing?"

"One of them. Now I'm getting into some other thrills. I want to fly a plane, try kite flying, skydiving—I want to try them all.

I need those thrills, the excitement. I like robbing death or defying fate, or whatever they call it. This is my personal story. I thought things were given to me pretty easily as a kid. I got everything I wanted and was told I could have anything else if I wanted it. So there was no fun, no challenge. Kind of a bore."

Roche suddenly pulled his orange vest out and began putting it on. It was pitch black outside now, and inside the place was completely full. "I have to run." Roche began to get up. "I'm sure it's past my responsibility time or obligation time or whatever."

Sloman picked up the check, to the protestations of Roche, and the two men walked outside into the cold night air on Boylston Street.

"I really gotta run." Roche was apologizing, obviously as dazed as Sloman was after that intense experience. "I take out a little brother tonight, and we're going skating. I'm getting sentimental, I guess. I joined Boston Big Brothers, felt I had a social responsibility . . ." Roche smiled at his own pomposity. "But I really feel I should give for some of the things I took."

The two shook hands and promised to meet again, although Sloman never expected to see this kid whose name he still didn't know, but whose story had really touched him. The reporter was headed down Boylston toward his car and the long drive back to New York City when he heard Roche's voice calling from the other side of the street.

"See ya, Larry," the dealer cum race car driver shouted. "Drive safely."

CHAPTER 18:

The Only Semi-Legal Pothead in America

The circle closes. Although the vast majority of people who use marijuana today do so for recreational purposes, there has been increasing attention paid lately to the drug's relatively unexplored medicinal potential. In one sense, William Woodward of the AMA was prophetic in those 1937 hearings when he decried the Marihuana Tax Act because it would strike a death blow to the possibility of discovering medical uses for cannabis. Now, some forty years later, scientists at major universities and research labs are finding new therapeutic applications for the drug.

But in reality these applications are not that new. Thanks to the efforts of Anslinger and his crowd, marijuana was dropped from the Pharmacopoeia in 1941, but its possible use as an analgesic-hypnotic, appetite stimulant, anti-epileptic, anti-spasmodic, and anti-depressant was known long before reefers were being peddled outside the Savoy in Harlem. Today marijuana is being prescribed for cancer patients as an adjunct in an attempt to stave off the horrible side effects of chemotherapy.

One recent promising use of the drug is in the management of the debilitating effects of glaucoma. As early as 1971, scientists at UCLA who were studying the effects of marijuana on driving reported that marijuana lowered intraocular pressure, a finding that suggested its use in the treatment of glaucoma. After these studies were replicated and found to be accurate, NORML in 1972 petitioned the federal government to reschedule marijuana so that physicians could prescribe it. However, NORML's action seemed theoretical, since they did not have an actual person who was being injured because of the present classificational scheme.

In 1975 Robert Randall, a mild-mannered part-time speech instructor at a junior college in the Washington, D.C., area, came out of the medical closet. Actually, he was forced out when in August of that year, Washington, D.C., police stumbled across four marijuana plants growing discreetly in his backyard. Another possession case—bring him in, let him cop a plea, pay his fine, that's that. Only this wasn't another possession case. Randall wasn't an amateur botanist searching for the ultimate Colombian. He wasn't growing for a community of users. He wasn't greenthumbing it to save money for the real stuff, like Quaaludes. No, Randall was smoking marijuana for a simple reason: so that he would not go blind.

It all started back in Florida in 1969, when Randall, who was a college student then, consulted a local eye doctor because he began experiencing visual rings and halos. The doctor chalked it up to student eye strain, but by 1972, after he had moved to Washington, Randall realized he was suffering from glaucoma. So naturally he began the conventional treatment of therapy.

However, Randall found that he developed tolerance very quickly to the standard medications. Then one day in 1973 the young instructor fortuitously happened to smoke two joints, being an occasional user of grass since 1968, and forty-five minutes later the rings vanished. Being a pragmatist, he denied his own senses, but four months of daily use convinced him that he had found the proper therapeutic regimen.

Of course, Randall was still too much of a nice middle-class young man to do anything rash. In fact, it would be years before he could screw up his courage to even tell his ophthalmologist the reason his intraocular pressure exhibited such weird variations. So the bust in 1975 sort of forced Randall's hand.

With NORML as an ally, Randall went to court on that possession charge, and at the same time petitioned all the governmental agencies that deal with marijuana for immunity to prosecution and access to government stocks of the drug. In the meantime, Randall journeyed out to UCLA to take part in a glaucoma study, in the process collecting data for his court case.

After spending time (and money) establishing that marijuana relieved his intraocular pressure, and proving that the conventional drugs did not work in his case, Randall went to trial in federal court in D.C. While awaiting that court's decision, which was ultimately favorable, he reached an agreement with the National Institute on Drug Abuse whereby he could receive marijuana as part of a pilot program administered by Dr. John Merritt at Howard University. Merritt's involvement was fortuitous; he knew nothing about Randall's case, but merely requested government approval to study the therapeutic use of marijuana, since glaucoma was a disease that struck down a disproportionate number of blacks. So Merritt's and Randall's pairing became a medical marriage of convenience.

Randall received his first government grass in November of 1976, and all went reasonably well until a year later, when Merritt decided that he was going to move from Howard. This left Randall without a doctor and faced with the almost impossible task of finding a new ophthalmologist who could meet the tremendously exacting government strictures that had to be satisfied before one could be entrusted with a substance that could be easily purchased one block away from the Drug Enforcement Agency's headquarters in downtown Washington.

So Sloman decided to pay a visit to the thirty-year-old whom he had seen speak that summer at the stirring smoke-in. It was a rainy afternoon in December, and somehow Sloman thought it was oddly fitting that he should be heading toward Randall's modest apartment just a bit southeast of the Capitol, directly across town from the DEA library. Sloman trekked up the stairs, wiped off his feet, and plopped down into an easy chair in the cozy apartment. Randall, who really did look professorial in a beige turtleneck under a blue dress shirt and white jeans, took a seat on the couch and began recounting his experience.

"I guess this is one of the first demilitarized zones of grass," Sloman cracked, surveying the living room, which was decidedly unextraordinary. "Do they expect you to smoke your issued marijuana in a special place?"

"They could expect almost anything." Randall's tones were firm and well measured, testimony to his master's degree in speech. "They've expected any number of things just getting to here. There were a series of initial negotiations where the DEA, through other agencies, wanted to put me in a hospital on a permanent basis. I was going to be a research subject. Schedule I drugs you're not allowed to use outside of a hospital. Ergo, if you want to use this drug you can volunteer to be in a hospital on a permanent basis. I indicated this was unacceptable. Then they wanted to have me return to the hospital each time I needed to smoke this drug. I could be released when I actually didn't consume the drug, run around the city, and then dash back in when I needed my next fix. They were coming at it from a very abuse-oriented notion. I was safe to roam the streets, but I wasn't safe to use the drug."

"That's a strange notion," Sloman marveled. "Even the old morphine clinics in the twenties, they'd have the addicts come in, get their dose, and then split. They weren't residents."

"I talked about Bibles a lot"—Randall smiled—"chained to churches. I kept trying to make analogies. I kept saying this won't look good. So they realized it wouldn't float, and they said, 'We'll let you take it home.' But because it's a Control I substance, there's a great deal of security necessary. They wanted me to buy a 750-pound safe or a 250-pound safe embedded in concrete and bolted from the inside to the floor. I told them that I rented here so that might be unfeasible." Randall chuckled, a hybrid laugh somewhere between a giggle and a high-pitched guffaw. It was nice to see that he still had a semblance of a sense of humor after fighting the Washington drug bureaucracy for three years.

"The whole thing broke down really oddly, though," Randall remembered. "A doctor was found suddenly. This had been a negotiating process of six months, May to September of 1976. Throughout that period I was looking for a physician willing to meet their requirements. Every time I found a physician half-interested, he would be informed of the requirements and he would withdraw violently."

"What were the requirements?"

"His background must be subjected to a security check by the DEA. DEA agents come into his office and review his office security. His medical files are open to examination. Should his secretary make an accounting error in accounting for a Control I substance, he could be fined $25,000 and end up in prison for five years. That's a powerful disincentive for a doctor to get involved. But as soon as this doctor entered the process, my contact with the agencies broke off. I was informed at the last moment that women and children would not be allowed into the program, that I would be guaranteed marijuana on a once-a-week basis—I would not have to report anywhere under any awesomely strange condition—and that the doctor would have control over the drug. Those were the basic things I wanted."

"What were you doing before Merritt's program? Were you abstaining?"

"I smoked five joints a day if I could get it," Randall remembered. "I hardly could get it. There'd be large gaps of maybe a week at a time."

"What were those periods like when you couldn't score?"

"Physiologically it was whatever glaucoma is—high pressure in the eye; there's no pain involved. But there are ocular symptoms, like halos around the eyes. It's very strange. If you smoke marijuana on a fairly continuous basis that doesn't happen and you almost disassociate the effect with marijuana. Then it happens and you just get mad. But without smoking, vision goes to white, like highly overexposed film, and that occurs at very high pressure levels and is very damaging. And to prevent that, I was throwing myself on what are essentially incredibly toxic drugs. One of them is Daranide. There's a whole series of drugs that are systemics. They are basically diuretics. Daranide is the strongest. It simply leeches the body of trace elements to the point where a person becomes extremely fatigued, very easily depressed. I quit taking the drug because it began to hurt my kidneys quite badly.

"It's a terrible drug. I didn't use it long enough to understand just how frightening it was. There are other people who have used it for longer periods of time who apparently become impossible to live with, their spouses report. Any number of terrible depressions, kidney stones, renal failure, gastric ulcers, inability to walk because the muscles have constricted so badly. It throws the pH in your body into hyperacidosis. It's a strange drug."

"What other good conventional drugs did you take?" Sloman smirked.

"I still take phospholine iodine. I really like it at low dosages, about .06 percent in solution. That dosage only constricts my pupils and makes the world quite dark. But at a high dosage, about .25 percent, it creates terrible spasms in the muscles around the eyes. I've never used it for a long time."

"So when did Uncle Sam give you reefer?" Sloman was chomping at the bit.

"I had been seeing Merritt since September of 1976. At first he wanted to get my pressures without marijuana use, for baseline data. In October I got five milligrams of THC orally as a test. That was the first indication that any of the shipment of the drug had come in. I had seen his safe coming in a couple of weeks earlier. Then one time in November, I saw this other guy there, a black guy in his fifties, and he was smoking marijuana. I don't really think Merritt wanted us to see each other initially, but the man was apparently having trouble smoking so he brought him in and asked me to show the man how to smoke. So I tried, but I couldn't smoke myself because I was on the oral dose, and for control reasons I couldn't actually demonstrate how to do it.

"That day I waited around for two or three hours; I spent a lot of last year just sticking around. Merritt finally concluded that the oral doses weren't going to work, so he gave me about fifty joints, and said, 'I'll see you next week.' I was really surprised."

"How did he give it to you?" Sloman was all ears.

"Wait, I'll show you." Randall walked into the next room and resurfaced with a clear plastic container with a label on it. "This is the basic marijuana packet." He tossed it over to the reporter.

Sloman felt that he was holding the future in his hands. The label read "15 Marijuana Cigarettes—For Investigational Use Only—Material Furnished Free." Inside the packet were perfectly rolled normal-looking cigarettes. Already, just by looking at them, he could tell that it wouldn't be as much fun. He gingerly handed the packet back to Randall.

"It was just so strange to walk out," Randall remembered fondly. "No one had ever walked out of a hospital before with it. Merritt let me titrate it, so I just went home and started smoking. UCLA indicated that I'd probably need nine or ten joints a day. I went through about ten a day, because I was back there in five days. He went, 'No, no, no. Too high.' He tried to get control over the dosage and put it back down. I think again it wasn't a reflection of how he felt medically, but some sharp bureaucratic reaction to the sudden drain. So we tried to get it back down to six, but we couldn't establish control, so we went back up to between eight and ten, depending on the weather. The pressure base appears to be seasonal."

"What about the side effects of smoking? Like getting high?" Sloman found it very curious to conceive of it that way.

Randall smiled. "I always thought the high was related to the amount of relief I was getting. Apparently this is a very strong impression of the people who use this drug for chemotherapy. If they are not high, then they don't get the relief. I really don't know what that says either. UCLA indicated that you can get the reduction in pressure without the high. In the last year, I've had a very hard time getting high off the marijuana I'm getting (because it's always the same), yet I'm getting pressure reduction consistent enough to make my eyesight stable."

"In other words, you're almost forced to buy street grass again to get high?" Sloman laughed at the irony.

"Yeah. I haven't been able to afford that luxury in the past year simply because I haven't had a steady job. But being at the NORML convention was interesting, because it indicated to me that the marijuana I could get on the street is probably more effective than the marijuana the government is providing.

"The government has more Delta 9 THC, because it's the most psychoactive constituent, not the most medically utilitarian. This grass contains no Delta 8 THC, which is the most effective of the Deltas in reducing eye pressure. I think the names of the agencies indicate what the basic problem is. The National Institute on Drug Abuse. The Drug Enforcement Agency. These are all agencies who have a perspective of abuse. You're not supposed to use this drug to benefit. The research that's done is to find out what happens when we give the most abused part of an abused drug to a person. That's not the best way of approaching a therapeutic situation. But that's the way they're forced to approach it because of their perspective."

"So you're getting an adulterated product?" Sloman railed.

"Very adulterated. For purposes that are surely distinct from mine."

"Do you have any idea of the origins of the marijuana other than that it comes from the government farm in Mississippi?" Sloman wondered. "Do you know where the seeds are from?"

"I have different stories. Mexican is like a universal guess. But there are at least a hundred different kinds of plants at the Mississippi farm. Some people have told me it's Mexican and Afghani mixed together. Some say it's a blend of twenty different kinds. I don't know. The fact that they freeze-dry it and dice it and flake it and process it—all of that detracts from whatever exotic image it may have. It's the Pringle's Potato Chip of pot. I don't want to say that it's an inferior product, because that might offend them, but they're producing a product to be looked at from an abuse standpoint. Some of the stuff I've been smoking is from the dark ages of the Nixon administration. It's really back there, some from 1971."

"How do you know that?" Sloman was intrigued.

"Oh, it's vague knowledge." Randall laughed coyly. "It's apparently refrigerated. It's dose-qualified as it leaves. But who would really want to smoke a cigarette that had been in cold storage for maybe five years? A good fresh taste, y'know."

"What does it taste like?"

"It tastes stale," Randall protested. "It has an overpowering but very strange smell. Some marijuana smells very heavy. This doesn't smell very heavy, but the smell is very penetrating. I've been in a room in a very large building and had someone five floors above come down and report that it had penetrated through the ducts."

"Where do you smoke most of your joints?" Sloman had visions of Metro buses emptying, people fleeing in panic.

"Here. This is where I live," Randall giggled. "It would be silly for me to go anyplace else. Although I do smoke in public. A lot of the initial press reports were 'Man Gets to Smoke at Home.' Home can be a prison too if you can only leave your home for two hours before you have to get back to it. I think the obvious interpretation is wherever medically necessary. The last time I really avoided doing that was in Mississippi. I was down there to testify at decrim hearings in the Mississippi Capitol Building. I didn't feel like I should intrude during the hearings. Everybody else was smoking cigarettes. The place is amazing—incandescent lights like a showboat. I didn't smoke there, and I got out four hours later and my pressure was incredibly high. I decided never to do that again.

"I tried smoking once in an airplane. A person very far away began to cough, and that made me nervous so I put it out. I find that it helps to put the stereo headphones on when smoking in airplanes, because then you don't believe you're there yourself. The stewardesses didn't seem to notice, or if they did, they didn't care. Only once has someone walked up to me. That was in one of those empty departure areas where I had run to five minutes before the flight, nobody around. So I started smoking, and this girl sat down and I didn't think anything of it. I got done with one joint and started smoking another, 'cause it was going to be a very long flight. This girl then came up to me and said, 'Is that marijuana you're smoking?' and I went, 'Yes.' She said, 'Can I have some?' I didn't realize until later how strange it must have sounded, but I said, 'No, you can't. This is legal.' She got very strange-looking and walked away. I don't know if she ever connected it, 'cause I sure didn't understand what had happened."

"Was that basically your own prudence, or did you ever get any directives like 'Thou Shalt Not Pass These Joints'?"

Randall smiled. "No. I make the assumption and go from there. I have a feeling I would be sucked into the sky if anybody ever touched one. Seriously, I have no idea. The government did a good job of not informing me."

"That's the abuse model at work," the reporter realized. "By not giving you these guidelines, they're saying . . ."

"You make a mistake and we'll tell you about it," Randall finished.

"You make a mistake and we'll bust you for it." Sloman was a bit more cynical. "They're putting the pressure on you to be an exemplar."

"The system lends itself to intimidation," Randall philosophized, as he cleaned his thick rimless glasses. "I would say that's a basic component of it. Even if that is not the intention of the individuals who are behind the system or the agencies, the whole system is just running against the grain. What are these yo-yos doing with this drug? I'm not dealing with ophthalmologists when I'm dealing with NIDA, FDA and DEA. I'm dealing with a bunch of entrenched bureaucrats who have a political perspective on this drug. I'm really tired of it after a year of it.

"I could have just paid the fine after I was busted. They probably would have fined my girlfriend and me $250 each. But finding that the government had known for five years that marijuana could be effective in the treatment of glaucoma and having a good sense that the government didn't really try to do much to pursue the issue made me mad. Initially I just didn't want to be a criminal. It was very shocking. It left me very insecure. But then to find out that these goons had one branch of their government discover that the drug is not only not too bad but it's really beneficial."

"How did your family react to all this?"

"It was fine with them. I don't know how to characterize it. How will a mother react? No mother is overly excited about her child going blind. I think it's simple commom sense—if it was going to help me, fine."

Randall suddenly reached over to the table. This was it. Sloman watched with fascination as he slowly pulled a perfectly rolled cigarette out of the packet and then inserted it into a strange oval-shaped stone. Randall then lit a match and took a deep drag off the joint. An overpowering odor filled the room.

"What's that you're smoking it with?" Sloman was curious.

"This? Just a stone. No medical significance. My fingers got incredibly yellow initially. It looked like I was going through a racial change. I could just imagine one of the doctors saying, 'My god, it's causing a racial change.' You could expect that from some of the yo-yos who research marijuana."

"Well, that's one of Anslinger's favorite warning signs, a telltale yellow discoloration of the fingers, and he was talking about real chronic addicts like yourself," Sloman jibed.

"There were some incredible things. Tokyo Rose was mentioned in my court case. Why, I don't know. The prosecutor brought up Tokyo Rose right after he brought up that the Constitution didn't protect people's eyesight. The judge got very upset toward the end of the trial. The guy said at one point that I shouldn't be allowed to use marijuana even if it did help my eyes because it might cause my legs to fall off. No evidentiary base for that. He just threw it in because he thought it sounded good. The judge really didn't know what to think. At the end of the trial he said, 'What are you recommending? You want to let this guy go blind because in forty years his legs may fall off?' I think the judge got genuinely upset about the quality of the case the government was presenting."

"When did they finally rule in your favor?"

"It was decided on November 24, 1976, after I had already been receiving marijuana from the government. It was a very strange period of time. I was getting marijuana from the government while being under indictment in the District of Columbia. The government moved to settle my petition when it realized that the court, having not responded in such a long time, was obviously going to rule in my favor. If the government had not made marijuana available to me through a mechanism it set up (which is very confusing), then it could probably be made to do so through the courts. That's probably where I am again. It's a year later now. My doctor is getting ready to leave. So as he leaves, he leaves this problem: I don't have formal immunity from prosecution, for they set up my access to this critically important drug through a research program that's never been funded to conduct research. For the past year I've been saying to these agencies that these are terribly irregular procedures. What does it come out to? You can't make this drug a ransom. They have done that. They have made me a research subject. FDA came to me and said—this was ten months after I had been receiving the drug—'if you don't sign the consent form to be a research subject, we'll take the drug away from you.' I don't feel I have the financial ability to carry on a continuous legal conflict with the government. I signed the forms and indicated that they were signed under duress, without willing consent. If I didn't sign these forms, I was deprived of my medication.

"My doctor's leaving means the government's only solution for me at this point is to turn around and say, 'Find another doctor.' Well, I've been down that road. That's Catch 22. It takes six months to fulfill the requirements. I can't afford six months of waiting around. So I'll probably have to go to court. Take all the agencies to court and ask that they be detached completely from my medical care. Ask either for a continuation of this supply or for a supply through the police, which would ensure that the drug had not been refined or manipulated beyond a certain point."

"Have you perceived any side effects from being such a chronic user of marijuana?" Sloman wondered. "For me, I find if I smoke a lot I get very paranoid, too introspective and self-conscious."

Randall stretched out on the couch, and he fingered his small mustache. "That's hard to determine in my own situation simply because I've been placed in a situation where my unique environment causes a great deal of introspection. Because one has to wonder, 'Why me?' " He laughed again, an endearing laugh. "Certainly my arrest made me much more paranoid than any marijuana smoking I've ever done."

"But until this year, you were basically high all the time," Sloman interrupted.

"I was high a good percentage of the time," Randall admitted. "I enjoy being high. I don't enjoy not being high. I think it's sad to have lost whatever it was that was there that I found pleasurable. I was much looser as a human being. I had barely gotten over my adolescence. I was just coming to grips with what it meant to be an adult. What it might mean to be a member of the middle class. All of that was occurring, and then suddenly I got arrested. It's been weird since then. It's strange to become an adult knowing that there are three federal agencies who have control over a drug that you need. I won't get paranoid about that.

"I think it was John Mitchell who said that the marijuana laws were like a never-never land. There have been points where I've stopped and thought for a considerable number of weeks, especially after I got the marijuana from the government, what do I do? Do I run out and say, 'Hey, everybody with glaucoma line up!' It was strange being placed in such a position; I didn't want to manipulate people's hopes. So you live in a very narrow line. You just say this drug works for me. It's reasonable to assume it would work for others. I wouldn't tell someone who had glaucoma to run out and use marijuana. I would say the best situation they could be placed in would be one in which they could go to a doctor and that doctor could say, 'Okay, let's try it.' Anything less than that is sort of silly. The drug is everywhere. People will go and do it.

"There are a lot of illusions here. I think it will take fifteen years to get an eyedrop from marijuana if you put it through FDA. The government is ideologically opposed to marijuana in smoked form, even though it's a perfectly good drug. Some people obviously won't be able to smoke it. That's life. Some people can't take penicillin. Some people won't like the high. All drugs have problems. But if someone wants to do it, he should be encouraged to do it."

Randall removed the butt from his stone and immediately lit up another cigarette. "The essential problem the way I see it is that I have a medical problem and need a medical response. I do not need this huge, clumsy, cumbersome machine which is constructed for abuse. That's what we'll probably end up in court about. I've never really understood the level of emotion that NIDA in particular has demonstrated toward me. One individual there has accused me of distorting reality on a continuing basis—one of my favorite quotes. The FDA indicated that I was psychologically dependent on marijuana. I pointed out to the FDA that according to the law that was addiction, and that if I was called an addict again I would send a lawyer off to discuss it with them and sue them for libel. Now it's a situation no one wants. I had been willing for a year to not go back to court, because the system is slowly trying to slide towards something more amenable. But the doctor was critical to the convenience, so it all snaps open again."

"Don't you sometimes get nostalgic for the simple days when you were just another recreational drug user?" Sloman was impressed with the tenacity of Randall's commitment.

"I get nostalgic for the days when nobody knew nothing." The patient sighed. "When I taught school. I liked plants. I *used* to like plants. It's been a very hermetic kind of experience. Because no one else can experience it firsthand except Alice, my girlfriend. Beyond that, it's a lot like your thesis. People ask how it's going. No one cares. It's too burdensome to know how it's going. There's too much detail. It's too confused. The primary disincentive the government's got is they've created a system that's so complex and so difficult to understand that people always blame themselves for not being able to understand it, rather than blaming the system. This makes no sense. Reasonable people can't understand why something that costs so much money can't make any sense."

"What are you doing these days for money?" Sloman followed up.

"I'm becoming excellent at begging, which is frightening." Randall laughed softly. "I don't know what I do for money. I've already consumed my life-insurance policy, which is a liberating experience. I'm going along here getting more and more liberated." Randall and Alice, who had joined the conversation, laughed in unison. "My entire entry into the middle class has been deferred."

"You'll wind up a Yippie," Sloman joked.

"I don't think so. I'm gonna end up on food stamps. I don't know what we do for money. I borrowed a good deal. I work on and off as a Kelly girl at the Australian Broadcasting Commission—which I really enjoy doing. I just enjoy getting out of this environment, thinking about other things. I decided not to go back to teaching for the time being because the experience was getting much too strange. I've heard from hundreds of people who have the exact same problems who aren't finding any solution."

"What do you mean the experience is getting too strange?"

Randall paused. "These people have the same problems I have. They're asking for the same relief I have, and they can't get it. It's because they don't have the proximity I do in this area to be able to pursue three federal agencies to the ground. Probably they don't have the inclination to do that. I do, for some reason. It's all very burdensome, but I'm young, so what the hell. It's also very interesting. I do know a lot about the government."

"Has Nader been interested in your case at all?" Sloman asked the logical question.

"No. I called his group once. I think the question is more bizarre than people want to get involved with. Initially there's very little comprehension. Maybe that's why the government paid so little attention to it. It's very hard for someone who uses marijuana on a social basis—and I think that everyone I dealt with including the bureaucrats and politicians uses marijuana on a social basis—to understand, because they come from that perspective, and the laws are designed to meet that perspective. They're so fixated in that direction that it must almost seem like a trick that marijuana works to help glaucoma. And this trick is refined only in me. Somehow it's not the same trick for two million other people in this country. There's never the honest admission that this drug works and it affects two million people's health."

"Isn't there a National Glaucoma Society?" Sloman tried another tack.

Randall smiled. "There are two foundations for the blind. They don't want to know. One is very establishment oriented. The other is having its own problems. The person that I talked to there had gone blind from glaucoma, but he wasn't interested in what happened before blindness. He was now only interested in blindness. I can understand that perspective. I may well share it some day. It would be foolish to say that I got into this to save my eyesight, because I can save my eyesight legally or illegally. That's very simple. I think I got into it because I was very angry. Also because I thought it would be an adventure. What you don't understand when you get involved in an adventure like that is that adventure by its very nature is a very painful experience that lasts a lot longer than you thought. And you don't have control over it, so it just keeps spewing out.

I really thought it would have an end. But I don't even see the twilight at the end of the tunnel."

They both fell silent. Sloman was beginning to feel a bit uncomfortable and a bit angry. "No pun intended, but it seems like you're living in shadows. Even NORML seems to be concerned more with just recreational use."

"I'm running through an area that no one else has ever run through before, I think. That alone makes the whole situation very strange. It's gonna take a significant amount of time for people to simply comprehend the dynamics."

"But there was a tremendous use of marijuana for medicinal purposes way before there was an inkling of its use in America for recreational purposes," Sloman recounted.

Randall smiled benignly. "Yes, and so we come full circle. I'm lost in my own perspective. This is a result of having been involved in it now for two years. But I think it's obvious to me that this is the critical question involved with marijuana. It is medical. I appreciate NORML's feelings about the question being about recreational use, but I feel all NORML can do with that is use facts as a secondary approach. They can use facts to say, 'No, the drug is not as dangerous as you're making it out to be,' which is an argument beginning in the negative. That suits itself to political compromise, but not to really looking at the drug itself. I think the issue turned in my direction is to begin with what does the drug do medically. As soon as you answer that, you shatter everything else beyond that. You find out that it's a beneficial drug, and that alone has symbolic value, in addition to its practical value."

Sloman was by now totally amazed that Randall could still talk about this so dispassionately and reason with such logic, and even maintain a droll sense of humor about the whole ugly affair. "Given your perspective, what kind of attitude do you have toward recreational users? Do you get pissed off at them for using the drug so frivolously?"

Randall smiled again. "No, the same attitude I've always had. Some of my best friends are recreational users." They both laughed.

The conversation seemed to be winding its way down, and during the lull Sloman could hear the sound of the falling rain on their rooftop. He had a long trip back to Virginia, where he was staying with friends, and he realized that he wouldn't have minded a hit or two off that government stash. But he also felt weird about asking, and he admired the incredible restraint Randall exhibited by not offering.

"You know, maybe the reason they gave the grass finally was so you'd fuck up?" Sloman mused aloud. "Then it would just be a self-fulfilling prophecy; you'd go down the toilet and their paradigm would still hold."

"I would think that's maybe what the government thought," Randall agreed, to Sloman's surprise. "Give him the drug and he'll become amotivational, lose his short-term memory. There are times when I really believe they read their own pamphlets and were sold. It's like the guy who makes polyvinylchloride being convinced that plastic is the way to go, so his whole house ends up that way. It's crazy. He didn't become amotivational. What a shock!" He laughed.

"In fact, he's got such motivation, the fucker is going to sue us!" Sloman quipped. "You've let them down again," Sloman smiled.

Randall nodded agreement. "I do let them down a lot. I don't live up to their expectations of action. I would think they probably have a psychiatrist dedicated to my Minnesota Multiphasic saying 'I vould think he vould do this next.' I don't know what model they're using. Who can tell? But it's obviously going to have to end somewhere. I'm counting on that. Because then I'll be able to step aside and think of how interesting it all was. Then it won't be so painful after it's over with."

"So then what are you going to do?"

Randall thought a second. "I'm going to go back to teaching college. If I still have my sight. It depends on how long the whole situation goes on. I used to have a sarcastic joke that I would tap my way to the stand when I was waiting for the court decision that seemed like it was never coming a year ago. The more it goes on, I really wonder if that could possibly occur. It does keep spewing out. And I would have never believed that it would have gone on so long."

So Randall sits and waits. He waits for the day when the vast majority of marijuana users, the recreational users—the ones who smoke to escape, to relax, to play tricks with their consciousness, to hear different things in their music, and to see flashing light shows when they stare at a neon sign—force the pot question to get fully played out in that arena. And then, maybe, he will have no obstacles to prevent him from smoking this playful substance so that he can get rid of those flashing lights and psychedelic exposures and halos that surround everything he tries to see. But in the meantime he just patiently waits.

CHAPTER 19:
The Cottage Industry

The American way of preparing hemp for smoking is very simple; in fact the simplicity is in striking contrast with the practice of the United States tobacco trade which deems it essential, according to the advertisements, that the cheapest cigarettes must be toasted or freshened, super-dried or super-moistened, before they can be offered to the consumer. No such refinements have yet percolated to marihuana manufacturing circles; on the contrary, the leaves and pods of the plant are merely chopped up coarsely and then roughly made up into a kind of cigarette of which three or four long puffs deeply inhaled are generally enough to cause a novice to fall into a sort of trance.

—From *The Last Plague of Egypt*
Baron Harry d'Erlanger (1936)

Little would Baron Harry know. The coarsely chopped, crudely rolled joint has in the seventies gone the way of hemp clothing. But of course that was inevitable, because the new marijuana ethic today is closely allied to a general consumerism that sooner or later was bound to intrude on the consciousness-altering ritual of smoking weed.

Along with a number of long-standing industries that the marijuana boom has helped (check out the stats on stereo-industry sales or notice how many fast-food places are springing up), an entirely new allied business, the paraphernalia industry, now grosses close to $200 million a year, according to some estimates. And provides another cutting edge in the struggle to eventually legalize grass.

No longer does a poor pot smoker have to suffer through

smoking seed-filled, hand-crushed marijuana clumsily rolled in paper that was designed for Bull Durham's best. No, today, thanks to the marvels of technology and consumer preference polls and cost-benefit analyses, there is an industry that is totally devoted to making sure that the illicit drug the average American is clandestinely consuming enters the body in the most pleasurable, efficient, hassle-free manner. So smokers rejoice! You can take your pick of at least 140 different varieties of rolling papers, from flavored ones to double-width numbers to those with built-in roach clips, filter-tips, even one that features Watergate atrocities courtesy of reprinted headlines. Then there are luxury reefer rollers, herb cleaners, filigreed stash tins, sophisticated scales, smoking stones (to avoid that telltale yellow stain), and all sorts of roach clips.

And for those who find the cigarette too pedestrian a smoking format, there is always the option of the endless varieties of pipes, masks, water pipes, tokers, ceramic bongs and power hitters. Throw out the corncob—the American head industry is about to make your smoke elegant. Just listen to this blurb from the most recent NALPAC 1977–78 Paraphernalia Dealers Handbook:

> Cocobolo is an exquisite exotic hardwood imported from Costa Rica. Each piece is unique in itself. Its colorful grains, seemingly hand painted, enhance the warm, rich hues of the wood. Its high durability and beauty make it a very versatile product. Any of the styles of cocobolo pipes would be a welcome addition to the connoisseur's pipe collection. The stash jars and boxes would grace any setting. Cocobolo with its high volume turn-over is a proven profit maker for any retail outlet.

And why not, with prices that begin at twelve dollars a pipe, wholesale? Which brings up the issue of the eventual legalization of the substance that gets crammed into these elegant pipe bowls. What the paraphernalia industry has proven is that the marijuana culture in no way threatens the American Way of Life. Amotivational freaks do not build up a $200 million industry. Revolutionaries do not spend twenty-five dollars on a water pipe.

No, the paraphernalia industry is peopled by hip, enterprising young capitalists who, in the best spirit of entrepreneurship, saw a crevice in the corporate supply side of the ledger and hustled like hell to fill the demand of a disenfranchised clientele. Never mind that the products would be used to facilitate illegal acts, let the law follow the mores, let the chippies fall where they may.

Burt Rubin is a fine example of this new breed of hip entrepreneur. He co-owns Robert Burton Associates, the makers of E-Z Wider Products, a paraphernalia line that grossed almost $7 million last year. At thirty-one, Rubin is one of the new Marijuana Millionaires. And a mother's dream. A Westchester boy, he was graduated from N.Y.U. in 1968, went to law school for a little while in Miami, and then got a job in New York with the largest fertilizer company in the world, training to be a metals trader.

But Rubin was also a pot smoker and a shrewd one at that. He noticed that he and every one of his friends always used two papers stuck together when rolling their numbers. Necessity being the mother of invention, the budding metals trader decided to go into the wide-cigarette-paper business. So along with his friend Bob Stiller, who was working as a systems analyst at Columbia University, the young entrepreneur set about breaking into the business.

This entailed reading every last piece of literature on marketing, advertising, packaging, printing papers. They visited four printing plants, five paper mills, numerous ad agencies. They wrote to every booklet manufacturer in the world, all of whom replied nada. Undaunted, they finally persuaded a small manufacturer to do up a test order in June of 1972. A few months later, they were responsible for all his production and onto their third outlet.

To ensure adequate distribution for this tainted product (it was obvious what was to be rolled in these extra-wide papers), Rubin developed a tobacco that was sold with the boxes of papers. To no one's surprise, the tobacco stiffed, the papers took off, and the distributors came back begging for only the papers.

But they would not stop at mere papers alone. Rubin developed what he calls his R&D staff, and soon innovative head products were rolling off the blueprints. A senior design engineer with Polaroid developed a fantastic new water pipe that was spill-proof and featured a disposable cleaning cartridge, similar to a razor system. The same people who brought you the interior of the Boeing 747 worked up a rolling machine complete with finger grips.

In the marketing arena, Robert Burton Associates regularly engaged in survey analysis, conducted in shopping center malls in six major American cities. The results were tabulated by computer and were utilized in ad campaigns and in product development. Rubin now employs over forty people in his Lexington Avenue office, and scores more in E-Z Wider's lower Manhattan factory.

It was into the elegant Lexington Avenue offices that Sloman ventured to talk to Rubin. And in a spacious, carpeted office, forty-four floors above the teeming streets of Manhattan, the young entrepreneur served the young journalist tea on a fine marble conference table and reminisced about his career in paraphernalia.

"I have a sort of sociological view of marijuana in terms of why here, now, etc." The handsome, casually dressed businessman began expounding his theories. "I think in the past when people worked in mills, worked in factories, worked in general, their days were very boring, and so at night, when they came home, they wanted something that was going to blow it out, ya know. Whereas today, with so much craziness of input, TV, radio, boom boom boom, and the rush crazy life, people want to have spare time, they wanna take it easy, relax, sit back. That's what marijuana does—puts a shit-eating grin on your face. It's like the opposite and equal reaction to the rush rush rush. People don't want to get blown out; they want to be relaxed."

"Basically your innovation was the double width?" Sloman really was not sure what E-Z Wider meant.

"Yeah, the double width." Rubin patiently explained, "I don't think, though, that that was the thing that per se made us great sales. I think that the image and the thing we put around E-Z Wider was as important to its sales as the paper.

"What are we doing with a racing team?" Sloman vaguely remembered seeing a huge photo of a formula race car as he entered the offices. "Well, it's at the racetracks. People see it, but it also shows people that smokers are not sitting around all day just smoking, doing nothing. They're active people. We have a formula car. Did you see the two pictures in the lobby, the car and a hang glider? We also have a hang gliding team. We're the only commercial sponsor of a hang gliding team.

"We sponsor rock concerts. We had Joe Cocker, the Atlanta Rhythm Section. We're trying to say, 'Hey, we came out of this time with you; we're part of the whole thing. *We* didn't make papers from 1722. We made rolling papers; we didn't make cigarette papers.' "

"What did your parents make of all this?" A dutiful Jewish son, Sloman never avoided asking this question of those who might be tainted by their association with the illicit substance.

Rubin smiled broadly. "They didn't know what to make of it. They may still not believe I smoke grass. But we've gotten real legitimacy. *Forbes* magazine wrote a full-page article about us last issue. The *Wall Street Journal* wrote a full-page article. Six years ago when I started the business and I'd tell people what business I was in, any businessman's next question was 'What do you do full time?' Three months ago I was invited and went down to the Wharton Graduate School of Business to give a speech on entrepreneurship. Five years ago they were laughing at me, and now I'm teaching their kids how to do it.

"It's a definite planned progression. For instance, we had Mickey Mantle down at the convenience-store convention a year ago September, giving out E-Z Wider Mickey Mantle bats."

"No," Sloman nearly spat out his tea.

"He's one of the Louisville sluggers." Rubin smiled slyly. "This wasn't in public. I mean Mickey Mantle didn't go out and say, 'Hey, I love E-Z Wider' to the public, and we put it in *Sports Illustrated*. But he was down there at a convention. *Hustler* had all the tits and ass they could afford, *Playboy* had all the tits and ass, *Oui* magazine, and where was everybody? Waiting in line to see the Mick. And you know it legitimizes it."

"Is Mick a head?" Sloman was delighted with the prospect.

"Nah," Rubin shrugged. "But his kids use our Roach brand. He took two boxes of Roach back. He's a nice fella, you know; he said he's tried it but it just wasn't his thing.

"Then we gave out the Marty Mouse Award. That one was fabulous. I'll show you a picture—this one'll kill you. All right, Marty Mouse. The San Jose Police Department was confiscating marijuana, and they found that this mouse was eating the marijuana. The Police Department was having an image problem at that time, so this mouse became a rallying point with the police and the people. Like they got together on it. In San Francisco, when Marty Mouse died, I think 2,000 people showed up at his funeral. Something crazy, ridiculous. So what we did was we gave a Marty Mouse Award to the Chief of Police of the San Jose Department, Robert Murphy. We presented him this award at the Hyatt Regency House in Los Angeles. I don't know if he still is, but this statue award of Marty Mouse was standing for over a year encased as you walked into the San Jose Police Department. There was Marty Mouse with an E-Z Wider hat sitting out there."

"What about advertising?" Sloman inquired.

Rubin smiled again. "We won a Cleo Award last year. We beat out Kodak and McDonald's in our category for our radio ad. Have you heard it?"

Sloman shook his head, and Rubin was back in a flash with a cassette and a tape machine. Seconds later, a silky female voice began a frantic spiel:

> E-Z Wider, the double-width rolling paper, knows that by now a lot of people are used to sticking two little pieces of rolling paper together in order to roll a good smoke, and why not? All you do is pull out two leaves of any ordinary paper, then carefully examine each to determine which pieces are striped with glue. Once you know for sure, take one of the papers and place it on the table. Then, holding the second paper with the thumbs and fingers of both hands, bring the paper to your mouth, stick out your tongue, and in one or two strokes, depending on how dry your mouth is at the time, lick the entire end of the paper, preferably the one which contains the glue. Then quickly reach for the paper you placed on the table earlier, and carefully affix the underside of the paper which does not contain the glue to the glued end of the paper that you just licked. Be careful to line the papers up correctly before connecting them, and try to avoid excessive overlapping. Then all you have to do is wait for them to dry.

The foregoing was delivered at a rapidly increasing breakneck rate. After a welcome breath-taking pause, the ad ended:

> Of course, now there is another way to do it. Just pull out one E-Z Wider double-width paper and start to roll. That's it. E-Z Wider is double width so you don't have to stick two papers together. The next time you buy papers, ask for the brown and white pack that says, "E-Z Wider, E-Z Wider, E-Z Wider."

Rubin was all smiles. "So that won a Cleo for us. I mean, that itself doesn't sell papers, but it's the kind of thing where here's a little company coming out against Kodak and McDonald's and winning."

"What if it's legalized?" Sloman didn't think that an odd statement, sitting in this luxurious office on the forty-fourth floor that grass built. "What then?"

Rubin thought for a minute. "If it is legal, I know for sure that the name, the association of E-Z Wider is a strong one, so that we would have a brand identification and we could say, beginning day one, 'More joints have been rolled with E-Z Wider than anything else.' If it's legalized, I'd say we'd go into it. The dollar value of the marijuana market is say $7 billion a year. If I take 2 percent of that $7 billion, that's $140 million. If I have 50 percent of the whole cigarette-paper market, I'm $10–$12 million. But I don't see legalization happening for quite a number of years."

"Do you sometimes feel tainted because you're supplying a product that gets used for illicit purposes?" Sloman wondered. "I mean, do you question the morality of what you're doing?"

Rubin was straightforward. "If you think of it, the government statistics say that forty million people have tried marijuana. Now if you add the population required to make families from that forty million, you get sixty or seventy million people in terms of direct families involved in that type of thing. Which is larger than Great Britain, Germany, Italy. I mean, it's a country. Forty million people are enough for me. If forty million do something, it's not a question of morality anymore—it's freedom. They're not getting high because of my papers. If all papers and pipes were made illegal, they'd have to make stationery and paper bags illegal. You know, I have friends out in the boonies. Marijuana's become the second media of exchange after money there. You could trade marijuana for milk. You grow it, you can get eggs, milk, beets, clothing—you can get anything. It's become barter."

"It's interesting." Sloman felt a little disoriented by the straight-ahead mercantilism surrounding the drug. "Did you ever experience grass in a political context? Even back in the sixties, when you first started smoking?"

Rubin shook his head. "I've never viewed it as a political thing. For me it was always a recreational thing. I've read quotes from the stereo music business attributing the growth of that industry to a great extent to marijuana. That was one of the first things people told you when you were gonna smoke. You're gonna get thirsty, you're gonna get hungry, and you're gonna really love music. I'd say *Sergeant Pepper* did more for the increase in smoking than anything around. You know how much money ITT Baking sells in Twinkies a year? Twinkies.

Seventy million dollars' worth of Twinkies. Go to any 7-11 store, they'll tell you people buy a pack of E-Z Wider, they buy a can of cherry soda, two Yodels and a Twinkie, and a few minutes later they're back for more Twinkies."

Sloman and Rubin talked on, Rubin bringing out surveys, computer printouts, cross tabulations, all demonstrating the scientific approach used to conquer the heads of America. Sloman was amazed to learn that only 20 percent of E-Z Wider's papers were distributed to head shops, with a full 80 percent winding up in 7-11s, K-Marts and other mass chains. But the thing that impressed Sloman the most that visit was a simple full-page magazine ad for E-Z Wider that featured a pack of the papers and a lush background of delectable chocolate-chip cookies and a tall frosted glass of milk. What could be better?

"Yeah, I thought that was great execution," Burt laughed. "We did one with earphones for the music, and this one for the food, you know."

"But what could be more wholesome than cookies and milk, man?" Sloman was rhapsodic. "Chocolate-chip cookies and milk. I do that every night, right before bed."

"Really, that's what we were trying to show. It's apple pie, it's a donut, a cup of coffee. And that's what it is. It really is that way. It's not trying to show anything that it's not." Rubin seemed to be speaking in code.

"Yeah, but it's also convenience. 'Get off easy.' I mean, it's that whole American notion."

"We've taken our campaign now and generated it into 'Take it easy,' " Rubin reported.

"That's it, the perfect slogan for a leisure society." Sloman began to bubble.

"Yeah," Rubin smiled proudly. "This is the marijuana ethic. Take it easy."

The two got up, and Rubin gave the reporter a short walking tour of the offices. They occupied the entire floor, and Sloman followed Rubin around obediently, peering into offices, smiling at secretaries, checking out expensive-looking hardware.

"Here's our Salsa paper." Rubin handed Sloman a packet. "It's for the Spanish market. It means hot sauce."

"I like the music too." Sloman fingered the papers as they continued down the hall.

"Here's advertising; this is marketing, the computer room;

this is invoicing, accounts receivable, personnel director, salespeople, telephone solicitation, shipping." They trooped around slowly.

"Have any problems with employee theft?" Sloman joked.

"No, not here, but down at the factory we had about fifty thousand dollars' worth stolen from us." Rubin looked grim. They passed his partner's empty office and stopped at a huge room.

"Here's the board room," Rubin announced proudly.

Sloman peered at it. It was certainly impressive to his untrained corporate eye. In fact, sizing up the large conference table and the plush decor and elegant drapes, Sloman thought it was indistinguishable from the board room of any Fortune 500 company. Except for one difference. There was a large functional ashtray poised before every seat at the table.

Part 3
The Politics of Pot

"To talk of legalizing marijuana is academic. It can't be done," Anslinger *stated. . . . "If marijuana is not a problem, then why has every country in the world enacted marijuana legislation prior to international treaty?" he went on. "Why should the U.S.A. reverse world order?" . . . Harry Anslinger has been in the area of narcotics for nearly forty years. When asked if he had some evangelical fervor, he laughed. "No, the government gave me a job to do, and I did it."*

—From "Harry Jacob Anslinger: Distinguished Citizen"
by Carol Parks, which appeared in 1968 in
Town and Gown, Pennsylvania State College

CHAPTER 20:
The Aborted Pie-Kill

The scene was the luxurious Hyatt Regency Hotel in downtown Washington, weekend home for the Sixth Annual NORML Conference. For three days, December 9–11, 1977, representatives of the lobbyist group from all over the country gathered to attend workshops, hear speeches, make policy, but mostly to smoke marijuana in one another's presence.

Keith Stroup, who has been synonymous with the organization since its inception and still serves as its national director, had taken a back seat during this conference to better hone the leadership skills of some of the fledgling regional coordinators, one of whom was Marc Kurzman, another esquire, and a man perfectly cut from the NORML-liberal-lawyer mold. Kurzman is young, bearded, neat, authoritative, punctual, stiff, pompous, boring and totally devoid of any sense of humor.

At least that's the way he appeared to Sloman, who by Sunday afternoon was completely intolerant of Kurzman's repeated attempts to maintain order by cutting off relevant substantive discussion of the issue at hand. It seemed to Sloman that what Kurzman objected to was not that the discussion was not germane, but that ofttimes it was coming out of the mouths of the twenty-five or so Yippies, led by superspokesperson Dana Beal, who had crashed the conference in an attempt to broaden the perspective of the conferees on the marijuana issue.

That certainly was what happened Sunday afternoon at the last big conference session in the spacious Yorktown Room. The meeting was on the international control of marijuana, and the panel was composed of Richard Bonnie, a law professor who served as the Associate Director of the 1972 National Commission on Marijuana and Drug Abuse, Joseph L. Nellis, the Chief Counsel for the House Select Committee on Narcotics Abuse and Control, and Bob Angarola, the General Counsel for the Office of Drug Abuse Policy at the White House. An impressive array of experts who were in the middle of being lambasted by the red-haired Yippie Dana Beal, who waxed eloquent at the mike set up in the audience.

"I would like to know why, with its much-heralded interest in human rights, the Carter administration is not concerned with the human rights of potheads the world around, of whom there are 200 million tribal Third World people who traditionally use marijuana and now are being crushed by Western-style totalitarian governments as part of an international conspiracy." The audience interrupted with cheers.

"I am here not as a member of NORML but as a representative of the marijuana smokers, and in our Constitution there are no limitations. We agree with the Alaska decision that marijuana is a constitutionally protected right. Not only that, the Washington, D.C., police agreed that it is a constitutionally protected right, because for some reason they let us smoke-in outside of the White House last July Fourth, and we would like to see them try to prosecute a smoke-in, because we think that regardless of whether it's protected privately, certainly when we're out demonstrating for civil rights our clinical rights override any harm that might come to society for smoking marijuana. So I want to know which comes first, the Bill of Rights or foreign treaties?"

Leave it to Beal. The Yippie agitator had just raised the most crucial issue regarding the eventual legalization of marijuana in America, the issue that Anslinger was so spooked by that he ramrodded his beloved Single Convention down the Senate's throats a full six years after he denounced it as being too wishy-washy. So Beal was resurrecting the specter of the Single Convention and, with it, the ghost of Harry J. himself.

But not if Marc Kurzman could help it. The bearded bureaucrat seized the mike on the dais, cutting off the lingering applause for Dana's question. "I would like to suggest that since there has been so much interest generated and some of the sessions had to be cut off, what we have done is to arrange for the Continuing Legal Education Seminar which is scheduled for here to continue in a room across the hall. Now what I'm going to have to do again because of people's flight schedules to get out is I'm going to freeze the people at the mike now, two minutes apiece for questions relating to international aspects.

At that point, Mike Stepanian is going to address the group. Okay, Craig, you're next." Kurzman recognized the next questioner.

"We didn't get an answer to the last one," Sloman shouted out at the dais.

"Excuse me." Kurzman's voice dripped contempt. "This panel is on international aspects."

"That was on international aspects—what comes first, the Bill of Rights or foreign treaties?" one Yip yelled out from the rear of the room.

"All right." Kurzman reluctantly turned it over to the panel.

Nellis signaled his intention to field it. If ever there was someone to come to bat for Anslinger and the old guard, it would be Nellis. He was a broad, stocky man in his late fifties, with a face that combined the best features of Anslinger and Hoover. In his black Banlon shirt and casual slacks, he could have passed for a mobster on his way to the links. But of course he wasn't that; he was only the chief counsel for the only House committee to hold hearings and come out against decriminalization. He was not a favorite of the NORML crowd, and his appearance on the dais was clearly an experiment in peaceful coexistence.

"The only part of that alleged question that I can answer is the part that he ended when he said the Bill of Rights takes supremacy over treaties." Nellis's tone was jaunty. "That's not so. Treaties are the law of the land. They are supreme over everything else." An avalanche of boos descended on the dais. "As long as we are—as long as we are"—Nellis was continually interrupted by catcalls—"as long as we are signatories to the Convention, no legalization is possible." More catcalls erupted.

"Excuse me," Kurzman grabbed the mike. "I would appreciate it if those of you who think you know about the law but do not would keep your opinions about what constitutionality and supremacy is to yourselves."

"Fuck you; we're talking about justice," an angry voice bellowed out. It belonged to Aaron Kay, the Yippie who had made a worldwide reputation as the lone assassin for Pie-Kill, a group that symbolically destroyed fascist insects by hurling, or attempting to hurl, various varieties of pies into their faces. Among Kay's victims were Howard Hunt, former N.Y.C. Mayor Abe Beame, and G. Gordon Liddy. There were rumors of another pieing at this conference, and a half-eaten lemon meringue at Aaron's elbow did nothing but add to those reports.

Craig Copetas, a reporter from *High Times*, stepped up to the mike. "My question concerns this concept of interdiction overseas."

But before the words tumbled out of the eager reporter's mouth, a bloodcurdling yelp descended on the arena, and the swift shadow of 250 pounds of Yippie flesh, carrying a half-eaten lemon meringue pie, flashed by Sloman's eyes. The next thing he knew Aaron Kay was hurling the pie square at that bulldog face of Joe Nellis! However, at the last moment, the swift arm of Marc Kurzman shot up and deflected the pie ninety degrees off its course, causing it to flutter harmlessly onto the table, leaving a scant trace of topping on Nellis's jet black shirt.

The chief counsel meanwhile had leaped to his full five feet eight inches and was wielding a water pitcher. "Crank," he sputtered at the Yippie down below. "Don't swing at me, man." He had the pitcher poised.

Aaron screamed something incomprehensible and was gone as fast as he had come.

But immediately Kurzman seized the mike. "All right." His voice sounded strangely rehearsed. "I am very sorry this happened for a number of reasons. One of them was that this was sponsored by an individual in this organization." A dramatic pause. The whole room was eerily silent. The other two panelists had already retreated, papers and portfolios in hand, to the safety of the wings.

"That individual is the individual who is the Executive Director of this organization." Kurzman was attempting to prolong the drama.

"Now this conference is not to make people happy, it's not a social event, it's not a fun time. If you want to have those things around the parameters of the conference, I have no objection to that. Those of you who still believe that the answer and the only way to reform is to play games, is to put on demonstrations, is to make pictures for the *Yipster News* or the *Daily News* or the *New York Times*, I would suggest to you that you have been passed by by the reform movement that perhaps even you started. There are more people involved now, there are more issues. People don't enjoy it and are offended by it."

The room was still deathly silent. Kurzman raised his voice to a fever pitch. "Now I am offended by the fact that I was asked to chair a conference. That I, in good faith, asked people from the government, from agencies, from organizations to come together. That I, in good faith, negotiated with various groups wanting to have input for the first time in that group which is being credited with having influence on legislation. I am not happy. It is not your fault. I suggest for those of you that are sitting here that you join with me, on behalf of myself and on behalf of those people seeking to influence policy in regard to marijuana, in condemning the actions of the Executive Director of NORML as an individual act, and as, in my opinion, an extremely immature act. If you wish to continue with this discussion, we will do so. I don't know if the panel will stay . . ."

"Excuse me, pardon me." Copetas was still at the speaker's mike. "Could you please identify who you're talking about as responsible for this act?"

Kurzman paused one more second, milking this as much as he could. Finally, with feigned regret, he spat into the mike, "Keith Stroup." Murmurs ran through the crowd.

"Wait a minute," Copetas screamed out. "Are you accusing Keith Stroup of masterminding that pie-kill?"

"I was informed . . ." Kurzman started.

"What was your source, sir?" Copetas was back. Suddenly it turned into a parody of a press conference.

"I'm not gonna get into that." Kurzman sounded like Nixon. "Now, are we gonna go on with the conference or not?"

"Excuse me," Copetas again. "Keith Stroup, the Executive Director of the National Organization to Reform the Marijuana Laws, has just been accused of masterminding a pie-kill on Mr. Nellis. I would like to know if this is true or not."

"We'll have to discuss that after the conference," Kurzman brushed it off.

"Who gives a shit about politics? Let's hear what they have to say. We'll worry about Keith Stroup later," someone yelled out.

The questioning resumed, but a pall hung over the room.

"That was incredible," Gene Schoenfeld, known to thousands of hippies as Dr. Hippocrates, whispered to Sloman. "Looks like Kurzman wants to be the next Executive Director of NORML."

"Not at all," Sloman snapped. "I just think he was talking to Nellis and the guy from the White House. Giving them his résumé." They both laughed and accepted a huge stick of Californian homegrown that was lazily making its way around the room while Nellis was reiterating the supremacy of treaty over rights.

CHAPTER 21:

Jack Cohen Is Normal

Sloman must have seen the ad at least a hundred times that winter, between the periods of every New York Rangers and Knicks game. It's a short one, a subliminal spurt, with a weird post-psychedelic soundtrack that resembles a disco band on Quaaludes chanting "la la la la la lah" over and over again like some perverse mantra. The visual consists of a tall, bushy-haired, mustachioed guy jogging in Central Park or someplace like that, accompanied by his huge Irish setter, whom he has genteelly on a leash. And this guy travels in style with what looks like a goddamn Yves St. Laurent color-coordinated sweat suit and fifty-dollar Adidas.

But the deep, solemn voiceover tells the story:

> Meet Jack Cohen. Ten years ago he was protesting, demonstrating, resisting the establishment. Today he's part of the new establishment, a group of young men grabbing at life in more ways than you can probably imagine. The most vibrant prospects American business has been blessed with since the post–World War II boom. And more of them read *Playboy* than read *Time, Newsweek* or *Sports Illustrated*. The *Playboy* Reader. His lust is for life.

And then Jack's gone, jogging off into the sunset. But you can bet your last *Playboy* key that Jack Cohen and his cohort boast of some other interesting demographics. They consume! Everything: stereos, color TVs, tequila, tennis rackets and, of course, marijuana. Why, according to conservative government estimates, the illicit marijuana business came to around $5 billion gross last year. Some studies estimate that 25 million Americans regularly smoke pot now. Which means that Jack Cohen, who ten years ago was deviant when he lit up a joint inside the administration building his campus SDS was occupying, today is normal. And is a consumer in need of a lobby.

By 1970 it was apparent that there was a tremendous change with respect to the role that marijuana was playing in American life. Marijuana could no longer be seen as having a political function—that is, as being a core element in a constellation of anti-establishment, anti-authoritarian values. Historically, marijuana had always been used recreationally in America, whether it was being smoked by a beet-farming wetback in Colorado or a horn-tooting black hipster in Harlem. With the advent of a new ethos in the seventies, a narcissistic, hedonistic Me-Firstism, marijuana slipped in the back doors of nearly every split-level in suburbia. Grass was almost respectable. But it was still illegal.

Which meant that it was only natural that respectable, solid, middle-class, concerned citizens would begin to devise respectable, issue-oriented, quantitatively sound arguments for the removal of the prohibitions on the use of what they felt was an essentially benign substance. Enter Keith Stroup, who, at twenty-seven, with a law degree from Georgetown University and two years' experience as counsel for the Product Safety Commission doing Nader-type consumer protection work, was about as normal as, well, Jack Cohen.

Stroup had this idea. He was an ambitious kid from the Midwest, a Southern Baptist farm boy from Southern Illinois, son of a building contractor with heavy connections in local Republican politics. Keith dreamed of going into politics someday; the scenario had him studying law, working for a Senator, and then returning to run for Congress from his hometown.

So like any budding politician, he went to college at the University of Illinois, where if you weren't Greek you were shit, and he went Greek. Vice-president of the fraternity and social chairman to boot. It looked like Capitol Hill '78, except for one thing. Stroup was a bit of a fuck-up.

Which in 1962 meant that he liked to enjoy life a little, put down a couple dozen beers, fraternize with the sorority sisters, steal pizzas. Steal pizzas? Exit Mr. Stroup from the hallowed halls of S.I.U. So the next logical thing in that what-can-you-do-for-your-country era was to join the Peace Corps. Which lasted about eight weeks, ending when Keith fired off a hostile letter to his director, upset that his program was being trained to build adobe shithouses in rural Colombia. Exit Mr. Stroup.

Lacking a parchment, the would-be politician and known troublemaker finally found a school that would accept him, a Kentucky bone-dry Southern Baptist teacher's college, where Keith promptly got straight As on two hours a week of work and made some nice pocket change bootlegging alcohol to his classmates. Even then he knew.

It wasn't until Stroup was graduated from Georgetown Law that he got high. He had tried marijuana once in 1967, but he had failed to get off. However, a few years later, while playing bridge with some of his colleagues on the Product Safety Commission, he got shitfaced. Bye-bye, Capitol Hill.

Then another Meaningful Event occurred. In late 1969, a friend of Keith's, a special friend, the man who had turned him on to grass, was pulled over by Washington, D.C., police, who, seeing the suspect's long hair, promptly scanned the van, tore it apart, and found three joints' worth of powdered marijuana. Keith took the case and won a dismissal. And found a cause.

Of course, marijuana reform was nothing new. A full seven years earlier, people like Allen Ginsberg, Ed Sanders and Tuli Kupferberg were cavorting around the Lower East Side of New York City, loosely organized into a group called LEMAR (Legalize Marijuana), doing things like picketing the local Department of Welfare (the closest official building) with signs reading 'Pot Is Fun.' On the West Coast, some early LEMAR people who had formed a full-fledged legalization group named AMORPHIA were generating funds by selling their own brand of rolling papers, Acapulco Gold. But these early groups had a distinct countercultural air to them. For them, the right to smoke marijuana was sacred, and the smoking of marijuana was a ritual that set one apart from the capitalistic, imperialistic Moloch that owned the White House. The early pot crusaders would have characterized themselves as anything *but* NORML.

Originally, Stroup was intent on calling his group the National Organization to *Repeal* the Marijuana Laws. But in Stroup's first lesson in practical politics, Ramsey Clark, the former attorney general, warned him of the negative implications "repeal" had. Stroup also was not quite clear on what policies the group would pursue with respect to the illegal status of grass. Should they come out for legalization? What about proposing a distribution scheme? A government-supported industry?

Of course, these questions were premature, since Stroup's

unenviable job was to get federal and state legislators, the guardians of our rapidly tarnishing morality, to sanction the use of a drug that for fifty-odd years had enjoyed a Pavlovian association with mutilation, molestation and Molochation, thanks to the vigilant efforts of Harry Anslinger and his Bureau of Narcotics.

NORML's job was made easier by President Nixon's Commission on Marijuana and Drug Abuse, known as the Shafer Commission. What this shrewd group did, in 1972, was to develop a new concept to deal with the deplorable fact that we were literally sending our own children to jail for the use of this controversial substance. The Shafer report struck on the brilliant idea of "decriminalization," which meant, in effect, the criminal penalties for the private use of pot would be removed. Never mind where you got your shit, smoking it would no longer be an occasion for criminal sanction. Stroup had a readymade, palatable strategy. Now all he needed was money.

Enter Hugh Hefner, who is a spiritual leader of sorts to people like Jack Cohen. It was *Playboy* magazine, and especially the *Playboy* philosophy, Hefner's personalized vision of the New Morality, that helped to usher in the chic hedonism that has defined the style of the seventies. Hefner told us to enjoy—without that layer of Jewish/Protestant Ethic guilt, whether we were enjoying women, cars, fine food, or good liquor. And naturally, as marijuana was perceived by more and more middle-class Americans, who comprise most of *Playboy*'s readership, as a much more efficient recreational drug than liquor, *Playboy* decided to throw some of their new moral weight behind the issue.

And what better forum to raise the issue of pleasure without payment than our antiquated marijuana laws? In some states, possession of minuscule amounts of marijuana was still subject to Byzantine fines and long prison sentences in the early seventies. So when Keith Stroup made a visit to Hef in 1970, after having been turned down by ten traditional liberal foundations, the *Playboy* patriarch threw $5,000 Keith's way, with a promise of more if NORML looked viable. One year later, to Stroup's credit, *Playboy* was budgeting $100,000 to the first professional pro-marijuana lobby.

Playboy got NORML off the ground, giving the organization a tremendous forum with which to reach millions of readers who were marijuana consumers, and, as such, were subjecting themselves to a huge risk of arrest and imprisonment or fine, a clear punishment for their harmless hedonism. So, armed with *Playboy*'s money and recognition, Stroup and the other early NORML organizers, most of them lawyers, set out to do battle against the laws, armed with a concept whose time had come: decriminalization.

The decrim fight produced its first result in 1973, when, much to the surprise of Stroup and his cronies, Oregon became the first state to reform its laws. Possession of up to an ounce was made punishable by a maximum civil fine of $100, which is nothing to a *Playboy* subscriber. But what's more, Oregon gave NORML a tremendous testing ground for this concept. Groups like the Drug Abuse Council made surveys which showed, basically, that the state did not go down the toilet with the loosening of the pot laws. Five years later, nine more states had followed Oregon's lead, thanks largely to the organizing skills of NORML affiliates.

One case in point was New York State. New York had one of the earliest NORML affiliations, led by a thirtyish mustachioed lawyer (what else?) named Frank Fioramonti. "We were the people who missed marijuana in law school," Fioramonti told Sloman one afternoon, sitting in front of his cluttered desk in NORML's small office above the Ed Sullivan Theatre on Broadway. "We all had straight political experience. Keith had worked for Senator Dirksen and Bobby Baker. I was working full time for City Councilman Carter Burden, who let me devote half my time to NORML. In fact, we used to call it the Carter Burden Marijuana Chair because, in effect, he endowed the marijuana movement about $10,000 a year."

Fioramonti, like Stroup, discovered grass after law school. In Frank's case it was on an all-night jag, and he woke up the next morning to find *Sergeant Pepper* going around and around on the turntable. But Fioramonti, unlike Stroup, has basically reduced his smoking to once a month, finding Transcendental Meditation and long-distance marathon running (watch out, Jack Cohen!) viable alternatives on the path to self-actualization. But that has not deterred the lawyer from becoming New York's number one advocate for pot law reform.

Fioramonti spent six long years lobbying for the decrim change in the Empire State, a process that entailed criss-crossing the region countless times, making thousands of speeches, shaking scores of hands, and buttonholing a few very key legislators. "Three weeks out of four I spent upstate in 1976," Frank remembered, "doing radio and TV appearances, working in the legislature. I did the 'Bowling for Dollars' shows at the small stations where the guy is a clown in the kiddie show, then he comes back as the M.C. on 'Bowling for Dollars,' and they mix it with public-interest guests. I was on with a chorus girl from the Barnum and Bailey Circus, the Fireman of the Week, and Miss Polish America." And he made news, of the "Marijuana Reformer Hits Town" variety.

By 1977, NORML's decrim bill, which, after being whittled down by the conservative legislators, called for a $100 violation fine for possession of up to twenty-five grams (about seven-eighths of an ounce), began to receive considerable support from the most unlikely sources. The P.T.A. endorsed the bill, as did key conservative Republican state leaders like Warren Anderson and Douglas Barclay. Legislators were lined up, conservatives courted, egos placated; the traditional stuff of lobbying was done with barely a dime in the state NORML coffers. "I was the straightest lobbyist there," Fioramonti chuckled. "All the business was done in the bars, but I never went there. The marijuana groupies were never called on; I never bought anyone dinner or lunch. I couldn't afford it. I told them I had no money."

But money or not, the bill was finally passed in dramatic fashion on June 28, 1977. Just a month earlier, the bill had gone down to defeat, due to a last-minute drive by the Conservative Party, who pressured a number of legislators who held their seats due to Conservative backing to nix the reform. The next day, New York Governor Carey condemned the legislature for the defeat ("He's got fifteen kids and they all smoke," Frank joked) and began twisting arms.

So when the same bill resurfaced in June, it passed the Democratic-controlled Assembly with a few votes to spare. But in the Republican-dominated conservative Senate, it was fingernail-biting time. Every vote was needed for this final roll call. Suddenly someone discovered during the debate that Roy Goodman, a Republican who was about to run for Mayor of New York City, and who therefore didn't want to be on record on such a thorny issue, had left his desk, and shortly afterward had had someone come in and collect all his papers. They checked the halls, they checked his office, they tried his hotel. Nada.

So in a state of total panic, the Majority Leader sent the state police after him. In a few minutes, they had troopers scouring the roads, helicopters along the side roads, and after two hours they found him driving home along the Taconic Parkway, allegedly going to a wedding anniversary dinner with his wife. They brought him back.

But that still wasn't enough, the vote looked that close, so earlier in the day, the Governor's private plane had been dispatched to Manhattan to pick up Senator Abe Bernstein, a Democrat who had had part of his leg amputated after a severe case of phlebitis. But a vote was a vote, so they yanked him out of bed, threw him into the plane, waited an hour at LaGuardia for takeoff clearance, and finally wheeled him into the Chambers amid much fanfare. The bill passed, and the next day the *New York Post* ran a picture of Bernstein, in his wheelchair, proudly casting his vote for decriminalization.

But besides battling state by state for decrim and supporting federal moves to decriminalize (which has earned the rancor of many civil libertarians, since marijuana decrim is included as a sop in Senate Bill S1437, which has been described by some commentators as a prelude to a police state), NORML, and especially Stroup, functions as a role model for middle-class users. Stroup is an unabashed public user, and as such is living testimony to the fact that regular daily use of marijuana does not addle the brain.

While in Washington doing research in the Bureau of Narcotics archives, Sloman took time off to pay a visit to the marijuana reformer at his downtown office. Since first meeting Stroup at the July Fourth smoke-in, Sloman had spent quite some time with him at the NORML Conference, and he had decided that he really liked Stroup, even if he had found him a bit jive at that first encounter. There was a certain awareness that Stroup exhibited, a certain "I understand that I'm bullshitting but it's all just a game" irony that Sloman perceived Keith understanding. Sure he still had that shit-eating Midwestern grin, but Sloman thought that he could detect a slight wink of Stroup's eye.

The NORML offices were housed in a three-story townhouse on M Street in the northwest section of D.C. Inside, workers stuffed envelopes, typed up press releases, answered phones, and filled orders for the NORML line of T shirts, bags and bumper stickers. Stroup had his office in the rear of the main floor, and as Sloman entered the room the bittersweet smell of marijuana still hung heavy in the air.

Stroup still looked collegiate, with his blue blazer (with gold buttons) covering his yellow NORML T shirt and his worn dungarees, and the impression he gave was of a funky academician, a Dean of Student Affairs at someplace like Antioch. He was surrounded by marijuana memorabilia, posters, photos, original Trudeau cartoons, books, but occupying an equally important place on the walls next to his desk were framed certificates attesting to the fact that Stroup had argued before the United States Court of Appeals, along with his two framed degrees. He was clearly a man who strode in both worlds.

"Did you get this memo yet?" Stroup handed Sloman a four-page memo that explained the reasons behind the pieing of Nellis, which had become a *cause célèbre* in the marijuana circles of Washington. Word had it that Peter Bourne's White House Office of Drug Abuse Policy had had it with the cheeky reformer after the Nellis imbroglio.

"This is sort of my mea culpa," Keith smiled. "It's just my first thoughts; I threw them onto the machine. Basically it says, 'Back off, motherfuckers; a pie is not that important!' "

"Right on." Keith's secretary Leslie had overheard the explanation and echoed her support.

"That Nellis thing was something else. That was the first thing he wanted to talk about when I went to see him the next day," Sloman remembered.

"Nellis is a pig." Keith screwed his face up in disgust. "It was a calculated out-of-bounds play. I gave Aaron five dollars for the pie, and he asked me who to hit, and I told him Nellis would be the one to get. His was the only committee that had hearings and didn't come out for decrim. But I wouldn't have authorized a pie for someone we'd have to send legislation through. Nellis's committee doesn't even write legislation," Keith sneered.

Stroup seemed to be finished on that topic, and Sloman noticed that he was crushing some buds on a NORML leaflet on his desk. "When we were setting up NORML," Keith related in his urgent clipped tones, "it was our perspective that the marijuana smoker should be represented in a kind of traditional middle-class way. The same way that Nader had very effectively begun to represent the general consumer that gets shocked by her refrigerator door. Do you ever think about why

Hugh Hefner would put so much money and effort behind us all these years? He's given us hundreds of thousands of dollars, ad space, editorial support, *Playboy* interviews. What caused him to be there? I think it was a cross between smoking himself and being a libertarian. He saw the issue of privacy. He took a lot of heat. He's worth a couple of million; he didn't have to go public. They wouldn't have busted him. He did it out of some altruistic sense.

"We're trying to organize a constituency that is hiding out." Stroup resumed his rapid monologue after extracting some stems from the pot on his desk. "We have had to get people to understand that before they are going to lobby their legislator, they have to feel good about themselves. And the fact that they smoke dope is no different than their buddy they work with who goes down and gets drunk every night.

"We are marijuana smokers; we don't deny it. We're not ashamed of it. I expect to be a marijuana smoker when I die. But that really doesn't mean anything more to me than the fact that my father is an alcohol drinker. I am a hedonist, to be quite frank about it. I like a lot of kinds of pleasure. I just don't buy that Calvinistic guilt bullshit."

Keith finished his preparations and expertly rolled a fat joint, took a long hit, and passed it to me across his desk with a sly smile. "Don't you sometimes wonder whether by promoting the use of marijuana, which in effect you do, you may be contributing to a larger problem in a drug-saturated society?" Try as he could, it was hard for Sloman to be the devil's advocate on that one.

Stroup took another toke and answered in his machine-gun style. Sloman began wondering whether grass had the same kind of reverse effect on him as Ritalin did on hyperactive children. "Not only don't I perceive it as being a threat, but I think the only impact it will have will be slight and positive. It will never likely become the dominant drug of this culture. As marijuana loses its stigma—and that's what decrim does—the market will continue to grow. The only difference will be that you may have a slightly less aggressive constituency. Alcohol is an aggression-producing drug. Marijuana tends to produce passivity. Not like the hippie thing, but that you don't drive as fast, you don't pass as often. We really may be a country that needs a little more of that Eastern passive quality and less of that Teddy Roosevelt big stick."

Sloman was still getting over the reference to marijuana users as a constituency as Stroup began to light up another joint. It's clear that this is his business—he is compelled to smoke with every NORML advisory board member, local organizer, marijuana groupie, ambassador from YIP and inquiring reporter (in an updated version of who can drink whom under the table), so the fucker must not even get high anymore. The preceding had taken about three minutes to register in Sloman's befogged mind, as Keith did cop good shit, and by the time Sloman focused on the lobbyist, he was off and running.

"There was a time period when you made your choice—marijuana or alcohol. Well, I made my choice for marijuana; fuck the alcohol. I threw it out of my life. I used to get up with hangovers, miss work, all that energy drain. Now I go blast out as late as I want, and I get up and come to work in the morning. With no hangover." Stroup suppressed a giggle and passed Sloman the joint.

But here was the classic case being made for marijuana as a seventies drug. Middle-class people like marijuana because it's efficient. It's clean. You can smoke your brains out, listen to *Hotel California* on your $2,000 stereo system, screw well into the night, and get up the next morning ready for the office without once having puked your guts out all over your leather Nikes. Pleasure without payment! Unless you get caught running a light holding the baggie. Which is why NORML is there.

Certainly Stroup deserves a lot of credit for building NORML into a high-powered lobby that has achieved hegemony over the grass issue within a space of a few years. From that skimpy operating budget of $5,000 NORML now boasts a yearly gross income of $450,000. In addition to *Playboy* and *High Times* (which has become one of NORML's leading contributors), Stroup has wooed the marijuana liberals, millionaires like Max Palevsky (of Xerox fortune and fame) and Stewart Mott, both of whom kick in money and organizing skills. A lucrative NORML merchandising industry (T shirts, tote bags, buttons, etc.) has begun. Thirty percent of the cash inflow in 1977 came from direct-mail solicitations orchestrated by Craver and Company, a well-respected consulting firm.

But NORML is not without its critics. Many people in the marijuana movement see decrim as a sham. Some see the NORML lawyers as opportunists, with political-bureaucratic aspirations. Some feel that Stroup has too much of a stranglehold on the organization, at the expense of other nascent leaders. But it is likely that Stroup will weather these criticisms. And it is also inevitable that the premier pot lobbyist will go on to greener pastures soon.

At the last national conference he adopted a low profile. The suggestion that Stroup might leave NORML no longer evokes gasps of surprise from those who have been touched by his charismatic personality.

"This organization is no longer my little domicile." Stroup looked tired now, and the words came a bit slower. "For years it was, because no one else gave a shit. Or would ride herd over it. I don't want that role anymore. This thing no longer mystifies me. I am no longer turned on by finding out that some United States senator smokes dope. I know that senators smoke dope. There are a whole lot of other worlds out there. I think I would like to try to do the same thing in some other areas. New people. New subjects.

"You can always hang your shingle out and get clients because of your notoriety. It's a traditional way that Washington lawyers rip off people, but I don't want to do that particularly. I would like to make the juxtaposition from NORML to something else in a less expioitative manner."

The joint died, and Stroup was too preoccupied to notice. Sloman was too stoned to care. "You know, I'm sometimes overwhelmed when I look at the histories, with the inevitability of the movement we are now spearheading. Something that has involved hundreds of millions of people for thousands of years and which is finally surfacing here in a more legitimate way," Stroup smiled.

"You have to be impressed with how little we have to do with it and how much it has to do with historical movements, drug-use patterns, philosophies. It's both inevitable and positive. But it is fun to ride the elephant out right now to the end. In some respects, I think we are the luckiest people of all, because we are getting to see that little end part of it. And to live through the end of prohibition is fascinating. How many times do you get to do that in your life?"

The reverie seemed to have energized Stroup, and he began frantically searching for some documents to show Sloman, a copy of last year's budget to study, all the while attempting to talk on the phone to someone organizing a Jimmy Buffett benefit show for NORML. But Sloman had had one hit too many, and it was hard for him to concentrate on cash flows and expenditures and the like. All he could see was this strange rose-colored hallucination.

He saw a park, a real bucolic scene, and somewhere in the distance he saw three joggers headed lazily in his direction. As the mists receded, he could recognize the figures. It was Keith, Hef and, of course, Jack Cohen with his dog. They were all smiling, with nice tans, looking quite trim and fit. They were obviously past their second wind, stretching their endurance to the breaking point, living on the edge, lusting for life. They were also passing around a joint as they ran. It was when Frank Fioramonti came out of nowhere to pass the trio that Sloman got up and left Keith's office.

CHAPTER 22:
The Man Behind the Pie

Sloman was sitting in the Lower East Side Yippie office-house listening to Dana Beal give his convoluted account of the ten-year history of smoke-ins. Beal was quite distressed that the Yippies had been unable to get adequate coverage from the media, and that when they did rate a mention, it was usually in connection with the marijuana issue.

"Do you think Yips have been overidentified with the marijuana issue?" Sloman asked Beal.

"Because we took that position in 1972 at the Democratic convention, this particular outgrowth of Yippies will always be thought of by the rest of the movement as being cultural nationalists on the marijuana issue, know what I mean? But I don't think that's true. What we're saying is that it's a bellwether issue, a litmus-paper issue. The media treats us like in terms of 1968." Dana fell back into thought.

"You know how the media treats Aaron?" Sloman nodded over at the pie-man, who was getting a cup of coffee in the kitchen. "As a deranged lone assassin. The Lee Harvey Oswald of Pies. I don't think they perceive Aaron as an organizational man. I'm sure they see it as theater, but they see him as a loner."

"Maybe the time has come to have Aaron do some other type of action," Dana wondered. "And never have him do the pieing. Have the women do the pieing. Their tolerance toward Aaron is about over."

"I can make the phone calls, engineering the pieing," Aaron brightly suggested.

"You don't have to," a skinny Yippie disagreed. "You have a reputation. Be elusive; let them call you for interviews when there's a pieing."

"I think Aaron's act should be seen as an act of agency,"

Sloman suggested. "For example, if it's homemade, he should give credit to the person who baked it. It's a collective action."

"Well, the reason we don't credit is it's usually store-bought and we don't want to give credit to another big company," the skinny Yippie argued.

"Does a pieing come out of a stoned consciousness?" Sloman suddenly asked Aaron. "I mean, that whole munchie sweetness thing."

"No." Aaron shook his head. "It comes out of a revolutionary consciousness."

"You can't blame it on pot," Dana agreed.

"I got the idea when I used to read about the Chinese cultural revolutionists," Aaron related, "the Red Guard, who grabbed capitalist roaders and subjected them to humiliation and ridicule with dunce caps. I use the same tactics but with an American twist. I use the tactics of the Marx Brothers and the Three Stooges. Bringing vaudeville back to politics. I may as well throw revolutionary American culture at their faces. Like here's some fat cat giving a spiel, like Beame. Beame was giving this commercial, 'I made tough decisions.' Then some guy screamed, 'Liar!' Then I ran in front of the camera and I tossed it at him and put everything in disarray."

"What was he talking about when you did it to him?" the reporter wondered.

"I wasn't even listening. It's all garbage anyway," the pieman shrugged.

"Tell me about the Nellis thing," Sloman implored.

"Sometimes you have to know how to hold off," Dana interrupted. "Like that Beame thing. Initially Aaron held off because the place was full of cops, the cops were superheavy and on top of it. The time wasn't right. So Aaron came back and ate the first pie."

"What about the Nellis thing?" Sloman repeated.

"Bad timing," Dana pronounced solemnly. "When you control the main meeting, you don't need a breakaway. You don't need to disrupt it."

"Whose idea was it?" Sloman prodded.

"Keith Stroup," Aaron revealed. "The night of the party. At first I was thinking of pieing Peter Bourne, but I wasn't equipped. So the next morning, Sunday, Keith gave me the money to go out and get a pie."

"Apparently this was a traumatic event for the marijuana movement, a real watershed. It's gonna come down to those who are for the right to smoke as opposed to those against. The decrim people have tried to bridge that gap," Dana observed.

"What do you mean right to smoke?" Sloman queried.

"That you have a constitutional right to smoke. All the decrim people don't believe that," Dana explained.

"Anyway, after lunch, some of the NORML people came over to me and told me I shouldn't pie Nellis," Aaron remembered. "But I had the money so I went out to this bakery on the hill. I had to walk about a mile, and I got a lemon meringue for three dollars. I pocketed the rest. So I came back and I hid the pie. I'd rather not say where. Then after all the NORML guys talked to me I wasn't gonna do it. I even started eating the pie at one point. But then I was talking to Dr. Hip and some of the big dope lawyers from California, and they seemed to be all for it.

"Then Dana was questioning Nellis, and Nellis said that the treaty supersedes civil rights. I got so mad at him I just charged up with the pie and I threw it. Kurzman stuck his hand out and blocked it. I heard from another source that I knocked over the water pitcher and the water got all over his pants." Aaron smiled.

"Some of the pie did get on him," Dana corrected. "You got him, Aaron. It was a hit. It was a pretty good pieing, though, but it was tactically the wrong timing. It was like hitting a gnat with a hammer." And with that, Dana finally took a huge hit off the joint that had been nested in his fingers, forgotten during the narrative.

CHAPTER 23:
The Old Guard Retreats

While in Washington, Sloman ventured over to the House Office Building to talk to Joe Nellis. Nellis, of course, was the lucky recipient of the half-eaten lemon meringue pie that Aaron Kay had attempted to hurl at the NORML convention, as well as the chief counsel for the House Select Committee on Narcotics, a committee finishing its second year studying the drug issue. Because it is a select committee, it cannot write legislation itself, and must attempt to persuade other congressmen in other committees to introduce any legislation it may desire.

But Nellis was interesting to Sloman because Sloman felt that he represented the entrenched old-time thinking on the hill. Originally from Chicago, Nellis began practicing law in Washington in 1947, and broke into the political arena as a counsel for the Kefauver Committee. Over the years, he had worked for six congressional committees.

The fact that a man like Nellis supported some form of decrim impressed on Sloman the near inevitability of the execution of the concept federally. Ever since the Shafer report of 1972, which Nixon promptly ignored, Washington policy makers on the marijuana issue have been moving toward NORML's position. In fact, in August of 1977, President Carter even gave his endorsement to the decrim fight. So with a number of decrim bills pending in the current Congress, Sloman decided to get the perspective of one of the old war-horses on the issue.

Nellis greeted the reporter and led him into a spacious office in the wing of the House Office Building that was still under construction. The counsel was dressed casually in sports clothes, but the famous black Banlon was nowhere to be seen.

"Were you there at that NORML thing?" Nellis immediately asked Sloman. "Wasn't that something? Do you know who paid for that? Keith Stroup. He's a crazy. There are some dedicated reformers like Kurzman, but there are also the crazies."

Sloman noticed Nellis had received Kurzman's résumé. "I've cooperated with Keith in the past," Nellis went on, "but you know what I'll give him now? Balls! I was worried. It's a good thing it didn't hit me—I had a new shirt on. It was a present. I picked up the water pitcher and hit his arm." A big grin crept across the lawyer's face. "Now I don't raise the pie incident as anything significant at all, but it does illustrate to me that the sixties haven't been purged from NORML, and NORML is still back in the Yippie days because this was all engineered by Keith Stroup. And he's a damn fool because to the extent that my alliance with his purpose is valuable to him, he's lost it."

"You know, I talked to the kid that tried to pie you," Sloman reported. "By the way, he's done some really famous people like Mayor Beame, so it's some sort of distinction to have been on his hit list, at any rate. He told me that the reason he did it was because of what you said about the treaty making the legalization of grass impossible. That got him very emotional."

"He doesn't understand the Constitution, it's clear. The average person does not know that the Constitution expressly provides that treaties entered into by the United States and confirmed by the Senate are the surpreme law of the land. They even supersede Supreme Court decisions, if they're in conflict. Most people who graduate from high school know that, but you'd be damned if they'd remember it. Now treaties have been revoked. The United States has had occasion to vote to revoke its adherence to a treaty, so it's like any other contract except that it's on such a high level and there are so many foreign-policy implications, it would create havoc among the international community if we were ever to revoke our signature to the 1961 Convention."

"Couldn't we just withdraw from certain provisions?"

Nellis shook his head. "No. You couldn't do it. It's a whole contract, and when you start taking the meat of the contract out, there's no more mutuality, no more mutual understanding."

"But the cannabis clause isn't really the meat," Sloman objected.

"My friend," Nellis began to lecture, "every drug that's named, beginning with cannabis and ending up with morphine base, I think it is, is subject to the same provisions that every other drug is subject to. And when it says that the signatories shall bind themselves never to make legal the use of any of the drugs named in Schedule A, that's what they mean. And if marijuana hadn't been on that list, I wouldn't have made that statement. Do you follow me? All right, that treaty has been in effect seventeen years. I'm in touch with the State Department almost every day, and there is not a chance that the United States, any government, Democratic or Republican, will come to the Senate and say, 'Let's revoke our signature.' "

"But . . ." Sloman was amazed that a document that laid dormant for seven years, only to be resurrected by Anslinger to get back at the hippies, the only social group that he claimed to fear, was still being heralded as the last wall of defense between the unsuspecting American public and the ogre of legal marijuana. But before the reporter could crystallize his thoughts, Nellis was off and running.

"But look, let's get down to business. There are two kinds of legalization, my friend. De facto and de jure. De jure, I say to you as I said to them, will never happen. De facto is—if you look around you will see that the states are not enforcing their marijuana laws, and very few casual users are being put in jail. Very few."

"But . . ." Sloman started to protest, but was cut off by a stern look from the counsel.

"So it's a matter of fact"—Nellis underscored the word *fact* —"not a matter of law, and it's a very bad situation, Larry, because any situation like this causes disrespect for all law, and that's a serious problem. As a lawyer I deplore it. I'd rather see a state go forward with legislation than instruct their police department not to arrest casual users."

"But what about the 400,000 people arrested every year for pot offenses?" Sloman charged. "Arrested, not fined like in the decrim states."

"Look, many states have diversion laws—Tennessee, Minnesota—so that these arrests don't mean anything. They come before the juvenile court, let's say, and the judge says, 'If you go to this program for six months I'll turn you loose and expunge your record,' and that's going on every day in every state of the union."

"Yeah, but what does all this stuff do to those people arrested in terms of their identity?" Sloman wondered. "It may not be on their record after a while, but what about on their psyche?"

"Well, you can't account for the psychological reaction of the individual involved. But I say to you we have to go back to my original thesis that we have, practically speaking, a de facto legalization of small amounts for personal use. It is not universal, but it soon will be in my judgment. And it's very bad."

"Let me ask you about this de facto legalization. How can one rationalize the fact that possession of small amounts is condoned but there is no way to legitimately obtain the substance?"

"My friend, I will tell you first as a lawyer, there is nothing necessarily wrong with a transaction in which the seller is committing a criminal act and the buyer is not. It is pervasive throughout the law, where the courts have even said that it is not necessary for both parties to a sale to be guilty of an offense, for the sale itself to be criminal. Do you follow? That's the legal answer. Now the other answer is philosophical. Sure it's coming in through illegal means; sure it's contraband, even when it's sold in one-cigarette amounts; but you've got to balance some sociological factors. Are you going to balance that against kids going to jail, the way they were thrown in in the sixties? I mean, a society like ours has to come to grips with what is the most reasonable, acceptable basis for proceeding. And apparently the states and even the federal government have decided that de facto legalization is better than de jure legalization."

"But can't you anticipate, ten years from now, a distribution system . . ."

Nellis gave Sloman a stare that could have extinguished a joint. "Never. Never. Never. Not even fifty years from now. Because there's a great body of public opinion in this country that feels, and has expressed itself this way in the polls, that there are enough harmful drugs on the market in the distribution system, and we don't need any more. We've got enough problems with this." Nellis smiled as he held up his lit cigarette. "The church groups, the community groups, civic groups—believe me when I tell you that the Single Convention is the umbrella under which they will all respond, but there are other motivations. We don't need marijuana. If a kid wants to get a joint and is willing to risk civil citation, I wouldn't interfere with him. I was yelling about arresting kids when I was in practice in the sixties."

"Have your views changed since 1947 on this issue?" Sloman wondered.

"Very materially. I was a hard-nosed prosecutor on the marijuana issue. I had been through World War II and I had seen very little use of drugs in the military at that time, but I had been exposed to the Anslinger model, and when we went into narcotics in the Kefauver Committee, Larry, I found that the dealers were largely—I don't want to say the Italians—the Mafia. Associating narcotics and marijuana smuggling with the Mafia, that did it as far as I was concerned." Nellis chuckled at his youthful folly. "Who needs it, right? I was in favor of putting every user in jail. I was a hard-nosed prosecutorial type. Then I got older, and listened more."

"What were your beliefs then?" Sloman prodded.

"I believed it was as harmful, that it was a steppingstone to heroin, number one, and, number two, that it was harmful to the young people because at that time the young people weren't using it that much, because they would be seduced, you see, into a drug culture from which there is no escape. I had the ridiculous notion that the Anslinger theory was probably correct. And I have changed very materially."

"But you don't foresee legalization?" Sloman reiterated. "How about a scheme where individual states legalized it?"

Nellis laughed. "The first case brought up on an injunction on the grounds that it violates the treaty would be the end of it. Because the treaty is the supreme law of the land."

"So are you comfortable with de facto legalization?" Sloman liked the sound of that jargon.

Nellis frowned. "No, I'm uncomfortable with de facto because it breeds disrespect for the law. I would much prefer to see the federal government enact a reduction-in-penalty statute and let the states follow in line. I'm totally comfortable with the notion that kids would not be locked up for being casual users."

"Well, not just the kids." For some strange reason Jack Cohen popped into Sloman's mind.

"Well, let me put it to you this way," Nellis hedged. "I don't care so much about adults, because they presumably have more experience and ought to have more brains than that. But it's the kids that I think about, the seventeen-, the eighteen-, the nineteen-year-old kids that don't know which side of their butts the world is coming from."

"Well, I interviewed families in Queens for my book where parents and children smoke together at ritual events like seders . . ." Sloman was getting carried away.

"Who am I to say what they should do?" Nellis smiled. "I don't do it in my family."

"And all that talk about amotivational personalities. I interviewed these middle-class entrepreneurs who were all using grass to inspire them into more creative ways to make money . . ." Sloman was gone.

"Well, for every inspirational story about what marijuana can make you think of, I can give you an equal story about depression and lack of motivation and so on. You picks your poison and you takes your choice." Nellis smiled and took a long, deep drag on his cigarette.

CHAPTER 24:
Moloch Revisited

After dinner, Peter Orlovsky began doing the dishes, and Sloman and Ginsberg lingered at the kitchen table. Ginsberg was in the middle of a long dialogue, making the argument that the mass diffusion of grass into our culture had really made a difference. That the sixties were not for naught.

"Within the limits of what could be done at all by any light-hearted means, short of violent physical revolution, which is impossible, it was the subtlest, most charming, pacific way of altering insight, perception and perspective. I think it left permanent effects on all the young lawyers, government administrators, bureaucrats and businessmen to come. You can't overcome the basic greed or passion, aggression and ignorance basic to egotism. But you can make a dent. I think it has led through acid and other things to a greater growth of dharma and contemplative practices in America. It led directly to vast meditation practices. Every single swami says 90 percent of his devotees have originally had drug experience. So it was a catalyst; that's all it was supposed to be. It wasn't supposed to be a revolution itself. From that point of view it was eminently successful. That's why it was battled so long. It was another culture, a nigger culture. The Third World asserting itself with all of its insights. What Kerouac originally proposed: it was fellaheen insight. The non-centralized, the non-city, the non-robotized."

"You think Anslinger intuitively thought that?" Sloman wondered.

"They were defending what they thought was Western civilization." Ginsberg got up and brought his plate over to the sink.

"In the sense that they were scared of some other culture rising from the deep just like Henry Luce was scared of it. All those ministers' sons were scared of something that was more Dionysian or black . . ."

"It makes them more sympathetic in a way." Sloman was groping for the right way to express his vague feeling that Anslinger might have been a victim of the relentless forces of history and social situation.

"Well, yes and no," Ginsberg chuckled ironically. "I accept sympathetic, but only as like all those people who killed six million Incas. They thought they were promoting Christ. And God. They came to America and killed off the Inca empire. Killed off the Aztecs. Burned the Mayan codices because they thought they were diabolical works. Very sympathetic. Just like Anslinger thought marijuana was the devil's weed. Very sympathetic. Not a madman. But so wrong—like Hitler, willing to arrest, torture and persecute people. People with nightsticks up their ass. Genitals with electrodes in Mexico. Sure, real sympathetic. It's like the Nazis. Hitler, a great idealist, believed in God. Marvelous. I'm sympathetic to him. I mean they got a bad deal in Germany—he was trying to reform it. Stalin was just trying to make Communism. A very patriotic man. LeRoi Jones still thinks Stalin was a great man. Very sympathetic. Anslinger's sympathetic. Burroughs sympathized with him for years because he felt that Anslinger took all the bad karma of the whole world on his back. They concentrated all the stupidity, ignorance and power drive into one person. From the point of view of white, Protestant, racist, patriotic, sure, he was real sympathetic."

CHAPTER 25:
The Pendulum Swings Back

Sloman was on the phone with Emmitt Corrick, who held the record for longevity within the Bureau of Narcotics—forty-five years. Corrick had been a statistician and record keeper for the Bureau since its inception, and a few years ago he had retired to Florida, which is where Sloman tracked him down, to get more Anslinger data.

"Well, there was only one man like him. He was a dedicated man to the work that he was doing. He could have gone out of the Bureau at any time with any of the drug manufacturers at ten to twelve times the amount of money he was receiving from the Bureau, but he was not interested in that."

After a few more minutes of conversation Sloman was thoroughly amazed at the reverential way Corrick still spoke about Anslinger, referring to him as "The Commissioner." Sloman was also a bit surprised that Corrick still clung to the marijuana myths that Anslinger had so fervently propagated.

"Way back in the Aba Baba [*sic*] days they smoked marijuana before they went on the raids," Corrick was rehashing the old stories. "That's the assassins. When a person's under the influence of marijuana they're not fully conscious of everything going on around them. I'm one of the old believers. I still think habitual use of it leads to something else. I don't think a person is satisfied with popping off once or twice with it. I think it gets worse as it goes on. Now, in our records, we had cases of terrible crimes that were committed while under the influence. I'm amazed myself at the number of people who like to go home and take a smoke in the evening to relax and get their minds off of everything. That's the same as taking a shot of something."

They talked on, and Corrick began bemoaning the breakdown of law and order in today's society, as opposed to the time when people like Anslinger and Hoover reigned supreme. "We had laws and we had courts, and if a person broke the law he was punished for the law. Today I can go out here on the street and I can stab a man and they'll have me up before a court and they'll say that I was temporarily insane and that it was a disease. And they'd put me in custody for maybe five years, and if I behave myself in three years they'll put me out on the street. Then I can go out and do the same thing again. It's been too much of the softness that's been allowed to creep in." Corrick's voice was mournful. "You take your penitentiaries today. They used to be sent to the rock pile and hard labor. Now they go to the penitentiary, and if they do any work they get paid for it. And in the evening they gather and they get all these television programs. They do everything except knock off at four o'clock and have tea."

Sloman brought up Anslinger again. "The Commissioner was a very demanding man." Corrick measured out his words. "He was demanding in everything that he wanted. And he was a little stern. But if I had my choice to work for anybody, it would be him. He was determined in his ways, knew what he wanted, and he appreciated what he got. He believed in everything he was doing."

"Do you keep up with the recent developments in the field?" Sloman wondered.

"Every now and then I pick up the paper and I'll see something and it makes me so disgusted I'll lay it down," Corrick chuckled.

"Florida's a major area for most of the pot that comes in," Sloman couldn't resist.

"They're getting boats every day," Corrick rejoined. "But what happens to the people that bring it in? They don't do anything to them."

"What do you think they should do?" Sloman asked.

Corrick laughed softly. "I think a few stiff penalties would straighten out a lot of things. You know they don't have much trouble with them in Mexico. If they catch anyone down there with marijuana, they slap them in jail. And we're getting about 300 of them back from the prisons down there now that were there for seven or eight years. Now that's what they do with them. And I'm telling you right now, if some of these people that are committing murder and rape and muggings and all, if they had the law set at them and they didn't send them to a plush penitentiary where all these softhearted people say they have to be rehabilitated. . . . You just can't rehabilitate a lot of them. There's only one way, and that's sweat it out of them. Of course, I'm hard-hearted." Corrick laughed ironically.

"What do you think about NORML?" Sloman wondered. "A middle-class lobby trying to get the laws changed, backed by *Playboy* magazine."

"The world's changing. Who ever thought the day would come when they wanted to change the laws about homosexuality? There's something wrong somewhere."

"It does almost look like the Roman days, doesn't it?" Sloman's tongue scraped the inside of his cheek. "All that partying, drugs, homosexuality . . ."

"That's the way the world turns." Corrick sounded resigned. "The pendulum will swing one way and then swing back. I think now it's on the verge of swinging back. You don't see quite as much wild haircuts and things like that as you used to. I think, I'm hoping that the world can look forward to a better world than the world we had the last twenty years."

"That's what Anslinger said in a commencement speech I found. He also once told an interviewer that the only people he feared were the hippies," Sloman remembered.

"Well, we all came from a different generation. Our generation believed in manners, neatness in dress, and putting forward the best front you could. Look your best and be presentable. Well, they're far from that today." Corrick shuddered.

"What does it mean that we're living in a society where 25 million people smoke marijuana?" Sloman asked the old prohibitionist. "Is that scary to you?"

"It scares the hell out of me," Corrick snapped back. "I'm just happy that I won't have to live in it too much longer. It's a terrible thing, a terrible thing." The chill in Corrick's voice traveled all the way up from Florida.

CHAPTER 26:
In the Bunker with the Last Straight in America

Corrick was right. The pendulum has begun to swing back a bit with respect to the marijuana issue. With the rapid success of NORML, more and more anti-marijuana spokespeople are attacking the decriminalization of the drug. NORML dismisses these people as the "reefer madness crowd," but it is clear that they are a vocal and organized minority.

One group that has organized to lobby against NORML is the American Council on Marijuana and Other Psychoactive Drugs. Marshaling some of the most famous anti-pot partisans under their umbrella (figures like Gabriel Nahas of Columbia, and Nicholas Pace of NYU), the Council has begun an education campaign aimed at exposing the severe dangers of pot smoking. They argue that as little as one joint a day can lead to extensive brain damage. In this regard, they have enlisted the celebrity support of former boxer Floyd Patterson, who apparently is an expert on the subject.

The Council's ranks were depleted in March of 1978, when Berkeley physiologist Hardin Jones died. Jones was widely noted for his belief that smoking marijuana led to, among other things, urinating in flour bins. In fact, Sloman was intent on talking to Jones for his research, and when he heard of the news, began to cast about for another spokesman for the extreme anti-pot position. Sociologist Erich Goode alerted him to the work of Alfred Miliman, head of the Maryland Drug Abuse Research and Treatment Foundation. He was based in Baltimore, and Sloman had an old friend, Roger Friedman, brother of country-pop star Kinky Friedman, who was living there. It was a good opportunity to kill two birds with one stone on the way back to New York from Washington.

So early one Saturday morning in March, Friedman and Sloman drove to downtown Baltimore and located the dingy basement offices of M-Dart. The two visitors filed off the self-service gate elevator and walked to a small office in the back of the basement.

"You must be the writer?" A huge, 300-pound man in shirtsleeves and brown tie pumped Sloman's hand, then greeted Roger and pointed them to seats. "Well, I'm Al Miliman. I'm the leading expert in America on marijuana. I know that's a pompous statement, huh?" Miliman laughed, an infectious laugh, then gingerly settled his corpulent frame back into his desk chair. Sloman instinctively began surveying the office, the wood paneling, the framed picture of John Kennedy, the bookshelves crammed with anti-marijuana tomes, the Jaycees plaques, the standard photos of the kids on the desk. He then snuck a glance at Miliman, who was stuffing out a cigarette in an already loaded ashtray, and realized that the drug counselor looked nervous.

"We have problems in this country. The social workers, the sociologists, the psychologists, the psychiatrists, they all believe that drug and alcohol abuse are symptomatic, not causative. We have a tremendous amount of data. I have a study here that I will give you, if it doesn't turn you off. For example, of 212 adolescent admissions to psychiatric hospitals from '72 to '77, at least 180 of 212 were chronic marijuana users." Miliman was off and running before Sloman had time to even set up the tape machine.

"Is it on?" Miliman finally asked. "I'm Al Miliman, of the M-Dart; glad to see you two fellows. I have worked in the drug and alcohol abuse field extensively since 1965. I began working in a private proprietary psychiatric hospital, and in 1966–67 I began to observe an interesting phenomenon. The psychiatric, psychologic, sociologic theory is that drugs do not cause mental disorders. The symptoms that follow drug abuse are symptomatic of some deeper underlying disorder. Now I saw kids who had used marijuana for seven years, and it was never mentioned in their psychiatric charts." Miliman shook his head in disbelief, and Sloman was impressed with how red his nose was.

"We think marijuana causes a brain syndrome and/or a thought disorder," Miliman continued, nervously tapping his cigarette into the ashtray. "I saw these kids come in. I saw what we call psychiatric symptoms, regression—who the hell understands regression? Regression is a change in the nature of your thinking where you revert to juvenile or infantile or primitive-type simplistic emotion-oriented thinking. I saw this in just about everyone who had been a regular chronic marijuana user. I saw the adoption of ego protection clauses. I saw a sixteen-year-old foam at the mouth on the subject of sound pollution—the SST transport. He knew nothing about it, but he turned fanatical; the intensity of the passion of these people is very interesting.

"In this country—and please don't be turned off; I'm telling the truth, the facts as I see them—for the past ten or twelve years there has never been, to my knowledge, a straight violent revolutionary. Never. You know, Abbie Hoffman, Jerry Rubin, Cleaver, Seale, Angela Davis, and there is a process here which we call a thought disorder. But we have had trouble getting the proper forum. I've told legislatures that they'd better be careful about who they listen to in connection with marijuana. The psychiatrist doesn't care about the drug, the drug is symptomatic. He will never make the connection. And remember the marijuana user really enjoys the drug. You two perhaps know this by personal experience, do you?"

Miliman asked the last question slyly, and Sloman decided that to get him to open up about the cannabis marijuana syndrome, he should take a prudent tack. In this case, he would attempt to out-Miliman Miliman.

"Ever hear of a Dr. Munch?" Sloman suddenly asked in response. "He was Anslinger's top marijuana honcho, and to be objective he tried it once. Well, in that same spirit, I did too." Sloman tried to keep a straight face. "He described it as being at the bottom of an ink well for two hundred years."

"But again, he's not into it right." Miliman smiled. "It is a very pleasurable drug. In India a thousand years ago they worshipped it as a god. They wrote poetry to it. They didn't smoke it; they ate. You ought to see some of the recipes. Remember, the marijuana smoker also does magical thinking, and this isn't related to magic. Opinion becomes fact. The thought connotes the deed or act. If he has an application in for an interview for a job, he says, 'I got the job.' If he has an opinion about something, *e.g.*, marijuana, he doesn't think it's harmless, he knows it's harmless, and you want to be very careful about arguing with some of these people. They can get verbally violent, at least." Miliman laughed again.

"Our research indicates that probably after eight or ten days, 30 percent of the THC is retained in human tissue, human fat. After a while, for the person who smokes once in every eight days, there will be trouble. It may take five or ten years. But if the users are honest, many users who smoke it and enjoy it find that in two years they have to give it up. They begin to get paranoid. Now we know in the dormitory at College Park, Maryland, University of Maryland, marijuana use is about 95 percent. They have people believing that if penalties are made lower, decriminalized, less smoking will be done. You would have to be retarded to believe that." Miliman laughed sarcastically.

"Why do you think people react so strongly to what you have to say?" Sloman was being very diplomatic.

"Because of the effect on them of marijuana." Miliman was as logical as two plus two is four.

"It's part of the syndrome?" Sloman asked. "It makes them defensive?"

"Defensive?" Miliman exploded. "Offensive! They know it's harmless, not only harmless but beneficial. Look at Leary and LSD. This is what we call regression, this mystical thinking, magical thinking, this introversion. We believe that—and this is partly theoretical—the left hemisphere of the brain is kinda knocked out. That is the hemisphere that deals with reason, science, logic, mathematics. The right hemisphere is talk, music, poetry, fantasy, imagination.

"Why can't we get dissemination of our information? For example, Dr. Nahas, a brilliant man, this is a hell of a dude, in one of his books reports findings in animal studies where not only the feces in the unborn animal but even one generation removed with a control group finds mutations in animals, lower species, genetic implication. So Nahas had a press conference in Helsinki on the latest laboratory findings. I wanted to read about it in the paper. Two weeks later, nothing. So I called the *Sun* papers, finally got a young fellow named Greenwood on the copy desk. I told him I hadn't seen the article on the new lab findings on marijuana; 'Haven't you printed it yet?' He said, 'No.' I asked him when they'd print it; he said they wouldn't. I asked why and he replied, 'I don't think it was important.' Believe me, the media is so responsible, the communications media, the academic profession. We can't get this information disseminated."

"And you think it's because a lot of the media suffers from the syndrome?"

"I know it." Miliman exploded again. "Look, we were interviewed by about ten or twelve reporters in the last seven or eight years, and I have not met a straight one yet. We know it can cause paranoia and depression. I personally believe that it is responsible for thousands of adolescent suicides. A simple little principle of physics, for every action there is an equal and opposite reaction. This high, this pleasure, this up, this feeling can be followed and often is by an opposite feeling, and, of course, you have the thought disorder, the regression, people having to adopt great causes. It's a very ego-protective psychiatric defense mechanism. Having to be critical of authority, of parents, of the establishment, of Vietnam, of Richard Nixon, every damn thing."

"It is fascinating," Sloman tried to keep a straight face as he peered over at Roger, who was sitting staring in amazement at the lay therapist.

"Well, you have an open mind about it." Miliman seemed taken aback by the reporter's warm reception. "That's unusual. The people from Consumer's Union, from Harvard, they don't have open minds."

"I'm trying to get a sense of use patterns," Sloman noted. "When it began on this scale . . ."

"It began in 1964," Miliman cut in. "Before that I knew people in show business who used to smoke, and I thought they were fine, I thought they were normal. But when you think back and examine their personal or private lives, they screwed up their marriages, their families, all kinds of things. Let me not forget to mention the effect, particularly in the young, of this brain syndrome. There is a lessening of concentration span, attention span, ability to do complex thinking, impairment in the ability to learn. Take one of our kids, Iris, a young black male—race is immaterial—in eleventh grade. He is not stoned—he is fine. This is not when you're stoned, this is the gradual condition that develops. But there are two pints in one quart and four quarts in one gallon. Iris can't tell me how many pints there are in one gallon. That is the simplest kind of complex thinking. But what it does to the brain the user is unaware.

"The political aspects are fascinating. The conservationists, the anti-war freaks, anti-pollutionists. Imagine that they had the media and the people believing that there was a civil war in Cambodia, Laos and Vietnam. Fantastic! Barry Commoner was telling people that solar power is cheaper than nuclear power. That is absolutely asinine. It's still going on. It's more dangerous now, because it's more subtle. You are going to find that these people have these crusades. Now this is only a theory out of my half-cocked brain, but I maintain that not only the Alaska pipeline sabotage but the chlorine car sabotage is by people who have this particular mission. They are going to prove the danger to the economy and the environment of this asinine type of activity. Regression. Go back to the land, go back to the forest, go back to nature and everything. Communes—I have been to some communes where human feces are right outside the front door." Miliman screwed up his red nose at the thought.

"Are there any specific clues that give the victims away? If you saw someone on TV, could you tell?" Sloman leaned in for the answer.

"In some cases, absolutely." Again the tap tap tapping of the cigarette was beginning to drive the reporter bonkers. "I watched Sterling Hayden on the Snyder show. He is an obvious one. He admitted it. I watched Jane Fonda from way back. For a girl like this, a brilliant, talented actress that she is—she is a Marxist and thinks North Vietnam is the greatest country in the world—for a girl like that to get a mind warp, we don't think it would be possible without marijuana."

"What about the Moonies? Don't they start out on drugs?"

"We believe it couldn't happen without it. We have not found a straight person in the SDS, the Black Liberation Army, the Black Panthers. None."

"I wonder if you could define the cannabis syndrome," Roger asked softly from his seat across the room.

"It is a condition which develops with marijuana use."

"How much?" Sloman pressed.

"Depends on the individual. If a person is a so-called social user, it might take a couple of years for these symptoms to develop, even longer. If he's a chronic or daily user, you can expect it much sooner. Now, he gets a very flat affect, he gets a speech blockage. This means, in some cases, unless it's memorized rhetoric, you have to be careful of how fast he talks or he will lose some coordination between his mouth and his mind. You often get a disassociation between thought and mood. You have to observe him, be with him, talk to him, and he gets an attitude that is totally inappropriate for the subject under discussion. The thought disorder is the key. If they are emotionally oriented, if they are passionate about things, major issues in this great society of ours which they have no technical knowledge of, then you have to be a little bit careful. Take Gary Wills, the famous columnist. Someone ought to talk to him about his pot use sometime. I have his columns from the late sixties; Johnson is a Hitler, Nixon is a Hitler. When people who have conventional American upbringing get that passionate, you'll always find it."

"But you say they have both the passion and the intensity as well as the flat affect?" Roger tried to sound friendly.

"Ordinarily you have a flat affect," Miliman admitted. "But they can get passionate. You should see them in Washington when they jump up on Volkswagens and pull the hood up and try to rip out the distributor wires. Take Vietnam; they had a cause there. What happens to society where the drug is legal? Egypt 1500 or 1400 B.C. Fantastic society, they constructed the pyramids, the Sphinx, engineering achievements like crazy. We believe that marijuana came in and they have not had an engineer or scientist in Egypt since. That's an exaggeration. In 1967, the Russians still had trouble teaching Egyptians to take apart, clean and put back together an infantry rifle. Of course, the hash in Egypt is fantastic."

"Well, that story doesn't make me sad," Sloman smiled.

"Now, when I talk with rabbis who might be saying how good marijuana is, I tell them they ought to thank God that it isn't that heavy in Israel yet, because I think marijuana is the cause of Israel's existence today. Fifty million Arabs, if they had any, any technical ability . . ." Miliman just shook his head. "Take the Minoan civilization. Remember the island of Crete, one of the most advanced people in history? In 1200 or 1300 B.C. they had commerce, industry, shipbuilding, everything. To this day they do not know why their society stagnated. Invasion, typhoon, tornado, hurricane, they really don't know. M-Dart thinks we know. We think marijuana came in, and remember that it was very pleasurable. We think it's the cause of the decline of the Minoan civilization. But again this is a theory, don't print it as fact. But we studied their art and sculpture, vases. We have pictures of this. In 1400 B.C., the vases had geometric concentric designs, everything. In 1200 B.C. you got psychedelic art, art that lets your imagination do what it wants with no design."

Sloman was amused by Miliman's use of the editorial "we," since the lawyer, who started M-Dart as an avocation, and who now gets referrals to his law practice from the juveniles he works with in the counseling center, seemed to be the director and only staff member. During the interview a number of young kids kept popping in and out of the office, and the put-down banter between them and Miliman suggested a relationship that transcended the typical therapist-client roles. Despite themselves, Sloman and Friedman found themselves liking this anti-marijuana crusader.

"I just interviewed a guy in Washington, Bob Randall, who used marijuana for his glaucoma," Sloman reported. "He's not a hippie, or crazy."

"Are you kidding? Priests, ministers, doctors, judges, lawyers, presidential candidates have smoked." Miliman recited the litany of the ignoble. "Jody Powell has been a smoker, Hamilton Jordan. What are you talking about? You've got me on record, I'm Al Miliman. Ever see *High Times* magazine? They talk about it in there; they don't deny it. It's not a rumor. Keith Stroup was on the Tom Snyder show one night, and Tom is talking to him about marijuana and what he thinks of Carter, and Stroup says he had a commitment from Jody Powell that young Carter would go with him to a state hearing on decriminalization and he didn't live up to it. Those people smoke, Jody Powell, Ham Jordan. Why are they so hypocritical about it? That was on national TV! I believe the two smoke because I have tied in their behavior with the social smokers—hip, flaky, they give simplistic answers to complex questions. They're beautiful talkers. They can solve the problems of the universe. They talk for hours."

"Have you done any research on populations of risk?" Friedman thought he was back at the University of Maryland.

"The adolescent population," Miliman ad-libbed. "The vulnerable ones are now smoking at the age of seven or eight in Baltimore City. Parents are trying it on their kids. It used to happen in Mexico, in South American countries. We're studying four families now; we think there is a genetic implication with marijuana."

"Genetic?" Friedman looked puzzled.

"Let me tell you why," Miliman continued. "Any drug of abuse has to reach the brain, it's got to affect your feeling. Drugs of abuse are tried for the first time by 99.9 percent of the people because of curiosity. The use is continued because of one thing—98 percent of the time because of pleasure. Why do people abuse Valium? It gives you a good feeling. Again, this is why, if you want to get into the social work theories and blame the parents and the pharmaceutical manufacturers, you're wrong."

Miliman's rapid delivery and convoluted thought patterns were beginning to make his visitors feel a bit dizzy. The endless tapping of those Winston Golds was driving Sloman nearly to distraction. And after he had killed a large cockroach that was crawling across his notepad, the reporter was intent on firing off a few more questions and getting the hell out of that wood-paneled cell. "What about violent crime?" Sloman sounded accusatory. "They used to link it to marijuana in the thirties."

"There's no question about it," Miliman shrugged. "Marijuana is related to crime in two ways. First, brain syndrome combined with a thought disorder. The lowered intellectual achievement, the decline in grades in school, the dissatisfaction at home. Marijuana has been an alienating and polarizing drug for 3,000 or 4,000 years. What is a man going to do if he drops out of school? It's easy to get money illegally. This causes the beginning of what we call a sociopathic-type symptomatology.

"The other type of crime is the sabotage bombings. People don't realize that in the years 1967 to 1972, there were 12,000 bombings in this country by 'dissenters.' These people are not political. Bombing is a violent act. I wish everyone could be exposed to a bomb so they could see what it means. You have people like Cathy Boudin, the Brandeis University graduates who robbed a bank and killed a guard in Boston. All these girls have been into marijuana. This is a thought disorder where they regress, the psychiatric defense mechanisms operate. Their psyche won't permit them to see how rotten and stupid they are. So they twist, they project, and it is the fault of society, the establishment, the drug manufacturers, their boss, mother, father, Vietnam, Richard Nixon, the military-industrial complex." Miliman paused for a breath.

Miliman was about to resume when a young kid in Western denim clothes walked in. The counselor sprang to his feet.

"Tommy, I want you to meet Larry Sloman and Roger Friedman. Larry's doing a book on marijuana. What you got for me there?"

The kid handed Miliman some papers. "This is all she got done."

"His girlfriend's doing some typing for me. To get out of his legal fee. Now Tommy here was a clean, upstanding young person. How old were you when you smoked your first joint?" Suddenly it was show-and-tell time.

"Seventeen," the kid answered laconically.

"Did you enjoy marijuana?"

"Yeah, thought it was pretty nice," Tommy drawled.

"Then you got into acid?" Miliman led.

"Little bit." The kid smiled sheepishly.

"Then you got into the big leagues, didn't you? He became an addict. Got on a methadone maintenance program, and he's had all kinds of trouble since. But he has a job now; he's off methadone."

"Guess what," the kid started.

"I don't believe you," Miliman snapped.

"Thursday the supervisor took me off punching a time clock and they put me on salary, gave me a $1,800 a year raise and three more departments to take care of."

"Honest to God," Miliman smiled. "That's fantastic. Maybe you can afford some Hawaiian blue now, $140 an ounce. How have you been doing? He still gets stoned. You smoked how many times the past week?"

"Every day," Tom smiled.

"See, he smokes and he has this job. He functions. Of course, he has a meaningful relationship with a young lady. During the process, though, he did some sky diving without a parachute, has been involved with the law, and nearly broke his neck and hip. It's a long process. But his brain has practically gotten inured to grass. I would predict that from two to three years from now he will get paranoid. He has become somewhat sociopathic. You don't get excited about little things? Do you ever cry in the movies?"

"Nah." The kid turned macho.

"I did the other day—I saw an old Bette Davis movie. He looks perfectly normal, good job and stuff, but odds are that before long, unless he makes some changes, there will be some serious consequences."

"Are you worried?" Sloman asked Tommy.

"He doesn't worry about anything," Miliman answered. "Are you kidding? The only time he worried was when he was laid up in a hospital."

"Do you think starting out on marijuana leads to more dangerous drugs?" Sloman felt compelled to ask that.

"I don't know of a PCP user who didn't first get indoctrinated into marijuana. Heroin use in our data shows 80 percent of whites and 70 percent of blacks start with marijuana," Miliman reported. "But nineteen of twenty don't get past hash."

"Do you know of any people who have smoked marijuana who have achieved great things, say in science or poetry?" Sloman inquired.

"I don't know of any." Miliman leaned back in his chair. "At Maryland Legislature hearings NORML had a girl there who had been cured of multiple sclerosis by marijuana—I'm not kidding. And when we had this symposium someone called in and said their migraine headaches were cured. You're going to see cures for gonorrhea, piles." Miliman chuckled at his humor. "The drug has an appeal. It's the most pleasurable thing you do maybe outside of sex, but of course you're weak at sex," he ribbed Tommy, who just at that moment was joined by his girlfriend, also outfitted in hippie cowboy drag. "Say hello to these two gentlemen," Miliman instructed. "Normal, right? Seems normal. You smoke?"

The girl nodded yes.

"So what's wrong with her?" Miliman continued the diagnosis. "I don't want to upset her, but she has a brain syndrome. Tom over there can't answer sixth-grade questions. But keep typing." He smiled.

"I need another typewriter," the girl said apathetically.

"Jesus," Miliman moaned.

"It's okay, I got one," she reassured him. "There's lots of big words though, and I don't know if I'm getting the names right."

Miliman grabbed the transcripts the girl had done and began reading from one section. "Let's see, a twenty-three-year-old parking lot attendant first used marijuana at age fifteen and used it regularly from seventeen to the present, smoked twenty joints daily. Ha! And no relevant medical illnesses. See, this is absolutely asinine. Okay, you two go. I just wanted to see how great marijuana was."

The pair left the office, and Miliman lowered his booming voice to a whisper. "That relationship is doomed to failure. Those two spend about two or three hours a day getting high. Have to be an idiot not to know what's happening. Their intellect is declining so bad, but I don't want to upset them. If that relationship lasts more than six to twelve months, I will kiss your rear end in the middle of . . ." The pair suddenly walked past the open door.

"Take care," Miliman yelled, then called them back in. "I don't want to talk behind your back. I just said when chronic pot users get together the relationship is doomed to failure. Too pleasure oriented. But you're having a good time while you're doing it, so go on. Make sure you close the gate on the elevator."

The pair left again, a little bewildered.

"She's a pothead"—Sloman to the attack—"and she's typing up your papers. Aren't you afraid she might sabotage them?"

A glimmer of fear passed through Miliman's eyes. "Naw," he protested. "She's a good kid. The decline is in the intellect. They have a good source of grass; he's always in hock. Their ability to manage anything is pitiful, except their ability to obtain and use marijuana."

"But it seems to be so pervasive, even all the cops are smoking it," Sloman complained.

"Maybe in New York or parts of California. But here less than half of 1 percent of Maryland State Police smoke. But you're right, and you'd better be careful of these people. Not the guns so much, but the ideation they get into. They are going to save the world. Calley was a marijuana user, and you know how he wasted the people of Vietnam."

"Could you give us some names of famous people we wouldn't expect . . ."

Miliman anticipated the question. "Governor Brown of California, Jody Powell, Hamilton Jordan, Father Berrigan, there are so darn many of them."

"What about Anita Bryant?" Miliman's Miliman piped up.

"Are you kidding?" The therapist was aghast. "She's superstraight. Her religious convictions alone would keep her away."

"But she's in show biz." Sloman smiled.

"Most of the people in the drug abuse field are potheads. Andrew Weil, do you know him? He's a bearded freak now. His latest recommendation is that we put cocaine in chewing gum. I'm not kidding. He comes up with a medical excuse."

"How about the role of popular music?" Sloman was touching all the bases.

"The largest incidence of marijuana use is in the rock scene," Miliman noted without blinking. "And I know people who are stoned who would be fascinated listening if someone pounded on a garbage can. When you are stoned, you really have an imagination, you sense things, hear things, feel vibrations. If you start having sex, you can feel like you're coming for five minutes—believe me, it doesn't last that long."

Sloman was beginning to perceive that sordid feeling, the strange fascination of the prohibitionist for the contraband, the same feeling he got when he read Anslinger's accounts of the opium dens and the white slave rings.

Miliman had gone on to talk about Vietnam and how the pothead press cost us victory. "Daniel Ellsberg"—Miliman grabbed another name out of the bag—"he was a dedicated government servant until he started smoking."

"Pothead?" Sloman almost sighed.

"He had the lights and everything in his own home. He started in Vietnam."

"How about Woodward and Bernstein?" Sloman asked.

"Only one of the two. Absolutely. I consider these people pimples on the asshole of mankind. They're the sneaks, and they got a big Pulitzer Prize. Shows you how crazy we are."

"Have you had any contact with Keith Stroup?"

"Yes." Miliman laughed. "He and I are pretty friendly. He and I disagree. Do you really believe that Keith Stroup is in this because of his great concern for a young person who gets eighty years for having a speck of grass?"

"Why are they in it, then?" Sloman played gullible.

"He loves marijuana! He thinks it should be legalized for a great free society. He loves it, and he knows it like you're sitting in that chair."

"Is that an ideology that is ego defensive?" Roger asked.

"I think his mind has changed so much that if you gave him a polygraph, he would answer questions that marijuana is helpful. He's absolutely sincere. Ellsberg, all these people are sincere as hell."

"They just need help," Sloman said sarcastically.

"Don't ever tell them that," Miliman warned. "Of course they need help."

"So you'd be happy if in America the trend away from alcohol to pot would be reversed?" Sloman was trying to sum up.

"Look what happens to societies who go to cannabis. Eastern civilizations went to cannabis—Africa, Arabs, Asia—and the Western ones went to alcohol and wound up with achievement, productivity. You ain't gonna get that when you have a substance soluble in the brain affecting your concentration, attention, memory spans, ability to do complex thinking. You will have an opportunity in your book to really do a job if you put in some of this other information, like the connection between the violence of the crusader, the anti-war, anti-pollution conservationist—they used to put in their newspapers that to end the war we should stop the war. We never had the power to stop the Vietnamese war.

"So we have been a party to such misinformation, such crazy things; let me give you some examples. I am not positive that Judge Sirica is a pot smoker, but I suspect it. He convicted six people of breaking into Watergate and found them guilty. He called them up to the bench and he said they were guilty and if they didn't talk they would get the maximum sentence of thirty-five years. A judge who does this should be put in jail."

Miliman raved on about Sirica and Rosemary Woods, but Sloman mercifully cut him off. "What about the Kennedys?"

"The sons have. Again, I'm not sure about the President or Bobby. But Ford's sons, Carter's, Agnew's daughter."

"What about Carter himself?" Sloman couldn't resist.

Miliman looked furtive. "I am not going to answer that question. But his emotionalism, his talk, his simplistic thinking seem significant. But I don't know."

"When can you be sure, in your own mind?"

"You can never be 100 percent sure," the therapist admitted. "Sometimes the symptoms are so apparent, though. In the movie business, take Kris Kristofferson, or the guy who played the part of Al Jolson and in six months became a bearded drug freak. Larry Parks."

"What about TV people? Johnny Carson?"

"You can tell quite often. Carson, no way; he's as straight as hell. But what about the Gong Show? That girl, what's her name? She's a famous head."

"What's your prognosis for the next couple of years?" Roger brought the conversation back on track.

"Unless we educate the public to some of the reasons for these way-out stupid activities and causes. . . . Like Women's Lib is a good example. You won't find a straight fanatical Women's Libber. I got files on them all. We got to get to the public the possible connection between marijuana use and the fanatical crusades for causes that are so asinine. Women, the exalted species. You laugh, but they're denigrating the role of housemaker and housewife, and there's no more important role in the country. You should see their writings; they talk about a housewife or a secretary as having ghetto jobs. They're so stupid." Miliman began to stew and crushed another cigarette out.

"What are some of your sources of pleasure?" the reporter was looking for substitutes.

"The achievement, the smile on the face of someone you love, the accomplishment. When I talk to a woman who calls me crying and her son came home, a miserable rotten slob, unthinking, unfeeling, and she's crying on the phone because this kid came up to her and said, 'Mom, let me help you wash the dishes,' with no ulterior motive, she broke into tears of happiness. That makes me high. I have ex-addicts who are making $25,000 a year, executive salesmen, career military people. For the most part these people have discontinued. They wouldn't smoke any more than they'd eat horseshit."

"What's your family like?"

"I have a wife, three daughters, two grandsons. They're wonderful."

"Did any of them experiment with drugs?" Sloman was waiting for the horror story, the LSD leap or the Quaalude coma.

"Well, the youngest one did briefly. I can't prove any connection, but she dropped out of school. Now she's got her Masters and she's doing fine. She told me she had done it. She only smoked a few times; her roommate was on it. One of our men went to Fort Hood, Texas; he's an engineer. Assigned there and he's doing great. He goes into an eight-man tent and the other seven guys light up. This is the United States Army! This guy was an addict, so you have a problem." Miliman laughed heartily at the irony.

"This is not out of disrespect"—Sloman trod carefully—"but I get the feeling sitting here that I'm in a bunker, and out there it's a nation of potheads and we're going down the toilet."

"It's only 20 million," Miliman tried to reassure the reporter. "It may take two or three generations. I hate to have you feel you're in a bunker, though. You're nice guys. We have no armament or fortifications here, and all I can say is that you have an opportunity to present some information to the public."

"I mean, it seems you could use some money or people or something," Sloman went on. "Have you ever tried to apply for foundation money?"

Miliman rolled his eyes. "We went to Washington. Two of the four people at the conference table were potheads. Of course, we could tell; they didn't have to tell us. It was so apparent—hairy, freaky, flat affect, simplistic thinking, emotion-oriented. We had no hope of getting a grant. These people up to a year or two ago were marijuana lovers, and I'm talking about the teachers, the authorities. Robert DuPont, head of NIDA, has admitted to trying marijuana. Peter Bourne, from the White House, has admitted to trying marijuana. Andrew Weil, we know he's been into every hallucinogenic drug there is. These people are in positions of authority."

"It sounds like a real conspiracy." Sloman laughed to himself.

"It's no conspiracy. It's an attitude that they can't help but develop. It's one of the symptoms of the cannabis syndrome. You know the drug is harmless. I'm talking now about newspaper reporters, editors, professors, instructors."

"What you're saying is in effect there are 20 million people, a Fifth Column of sorts . . ."

"They're a Seventh Column," Miliman worried. "They don't know what is going on, but they know they're right. You ought to talk to some young people."

"Senator Eastland called them a nation of zombies," Sloman fueled the fire.

"That's only in certain Arab areas, some sections of Mexico, Central and South America. Not here yet. Maybe two or three generations. You'd have to go to the African history, and can you picture a hashish bowl that diameter?" The lawyer spread his arms far apart. "In certain African tribes they had those with all these different stems coming out. No one did anything. It was a great mother's helper. Some cultures, the kids would get a marijuana cookie to nibble on and you wouldn't have to touch the kid all day. They'd play, be happy. I'm talking historical facts. The anthropologists should have gotten into this, not me, but they're all potheads. Great mother's helper, though. It really ruins the kid."

"Did you read *Cannabis and Culture* by Vera Rubin?"

"I will get it and try to read it, but it is such unmitigated horseshit that it bothers me," Miliman ranted. "And Zinberg. Another pothead, for godsakes. But again, an intelligent man with a bias that just won't quit. He wrote an article for *Psychology Today* that is the most ridiculous horseshit. I use the word pothead loosely to mean people who have been affected by marijuana use without their knowledge or awareness."

"So what does Alfred Miliman do, since he doesn't do drugs?"

Miliman killed the last of his coffee from Little Tavern and leaned back in his chair. "I enjoy everything I do. I enjoy eating. I'm a philatelist. I belong to the International Society of Criminology, American Judicature Society, American Bar Association. I'm a tournament bridge player. I used to fish. Gourmet eating is my specialty. But why is it so bad to enjoy your work? There's nothing more rewarding. When you finish your book and you do a good job, you will get high from it, believe me. Personal achievement, personal productivity are great sources of pleasure. That's where I make my mistake. If I get a good result in a law case, I feel wonderful and I reward myself with a big fat dinner. That's how you get high. From the smile of someone you love. If my grandkids or my wife of thirty-six years smiles, I get high. I can't describe that feeling to you. When I saw that Bette Davis movie, it was so great I had tears in my eyes. The pothead can't do this. You develop sociopathic symptomatology with this and other drugs too. These feelings are real, but we don't talk about this, we experience it. People who talk about feelings to me are suspect. And they're not going to work with any of my addicts or drug-dependent people or my drunks. Because to me they don't know what the hell they're doing."

"If you're suffering from cannabis syndrome . . ." Roger started a question.

"You use the word suffering. These people are happier many times than you or I," Miliman smiled.

"I can't say victim, because they don't consider themselves victims, but if they have the syndrome, then . . ."

"Let's get the record straight," Miliman interrupted again. "You can have the syndrome from .1 percent to 90 percent. An

M.D. who smokes, a biologist who becomes an expert on ESP, he still functions. Jody Powell still functions. They're not hurt too badly. The only people who are directly hurt by it are those who are young and have that learning impairment and also those who get involved in this ego-protective cause business."

They had been inside that stuffy office for nearly three hours, and the afternoon had turned into a cold Saturday night. Sloman had a late train to catch to New York, and Friedman was showing signs of advanced wigging, but Miliman, oblivious to the two casualties in front of him, was ranting on about the cannabis marijuana syndrome and regression and ego-protective devices. But with all the bullshit taken into account, Sloman still kind of liked the guy. He was obviously suffering from every facet of the cannabis syndrome that he was skillfully projecting onto the potheads. And without the pleasure of the puffing too, Sloman thought, and savored the irony. The reporter was really tempted to try to turn Miliman on, but in that world of vipers he was without any grass. So he settled for a last question.

"The local press doesn't cover you, right?"

"Are you kidding?" Miliman shook his head. "They're all potheads."

"So why don't you just forget about talking about the cannabis syndrome and talk about the great job you're doing with these junkies?" Sloman thought that was a great suggestion, because he really was struck by the split between Miliman's ideology and his practice. On the one hand, he thought these kids were clinically diseased with an ailment that their own mindless hedonism brought upon them. On the other hand, he was practicing some hybrid form of gestalt therapy and giving these kids a lot more attention and care and warmth than most liberal bleeding-heart social workers, carrying a caseload that would choke a rhino. But Miliman would not hear about suppressing the syndrome.

"What purpose would that serve?" He looked hurt and vulnerable. "Self-aggrandizement, I guess. But we've got to get this marijuana stopped. That's the point: if we don't get that thought disorder concept understood, we're dead. Dead."

Sloman waited a minute and then clicked off the recorder. Miliman looked totally wasted and confused. He had envisioned two hostile reporters—potheads, of course—laughing at his concepts, but instead he got a social worker who dug what he was doing therapeutically and a reporter who was convinced Anita Bryant was a submerged agent for NORML. It was all too much for the fat man to digest.

"Well, good luck with your book." He extended his hand and Sloman took it. "Listen, ask Bobbs-Merrill if they want a book on marijuana with case histories."

Sloman looked at the lawyer-analyst with compassion. "I would, but I think my editor is a pothead," Sloman whispered with a shrug.

Miliman just shook his head. "Yeah." He sighed. "I understand." Then he said good-bye and asked the visitors to make sure the elevator gate was closed when they left.

CHAPTER 27:
Ambush at the Calvert Café

After the pie-ing of Nellis, the rest of the Sunday session at the NORML conference was an anticlimax. But Gene Schoenfeld, the nationally syndicated counterculture medical advice columnist who's known as Dr. Hip, invited Sloman and NORML photographer Shep Sherbell to a small party at the house of Blair Newman, who was one of the first members of AMORPHIA. Actually, it was at Blair's mother's house, as Newman was now living in California and working for the Rand Corporation.

But somehow, when the trio drove up to one of the most exclusive apartment houses in Washington, they began to realize this might be a stranger party than they had anticipated. And Blair, greeting them at the door, confirmed their fears.

"This is gonna be a little strange," Newman whispered, peering anxiously into the living room. "It's just my mother and some of her old media friends. Helen Thomas is here. So be cool." He took their coats, and the conferees walked into the living room. Ten wizened eyes cast suspicious glances in their direction.

Sloman immediately recognized Ms. Thomas. During the Watergate years, he had thrilled at her insistent attempts to get her explosive questions at the lame President. He loved her cheeky style and gutsy manner. And he was excited to hear that familiar voice ask the first question.

"Where were you people? Dorothy said it was some marijuana conference?" The other four people peered at the newcomers as though they were specimens of some sort.

"We came from the NORML conference. We were discussing changing the laws with respect to marijuana." Dr. Hip became the group's spokesman.

"Well, isn't that stuff dangerous?" Helen to the attack. "Doesn't it lead to violence? You don't use that stuff, do you? You don't actually smoke that? What about heroin—that's next, isn't it? Have you ever been to 14th Street, that corner where they just wait in droves for the pusher? It's disgraceful how that drug takes the kids into a demimonde."

Gene attempted to patiently explain that these were all myths associated with marijuana, that marijuana in itself was a beneficial drug. But somehow he wound up answering one of Helen's questions by noting that he thought it was okay for people to use heroin. This libertarian position did not sit too well with these senior citizens.

"Are you married?" one of the old women croaked at Gene.

"I'm divorced," he explained.

"Was she white?" The old woman was dead serious.

Sloman began to feel like Jacques Cousteau. He had the impression that a cell of the Woman's Christian Temperance Union had been discovered intact, fresh from a 1937 meeting where Anslinger was the keynote speaker and *Reefer Madness* had been screened to much applause. The reporter began to feel Mexican.

But Dorothy Newman, Blair's mother, came to the rescue and suggested that the party move to the Calvert Café, where their dinner awaited them. The Calvert was a greasy-spoon Middle Eastern dive that had been discovered by the chic Washington crowd. Kissinger had made it one of his hangouts, and the sycophants rushed to it in droves. Rumor had it that behind those stucco doors was a hotbed of support for the P.L.O. Sloman did not think he would feel quite that comfortable sharing Baba Ganoush with P.L.O. sympathizers. The reporter began to feel like Victor Licata.

But once at the restaurant, everything was dandy. The women had each attached themselves to one of the young guests, and the wine flowed and flowed. Ms. Thomas got loose and began criticizing the President and the First Lady. Recalling a particularly unpleasant interview with Rosalynn, Thomas noted, "She could have marched in Hitler's army." That characterization drew a long laugh from the table, much to Sloman's surprise.

After a few carafes, the old women got up and, requesting music, began doing a strange lewd variation on belly dancing.

They tried to drag the reporter into it, but he was able to resist.

But it was hard for him to resist the advances of the seventy-year-old to his left. From the appetizer on, she had been sneaking her wizened right hand onto his thigh. He had somehow managed to shake it off without appearing that he knew the errant hand had ever been there. But by dessert, it was almost a hopeless cause.

"Oh, this is so nice." The drunk old lady squeezed Sloman's hand and cooed. The reporter forlornly dipped his pita into some cold hummus.

"You're such an interesting fellow." She had forgotten all about the marijuana and the heroin and Dr. Hip's white wife, and without warning snuck her hand back onto his thigh. Sloman quickly scanned the table. Seeing that the others were in similar dilemmas, he then turned back to his plate. There was nothing left to pretend to eat.

"Do you dance?" his drunk seducer squealed, and the reporter just sighed and wished he had a joint. Or at least a Tom Collins.

CODA:
Reefer Madness: Reprise

Sloman had finished his research and was celebrating at Cusimano's Manhattan apartment. Cusimano marked the occasion by rolling big fat joints, each of which Sloman politely refused. After eight months on the marijuana trail, the reporter couldn't care less whether he ever saw a baggie full of primo again. Not that he begrudged Cusimano his choice of intoxicant—it was just that he had ODed on the concept of marijuana. Sloman was celebrating with an Entemann's chocolate donut and milk.

"You were right," Cusimano hacked between pulls of his joint, the fat rolling on his belly like a bowl of Jello caught in a hurricane. "I really thought grass was a dead issue in the seventies. But shit, it's not. It still has so much meaning in all those people's lives. Barbara and her friends, Dana Beal and the Yippies, the fucking guy with glaucoma."

Cusimano absentmindedly offered the joint to Sloman, who waved it away cavalierly. "It's a weed whose time has come." The reporter was feeling cocky enough to make such glib statements. "Look, it basically took the honkies of America thirty-five years to discover what the Negroes and Mexicans knew back in the thirties. You smoke a little reefer, you get high, you forget about your tsouris, you get laid, you have a good time. Eat some ribs, or tacos, or Twinkies, whatever."

Cusimano nodded and exhaled marijuana smoke, accompanied by a full minute siege of fierce coughing. "Look, it's the drug for the seventies," Sloman continued as Cusimano flicked on the cable TV and looked for a sex show. "The New Hedonism. Get high efficiently, cleanly, with no puke scenes or guilt hangovers. I mean it's a whole leisure-time industry. Look at the paraphernalia industry. The only thing they don't have is chocolate-covered roach papers for those first pangs of the munchies, and I bet that ain't far down the line if Burt Rubin has anything to say about it. And you can bet your ass that as soon as it's legal, you'll see NORML filtertip joints. I mean, Madison Avenue would pay millions for the consumer recognition factor that NORML has."

Cusimano was taking this all in, draped over his sofa like a reclining Buddha. "Jesus, I'm getting hungry," he moaned, and snatched a donut from the box. "The way I see it . . ." the reporter continued, and there was no stopping him. The eight months of research had turned Sloman into a 180-pound ounce. Whenever he was in the presence of burning reefer, he began with his Harry Anslinger stories and even gave long verbatim readings of the transcripts of the Tax Act Hearings of 1937. It was amusing to his friends for the first week, but now they were starting to get worried. It seemed that he had terminal marijuana data overload. They only hoped that this marijuana work would not lead him to harder stuff, like doing research on heroin.

"The way I see it, legalization is inevitable. I mean, all the economic arguments are overwhelming. A multibillion-dollar drain, going to Third World countries at that, when American industry could be cleaning up on government-approved Grade A shit. The amotivational syndrome is so much bullshit, Barbara and her friends being prime examples. You can't argue with the medical users unless you take the position that better thousands go blind than a few kids crack up their car or knock up their girlfriend. They'd probably do both anyway. And think of the tax revenues. I mean, guys like Rubin and the other marijuana millionaires have proven that good old American capitalist ingenuity can sell anything. And they plow some of the profits into race cars and gliders, not the Symbionese Liberation Army."

Cusimano had sat patiently though this lecture, puffing on his smoke, and punctuated the narrative with paroxysms of pulmonary action.

"So the cutting edge of the marijuana issue becomes the moral one again." Sloman was winding up. "What kind of person smokes marijuana? A bad person? A deviant? Someone capable of moral rehab? A Whiskeypalian backslider? It's like us versus them again, only this time it's not just a few wetbacks or jazz weirdos, its your fucking nephew who's right tackle on the football team."

The lecture had worked Sloman up, and much to Cusimano's surprise, the reporter grabbed the joint and took a long, deep toke. Immediately his eyes watered, his lungs felt as though they were on fire, and he exploded into a coughing jag that lasted for minutes. One of the reasons Sloman really didn't smoke much was because he really didn't know how to. Cusimano smiled paternally at the feeble attempt and immediately snatched the joint back.

"It's like the marijuana battle has been won." Sloman began to feel a little light-headed, a nice cheesy warm feeling creeping over his brain like the fog rolling in over Cape Cod. "I think the watershed was Operation Intercept by the folks who later brought us Watergate. I mean Liddy and them tried to close the border in September of 1969 and dry out the potheads of America, and all they could do was hassle thousands of tourists, lose a lot of jobs for Mexicans who commuted over the border every day, and get some sailors beat up in Tijuana. They didn't bust anyone. The smugglers were all too sophisticated, the demand was much too great, and Joe Tourist wound up getting pissed waiting six hours to bring his stuffed alligators back into the country only to go through a strip search. Operation Intercept lasted a little more than a month, and then Nixon had to eat it. And that was the beginning of the end for the Pothibitionists." Sloman smiled smugly and went into the kitchen to raid the refrigerator.

But his rummaging was interrupted by a low moan issuing from the living room. Cusimano had been idly scanning the newspapers when his eyes caught a startling story. "Jesus Christ, Larry, listen to this." The ripped PR man began to quote aloud:

> WASHINGTON—HEW Secretary Joseph A. Califano, Jr. today warned that marijuana contaminated with the herbicide Paraquat could lead to permanent lung damage for regular and heavy users of marijuana, and conceivably for other users as well.
>
> The Secretary issued the warning based on preliminary studies conducted by HEW's National Institute on Drug Abuse. Paraquat is an herbicide which is used in Mexico to eradicate marijuana plants. The contaminated marijuana, which may be disguised for street sales by mixing it with other marijuana, is not easily detected by the average user.

"What?" Sloman had heard rumbling about an herbicide that was being used in Mexico, but this announcement by Califano came as a bombshell. If HEW was warning a vast illicit minority about the dangers of smoking grass, there must be some very heavy reasons they were protecting their asses. "What else does the article say?"

Cusimano scanned the page. "It says there have been some reports of serious lung lesions"—he was getting paler by the minute—"and that the DEA provided technical assistance in the spraying. And that we've provided over $40 million in direct funding for this program. They're using all the high technology tricks they developed in Vietnam to spray the fields, and the fuckers have been doing it since the spring of 1975." Cusimano collapsed back onto the couch and coughed involuntarily. They both fell silent for a few minutes.

"Jesus." Sloman's mind was racing back to his research about the marijuana eradication programs of the thirties, where the big debate was whether or not to use the Boy Scouts to de-weed the nation. Anslinger nixed that idea quickly, convinced that the little buggers might come up with a merit badge for joint-rolling. But somehow his mind became fixated on those early headlines, the ones about the Killer Drug that was making its way into America from Mexico.

"What a bummer," Cusimano was slapping his balding head, not even noticing that the American Blue Show was featuring an interview with an S&M dominatrix and her slave.

"The Killer Weed," Sloman kept muttering. "The Killer Weed. Back again." And for one eerie moment the stoned reporter thought he heard laughter rolling in slowly all the way from San Clemente. Or maybe just Hollidaysburg. But the reverie was interrupted by the sound of Cusimano stumbling back into the room, carrying a large water pipe.

"This should take the edge off this contaminated shit." Cusimano set up the apparatus and began filling the pipe bowl, the concentration etched on his stoned visage. He lit up the suspect grass and took a long, deep toke. The only sound in the room, apart from the TV, was the gurgling of the water.

Cusimano was making a valiant effort, but it was no use. A torrent of coughs racked his body. "Shit!" he screamed, slamming his baggie down on the coffee table. Slowly he focused on Sloman, who was silently observing this scene from his perch on the sofa.

"You still know how to get in touch with Mr. Roche?" Cusimano's voice took on a tone of urgency. "I gotta find a connection for some good Colombian." And then he shook his head and grabbed the water pipe and knocked a pile of magazines off the coffee table looking for the matches.

THE MADNESS CONTINUES

Michael Simmons

I. MORE OF THE SAME

It's 1998 and in spite of all the rosy crystal-balling that by the end of the twentieth century we'd be living on an enlightened planet in which the very notion that marijuana is an evil weed would be antiquated and absurd—*reefer madness prevails.* Peasants who drank coffee in sixteenth-century Europe were publicly caned, while its use by the clergy and aristocracy was condoned. Now we have a president who, while acknowledging having held marijuana in his slick little fingers, continues to insist that anyone who does the same be subject to criminal penalty. The oxymoron known as civilization is an endless repetition of momentary whim, carried out with a cruel and unusual brutality, unanswerable to any logic or rational discourse.

Meaning that it's 19-fucking-98 and marijuana is *still* illegal in the United States of America. Larry Sloman, or "Ratso," as he's known to many, wrote his definitive tome nineteen years ago and yet the blindly stupid and downright venal marijuana laws in this country, and the lawmakers and cops who write and enforce them, are still, more or less, in place. So on the surface, it may seem as if nothing has substantively changed since the publication of *Reefer Madness* in 1979.

But it hasn't been for lack of trying, and thanks to a diverse cross-section of hemp activists, countercultural potheads, civil libertarians, and medical reformers, the issue has been kept well lit. Of the many evils attributed to marijuana, amotivational syndrome—or the lie-on-the-couch-and-watch-TV-and-eat-potato-chips disorder—is one of the most laughable. Pot activists are highly organized, highly committed, and highly knowledgeable—even while high. Interestingly, though, it was the gay community's reaction to the AIDS crisis and the issue of medical marijuana that precipitated the political activism that kicked the most bricks out of the Berlin Wall of Pothibition.

II. COPS BREAK NUN'S ARM IN POT BUST

Nobody knows for sure when the first AIDS patient realized that the reefer he'd been smoking recreationally made him feel a hell of a lot better. But cancer is one of the many opportunistic diseases that AIDS invites and cancer patients have been smoking pot for years to combat the nausea from chemotherapy and radiation treatments. A myriad of therapies have been utilized in the almost twenty years since the AIDS plague descended upon us, and many of them rob the patient of the ability to hold his or her food down or of an appetite in which to attempt to do so. One of the perennial pothead in-jokes has been "the munchies"—the insatiable desire to consume massive amounts of food once one has cannabinoided oneself. Between the nausea and the AIDS wasting syndrome, in which the patient loses muscle tissue, the disease was having what some referred to as the Auschwitz effect. Those afflicted often resembled the walking skeletons of Nazi concentration camps.

Before you could say Chong or bong, the munchie jokes weren't jokes anymore. The munchies—a term that, like much drug slang, has entered the mainstream vocabulary—became a matter of life or death. In San Francisco, the American city with the largest percentage of gay *and* countercultural communities in the United States, there already existed an infrastructure to deal with large-scale distribution of marijuana for the sick. To a large degree, that infrastructure was the work of one diminutive gay hippie named Dennis Peron.

Peron had smoked pot on his native Long Island as a teenager in the mid-sixties to relieve what he called "parental stress syndrome." Drafted into the army and opting for the air force in 1966, he was given a thirty-day leave in San Francisco prior to being sent to Vietnam. He arrived in early October, just in time for the "Death of Hippie" demonstration: a protest against the commercialization of all things "hippie" by the mass media, which symbolically ended the legendary Summer of Love. The nineteen-year-old kid embraced the ethic of love and peace and its sacrament of grass. In Vietnam, Peron smoked dope through the Tet Offensive of '68 and, under the rockets' red glare, made love to a male soldier in a bunker. On his return to San Francisco in 1970, he brought two pounds of pot back with him and breezed through customs, looking the role of all-American soldier boy. As soon as he returned, Peron unfurled his freak flag, which had been closeted in Nam: "I left as a hippie and returned as a hippie."

Peron lived with a dozen other freaks in the Big Top Commune and began his life work as the Bay Area's most famous pot dealer. The Big Top morphed into the Big Top Supermarket, a brazenly open reefer retailer and pot den that became the largest marijuana outlet in the city, possibly the planet. In 1974 the SFPD busted the Big Top, yet in spite of the enormity of his operation, Peron plea-bargained himself a six-month work-furlough deal. These were the days when the prevailing winds of decriminalization were wafting across America. Two years earlier John Sinclair, a political and cultural activist and the most famous pot prisoner in America at the time, had been released after serving twenty-nine months of a ten-year rap for possession of two joints. Sinclair, chairman of the radical White Panther Party, had been busted by Detroit narcs to be made an example of for his pro-pot activism. Not only did Sinclair legally challenge the pot laws, but John and Yoko, Allen Ginsberg, and other celebs spoke out publicly and loudly on his behalf, and when Sinclair walked on appeal, the Michigan State Legislature reclassified marijuana from a narcotic to a controlled substance and reduced the penalties from ten years to one year max for possession and from a mandatory twenty down to four years for sale. Subsequently, forty-three other pot prisoners were discharged after the state laws were declared unconstitutional based on Sinclair's appeal. The period from 1970 through 1978 was an increasingly enlightened one for pot. Eleven states decrimmed it and all thirty-nine others lowered penalties. With Tricky Dick's resignation in '74, there was a palpable feeling that if the counterculture hadn't exactly realized its dream of Woodstock Nation, at least Budweiser Nation was becoming more tolerant.

Instead of keeping a low profile, Peron began renovating an old storefront and opened up the Island Restaurant in December of '74. The Island became the world's first health food eatery cum pot parlor. One could sit and puff on a joint in between bites of one's veggie burger. "It was a little oasis," remembers the man who coined the name *Yippie*, *Realist* editor and satirist-activist Paul Krassner. "The food was good, the atmosphere was great. They had a little stage and I did a little comedy one night." Everyone from Frank Zappa (an avowed abstainer) to the Tubes to Jerry Rubin to local progressive

San Francisco politicos hung out there. Meanwhile, the Big Top Supermarket reopened upstairs. "I was part of the family," says Krassner, "so I'd be invited upstairs. It was an after-dinner smoke. If you didn't want dessert before, you wanted it now." The Island closed in '77 as a result of its inability to turn a profit, but the Big Top remained open until June of that year, when the SFPD once again shut it down, this time in a huge paramilitary operation that grabbed an incredible two hundred pounds. Peron was shot in the left leg by Officer Paul Mackavekias, and his femur was shattered. Mackavekias had nabbed Peron in '74 and later, in the presence of four lawyers, allegedly called him a "motherfucking faggot" and "said that he wished he had killed me so there would be one less faggot in San Francisco." While Mackavekias's testimony was later thrown out of court, Peron got six months in the county jail for possession of one hundred and ninety-nine pounds of marijuana (the cops claimed that one pound was eaten by rats while in evidentiary custody). In the meantime, Peron and his supporters collected sixteen thousand signatures for a citywide initiative, Proposition W, which called for the complete legalization of marijuana. The Board of Supervisors, with support from Mayor George Moscone and Supervisor Harvey Milk, planned a revision of the city charter to allow for more direct community control. Peron declared himself a candidate for the post of charter commissioner while sitting in the hoosegow. "I'm the only politician who started his career in jail," quips Peron who lost by two thousand votes, "most of them just end up there." But Prop W passed by 58 percent. Though merely symbolic, it clearly painted San Francisco as a bastion of free spirit and common sense.

But a tragedy of biblical proportions was quietly unfolding. As a portend of bad tidings, Moscone and Milk were murdered by a former member of the Board of Supervisors named Dan White. White was a homophobic ex-cop who hated the openly gay Milk for many reasons, including Milk's support of his friend Dennis Peron. As a state senator Moscone had authored the Moscone Act, which made possession of an ounce an infraction punishable by a one-hundred-dollar ticket. Moscone and Milk's fight to revise the city charter had enraged the city's conservative business elite, including soon-to-be-mayor Dianne Feinstein, who engineered an election after the murders of Moscone and Milk and successfully reversed the changes in the charter. There are those who to this day believe that Dan White was a paid assassin. White was found guilty of the lesser charge of manslaughter based on the infamous "Twinkie defense," in which he claimed that overconsumption of sugar had rendered him temporarily insane. White was released after serving four and a half years and eventually killed himself, perhaps after a bout with an Entemann's coffee cake. The local politico scene became more conservative as America slouched towards the Reagan era.

And then gay men started dying.

AIDS galvanized the gay community into action. Any and all treatments or approaches to ease the suffering were investigated on a grass-roots level, since the grass roots were the only sector who initially gave a shit about the crisis. Because of its historical outsider status, the gay community was good at taking care of its own. Marijuana was found to be a miracle drug for AIDS patients. In addition to preventing the previously discussed AIDS wasting syndrome by working as an appetite enhancer, pot is a miraculous painkiller. The benefits that marijuana held for the afflicted were as varied as the symptoms of the disease. Peron went from being a pot dealer to a de facto pharmacist. The wags tagged him "The Prince of Pot."

At the same time, another man was on a path that would cross Peron's and end up changing history. One could glibly remark that Imler's consciousness was raised so quickly that it was as if a tree had hit him. In fact, that's exactly what happened.

Scott Imler was born in 1958 in Kirkwood, Missouri, into a white middle-class family. His father and grandfather were both golf course superintendents; in other words they grew grass—the kind with divots. Other ancestors included a farmer and a pharmacist. These occupations would make amusing genetic sense when Imler later found his own calling. When he was a child in the early '60s, Imler's family lived in Birmingham, Alabama, where they witnessed civil rights demonstrators beaten and hosed down by Southern law enforcement, images that most Americans received via the evening news. The experience radicalized his mother, and Jane Imler became an activist and social worker, eventually working with Jesse Jackson on Operation Breadbasket in Chicago. The brutally raw, visceral experience also made a lasting impression on young Scott.

His family moved back to Kirkwood in 1967. A mostly typical suburban teenager, he tried pot in high school but was never much of an adolescent stoner. He was a shy and insecure kid and confused about his sexuality. Like tens of thousands of other small-town gay youths, he yearned for the indefinable *more.* And like many, *more* meant *California.*

He arrived in the Golden State in 1976, dabbled as an actor in dinner theater, and moved to Los Angeles for three months to explore show biz. "There were eighteen million other people pursuing the same goal, so I left." After coming to terms with the fact that he was gay, he arrived in San Francisco on May 21, 1979, the day Dan White was acquitted of first-degree murder, and found a citywide riot in progress to protest the verdict. "When I saw what was going on, I knew I'd moved to the right place."

In early September of 1980, Imler went to the Alice B. Toklas Democratic Club, named after writer Gertrude Stein's lesbian lover, who'd written a cookbook for bohemians, fondly recalled by many a head for its hashish fudge (the recipe for which she credited to Brion Gysin, William S. Burroughs's collaborator). There, Imler heard Dennis Peron speak for the first time. Peron had just returned from the Democratic Convention in New York where, in one of those maverick middle-fingered moves common at political conventions, he'd been nominated for vice president. The Prince of Pot was now running for the Board of Supervisors and told the assembled crowd: "People say I'm a one-issue candidate, but that's one more issue than the rest of you candidates have." Imler was impressed by this funny, charming character and he and Dennis Peron became friends.

Inspired by Peron's relentless commitment, Imler went looking for his own and found it in the antinuke movement. When the Unitarian Universalist Church, of which Imler was a congregant, became involved in a statewide nuclear freeze initiative in the fall of 1981, he became a full-time activist. The initiative, which became Proposition 12, required that Governor Jerry Brown send letters to both Washington and Moscow demanding the end of nuclear weapon proliferation. It was, to be sure, another symbolic gesture, but in those days of the cold war and Three Mile Island, the threat of nuclear holocaust didn't seem far-fetched. Imler became office manager of the Northern California signature-gathering effort and got his first taste of political campaigning. The initiative eventually gathered 1.2 million signatures and Prop 12 passed in November of '82 by 52 percent.

By the end of the freeze campaign, Imler was becoming a canny and skilled political organizer and enjoyed a good rep and good connections that landed him a job with Gary Hart's campaign staff in '83. In February, Imler went skiing with some friends in Squaw Valley. While on the slopes, he found himself doing an unintended pas de deux with a tree trunk and sustained head injuries that led to chronic seizures. Doctors loaded him down with Valium, phenobarbital, and Tegretol, which stopped the seizures but caused liver damage and left him somewhere between lethargy and catatonia. On the advice of a friend who was into the more arcane minutiae of cannabis pharmacology, Imler found that when he got an aura—a precursor signal to the seizure—a few hits on a reefer prevented the seizure. He quit taking all prescription medicine.

Imler eventually moved to Santa Cruz and became a special ed teacher, working with troubled kids. He grew his own medicine, only to find it confiscated by the local sheriff's department in September of '91. While no charges were filed, his paranoia was only surpassed by his rage. The terms of the debate over marijuana were shifting from recreational wacky weed to efficacious medication. The cops had taken Imler's medicine and he was pissed off.

Like a perpetual phoenix rising from the ashes of a burning doobie, Dennis Peron continued to sell pot. Only now many of his customers were not just stoners, but also sick people. Keith Vines, a prosecutor in the DA's office who'd served for two years on the Federal Narcotics Strike Force and a gay man with AIDS, is, to this day, a club member. Peron befriended a colorful elderly woman named Mary Rathbun, also known as Brownie Mary, who came to be known as the Alice B. Toklas of medical marijuana for the savory and potent pot brownies she baked for cancer and AIDS patients. Brownie Mary was busted twice by a cop named Stephen Bossard. In between her first and second bust, Bossard got drunk and was found shooting off his gun while naked outside the apartment of his girlfriend. Peron made a flyer that placed newspaper articles about Bossard and Brownie Mary's respective busts side by side with a headline that asked, WHICH PERSON IS MORE DANGEROUS? This bit of effective agitprop only increased the San Francisco Police Department's revulsion towards the taunting, undaunted, seemingly unsinkable Dennis Peron.

On January 27, 1990, Peron and his lover Jonathan West were busted in their apartment. When West revealed that he had AIDS, the cops put on rubber gloves and made homo jokes, but all they could find was a mere four ounces, which by Peronesque standards was like a roach in an ashtray. When the case went to trial six months later, a noticeably weak West testified that the pot was his. The charges against Peron were dropped; West died two weeks later. Peron credits West's death as the motivation for Proposition P, another citywide initiative that recommended that California legalize marijuana for medicinal purposes. On November 7, 1991, Prop P passed by an astounding 80 percent.

In September of '93, Peron opened the San Francisco Cannabis

Buyers Club. When after two years the patient base exceeded five thousand, Peron moved the club to the more spacious five-story 1444 Market Street. Its stated purpose was to distribute medical marijuana, but whether the SFCBC was merely the Big Top with a stethoscope—meaning that not everyone who was being serviced was sick—depends on whom you ask or whom you believe. Whatever the whole truth is, the fact remains that the club was tending to the legitimate needs of the AIDS patient base in San Francisco as well as those with cancer, epilepsy, arthritis, glaucoma, and the laundry list of diseases and ailments for which pot is a legitimate medicine.

After Imler's plants were seized in the middle of the Prop P campaign, Peron suggested that he organize his own initiative in Santa Cruz. Imler had gained considerable political acumen from his antinuke work and Democratic Party work in the ten years since he'd first met Peron. Measure A passed in November of '92 by 77 percent, requiring that the local Board of Supervisors urge all representatives of the citizens of Santa Cruz—from state reps through Congress and up to the president of the United States—to make marijuana legally available as medicine. In March of '93 Imler, along with fellow epileptic Valerie Corral, who'd been busted during the Measure A campaign and became the election's poster child, formed the Santa Cruz Medical Cannabis Cooperative, which distributed pot to the sick. The co-op eventually became the Santa Cruz Cannabis Buyers Club, the first strictly medicinal club in California.

In September of '93 Imler flew to D.C. to lobby the California congressional delegation and work with Patient Zero of the medical marijuana movement: the legendary Robert Randall. After becoming in 1976 the first American since the passage of the Marihuana Tax Act of 1937 to gain licit access for his glaucoma, Randall had worked tirelessly with his Alliance for Cannabis Therapeutics, lobbying Congress and state legislatures on behalf of patients. He had helped fifty sick people get their medicine under the Compassionate IND Program before the Bush administration stopped accepting new patients in '92 (by 1998 only eight people, including Randall, continued to get legal pot from Uncle Sam). He successfully pushed for various forms of medical pot legislation in thirty-five states. His most astounding political sleight of hand occurred in 1981 when he convinced four Republican members of Congress, including Newt Gingrich, to sponsor H.R. 4498, which would have legally allowed "for the therapeutic use of marihuana in situations involving life-threatening or sense-threatening illnesses and to provide adequate supplies of marihuana for such use." One can only assume that the bill reverted to spelling *marijuana* with an *h* because that's how it had been spelled back in 1937. Despite bipartisan support, the bill, introduced three times, eventually died when Congressman Henry Waxman, an alleged liberal from Los Angeles, refused to hold public hearings when he chaired the House committee responsible for overseeing health issues. Randall says it was always irrelevant to him whether it was a liberal or conservative who was trying to deny people their medicine.

After endless petitioning by Randall and NORML and two years of testimony by doctors, patients and public health administrators, the Drug Enforcement Administration's own chief administrative law judge, Francis L. Young, ruled on September 6, 1988, that "marijuana in its natural form is one of the safest therapeutically active substances known to man" and condemned its prohibition as "unreasonable, arbitrary, and capricious." Young ruled that the DEA should reschedule marijuana in order to make it available by prescription. DEA director Jack Lawn sat on Young's decision for fifteen months and then overturned it, claiming that the doctors who testified had ties to NORML and the patients who testified had smoked pot recreationally before they became ill. . . . *momentary whim . . . cruel and unusual . . . unanswerable to any logic or rational discourse . . . reefer madness!*

After three months in Washington, Imler returned to Santa Cruz and successfully challenged Sheriff Al Noren and local DA Art Danner in their attempt to expand the local CAMP program. CAMP, which stands for Campaign Against Marijuana Planting, is a federally funded paramilitary op that sends camouflaged cops in choppers after pot growers. Noren would retire by the end of the year and Imler ran the campaign of Danner's opponent in the next election (who lost by a narrow margin) and continued to operate the Cannabis Buyers Club.

Because of AIDS, medicinal pot had become a *demand-and-supply* issue of huge proportions. Three times the California State Legislature passed bills either supporting or legalizing medical marijuana. The bills that legalized med-mar were vetoed by Governor Pete Wilson, oblivious to the legions of the sick and dying and hiding behind the tired this-sends-a-bad-message-to-our-kids rap. Does morphine for cancer patients encourage teenagers to become junkies? Wilson is the Republican equivalent of Bill Clinton, a spineless bottom feeder with no conviction who says whatever's necessary to appease whichever constituency he's trying to appeal to at any given moment.

By January of '95, statewide activists were frustrated, furious, and desperate. Something *big big big* had to be done. Dale Gieringer, coordinator of California NORML, talked to Peron about taking the issue to the voters and appealing to their compassion. A month later Gieringer met with a group of wealthy potential contributors, including a millionaire named Peter Lewis. Also present were a professional political consultant named Bill Zimmerman, who years earlier had coordinated the same nuclear freeze initiative in which Imler had honed his activist chops, and Ethan Nadelmann, who ran the Lindesmith Center, a drug policy think tank that was financed by billionaire currency speculator and philanthropist George Soros.

Jack Herer, a bearded bear with a scholarly mind, had written *The Emperor Wears No Clothes* in 1985. In the book that became the bible of the hemp movement, Herer made the case that hemp (the whole plant of which the flowers and leaves are the intoxicants known as marijuana) could replace wood pulp for paper (eradicating deforestation) and be used for fuel, clothing, and building materials. For instance, hemp, unlike cotton, is naturally pest repellent (with the exception of the pests with badges and guns), obviating the need for chemical pesticides. In addition, Herer wrote of the medicinal uses of pot as well as the nutritional attributes of the protein-rich hemp seed and created a big-picture scenario of cannabis as the magic plant that can save the planet from environmental disaster, heal the sick, clothe the naked, and feed the hungry.

The Hemperor, as Herer is referred to, and the hempsters, as the adherents call themselves, are utopian visionaries with a unified-field theory of marijuana as an evolutionary, even revolutionary, tool with the power to create paradise on earth. Herer credits Sloman's book with inspiring him to pursue further research into the history of the plant. The Hemperor had his own petition for a ballot proposition called the California Cannabis Hemp and Health Initiative, which called for outright legalization. But polls showed that legalization wouldn't fly at the ballot box and Imler and other medicinal proponents were against sacrificing the rights of the sick and dying for those of stoners. It was a moot point; Herer was unable to gather sufficient signatures to qualify for the ballot.

In March of '95 Gieringer spoke to Imler about doing a strictly medical initiative. Imler was initially wary: "I didn't like the idea of putting our rights up to a vote." But Gieringer contacted the Drug Policy Foundation, the country's leading drug reform think tank. The DPF gave Californians for Compassionate Use, as the nascent movement named itself, a $25,000 seed grant to study feasibility, do a direct mailing, and conduct a poll. Polls showed strong support for medical marijuana. Led by Peron, the CCU spent months debating the wording of both the petition and the initiative.

In July of '95 Peron and pals made their yearly sojourn to the Rainbow Gathering, held that annum in the mountains of New Mexico. Imler and his partner George Leddy, a UCLA development policy specialist, who were not inclined to hobnob with hippies, went along for the ride. The Rainbow Gathering is a rural festival, usually held in federal parkland, of hippies, Deadheads, ravers, stoners, and nature freaks that's been an annual event since 1972. The CCU group settled in Fairy Camp, the gay enclave at the gathering. Living conditions are extremely spartan, even harsh, at the gatherings and after a couple of days, Imler felt like shit. And oddly enough, at the largest hippie fest on the planet, they ran out of grass and were unable to find anything but ragweed. Imler became dehydrated, had an aura, and then a full-blown seizure—and he had no medicine.

Peron and Leddy threw Imler into a van and bounced him sixty-five miles down the mountainside to Holy Cross Hospital in Taos. Peron credits himself with saving Imler's life, something Imler declines to dispute. Drifting in and out of consciousness, Imler remembers, he was consoled by Peron. At one point Peron made a prescient remark that's stayed with Imler to this day: "Don't die on me. I'm not going to be around forever. Someone's going to have to run this thing." Scott instinctively read between Dennis's somewhat cryptic lines. Imler believes that Peron knew, ultimately, that he couldn't trust himself to lead this movement into the mainstream. Peron's a wild card, too much of an old hippie to be a national leader on an issue that, because of the cultural baggage it carries, requires making it understandable to Middle America. Despite Imler's activism and the fact that he's gay—he *is* Middle America. The kid who'd grown up in Missouri and Alabama knew and liked everyday Americans. He's a Christian steak-and-potatoes Eagle Scout who never felt quite at home with the tofu-and-tie-dye crowd. And after the Rainbow Gathering, he didn't care if he never saw another woolly-headed Deadhead again.

Imler recovered and CCU continued meeting at the San Francisco club to plan their strategy. In addition to Peron, Imler, and Gieringer, other co-schemers included Valerie Corral, Peron's right-hand man John Entwistle, rocker-turned-lawyer Bill Panzer, Vic Hernandez (who later opened up his own Frisco club called CHAMP), Lynnette Shaw of the Marin Alliance for Medical Marijuana, Michael Petrellis of ACT-UP, Gilbert Baker (who'd designed the Rainbow Flag, the emblem of the gay rights movement), Mary Krell (who co-founded the San Francisco Medical Marijuana Delivery Service with Baker), anti-drug war warriors Chris Conrad and Ellen Komp and pot historians and anti-forfeiture activists Lynn and Judy Osburn. Peron asked Imler to be treasurer of CCU, which he agreed to do if he was allowed to do everything by the book and aboveboard. Imler felt Peron's bookeeping procedures were, to put it mildly, somewhat loose. Imler was developing a strategy he refers to as the "radical center," a concept in which you stand by your convictions, no matter how unpopular, but present them so that your opponents feel that you're more eager to work with them than antagonize them. This was the antithesis of Peron's in-your-face '60s-style activism.

The final initiative language was based on a bill that State Assemblyman John Vasconcellos had pushed through the legislature the year before, only to be vetoed by Governor Wilson. Basically it stated that seriously ill Californians have the right to use, obtain, and cultivate marijuana on the written or oral recommendation of a doctor for "the treatment of cancer, anorexia, AIDS, chronic pain, spasticity, glaucoma, arthritis, migraine, or any other illness for which marijuana provides relief." There was a provision for a designated caregiver, in case the patient couldn't provide for himself, and one that stated that physicians were legally protected for recommending pot. In addition, the initiative encouraged the state and federal governments "to implement a plan to provide for the safe and affordable distribution of marijuana to all patients in medical need." The Compassionate Use Act of 1996 was filed in Sacramento on September 29, 1995.

By November, Imler and Peron's friendship was fraying at the edges. Scott was tired of living under what he felt was Dennis's irresponsible leadership and acceding to his every command, no matter how well intentioned he thought they were. Peron ordered Imler to L.A. to direct the campaign in Southern California and start a buyers club. That month Imler opened up the Los Angeles Cannabis Buyers Club in a house in Santa Monica. Peron's inability to keep narrowly focused on medical marijuana culminated in his sending nonpatients to Imler to buy pot. The last straw was when Peron purchased quantity from a militia group, not the kind of folk usually considered to be gay-friendly (Peron has declined twice to respond). Scott was fed up. On January 14, 1996, Imler, as treasurer, and Anna Boyce, an elderly nurse who was coproponent of the initiative with Peron, flew to Sacramento and hijacked CCU. They legally changed the name of the group from CCU to Southern Californians for Compassionate Use and took over the existing bank account. SCCU had 150 days to get the proposition on the ballot. Everyone knew they had little money and time. But the lobbying of the fat cats was about to pay off.

George Soros eventually contributed $550,000. George Zimmer of the Men's Warehouse gave $100,000. Peter Lewis, John Sperling, Richard Dennis, Richard Wolf, and Laurance Rockefeller (brother of Nelson, sponsor of New York State's draconian drug laws) were good for several hundreds of thousands more. Gail Zappa, widow of Frank, not only wrote a nice check, she convinced *Hustler* publisher Larry Flynt to contribute. A quickie organizing op was set up, headed by Bill Zimmerman and later joined by former DPF staffer Dave Fratello, called Californians for Medical Rights. Chris Conrad became the community action coordinator for the petition drive. In late February of '96 Zimmerman engineered a crash signature-gathering effort and by April the Compassionate Use Act of 1996 had qualified for the ballot in the November election as Proposition 215.

The public relations war for the hearts and minds of California voters began. CMR took a poll that showed that while only 34 percent of voters surveyed supported full legalization, 62 percent supported legalizing medicinal use. A surprising one-third said they'd known someone who'd smoked pot for medical reasons. On the surface, the medical marijuana putsch looked like a cohesive movement with broad public support.

But behind the scenes, power plays, territorial squabbling, ego posturing, temper tantrums, and strategic disagreement had been rampant for months. Imler, Zimmerman, and Gieringer all had fallings-out with the mercurial, erratic Peron. By several accounts, one of Dennis's failings is his inability to listen to advice. The petitions weren't up to code and he'd almost botched the signature-gathering campaign by, for instance, failing to use the bureaucratically required type size. While the grass-roots activists were grateful for the fat cat cash, some felt that Zimmerman had barged in and taken over a campaign that they'd begun without consulting them. And the hempsters were loudly supporting Prop 215 and publicly allying it with their own agendas of hemp and recreational legalization. The last thing the strict medicinal advocates wanted was for Prop 215 to turn into a cultural war. "A lot of these people just operate on ideological impulse," says Bob Randall of both anti-drug warriors and reformers alike. " 'Gee, did I like Elvis or like the Beatles? Did I smoke pot or get drunk?' You're trapped in this incredibly trite conflict between these mutually insipid ideas."

The LACBC slowly built up a patient base. On August 1, SCCU

and the LACBC moved to West Hollywood in offices donated to them by author/publisher/medical marijuana patient Peter McWilliams. Three days later the feces flew into the fan when a hundred armed state Bureau of Narcotics Enforcement agents, under the direction of right-wing California attorney general Dan Lungren, raided and shut down Peron's San Francisco Cannabis Buyers Club. Agents hauled away 150 pounds of pot, $60,000 in cash, 400 plants, computers, client records, and, most outrageously, Prop 215 campaign materials. Lungren's office admitted that some 215-related materials may have been inadvertently seized but insisted that they'd be protected. "The timing of the raid smacks of fascism," said Assemblyman Vasconcellos. Carried out almost three months to the day before the election, the bust stunk of politics. The virulently anti–medical marijuana attorney general was suspected of staging the razzia as an anti-215 PR ploy. "This is nothing more than an obscene effort to win with guns what they can't win at the ballot box," was Peron's reaction. "Lungren's trying to ride to the governor's office on the backs of sick and dying people."

Lungren, who was planning a gubernatorial run in '98, had run a sting operation by setting up phony doctor's offices and phone numbers so that if someone from the club called the physician to verify a recommendation, they were actually talking to a narc. Lungren also claimed Peron had sold quantity to individuals and dealt to nonpatients or those with minor ailments—and to four teenagers. Peron countered that the kids had leukemia and the permission of their parents. Peron conceded that the club was "not perfect," but said they'd tightened up rules and issued photo ID cards to prevent fraud.

It was no big secret within the activist community that regulation was not a priority of Peron's. While his concern for the sick was sincere, Peron remains an avowed legalizer. Privately, most in the medical marijuana movement think Pothibition is ludicrous. But the life-or-death raison d'etre for accessibility to marijuana for the seriously ill and the lopsided poll results when you ask voters if they support med-mar (yes) or legalization (no) demands that the issues remain separate. The SFCBC had somewhere between nine and twelve thousand members when it was closed down. But if you're an AIDS or cancer patient whose nausea is so acute that you can't even hold down pills to alleviate it, inhaled marijuana is your only option. Even if you believe that Peron ran a loose ship, nobody's questioned that most of the club members were legit. The raid resulted in an injunction by the state that kept the club closed for five months. Dan

Lungren had basically told the seriously and terminally ill to go fuck themselves.

But Lungren became the subject of national ridicule when *Doonesbury* creator Garry Trudeau ran two weeks of strips dealing with medical marijuana in October; one strip featured an elderly cancer patient who used pot and one starred Zonker Harris, *Doonesbury*'s resident hippie. Trudeau criticized Lungren by name for "raiding a sanctuary for dying AIDS and cancer patients." Lungren was furious. While one would think that an attorney general would have innate respect for that pesky little constitutional amendment known as the First, Lungren's anger overrode his legal training. He sent a letter to the president of the Universal Press Syndicate and to nine California newspapers and asked them to refrain from distributing any *Doonesbury* strips concerning the medmar issue. His request was denied. The press had a field day, portraying this as a battle between a flesh-and-blood Republican mucky-muck and a fictitious cartoon stoner. Brian Lungren, the AG's brother and adviser, made the dumb look dumber when he actually asserted that "Zonker's a real person in our society. He is not fictitious. And we should put Zonker behind bars where he belongs."

I'd just been assigned by the *L.A. Weekly* to cover the medical marijuana issue and I asked Attorney General Lungren what he would say to Trudeau if he could talk to him face-to-face. "I'd say we're members of the same generation," he replied, "the baby boom generation, and I would hope we'd have the same concern about our children, and that is, we wouldn't want them to be visited by the terrible tragedy of drugs that too many people of our generation were when they were young."

Lungren's response was my first exposure as a reporter to the hollow clichés from the mindless drug war monolith: . . . *momentary whim . . . cruel and unusual brutality . . . unanswerable to any logic or rational discourse.* It has, unfortunately, not been my last. I asked Trudeau for his reaction to Lungren's reefer madness redux: "I hope to teach my children that it's more important to alleviate suffering than to advance a political agenda. If the state of California is able to safely regulate the distribution of morphine and other medical narcotics, then I have every confidence they can find a way to distribute marijuana without it falling into the hands of those for whom it's not intended. That's why we have pharmacists. It's insane that critically ill people with legitimate medical needs should be faced with a choice between suffering and lawbreaking."

I thought of the prank Peron had pulled with the Officer Bossard and Brownie Mary news items. Put Lungren and Trudeau's quotes back-to-back and then ask WHICH PERSON IS MORE COMPASSIONATE? WHICH PERSON IS MORE RATIONAL? WHICH PERSON SHOULD BE IN PUBLIC OFFICE AND WHICH PERSON SHOULD BE DRAWING COMIC STRIPS?

My assignment from the *Weekly* to cover med-mar came in the form of a phone call from news editor Charles Rappleye on September 18. Two days prior, the Los Angeles Cannabis Buyers Club had been busted by the L.A. County Sheriff's Department and were shut out of their office space. Unlike Peron, who didn't reopen until a judge modified the closure decision five months postbust, Scott Imler refused to abide by an immoral law. Imler, who had joined the Crescent Heights United Methodist Church soon after moving to L.A., accepted an offer of sanctuary from the Reverend Tom Griffith, the pastor of the church.

I was considered the house hippie at the *Weekly;* my most recent pieces were on psychedelic philosophers Terence McKenna and Timothy Leary. I'm a lifelong legalizer who believes that marijuana, along with psychedelics, are drugs that expand consciousness and therefore are crucial if we're going to transcend this simian phase we're still locked into. And, of course, they're fun. But when I walked into that church, I immediately saw that medical marijuana isn't about consciousness expansion or giggling with your friends or enhancing music or staring at a Picasso for two hours or . . . whatever. I was led into a stark room lined with chairs. Sitting in those chairs were club members waiting for their medicine. Mostly male. Many were emaciated. Many walked with canes. One could barely hold his head up. Some were spotted with Kaposi's sarcoma, the skin cancer that affects AIDS patients. Some looked pretty healthy. One of them, Richard Eastman, a forty-three-year old AIDS patient, told me his story.

Eastman had almost died after a bout with pneumocystis carinii pneumonia in 1994. "Approximately two months after I got out of the hospital, as soon as my lungs regenerated, I started smoking marijuana for medicinal purposes. I weighed one hundred thirty pounds. Now I weigh one fifty-seven. A lot of the pills we take take away our appetite. I asked my doctor, Dr. Charles Farthing of the AIDS Healthcare Foundation, if he would mind me smoking marijuana and he said no. So he wrote me a letter.

"I take thirty to thirty-five pills a day. Sometimes it feels like an explosion goes off in my stomach and I feel like I'm going to vomit. If I smoke, that goes away in ten or fifteen minutes. I smoke two or three tokes and within a half hour to forty-five minutes I get hungry. It's really important with AIDS to keep your weight on because HIV eats away at your body-muscle mass. I know it helps me and I tend to believe in a doctor more than a politician."

Standing at a table by the stained-glass windows was Scott Imler. Lean. Six foot five. Tie. Short hair. Hugging club members. On the table were bags of pot and a box full of brownies. It was a strange kind of culture shock for an old stoner to see reefer being distributed for what was clearly nonrecreational use. Standing there in that church, surrounded by AIDS patients with volunteers checking files and filling forms and clinging to clipboards—*I understood.*

The problem with the medical marijuana issue is that too many people don't understand it. Some of them are attorneys general and cops and some of them are drug reformers and hempsters. Some of them hate marijuana and everything that it stands for and some love marijuana and everything that it stands for. But medical marijuana has nothing to do with what marijuana stands for and everything to do with whether Richard Eastman's going to keep his food down or Scott Imler's going to have a seizure or Bob Randall's going to go blind.

Babaji Zeiger, one of the four L.A. club members nabbed in the raid, told me a funny story. On the wall of the raided club hung a puppet of a nun on which someone had placed a YES ON 215 button. The puppet became the club's mascot. In the process of rampaging through the little office, one of the narcs broke the arm off the puppet. "I could just see the headlines," mused Zeiger, "COPS BREAK NUN'S ARM IN POT BUST!" The anecdote was a metaphor for the overkill and misinformation from both sides surrounding the entire issue.

Charges were never filed against the club and the West Hollywood City Council adopted a resolution in support of the LACBC. Prop 215 (and Prop 200, its much-broader counterpart in Arizona) went from political campaign to full-blown war. Clinton's drug czar, General Barry McCaffrey, director of the Office of National Drug Control Policy, displayed his own cluelessness on the subject. "There is not a shred of scientific evidence that shows that smoked marijuana is useful or needed," said the general. "This is not science. This is not medicine. This is a cruel hoax that sounds more like something out of a Cheech and Chong show." McCaffrey's an intelligent man, a decorated soldier who once wrote an honorable treatise on the moral obligation of the U.S. armed forces to observe human rights conventions. But like too many in positions of power, he'd hit the impenetrable wall of reefer madness, that inability to see beyond the decades of false propaganda.

One of the conundrums of the med-mar debate is the issue of Marinol. Marinol is isolated THC, the psychoactive ingredient in pot that was approved by the FDA in the '80s as an anti-emetic and appetite enhancer—the same qualities attributed to marijuana. The problem is that very few patients can either keep the pill down long enough for it to work or titrate the dosage to where they can stand the psychoactive effect. In other words, the great irony of Marinol, "the legal pot pill," is that it gets you *too* stoned. "When I took Marinol, I found it anxiety-provoking and intense, like I had wandered into a short story by Flannery O'Connor," Bob Randall told journalist Elsa Scott. And how can it be said that marijuana can't possibly be medicine, when the government says that Marinol is?

. . . unanswerable to any logic . . .

McCaffrey and Drug Enforcement Administration chief Thomas Constantine both accused 215 of being a Trojan horse for legalization and criticized the out-of-state cash cows who'd paid for it. The hypocrisy of establishment types becoming apoplectic over campaign contributions to a cause they disagree with is incredible in light of the fact that the whole system is kept afloat by the donations of the rich.

. . . endless repetition of momentary whim . . .

Meanwhile, Peron and five others were arrested on October 21 of '96 and charged with selling and transporting marijuana in connection with the August 4 bust. Lungren filed the case in nearby Alameda County, despite the fact that the SFCBC was in San Francisco, leading to accusations against Lungren of "forum shopping." While polls showed voters still supported 215, the numbers were slipping, from 62 percent in April to 57 percent in September. Imler and others felt that Peron's unpredictability had become a liability and 215 opponents were pointing to the flaky operation of the Frisco club as evidence of the dangers of legalizing medical marijuana. In September, Imler publicly called for Dennis's resignation as titular head of CCU. Peron refused, but he admitted to the *Bay Area Reporter* that he ran the SFCBC "with my heart instead of my head. In my loneliness I ran the club like a country club instead of a medical facility. I apologize to the wonderful people who have supported the cause of freedom, if I have let you down."

In spite of opposition to 215 by Bill Clinton, George Bush, Jimmy Carter, Gerald Ford, Senator Dianne Feinstein, former U.S. surgeon general C. Everett Koop and virtually every cop and Republican politico in the state of California, it passed with 56 percent of the vote on November 5. In conservative Arizona, Prop 200, which medically legalized all Schedule I drugs (heroin, acid, methamphetamine, you name it) and decrimmed all first- and second-time drug offenders, passed by an even more astounding 65 percent. "*Doonesbury* won the election!" japed Loyola law professor Laurie Levenson, who'd become a minor celeb due to her O. J. punditry. "This may be the baby boomers taking control."

On the evening of the election, the LACBC opened up new quarters in West Hollywood and held a low-key, nonsmoking "potluck" party. The ashes of Patrick Eddington, an early club member who'd died of AIDS, were ceremoniously mixed into the soil of two plants. Up in San Francisco, Peron and company celebrated by lighting up for the news cameras. "I believe all marijuana use is medical—except for kids," Dennis proclaimed, displaying his predictable knack for playing into the hands of his opponents—hands which can easily turn into iron fists. Grandstanding aside, Proposition 215 was now Section 11362.5 of the California Health and Safety Code, meaning that with a doctor's recommendation, it was legal to possess and cultivate marijuana for personal medical use according to state law. Pandora's stash box had been opened.

Statewide law enforcement agencies were at a loss. They no longer had carte blanche to handcuff any dope fiend in a wheelchair. Lungren's "sounded slightly flummoxed," noted the *L.A. Times.* "This thing is a disaster," proclaimed the attorney general, who'd lost the PR war to the compassion of the voters. "We're going to have an unprecedented mess." On November 6 Lungren issued guidelines for police chiefs, sheriffs, and county prosecutors. He advised that cops and prosecutors interpret the law's language narrowly and require verification of a doctor's recommendation from any bustee claiming medical use.

Scott Imler's next move was to bring all local interests together. On December 20 the Christian radical centrist held a "peace conference" at the Crescent Heights church for patients, law enforcement, health care professionals, and community leaders to "discuss local implementaiton of Proposition 215 and to codify the LACBC admissions and operational protocols." Imler later noted in a report to a statewide Methodist conference that "representatives of the Los Angeles County Sheriff's Department attend the conference and declare that the law no longer obliges them to interfere with the LACBC's operations. Praise be to God." Imler developed a rapport with the West Hollywood Sheriff's Department and its commander, Captain Richard Odenthal. When any street shit went down near the club, Imler would notify the station. Odenthal was quoted in the press as saying that the neighborhood, a haven for street hustlers and speed freaks, had actually cleaned up since the club had opened and that he thought Imler had something to do with it.

After a month and a half of vague threats, the empire finally struck back. On December 30 General McCaffrey, Attorney General Janet Reno (who'd torch a baby but not a reefer), and Health and Human Services secretary Donna Shalala (an admitted pot puffer back in her youth) held an anti-joint joint press conference. They threatened to revoke the federal licenses of any doctor who recommended pot, thereby denying the doctor the right to prescribe controlled drugs. Lungren, who as attorney general of California had sworn to uphold the laws of that state, applauded the Clinton administration's chest thumping. Within two weeks, a group of doctors led by Marcus Conant, an AIDS specialist from San Francisco, filed a class action suit against the feds. While only one doctor in a secluded area of California was ever actually hassled, the threats had a chilling effect on physicians' willingness to recommend pot. The feds' action was a blatant violation of the First Amendments rights of doctors and the confidential relationship they share with their patients. Even the editor in chief of the highly respected *New England Journal of Medicine* blasted the federal policy and argued that pot should be rescheduled.

The feds were looking like bullies and thugs, even to mainstream America. McCaffrey, the man who only half a year earlier had said there wasn't "a shred of scientific evidence" to support medical marijuana, attempted to deflect logical criticism of the government's reefer madness by announcing in early January of '97 that the feds were going to plunk a cool mil into a comprehensive review by the Institute of Medicine at the National Academy of Sciences of existing clinical, medical, and scientific documentation—i.e., the shreds that purportedly didn't exist—on the safety and medical efficacy of pot. McCaffrey said the study would take eighteen months.

. . . endless repetition of momentary whim . . . unanswerable to any logic or rational discourse . . .

Soon after McCaffrey's announcement, in February, the National Institutes of Health convened a conference on med-mar. A committee of medical experts authorized by the NIH released a report in August concluding that there was sufficient evidence that pot had possible beneficial use in treating weight loss, nausea, neurological disorders, and glaucoma, while adding some concern about smoking's effects on the lungs and immune system. They suggested developing a smokeless delivery system. They were evidently unaware that one already exists. It's called a vaporizer and it heats the pot without burning it. It's available at finer head shops in your city. Once again, the NIH committee findings were met with *momentary whim, unanswerable to logic or rational discourse,* when White House spin wizard Mike McCurry's reaction to the expert's conclusions was, "the president continues to oppose giving marijuana to sick people."

While Slick Willie's minions were doing their best to appear tougher than thou on the drug war to ward off Republican headbaiters, one lonely figure in the White House piped up—literally and otherwise. I'd met Bob Hattoy when he was regional director of the Sierra Club for California and Nevada in the early '90s. I'd *taken* lunch (hey, I live in Hollywood) with him and a couple of friends from the ACLU and remembered his outrageous sense of humor. At the '92 Democratic Convention, Bob, along with the late Elizabeth Glaser, gave a poignant speech about living with AIDS. When the Slick One was elected, he made Bob the White House liaison to the Department of the Interior and a member of the President's AIDS Commission. I called Bob up in late January of '97 to hear what a gay man with AIDS thought about his boss's policy on med-mar. He was indignant.

"This whole rush by General McCaffrey and Attorney General Reno to criminalize doctors . . . is misguided and small-minded and mean-spirited. This attempt to impose an Eliot Ness kind of marijuana prohibition . . . is pathetic." The Hattoy Veg-O-Matic wit kicked in. "I screamed and yelled at [McCaffrey's and Reno's aides], 'It's so pathetic that you're trying to arrest doctors when Cabbage Patch dolls are eating the hair off of young children.' That's more of a threat to the children of America than giving prescriptions to adults suffering from AIDS and cancer."

At the time, there was a minor crisis of defective Cabbage Patch Kids dolls. I asked Bob if he'd ever used marijuana medicinally.

"Given the fact that I'm a government appointee, I don't want to answer that question. But let's put it this way: I had AIDS-related lymphoma five years ago and went through chemotherapy and had nausea and no appetite, and I used supplements to help me overcome the nausea and suppressed appetite, and I survived through a combination of supplements, alternative medicine, and chemotherapy, and I believe that I'm alive today because of that combination."

He'd answered my question.

Meanwhile, the new law was actually working on the street. Willie Perkins, a HIV-positive member of the LACBC, had criminal charges dropped against him after a bust when he presented his doctor's note in court. Sickle-cell-anemia patient Sister Somayah Kambui, who operates the Crescent Alliance Self Help for Sickle Cell–Project Hemp Is Hep, a cannabis and nutritional hemp seed club in South Central L.A., also had charges against her dismissed when she produced proper documentation. Not all patients were as lucky. Alan Martinez, an epileptic from Santa Rosa who was busted prior to 215, was forced to face charges in spite of the new law and was hesitant to use the medical marijuana that he said prevented his seizures. Tragically, Martinez was killed after he evidently lost control of the car he was driving in. An acquaintance who saw the accident said the car just drifted off the road and kept speeding up. Some suspected, including his lawyer Bill Panzer, that he'd had an epileptic fit.

In April the DEA raided Flower Therapy in S.F., one of the many cannabis clubs that had sprung up statewide. Particularly ominous was the inclusion in the search warrant of "books and/or magazines for growing marijuana, such as *High Times, Marijuana Growers Guide, Sinsemilla Tips,*" et cetera, among the items authorized for seizure. In Arizona, Governor Fife Symington, who within six months would resign and be convicted (a conviction that is on appeal) for real estate fraud, effectively pushed state lawmakers into gutting Prop 200. The new law, however, was temporarily saved by a new referendum that was to be voted on in November '98. The same month, Judge Fern Smith issued a restraining order against the feds, prohibiting them from hassling physicians for discussing pot with patients. However, she restricted the conditions for which recommendations could be made—nausea, glaucoma, and spasticity—and prohibited docs from any dealings with cannabis clubs. The issue had taken on the mood of a legal and emotional yo-yo. It was still trench warfare for those personally involved, but the media turned to more important stories, like Slick Willie and Paula Jones, Slick Willie and the Whitewater land deal, and occasionally even less trenchant topics such as Slick Willie's gutting of welfare. Then Todd McCormick got busted, and for a Warholian fifteen minutes medical pot was page one again.

On July 29, 1997, L.A. County sheriff's deputies and DEA agents raided a "mansion" in the hoity-toity Bel-Air area of Los Angeles, just down the road from where Ronnie and Just Say Nancy Reagan live. Inside the gray stucco faux castle on Stone Canyon Road, the narcs seized, according to their spurious cop count, 4,116 pot plants from drug reform activist, pot farmer, amateur research scientist, and cancer survivor Todd McCormick. The talking hairdos on television (or "sellovision," as journalist Danny Schechter calls it) had a field day covering what the *L.A. Times* claimed was "the largest indoor pot bust in Los Angeles County history." Two weeks postbust, McCormick was sprung when his pal, hempster and movie star Woody Harrelson, posted $500,000 bail. "I am helping Todd because he is a friend but more importantly because he is working to help others in a way that California voters have declared perfectly legal, in spite of the fact that the DEA considers this legislation a threat to their somewhat questionable reason for being," Harrelson told the press. The McCormick story immediately hit CNN and became international news. McCormick was indicted on federal drug charges and because of the alleged quantity, was facing the possibility of spending the rest of his life in jail.

Physically, Todd hardly seems a threat to anybody, standing five foot six and weighing 120 pounds. His diminutive stature is the result of his having had histiocytosis-X, a rare form of cancer, ten times between the ages of two and fifteen. When he was nine his doctor told his mother, Ann McCormick, a self-described hippie who'd given birth to Todd when she was nineteen, that there'd been studies that showed that pot could control the pain and nausea of the chemotherapy and radiation sessions as well as restore the boy's appetite.

So one day Ann gave Todd a joint. "It immediately removed my dizziness, my nausea, and gave me an appetite," remembers Todd. "I got home, wanted to play, eat some food—which was amazing—and my overall health increased." The first five vertebrae in his neck are fused as a result of the first of nine surgeries he had to remove tumors, causing chronic neck pain. Once again McCormick found that pot eased this condition. So instead of becoming infatuated with the usual preteen hobbies, the by-now twelve-year-old began a lifelong interest in researching and advocating marijuana.

In 1994, now twenty-four years old, Todd went to the Netherlands, was thoroughly examined by a doctor, and given an international prescription for pot. "My prescription is for ten grams a day, equivalent to seven to twelve joints, depending how fat you roll them." This scrip was tested in February of '95 when, after purposely notifying a DEA agent, he flew into Colorado from Amsterdam with his medicine. He declared his pot, showed his prescription, and was allowed—based on an obscure agreement in the U.N.'s Single Convention Treaty of 1961, which honors scrips from any U.N. member—to leave the airport. Reefer in tow.

In '95 Todd opened up the San Diego Compassion Club, lobbied successfully for a declaration from the local city council endorsing med-mar, and worked with Jack Herer on his Hemp and Health Initiative. In July of '95 McCormick was popped by an Ohio State Police five-car drug interdiction team with more than thirty pounds of grass in his car, which he was transporting to Rhode Island to start a club. He strolled when a judge ruled illegal search and seizure. Then, three days after the Ohio bust, the DEA raided the San Diego club, seizing literature, software, initiative petitions, and a small stash. No charges were filed. But it was obvious that McCormick was a marked man.

In November of '95 he split for Amsterdam, the Shangri-La of enlightened attitude and hashish coffee shops, which has become the planetary mecca for cannabis aficionados. For a decade an annual awards ceremony called the Cannabis Cup is held there, during which different strains are judged for their quality (the '95 and '96 winners were named "Jack Herer," in honor of the Hemperor). McCormick experimented with a variety of strains to determine which were most efficacious for individual illnesses. Ironically, he found that marijuana low in THC and high in a less psychoactive cannabinoid called CBD was most effective in controlling his neck pain. When 215 passed, he was contacted by Peter McWilliams, the writer/publisher/med-mar patient who'd briefly let the LACBC use office space, and returned to California.

McWilliams worked out a six-figure book deal with Todd. Larry Flynt visited the mansion to discuss a magazine project. And then, rumor has it, some paddy-wagoned female speed freak starting singing to the cops about this mansion in Bel-Air loaded with weed. Not that McCormick went to any lengths to hide it. Most of it was growing outside on a porch, clearly visible to anybody at a higher elevation, such as, say, a snooping copper chopper. When McCormick surfaced from the pokey, even the media seemed sympathetic to this childhood cancer survivor.

One notable naysayer was Scott Imler. Imler criticized McCormick for growing such quantity and expecting to be shielded by the new law, which stated that a patient or caregiver could grow for personal use. Todd had openly aligned himself with the legalizers and hempsters, and Imler was worried that operations like McCormick's were the kind of adventurist endeavors that could endanger the new law and therefore the thousands of newly quasi-legal med-mar users. Between McCormick and Peron and the dozens of willy-nilly cannabis clubs that were opening up overnight, Imler felt that some kind of organization was needed to keep the medical marijuana movement grounded and narrowly focused on the responsible disbursement of medicine and overall care of patients. So he pooled all his connections and resources and activist experience and energy and cash—what little the club had—and got to work.

I'll never forget it. The scene was straight out of some cornball campaign ad. Dozens of high school marching bands, in town for a convention, marched through Santa Cruz, California, on Saturday morning, October 18. But as they passed the corner of Maple and Center Streets, a different slice of American pie was clearly visible. In front of the Loudon Nelson Community Center, named after a freed slave who'd lived there in the 1850s and willed his estate to the school district, was a marquee that read 1997 CONFERENCE OF MEDICAL MARIJUANA PROVIDERS. Twenty-eight cannabis clubs, co-ops, delivery services, and wanna-bees convened for two days to discuss a set of principles and how to proceed with caution and solidarity. It was the largest, most powerful, most mature show of unity among med-mar advocates since the beginning of the diffuse and often fractious movement.

"I'd like to welcome any members of law enforcement who might be in the audience," dead panned Imler as he welcomed the 115 conferees. Micromanaged down to the choice of piped-in music and staffed by members of the L.A. club (which had recently changed its name to the L.A. Cannabis Resource Center), the meeting was a model of cultural sobriety and parlimentary discipline. To stave off the endless bickering that prevents many progressive gatherings from being effective, Imler, with input from other clubs, compiled a set of principles and guidelines, which included documenting verification of treating physicians and their recommendations, maintaining accurate records and the lowest possible prices, cooperation when possible with law enforcement, and more than a dozen other items meant to ensure that the integrity of the clubs was standardized. Various amendments to the guidelines were introduced and voted on. The most controversial was an amendment to remove the principle that providers refrain from behavior that blurs the lines between medical and nonmedical use.

The amendment was voted down, but it highlighted the chasm between the strict medicinal advocates and the hempsters. "I guess

I can understand their reasoning," said Hemperor Herer. "They're afraid to lose their freedom. But I would say all use is medicinal. It stops stress. It's a safe, therapeutically active substance that allows people who smoke it to live longer than people who don't do drugs at all." But Imler disagreed: "That's lunacy. We have a responsibility to implement the new law honorably, and that doesn't make all use medical. The wording of 215 said 'seriously ill.' "

Herer's comments echoed those of Peron's, which had been lobbed back at the Prince of Pot by opponents of 215, including Lungren, as proof that the new law *was* a Trojan Secretariat. Conspicuous by his absence at the conference was Peron or any rep from his newly named San Francisco Cannabis Cultivators Co-op. Peron said he'd felt obliged to attend the memorial service for his friend, former S.F. police commissioner Jo Daly, who had been a medical user of marijuana and member of Dennis's club before her death from cancer. "What was I going to add to it anyway?" asked Peron. "I'm glad people got to meet each other." But Imler maintains that Peron declined a personal invitation to the conference three weeks before Daly's death.

Bob Randall, who'd been diagnosed with AIDS in November '94 and whom Imler asked to give the keynote address at the conference, opines that one can't "look at Dennis in a one-dimensional way. He's obviously done a lot for people in San Francisco and he's also done a great deal to confuse the issue. You can't just make one concept of what Dennis has been."

But Peron's prediction to Imler two years earlier at the Rainbow Gathering had come to pass. "I'm not going to be around forever. Someone's going to have to run this thing," he'd said. The success of the conference, however temporary, was proof that Scott had become the grass-roots leader of medical marijuana. By displaying consistency and leadership; avoiding grandiose and rhetorical public statements or confusing medical marijuana with other issues; and repeating the mantra *"It's about sick people, it's about sick people,"* Imler had become the moral center of the movement. Randall, the godfather of this unique civil rights struggle, says of Imler, "He's the most focused, the most thoughtful. He thinks more deeply about the implications of actions and he's engaged on behalf of patients. Scott *got* it. Ever since I met him, he focused on how we can help people who are suffering. I have great respect for Scott.

"Mao said, 'Political power comes out of the barrel of a gun.' " Randall continues. "If you're not going to resort to firearms, the only true font of political power is legitimacy. And legitimate claims and grievances, if they have any resonance at all, have an innate appeal to the human heart. But as they become abstracted from that legitimacy, they become as trite as the rest of the political scene—which means meaningless."

While the Santa Cruz conference was empowering for those distributing pot to the sick, unbeknownst to the conferees, all the codifying and refocusing was too late in the game. Since the spring of '97 the DEA had been operating an undercover sting operation against the clubs, similar in structure to the BNE op against Peron's club in '96. Undercover agents were supplied with fake names, IDs and doctor's letters, then sent into the clubs claiming various illnesses. For instance, a "Brian Zanza" visited various clubs with documentation that he suffered from post-traumatic stress syndrome and irritable bowels. According to the DEA's own affidavits, when a club called the doctor's number to verify the letter, another DEA agent would answer the phone as the "doctor" and confirm the information.

On January 9, 1998, six clubs—two in San Francisco (including Peron's) and one each in Marin County, Oakland, Santa Cruz, and Ukiah—were slapped with civil nuisance suits by the Department of Justice and charged with distributing pot in violation of the federal Controlled Substances Act. The ubiquitous "Brian Zanza" visited all six clubs named. He can be identified as DEA agent Brian Nehring by matching the dates and testimony in Nehring's affidavits to the "Zanza" files at the besieged clubs. Nehring also attempted to gain membership to the L.A. center, but the admissions director called the purported doctor to confirm the recommendation and double-checked the doctor's ID number with state authorities. The ID number had expired and no doctor by the name on the letterhead existed. Further, the date of the diagnosis was later than the date of the recommendation. "Don't come back till you quit forging letters," the narc was told. The LACRC was not named in the suit.

On the other hand, affidavits compiled by DEA agents Nehring, Bill Nyfeler, and Carolyn Porras chronicled sloppy intake procedures at the cited clubs. Cannabis advocates agree that the clubs are staffed by patient-volunteers who are often inadequately trained. "Clubs were never intended to be the solution to the problem," said Imler. "They're a reasonable short-term alternative. Some of them are more reasonable than others. All of them are more reasonable than the street."

Which was the bottom line. If the clubs are forced to close, these folks will either be thrown back on the black market, forced to become horticulturists, or unable to obtain their medicine. The clubs exist in a vacuum. Attorney General Lungren ignored the provision in 215 that "encourage[s] the federal and state governments to implement a plan to provide for the safe and affordable distribution of marijuana to all patients in medical need of marijuana." The feds didn't give a flying Reno: "The federal court doesn't care whether marijuana is going to people who are sick," said Department of Justice flack Gregory King. "All they'll be determining is whether marijuana is being distributed."

. . . endless repetition of momentary whim . . . cruel and unusual brutality . . . unanswerable to any logic or rational discourse . . .

But Lungren, instead of implementing any plan as he's bound to do as chief law enforcement officer of the state, not only obtained a state appellate court ruling that Peron's club didn't qualify as a primary caregiver and therefore couldn't distribute under 215, but called for the closure of all the clubs and welcomed the federal incursion. Peron, now facing state criminal charges *and* state and federal civil suits and with seventeen busts under his belt and one strike left before he's *out* (according to the three strikes law), announced his plan to challenge Lungren in the June Republican gubernatorial primary. "I'm going to pardon every nonviolent drug prisoner," proclaimed Peron. "I'm gonna make Wavy Gravy head of the California Highway Patrol." Lungren, an avowed square, displayed a momentary sense of humor when his response to Peron's candidacy was "He has smoked more marijuana than even I thought."

If the clubs get shut down, how are the patients expected to get their medicine? Matt Ross, Lungren's flack, says, "A patient can grow, or if a patient cannot grow on his own behalf, then a primary caregiver can grow."

. . . unanswerable to any logic or rational discourse . . .

Imler conceded this is feasible for some: "That's exactly what some some of the clubs are—patients growing their own. They happen to be doing it together. But it's absurd to expect an eighty-five-year-old woman who's got forty-eight hours until chemotherapy to grow a plant. It takes four or five months. You shouldn't have to have a green thumb in order to access medicine."

The court date was set for March 24, 1998, at which time the feds intended to request a summary judgment against the six clubs and shut 'em down. Imler's unique form of liberation theology included the concept of "faith in action." He sent a letter to all participants from the Santa Cruz conference reminding them "that an attack on one Affirmed Provider is an attack on all Affirmed Providers." Imler announced "Keep Faith with the Voters: A Patients' March for Medical Rights" in San Francisco on the twenty-fourth. Mayor Willie Brown of S.F. and the mayors of West Hollywood, Oakland, and Santa Cruz all sent Slick Willie letters asking him to desist from pressing the civil suit. S.F.'s maverick DA Terence Hallinan warned that the city would distribute pot to patients and that local cops would stop busting pot smokers of any kind if the feds closed the clubs. Lungren's reaction was to threaten prosecution of city workers who distribute.

Imler and the L.A. club worked in tandem with Common Sense for Drug Policy, an advocacy group headed by former NORML director Kevin Zeese, and the Medical Marijuana Patients and Caregivers Fund, the front org for the civil suit defendants. But most of the planning and financing for the march and rally came from Imler, Gilbert Baker, and the LACRC. The morning began with a prayer breakfast at the Metropolitan Community Church in S.F., a gay congregation known for its activism and support of medical marijuana. Imler, the Reverend Jim Mitulski, and other ministers spoke, as did Assistant DA Keith Vines and Mayor Steve Martin of West Hollywood, the latter having traveled north for the event the day after he was sworn in. At 11:00 A.M. the march began and proceeded down Market Street. On the way, groups of Peronistas joined in, waving PERON FOR GOVERNOR signs. San Francisco was Dennis's town. But what was intended to be an event in support of beleaguered sick people and their clubs turned into a Peron ego circus. The marchers, now a few hundred strong, made a stop at the Civic Auditorium, where the National AIDS Conference was coincidentally being held. The marchers tromped through the hallway of the auditorium, chanting and making sure that "the experts" confabbing inside heard that medical marijuana, too, was an AIDS issue.

The rally was held at noon in front of the federal courthouse, where the trial was scheduled to begin at 2:30. Imler addressed the crowd in a fiery speech and made a point of crediting Dennis as the man who started it all. It was an extended olive branch that was not to be reciprocated. It seemed like every player in the dope opera was present: Kevin Zeese (who'd done one of the most comprehensive surveys of current lit on pot's medical efficacy); hempsters Jack Herer and Chris Conrad and Mikki Norris; Lynnette Shaw of the Marin club and the other defendants and their lawyers; Elvy Musikka (along with Bob Randall, one of America's eight legal users); outspoken patients Todd McCormick, Mary Gennoy, and

Dixie Romagno; Dale Gieringer from NORML; and, of course, Dennis Peron.

Zeese was against letting Peron speak, but Scott, even with his misgivings about his former friend, felt that Dennis was a defendant and ought to be given mike time. When the Prince of Pot finally did speak, he repeated his most controversial canard: *"All use is medical!"* The tone in his voice was venomous and it was clear it was a "fuck you" to all those who'd labeled Peron irresponsible—especially Imler. Imler stood in the crowd, shaking with rage, feeling betrayed by the man who'd initiated him into the medical marijuana movement and whose freedom Imler was there to support. *"Bullshit! Bullshit!"* Imler screamed, the veins popping out in his neck. But he was drowned out by the Prince, claiming eventual victory over Dan Lungren in the upcoming primary.

The hearing was substance by the defendants' lawyers over stonewall by the government. A whole battery of legal eagles were assembled for the defense, including Tony Serra (the famous radical attorney who was the model for James Woods's character in the movie *True Believers*), Santa Clara University law professor Gerald Uelmen (widely respected in judicial circles and a member of O.J. Simpson's "Dream Team"), and Bill Panzer. While Reno's mouthpiece, Mark Quinlivan, predictably argued that the clubs couldn't distribute because it was against the law, Panzer countered that the feds had "arbitrarily and capriciously" turned a blind eye to any evidence that marijuana was medicine. Citing everything from the 1894 Indian Hemp Commission findings to the 1972 Shafer Commission report under Nixon to Judge Young's 1988 decision to a 1995 Dutch government report—all of which found pot to be relatively harmless and/or medically efficacious—Panzer forcefully made the point that federal law is based on erroneous science. He called the government outright "liars." The ponytailed Serra, in a stentorian performance deserving of an Oscar, accused the feds of dishonesty and disingenousness under "the clean hands doctrine." Judge Charles Breyer was seemingly moved by the defense and postponed a ruling till after April 16, while he reviewed written briefs from the feds and the defendants. Among other things, he wanted to know whether Congress had considered medical use when they enacted the Controlled Substances Act in 1970 and whether any efforts were being made to reclassify pot as prescription medicine.

As Scott Imler prepared to load the bus for the trip back to L.A., he looked spent. He'd spent weeks organizing this show of solidarity for the other clubs, and while he was thankful that the judge hadn't immediately closed them, he felt very little solidarity in return. No one had even thanked him. After all, his club hadn't even been named in the suit. "I don't know whether I'm elated or depressed," he said as he slouched towards the bus.

The next day the L.A. club once again opened its doors and Scott Imler did what he does every weekday—distribute medicine to the sick and dying.

Faith in action.

III. ENOUGH IS ENOUGH

More than seventy million Americans have tried marijuana and one-fifth still smoke, if only occasionally. A recent ACLU survey of voting adults found that one third have acknowledged smoking pot at some point in their lives. More than eleven million have been arrested for it since 1965. In 1995, the last year the feds correlated such figures, the blue meanies popped almost six hundred thousand for pot, a record number. In spite of Republican politicking and kvetching about Clinton's drug policy, approximately 1.5 million weed users were arrested during the first three years of Slick Willie's reign of reefer madness, 84 percent for simple possession. The average number of arrests under His Slickness is 30 percent higher than under the evidently kinder and gentler George Bush.

Federal mandatory minimums—for those convicted of drug crimes by the feds—were enacted during the Dark Ages of the Reagan regime. If you're prosecuted in a federal court for possessing one joint—*one joint!*—you can get a year in prison and fined ten grand. Now former doper Newt Gingrich has sponsored legislation that would mandate the death penalty for a second offense of bringing over fifty grams (less than two ounces) across U.S. borders. Thirty-seven members of Congress have cosponsored the bill. "One cannot imagine how people do what the government is planning to do and then go home say 'Hi honey, I had a great day.' It's morally reprehensible," says Bob Randall.

Then there's the bill introduced by Mississippi state legislator Bobby Moak that would allow anyone nabbed for narcotics "to have a body part removed" instead of doing time. Some wag tagged it the "smoke a joint, lose a joint" law. It's not expected to pass. Even in Mississippi.

On February 26, 1998, Congressman Bill McCollum (who had supported the first medical marijuana bill in Congress in '81) introduced

House Resolution 372 on behalf of himself and eight other Re-pukelicans. Perhaps one couldn't characterize this proposed resolution as the *most* baseless, exaggerated, hysterical, distorted pack of lies ever entered into the *Congressional Record,* given that for more than two hundred years rich white men have been advancing their own social and financial agendas in the guise of representing their constituents. But let's put it this way: if McCollum or any of his co-nitwits had been George Washington (who, by the way, grew hemp), they would've sworn that the neighbor chopped down the cherry tree.

The resolution claims, among other things, that pot impairs normal brain function. A brilliant conclusion. If it didn't, it wouldn't be worth smoking. I've always believed, with two hundred years of history to substantiate my claim, that being an American politician impairs normal brain function. Marijuana, on the other hand, enhances creativity. Being a politician enhances predictability. There was some obscure study that showed brain damage in rhesus monkeys after long-term, high concentrations of marijuana smoke. No recent tests utilizing state-of-the-art methods have detected any harm.

The resolution erroneously babbles on: "marijuana is a dangerous and addictive drug and should not be legalized for medicinal use." It's infuriating to hear these Beltway jerks—you wanna grab 'em by the collar and scream: "Why don't you just go ask anyone who smokes pot if they're robbing the First National at gunpoint or hocking Grandma's prosthetic leg so they can score a blunt at the 311 show on Saturday night?" What's even more infuriating, as ignorant as some of these self-proclaimed drug experts in Congress are—some of 'em have smoked the stuff and *they know it's not addictive!* Both Clinton and Gingrich are two college-era inhalers. The only thing Clinton is addicted to is pussy and Gingrich's jones is for power and ego gratification.

(Or is it Gingrich/pussy and Clinton/power? I can't remember. Evidentally marijuana has caused me short-term memory loss.)

But Congressman McCollum recently announced that he's also opposed to researching marijuana. It's a variation on the "don't ask, don't tell" theme or the three monkeys covering their ears, eyes, and mouths. And ask any researcher who's tried to fire up a government-sanctioned or -funded experimental program. Between the DEA and National Institute of Drug Abuse and the Food and Drug Administration, scientists are forced to navigate a bureaucratic obstacle course in order to get a green light—and even then they're usually ultimately refused.

House Resolution 372 makes dozens of the standard absurd claims to explain why cannabis is a demon weed. Drs. Lynn Zimmer and John Morgan simply and cohesively refute each claim in their book *Marijuana Myths Marijuana Facts.* I suggest you read it. The antidrug warriors continue to whine about there being no empirical evidence that marijuana is safe. They should begin by checking out the LaGuardia Committee Report of 1938 (commissioned by New York City mayor Fiorello LaGuardia), which Sloman covers. Or the famous Jamaican study by Vera Rubin and Lambros Comitas. Or the 1997 Kaiser Permanente study that showed that regular pot use does not lead to premature mortality. The latter study and the 1972 Shafer Commission findings show that the greatest harm to the pot smoker are legal penalties. If they don't feel like dealing with the library or Internet, they should just look around them. With the advent of jazzbos, then beatniks, then hippies, then punks, then slackers, we've now had a century of subcultures in which pot was an integral shared social intoxicant. While many of these hedonistic societal reprobates have croaked from cigarettes, booze, heroin, or coke, where's the evidence that bohos are dropping dead from reefer toxicity? *Nobody's ever OD'd in the history of civilization from marijuana!!!!!!!*

There is hope. Drug Czar McCaffrey's Institute of Medicine study is due in December 1998, and if they're truly as nonpolitical and as scientific as they claim to be, they'll come to the same conclusion every other damn government investigation has, which has been to say, in stoner parlance: *"It's only pot, man!"* But in an even more startling development, the DEA has forwarded a petition by journalist-activist Jon Gettman and the Trans-High Corporation (publisher of *High Times* magazine) to the federal Department of Health and Human Services for evaluation. The petition presents volumes of documentation, including studies by the National Institutes of Mental Health and several prominent psychopharmacologists, and asks that pot be dropped from its current Schedule I status, which holds that it has no medical value and high potential for abuse.

By agreeing to hand the matter over to HHS, the DEA is implicitly stating by its own rules that "sufficient grounds" exist to reclassify cannabis. If HHS finds the petition valid, according to the Controlled Substances Act, not only would marijuana have to be removed from Schedule I but also from Schedule II, which accommodates drugs that have medicinal applications but are considered dangerous and addictive, such as morphine and cocaine.

The petition is the result of years of research by the forty-year-old Gettman, national director from 1986 to '89 of NORML (which is once again being run by founder Keith Stroup). The Virginia resident found that pot's status as a Schedule I drug was intended as a temporary measure by the Nixon administration until further scientific study could ascertain its abuse potential. Typically, the feds then forbade further research and ignored existing data. Gettman discovered that, in the meantime, the scientific community had adopted "a new model for assessing drug addiction. I realized from reading a report from a congressional agency that marijuana didn't satisfy the criteria of this new model for abuse—which, by the way, is centered on craving and repeated self-administration in animal models. This has been known for a long time, that you can't get animals to self-administer marijuana."

Which is just another way of saying, *"It's only pot, man!"*

Gettman says the review process could take one to two years to complete. "The DEA has examined the petition with extraordinary care and devotion to the law," Gettman says magnanimously. "If I'm right, then marijuana will have to be placed on Schedule III, IV, or V, or taken out of the schedules. The presumption that marijuana has a high potential for abuse is at the root of all aspects of marijuana prohibition, justifying the ban on hemp, medical marijuana, and recreational use."

The burgeoning hemp movement has further broadened the cannabis debate. Hemp has been utilized for textiles, rope, paper, food, fuel, and dozens of other applications throughout history. The feds subsidized hemp farming during World War II and advocated a "Hemp for Victory" campaign. Under the justification that hempsters, like medical marijuana activists, are using the issue as a cover for legalization, the DEA has forbidden domestic hemp production. However, American companies can manufacture products made from imported hemp and a multimillion-dollar industry has resulted. In 1989 hemp companies made under a mil. By 1998, Gettman says, domestic hemp products now reap about $25 million—and he emphasizes that that's a conservative estimate. Chris Conrad says that claims have been made that worldwide the industry rakes in anywhere from $100 to $300 million.

A domestic trade group, the Hemp Industries Association, has more than two hundred members, and according to Ken Friedman, president of HIA, "Imports [of raw hemp to the U.S.] are growing at more than fifty percent a year." *Hemp Times,* sister publication of *High Times,* is the leading promoter of hemp products, ranging from clothing and footwear and luggage to soap and cosmetics, as well as food and nutritional supplements. Adidas even came out with a hemp sneaker. Because hemp produces more pulp per acre than trees, because it's biodegradable, because chemicals are unnecessary to grow it, and because it contains more essential fatty acids than any other plant food (and is second only to soybeans in complete protein)—hemp is being touted as the most versatile, potentially profitable, environmentally friendly crop on the planet. Twelve states have legislation passed or pending to legalize or research hemp for industrial use.

Actor Woody Harrelson is the most well known hempster. He's an example of the shifting consciousness on cannabis that's manifoldly manifested itself in popular culture. A restaurant called the Galaxy opened in New York and its entire menu, from waffles to salad dressings, utilizes hemp seeds or oil. Paul Krassner recently wrote an article for *High Times* chronicling the resurgence of dope humor, usually based on firsthand experiences, in stand-up comedy routines. Musicians, who, like the Mighty Mezz, were among the first to recognize the mind-expanding properties of reefer as it applies to artistic endeavor, continue to publicly support legalization. The list of pot-positive musical rockers include Chris Robinson of the Black Crowes, rap groups Run-DMC and Cypress Hill, Chrissie Hynde of the Pretenders, Jello Biafra, Spearhead, 311, Primus, Liz Phair and Kim Deal of the Breeders, on whose lapel I pinned a medical marijuana emblem that she promised to wear onstage at every show. There's the first family of reggae—the Marleys—Rita, Ziggy, and Stephen. And, of course, there's pothead—and now hempster—Willie Nelson.

Movies showing pot use as a normal—even positive—aspect of everyday life include *Dazed and Confused, Short Cuts, Jackie Brown, The Big Lebowski,* and the first blatant stoner comedy since Cheech and Chong's heyday, *Half-Baked.* On television *The Simpsons* contains frequent reefer and hemp refs. Roseanne and John Goodman's characters got high on *Roseanne,* and *Murphy Brown* used medical marijuana when Candice Bergen's character's cancer was diagnosed and she had to undergo chemotherapy. The latter episode prompted a bit of reefer madness when DEA honcho, the byzantine Constantine, issued a press release decrying Murphy's toking as "trivializing drug abuse," restating his belief that cancer patients do not have the right to medication that improves their well-being. There was some talk that the DEA was investigating *Murphy Brown,* leading to whimsical scenarios in which a fictitious television *and* cartoon character (good ol' Zonker) could have criminal records.

What the establishment consistently fails to realize is that the hysteria over marijuana works against them. If they're so maniacal about pot, why should young people take them seriously about any other substance? "If there's any evidence that the culture is prepared to be less hysterical about the occasional use of marijuana, it can only be applauded," says UC Berkeley sociology prof and '60s rad Todd Gitlin. "The hard-and-fast view has been ineffectual. Most kids think it's ridiculous."

Though pop culture may be relaxing its standards towards cannabis, law enforcement is not. Pot penalties vary from state to state, but in forty-two states, simple possession of even the smallest amount subjects the pinched puffer to incarceration and/or a hefty fine. One of the most despicable examples of this is the case of Will Foster of Tulsa, Oklahoma. Foster has advanced rheumatoid arthritis, precisely the kind of ailment that seven seperate studies, presented to the Society of Neuroscience in 1997, proved marijuana to be extremely effective in treating. He was given 93 years for 60 plants (says the prosecutor) or 10 plants and 50 seedlings and clones (as Will and his wife Meg maintain). Meg Foster told me in her Okie twang that "I'm ashamed to be an American," and she apologized for choking up while trying to hold back the tears for the three kids whose father's in jail for 93 years . . . 93 years . . . 93 years . . . *momentary whim . . . cruel and unusual brutality . . . unanswerable to logic or rational discourse . . .* These kinds of stories can lead a nonviolent and humane person towards thoughts and emotions one would rather avoid. There's a saying among the less patient reefer activists and it goes something like this: "If they want a War on Drugs—fine. But when it's over, there will be war crimes trials held and those responsible for these human rights violations will have to answer for *their* crimes."

I'm sorry, dear reader, if I'm treading on vitriolic territory. But I'm tired. My pal Larry "Ratso" Sloman wrote the brilliant book you've just read and it's the best, most concise, informative—and tragicomic—history book on the subject. But he keeps calling me in that nasal voice of his ("Maaaahhhh-keeee! Ya done yet?") and hassling me to finish this afterword and I've been greeting dawns to tell you the story as I see it and I'm tired. I'm tired because the optimal rapid eye movement period of my sleep has been disrupted by overwork. I'm tired because I've been covering medical marijuana for more than a year and a half for the *L.A. Weekly, Rolling Stone,* and *High Times,* and I really want to write about the lovely exhibit by Japanese artist Yayoi Kusama I saw last week at the Los Angeles County Museum of Art. I'm tired of trying to be objective about an issue in which the government shows neither validity, common sense, nor basic humanity. Between $7.5 and $10 billion a year in federal, state, and local budgets are spent on the enforcement of Pothibition. A pot smoker is arrested every fifty-four seconds in America. And while only 20 percent of tokers are blacks and Latinos, in 1995 they made up 58 percent of those sentenced under federal law. That same year 71 percent busted for misdemeanor pot charges were nonwhite. The *cruelly and unusually brutal* federal mandatory minimums and forfeiture laws (which encourage drug busts so that law enforcement can make a profit off the property of bustees) is downright immoral. Trying to be objective about the marijuana laws in this country is like trying to be objective about racial segregation during the Jim Crow era.

I'm tired because I first publicly argued for the legalization of marijuana in my eighth-grade debate club and that was thirty years ago. I'm tired because pot smokers go behind the bars of prisons, while alcoholics go to the prisons of bars. (Mea culpa, folks. I enjoy the occasional eight-hour mandatory minimum stretch at my local pub.) I'm tired of the hypocrisy and the lies and the unconstitutionality of the illegal search and seizure suffered by heads, or even those suspected on baseless grounds.

At it's most innocuous, there's the young woman who told me that in order to be a video clerk at Blockbuster, she was forced to allow the manager to cut off a lock of her hair for a drug test. Perhaps management was worried she'd file *Schindler's List* under Comedy. At its worst, there's Donald Scott, a sixty-one-year-old Malibu rancher who was murdered after a team of L.A. County Sheriff's Department, LAPD, Park Service, DEA, Forest Service, California National Guard, and California Bureau of Narcotics Enforcement agents burst in on him based on a false tip that he was growing marijuana. Responding to his wife's screams and clueless as to what was going on, Scott grabbed a gun. Agents pumped two bullets into him. No pot or other drugs were found.

I'm tired of being tired. And, most egregiously, I'm tired of seriously ill people being denied something that helps them feel better and in many cases saves their lives. A patient once told Jack Herer that the difference between having cancer and not using pot and having cancer and using pot is that without pot you are *dying* with cancer while with pot you are *living* with cancer. In one of the research papers touted by the anti–medical marijuana forces, there lies an interesting statement: "Studies have shown that smoking marijuana produces undesirable side effects for glaucoma patients, such as elevated blood pressure, dry eye, and euphoria in the majority of patients studied." I have no idea whether the first two claimed side effects are true, but I know Bob Randall and thousands of other glaucoma patients say that pot keeps them from going completely blind. As for the third "side effect," the dictionary defines *euphoria* as "a feeling of general well-being." Evidently in 1998 in the United States of America, "a feeling of general well-being" is an undesirable side effect for those with glaucoma and cancer and AIDS. Undesirable for those in pain. Undesirable for the dying.

As discussed, marijuana has different meaning for different people. For former drug prosecutor Keith Vines it's medicine that prevents him from wasting away and keeps him alive. For Jack Herer it's manna from heaven that will reverse mankind's self-destructive course. For Chris Conrad it's a combination of personal, industrial, and medical use. For musicians and artists it provides aesthetic inspiration. For millions of others it's simply a harmless relaxant. While there's a life-versus-death, healthy-versus-sick urgency for medical marijuana patients that requires the issue being dealt with seperately—*no one who smokes, grows, or distributes reefer should be subject to prison, handcuffs, harassment, job loss, forfeiture, or even the equivalent of a parking ticket. It is time, once and for all, to legalize.*

I like marijuana because I like feeling euphoric. I like smoking marijuana with my friends and laughing and doing routines and trading stoned epiphanies with them. I like marijuana because I had two total hip replacements and have chronic bursitis in my shoulders and I broke my left collarbone and I have osteoporosis in my spine so acute that getting out of chairs or cars has become a chore and when I smoke marijuana the considerable pain of all these ailments goes away. I like marijuana because it opens conduits to synapses in my brain that encourage creativity and provide pleasure. I like marijuana because I just smoked a joint and I feel fluid and candid and open and the musician in me is blowin' and riffin' and I see that boundaries can be dissolved as a writer, as an artist, as an activist, as a human being. All the circuits are open.

When you're pleasantly high, and anything seems possible. Even when, in this mundane plane called reality—a plane goin' nowhere quick, if I may mix my metaphors—it may not be. This is why some heads become so evangelical in their advocacy. It's the old *"If only me and Newt could share a bong hit . . ."* This realization of consciousness is exhilarating, it's spiritual, and it's euphoric.

I like marijuana because I want to live in a euphoric world. I like marijuana because I don't buy that organized religion crap about how we're meant to suffer because Eve gave Adam an apple to eat or that life on earth is an inferior existence that's redeemed only after we enter the Kingdom of God. Which is to say, I like marijuana because I want to get to heaven before I die.

Los Angeles
March 1998

INDEX